Freedom's Frontier

Also by Donald Thomas

POETRY
Points of Contact
Welcome to the Grand Hotel

FICTION
Prince Charlie's Bluff
The Flight of the Eagle
The Blindfold Game
Belladonna: A Lewis Carroll Nightmare
The Day the Sun Rose Twice
The Ripper's Apprentice
Jekyll, Alias Hyde
Dancing in the Dark
The Raising of Lizzie Meek
The Arrest of Scotland Yard
The Secret Cases of Sherlock Holmes
Red Flowers for Lady Blue
Sherlock Holmes and the Running Noose
The Execution of Sherlock Holmes

BIOGRAPHY
Cardigan of Balaclava
Cochrane: Britannia's Sea-Wolf
Swinburne: The Poet in his World
Robert Browning: A Life Within Life
Henry Fielding
The Marquis de Sade
Lewis Carroll: A Portrait with Background

CRIME AND DOCUMENTARY
A Long Time Burning: The History of Literary Censorship in England
State Trials: Treason and Libel
State Trials: The Public Conscience
Honour Among Thieves: Three Classic Robberies
Dead Giveaway
Hanged in Error?
The Victorian Underworld
An Underworld at War: Spivs, Deserters, Racketeers and Civilians
in the Second World War
Villains' Paradise: Britain's Underworld from the Spivs to the Krays

The Everyman Book of Victorian Verse: The Post-Romantics
The Everyman Book of Victorian Verse: The Pre-Raphaelites to the Nineties
Selected Poems of John Dryden

Freedom's Frontier

Censorship in Modern Britain

DONALD THOMAS

JOHN MURRAY

First published in Great Britain in 2007 by John Murray (Publishers)
An Hachette Livre UK company

1

© Donald Thomas 2007

The right of Donald Thomas to be identified as the Author of the
Work has been asserted by him in accordance with the Copyright,
Designs and Patents Act 1988.

A CIP catalogue record for this title
is available from the British Library

ISBN 978-0-7195-5733-0

Typeset in Bembo by M Rules

Printed and bound in Great Britain by William Clowes Ltd, Beccles, Suffolk

John Murray policy is to use papers that are natural, renewable and
recyclable products and made from wood grown in sustainable forests.
The logging and manufacturing processes are expected to conform to
the environmental regulations of the country of origin.

John Murray (Publishers)
338 Euston Road
London NW1 3BH

www.johnmurray.com

For Morris Ernst and Murray Mindlin

Contents

Preface

ALMOST FORTY YEARS before completing the present book, my earlier
account of censorship, *A Long Time Burning: The History of Literary
Censorship in England*, went to its publishers. That book began and ended
with the same comment. 'The relevant question at any stage of human
history is not "Does censorship exist?" but rather, "Under what sort of
censorship do we now live?"' Anthony Burgess quoted the remark in his
1969 *Spectator* review and added, 'Just so. *Cunt* and *bugger* can get on the
literary omnibus only because *kike* and *nigger* have been ordered off.' In the
next four decades a good many new passengers would scramble aboard and
an entire lower deck would be ordered off.

The earlier book covered a period from the introduction of printing in
1476 until the end of the 1890s with a short epilogue on the earlier twentieth century. The remaining decades of that century were to turn
censorship on its head. *A Long Time Burning* was built upon my doctoral
thesis on the manuscripts of the Court of King's Bench from 1730 to
1911. Of some 30,000 cases in the parchments 455 were literary prosecutions, involving authors, illustrators, publishers or booksellers. The law of
the time required that all passages objected to as seditious, blasphemous or
obscene should be set out in full in the indictments. Sometimes this
included an entire political pamphlet or most of a book, which had been
thought lost but had survived in this form. If there was a moral in the tale,
it was that censorship in the long term did not suppress any of this material which was so obnoxious to the authorities. Indeed, it guaranteed its
survival and in some cases its reprinting.

As the earlier book went through its production process in 1967–8, a
scholarly and urbane Routledge editor, Colin Franklin, raised the possibility that we might face a threat of prosecution under the Obscene
Publications Act 1959. The text included excerpts from such titles as *The
School of Venus*, once purchased furtively by Samuel Pepys and subsequently
thought to be lost, or Paris-printed fiction for the Edwardian market. *A*

Long Time Burning was principally concerned with political censorship. However, the complete *Fanny Hill* had recently been declared criminal and no publisher in his senses at that time would have touched Sade's *Justine*. As *A Long Time Burning* appeared, a Bradford printer went to prison for two years for typesetting two volumes of the Victorian diary *My Secret Life*. The best advice, which proved correct, was that there would almost certainly be no prosecution of Routledge and, should there be, it would not succeed. Even so, some reviews expressed surprise that it was possible to quote from certain texts. George Steiner thought it no surprise that the book should be in the shop windows of Soho. Several well-wishers set out for Soho, where disappointingly the book was not found in shop windows or anywhere else.

As that book was being written, sections of it had appeared in the magazine *Censorship*. This stablemate of *Encounter* and *New China Quarterly*, under the aegis of the Congress for Cultural Freedom, was edited by Murray Mindlin, former literary editor of the *Jerusalem Post* and translator of James Joyce's *Ulysses* into Hebrew. The Congress originated in Berlin in 1950 to counter the Soviet-sponsored 1949 World Congress of Peace in Paris, Moscow's attempt to divert attention from artistic repression at home by lionizing Pablo Picasso, Jean-Paul Sartre, and Communism's sympathizers in the West.

Censorship certainly denounced Soviet repression but it often attacked restrictions on the arts in Britain and the West, usually when directed against the avant-garde on grounds of indecency or obscenity. Only after the magazine's demise did it become public knowledge that funding for the Congress for Cultural Freedom came solely from the CIA. Those who had written for its magazines could only reflect that it was better for the money to have gone into the pockets of their grocers than into the arms budgets of Washington's client states.

Now, as then, the critic over the shoulder wonders whether certain words or expressions or quotations had not better be omitted from an account of current censorship. They ought not. The words, of course, are no longer the same. Those which might have caused a blush or a blanch in the 1960s are now the small change of late-night television or kerbside chatter. A new tribe of insults and prejudices in a new century is identified by law and custom. If there is an historical distinction between the decades it is that censorship in the 1960s was concerned principally to ensure that the innocent were not depraved or corrupted by what they read or watched, while forty years later the greater fear appears to be that they may feel offended.

Those who protested that readers could not be depraved or corrupted must presumably have believed that they could not be improved by what they read either. The probable truth was that what would affect a reader depended more upon the reader than the book and was unpredictable. So it was that two boys convicted at Stratford Juvenile Court in October 1987 of demanding money by threatening letters had got the idea from Agatha Christie's Miss Marple. In 1996 a suspect during the United States 'Unabomber' attacks on public targets was alleged to have drawn inspiration from Joseph Conrad's novel *The Secret Agent*. In June 1979 a French mechanic was convicted of murder by poisoning, also copied from an Agatha Christie novel in his possession. In the wake of the child murder of James Bulger, a 1997 Home Office inquiry found, more plausibly, no conclusive evidence that watching violent films encourages such behaviour 'in young people who have not already shown a tendency towards violence'. The last qualification was the most important.

As the grounds of censorship shifted, new legislation was to criminalize speech or writing which might cause offence, harassment or distress on grounds of race, religion or sexual orientation. It was not necessary to prove that offence had been experienced. Instead, the new laws conjured up a phantom of the grim-faced bigot alert for the first hint of offence as an excuse for vengeance. In the shadow of this threat, words and images, religious symbols or celebrations were prudently outlawed by companies, councils or corporations who had the power to do so. It mattered nothing, for example, that the huge majority of Muslims or Christians were delighted for their compatriots to celebrate Christmas or Ramadan, nor that the Muslim Council of Great Britain had advised against making cuts in the National Theatre production of *Tamburlaine the Great* after four hundred years of freedom. The new laws delivered greater control over freedom of speech into the hands of present and future governments. Sceptics suggested that this was the true motive of the legislation, as a means of curbing dissent.

Freedom's Frontier, like its predecessors, *An Underworld at War* and *Villains' Paradise*, is the history of a period seen in the focus of a particular topic. Though the history is British, it cannot always be confined to Britain. Censorship and its opponents are sometimes international. The battle over James Joyce's *Ulysses* also belongs to the United States and the triumph of Morris Ernst, just as the defeat of the New York anti-Sadism law by the US Supreme Court in 1948 was to affect Britain dramatically in the 1950s. The downfall of Ezra Pound and P. G. Wodehouse is as much part of the 1945 taste for retribution as the execution of William Joyce. The example for such questionable forms of revenge was already set in France in 1944. At other times, from the Edwardian period until 1960, Paris was to play as large a part as London in the attempt to publish the most famous of banned books in English.

The bias of the present book is towards the printed word. Yet the censorship of literature or the press cannot be isolated from those other censorships of the theatre or the cinema and later of television or even advertising. Yet one book can hardly encompass them all. For that reason there are sideways glances from time to time, away from literature or the press, towards what was happening in those other areas, as there are towards relevant developments in France or the United States.

In one sense, this book began with the conclusion of its predecessor, so that my gratitude to individuals and institutions covers several decades. For some time I taught Muslim and other overseas postgraduates, on a course which prepared them for whatever further qualifications they aspired to. It seems only right, in the present climate and at this point in the book, to record that those Muslim students were uniformly delightful and charming – and would have been the first to wish a Christian 'Happy Christmas'. From one Iranian, the Christmas cards continued for many years, until his country fell under the rule of the Ayatollah Khomeini. The encouragement of terrorism by such regimes and their adherents is unhappily a matter of record. However, the figure of the scowling fanatic, alert for a first hint of offence as the inspiration to terrible retribution, is one I do not recognize. The need to impose so many laws, safeguarding security or outlawing 'offence' by the trimming or curbing of free expression, is one I cannot regard without great scepticism.

Two institutions in particular have made my work possible, the Bodleian Library and what was originally the University of Wales, Cardiff, but is now Cardiff University. It is a great pleasure to acknowledge the kindness and support of my colleagues Professor Martin Kayman, Professor Stephen Knight and Professor Martin Coyle of the School of English, Communications and Philosophy, and particularly the encouragement of my colleague Professor David Skilton, over the past twenty years, to continue the story of censorship into a new age.

To document the course of censorship over a long period of time has been made infinitely easier by the variety of information and suggestions from colleagues and friends. Among the first of these was the late Morris Ernst who, with great courtesy and gentleness, was one of the most formidable cross-examiners and lucid advocates of his day. As an American libertarian lawyer, he was a worthy rival in his skills to his British friend and colleague Norman Birkett. I was also fortunate in being published by Murray Mindlin, as editor of *Censorship*, at a time when he was working against the repression of authors in Eastern Europe. Colin Banks of *Studio International*, a friend for many years, encouraged my interest in the censorship of political cartoons. In the earlier part of this work, I was fortunate to have the guidance of Leslie Boyd, Clerk of the Central Criminal Court, and John Saltmarsh, Librarian of King's College, Cambridge. For finding material which left to myself I should have missed I am most grateful to Mr and Mrs Ben Bass of Greyne House Books, to Mrs Marie Elmer of Clifford Elmer Books, to Mr Jonathan Walker and for a great deal of press material to Dr Linda Shakespeare.

My thanks go to Mrs Dawn Harrington, Research Administrator, and to the Information Services of Cardiff University, especially to Ms Sue Austin, Ms Helen D'Artillac Brill and Mr Tom Dawkes, as well as to the Archives Centre and its Director, Mr Peter Keelan. Among other libraries and institutions who have supplied me with material, I should like to acknowledge the Bodleian Law Library and Modern Papers Room; the British Library Document Supply Centre; the British Library Newspaper Division; Cambridge University Library; Cardiff Central Library; the Central Criminal Court; the City of Bristol Reference Library; Leeds City Libraries; the London Library, and the Public Record Office.

This is the fourth book in my series of 'histories' which John Murray has published. It is a pleasure to acknowledge the enthusiasm and guidance of Ms Eleanor Birne, Ms Lucy Dixon, Ms Helen Hawksfield, Ms Caroline Westmore and the editorial skills of Mr Howard Davies.

I have much appreciated the advice of Mr Bill Hamilton of A. M. Heath Ltd, as well as the encouragement of the late Howard Gotlieb and Ms Vita Paladino, past and present Directors of the Howard Gotlieb Archival Research Center at Boston University. My greatest debt, as always, is to my family.

If they give you ruled paper, write the other way.
— Juan Ramón Jiminez (1881–1958)

With effervescing opinions, as with not yet forgotten champagnes, the quickest way to let them get flat is to let them get exposed to the air.
— Justice Oliver Wendell Holmes (1841–1935)

I

Watch Your Lip: The New Millennium

I

ON 28 SEPTEMBER 2005 Jack Straw, as Foreign Secretary, addressed the Labour Party Conference in Brighton. His speech was not particularly well attended and television cameras showed a swathe of empty seats. The Iraq War had not been on the conference agenda and almost the only reference came a few days earlier from a delegate of the Transport and General Workers' Union. Barry Camfield ended his speech by saying, 'We should bring our troops home – now!' From the balcony came a burst of applause and 'Hear! Hear!' Conference stewards approached the applauders. 'Be quiet,' they said. 'No more noise.'

The Foreign Secretary's point about the war was succinctly put. 'We are in Iraq for one reason only – to help the legitimate, elected government to build a secure, democratic and stable nation.' Another voice could be heard more faintly. 'That's a lie – and you know it!' The cameras and microphones deserted Mr Straw, bringing into focus a frail, white-haired figure, sitting almost at the back of the hall. Three burly stewards had reached him. As the world looked on, a steward who appeared twice the size of the interrupter was assisted by a companion to haul the elderly culprit from his seat.

The chairman of Erith and Crayford Constituency Labour Party, a few seats away, called out, 'Leave the old man alone!' He was also seized by two stalwarts and marched outside, where party officials and police were in attendance. The elderly man was Walter Wolfgang, eighty-two years old. A refugee from Hitler's Germany, he had been a Labour party member for forty-seven years and parliamentary candidate for Croydon North-East in 1959. He had also been Vice-President of the Campaign for Nuclear Disarmament.

A hand briefly covered the television lens but cameras and microphones followed the two groups into the foyer. An official was telling Mr Wolfgang, 'We want you to leave the premises.' 'On what grounds?'

I

'Causing an interruption in the arena.' 'I'm sorry,' said Mr Wolfgang, 'but you can't make me leave the premises. You know, I've got a right to my views as Jack has a right to his and what has happened is . . .' At this point he was led away.

The Sussex police, well drilled in implementing the Prevention of Terrorism Act 2005, made matters worse by detaining Mr Wolfgang as a security threat. He was issued with a 'Section 44 stop and search' notice, giving him a police record. He carried nothing more dangerous than a spare pair of glasses and a belief in free speech. There seemed little scope for a further blunder but Sussex police found it. They allegedly denied to the press that they had detained Mr Wolfgang under anti-terrorist laws, then had to admit that they had done so.

The Labour party chairman conceded that the treatment of Mr Wolfgang had been 'inappropriate', a non-judgmental cliché with an unfortunate reputation as the weasel word of 'political correctness'. Rank and file party members and MPs, opposed to the war, supported and applauded their dissident. The country was left to decide whether the party leadership was truly sorry for the incident or merely sorry as a burglar is sorry because he has been caught.

To those whose memories or reading of history went back far enough, the case of Walter Wolfgang illustrated a marked change in political responses to free speech. What some newspapers and readers now called a 'roughing up' of the heckler was once the preserve of the British Union of Fascists and its kind at rallies in the 1930s. As they struggled with stewards whose job was to evict them, protesters had chanted, 'One, two, three, four, what are the Fascists for? Thuggery, buggery, hunger and war', followed by, 'Two, three, four, five. We want Mosley dead or alive.' Compared with this, a single voice calling out, 'That's a lie and you know it', seemed a gentlemanly rebuke.

Walter Wolfgang's was the most publicized case at the conference but he was not alone. In all, he discovered 426 people were stopped in Brighton under anti-terrorist legislation during the week of the conference. None was found to have any connection with terrorism. They included the campaign manager of the Freedom Association, Mark Wallace, who was collecting signatures for a petition against the introduction of compulsory identity cards. He was detained and filmed. The video would be destroyed after seven years but his police record would be a companion for life. As he remarked ruefully, 'All I have done is to use my freedom of speech.'

Another police record was acquired by a man on Brighton sea front for wearing what his Section 44 notice called 'an anti-Blair T-shirt'. On 29

June 2006 a different T-shirt slogan, 'Bollocks to Blair', convicted a Norfolk retailer under the Public Order Act of 'causing harassment/alarm/distress'. He was fined £80 by the police. In dealing with dissidents, the aim was to avoid public trials or controversy. On-the-spot fining behind closed doors recalled the bouncers' first warnings at the party conference. 'Be quiet, No more noise.'

In October 2005, Maya Evans was arrested and charged under the Serious Organized Crime and Police Act 2005 after standing by the Cenotaph in Whitehall and reading out the names of the ninety-seven British war dead in Iraq. It was what she called 'a remembrance ceremony' for these forgotten soldiers. At Bow Street, on 7 December, she was given a conditional discharge but ordered to pay £100 costs. The law she had broken was originally intended, as its name suggested, to combat organized crime. Section 132 was added to make it criminal to hold an unauthorized protest within a kilometre of Parliament, or any other place decreed by the Home Secretary. A similar protest outside the 2006 Labour Party Conference in Manchester, by two women whose sons had been killed in Iraq, was banned in advance by the city council.

A private expression of opinion, made without any intention of causing offence and without the knowledge that it could be overheard, was still criminal. In January 2006, a commuter walking past a metal detector at Highbury and Islington station in North London remarked to his companion that this security device was 'a piece of shit that wouldn't stop anyone'. Detectors also have ears. He was surrounded by six police officers who used their powers under the Public Order Act to fine him £80 and also give him a record. Had he been alone and talking to himself, it would have made no difference. The law was close to monitoring those few cubic centimetres within the skull which even Winston Smith in *Nineteen Eighty-four* believed to be safe from surveillance.[1]

One of those who removed Walter Wolfgang later told him, when he defended his freedom of speech, that the Foreign Secretary's speech at a Labour party conference was 'not the time' for free speech. Mr Straw had the greater right to be heard without interruption or contradiction. To oversensitive libertarians, this might recall Nuremberg in 1934 or the Soviet Chamber of Deputies. Yet it was no longer as outlandish as it sounded. In January 2006, the European Parliament approved a code of discipline to ban heckling and enforce 'mutual respect'. Any breach of the code would make an offender liable to forfeit ten days' subsistence allowance and to be excluded from the Parliament for ten days.

The suspension of a democratically elected representative at the behest of unelected officials, for speaking out of turn, was also less of a novelty. In February 2006, the Mayor of London was suspended by the Standards Board for England after causing offence to an Associated Newspapers reporter whom he claimed was 'doorstepping' him. Ken Livingstone had just left an anniversary party for the first election of an openly homosexual MP. As the unwelcome questioning continued, Mr Livingstone told the reporter that his newspaper group was a 'load of scumbags' who supported the Fascists in the 1930s. He likened the reporter to a concentration camp guard, obeying the orders of such masters. The reporter had already said he was 'actually quite offended' because he was Jewish; he added, 'I've got you on record for that.'

There was no doubt what was said. Yet for an elected mayor to be suspended by three unaccountable officials offended democratic instincts. If Mr Livingstone was to be punished, the voters were the people to do it. If it could not wait, an action for slander by the reporter or his newspaper – or a prosecution under race relations law – might be heard in open court. That was where Mr Livingstone took the Standards Board, arguing that 'Elected politicians should be removed only by the voters for breaking the law.' He won his case. 'Surprising though it may seem to some,' said Mr Justice Collins, 'the right of freedom of speech does extend to abuse.' It was a useful reminder to those politicians who demanded that free speech should be inoffensive.[2]

2

Those who lived through the second half of the twentieth century were to witness a dramatic inversion in the nature of censorship. For most people in the 1940s liberty of opinion and expression, in the shadow of Fascism and Communism, had marked the frontier of all liberty. In Franklin Roosevelt's Inaugural Address on 6 January 1941, 'Freedom of speech, everywhere in the world', was the first of his famous 'Four Freedoms', even ahead of freedom of worship and freedom from want or from fear. Where there was no freedom of speech, the other freedoms were not likely to flourish anyway, from the Soviet Union in the past century to Robert Mugabe's Zimbabwe in the present.

When the Second World War ended in 1945, universal suffrage at twenty-one years of age was only seventeen years old in Britain. It had taken a hundred and eighteen years to achieve this after the first unsuccessful Reform Bill was introduced into the House of Commons in 1810. Not surprisingly, the new freedom was still valued. The greatest war in history had just been fought to defend liberty against tyranny and by no one more steadfastly than the British. In the 1945 election, liberty was to accomplish more by democratic and constitutional means than the blood-letting of many revolutions.

Freedom of opinion, speech and the press was taught to children at mid-century. Pupils at A-level examinations in 1953, for example, were set Milton's *Areopagitica* (1644) by the Oxford and Cambridge Schools Examination Board. They entered the room with at least one quotation memorized. 'For who knows not that Truth is strong next to the Almighty . . . Let her and Falsehood grapple. Who ever knew Truth put to the worse in a free and open encounter?' For the young it was a simple, irrefutable faith. All governments must now provide that free encounter which, just then, seemed rarely to have existed outside the British Commonwealth and the United States. In 1952, the same candidates would have confronted John Stuart Mill, *On Liberty* (1859), with its ringing defence of free speech in their minds. 'If all mankind minus one were of one opinion and only one person were of the contrary opinion, mankind would be no more justified in silencing that one person than he, if he had the power, would be justified in silencing mankind.'[3]

The spread of television by the general election of 1955 began to insulate electioneering within the sanitized world of studio discussion. Previously, most people who saw anything of the process did so at open-air hustings, on sports fields, castle greens, cattle markets or show grounds, up and down the land. Candidates had the right to declare their policies in whatever terms they chose and the voters had an equal right to answer back. That candidates should meet the voters in this way had been fundamental to electoral politics. Eighteenth-century hustings were already lively in seats like Westminster where a large number of residents had the vote. Though the throwing of offal or dead cats had been discontinued, candidates in the 1950s were routinely barracked and sometimes reduced to silence. In 1945, crowds greeted Conservatives with communal singing of a popular hymn adapted for the occasion. 'Tell me the old, old story – Tell me the Tory story.' In 1950 the Labour party was out of favour and the hymn, readapted, was sung to its candidates, along with 'Poor old Attlee's got the wind up', to the chorus of 'John Brown's Body'.

Anyone proposing to cut a figure in public life and hold power over others was assumed to have the moral stamina and mental agility to take the initiative against hecklers either through wit or a blaze of sincerity. Hugh Gaitskell, under assault at the Labour Party Conference on 5 October

1960, confronted his opponents fiercely. 'I have been the subject of some criticism and attack! I have the right to reply!' He was not, after all, merely the desiccated calculating machine which Aneurin Bevan thought. The storm of acclamation that followed was such as Jack Straw might have envied.

Freedom of speech had been inseparable from the right to insult and offend. As John Stuart Mill remarked, where offence was taken it was often a sign that an argument had been 'telling and powerful'. Yet those who employed insult had better know their business. The most famous faux pas was Lord Sandwich's comment on John Wilkes, 'By God, Wilkes! You will die either on the gallows or of the pox' – and the reply, 'That depends, my lord, on whether I embrace your lordship's principles or your lordship's mistress.' Few contenders got up from the floor after such a blow.[4]

No one who saw it would easily forget Harold Macmillan's address to the UN General Assembly on 29 September 1960, in the presence of Nikita Khrushchev, when the British Prime Minister advocated disarmament reinforced by international inspection, which the Soviet Union denounced as 'spying'. As the translation came through his headphones, Khrushchev was seen gesticulating and shouting, pounding his fists, taking off his shoe and beating the desk. Macmillan, in a gesture of urbane courtesy, replied, 'I'd like a translation, if I may.' A gale of laughter and applause swept the auditorium. In that moment the dictator who boasted of being the most powerful military leader on earth, the terror of the Lubyanka and the labour camps, was ridiculed before the entire world.

In the 1950s and even in the 1960s it was generally believed that freedom from censorship in comment and opinion was an unalterable British tradition. The principal battle was to free books, plays and films, some banned for years, on the grounds of obscenity. Censorship in this area was treated with a mixture of scepticism and ribaldry. A cartoon from 1946 showed the Board of Film Censors hunched in a projection box with one member saying, 'Perhaps we could see it just once more before we ban it.'

Mockery of censorship often capitalized on censorship itself. Kingsley Amis, addressing the Oxford Union in November 1955 on his experience of living in Wales and of its most famous poet, remarked, 'I only ever heard Dylan say three words about Welsh Nationalism. And two of those were – "Welsh Nationalism".' The polite laughter which followed grew to a roar as the full meaning sank in. This would have been impossible with the unspoken word in general use. Conversely, hilarity broke out in 1999

6

when a senior City of Washington official was sacked. As the mayor later explained in some embarrassment, the man's vocabulary was somewhat larger than that of those around him. He had used the word 'niggardly' and been dismissed for racial abuse.[5]

One man's reputation illustrated the state of censorship in public discussion. In November 1965 the gadfly of the British establishment, Kenneth Tynan, was the first person to use 'fuck' – in the form of 'fucking' – on live television. It seemed as if a bomb had gone off at the BBC. Mrs Mary Whitehouse formed her Viewers' and Listeners' Association within the week. Wags who wished to insist there was something they would not do at any price, now said, 'Not Tynan well likely.' As the *enfant terrible* of theatre critics, Tynan had also reviewed Orson Welles' performance as Othello: he called it the lordly and mannered performance in *Citizen Kane*, 'lightly adapted to read Citizen Coon'. This passed without comment. Forty years later it would instantly have drawn the attention of the police Community Safety Unit and the Crown Prosecution Service to the author and his newspaper. At the same time, the most famous four-letter word would be heard in the streets, endlessly and tediously repeated.[6]

Throughout the 1960s and 1970s censors of pornography or obscenity, increasingly presented as clowns or hypocrites, fought a losing battle. Among other absurdities, the Lord Chamberlain's control of the stage had led to the preservation of an obscene and unperformed work, alleged to be by Gilbert and Sullivan, in the guardroom of St James's Palace, where it relieved the tedium of guard duty. The cast list of *The Sod's Opera* included Scrotum, 'a wrinkled old retainer', the Brothers Bollox, 'a pair of hangers-on', and Count Tostoff. T. H. White, in *The Age of Scandal*, unveiled the British Museum's manuscript letters of the Marquis de Sade, deemed so inflammatory that museum rules allowed them to be read only in the presence of the Archbishop of Canterbury and two other trustees.[7]

Censorship of this type was also attacked as futile. Obscenity, like beauty, is in the eye of the beholder. One young homosexual became aware of his yearnings, not through pornography but on seeing a pious Victorian painting of the boy Nelson in a sailor suit. A young woman disclosed to the social historian J. P. Mayer in *British Cinemas and their Audiences* a masochistic fantasy inspired by a film. Like the heroine, she was tied, in imagination, to a post as if to be beaten by a brutal guard, though sometimes saved by a hero of her choice. The offending film was *The Bohemian Girl*. Its principal stars were Laurel and Hardy.[8]

Laughter at the expense of censorship was not confined to the temperate zone. Three young Australian poets in 1944 created a non-existent, deceased, native poet Ern Malley, whose 'works' were random lines from a variety of sources, including manuals on swamp drainage and the breeding habits of the mosquito. Malley's poems had great success in the avant-garde magazine *Angry Penguins*, as the work of Australia's first modernist, before the hoax was revealed. Unfortunately, some lines were considered indecent and a prosecution was brought. In a surreal twist, the investigating police officer, Inspector Jacob Vogelsang, was affectionately and literally translated as 'Inspector Birdsong'. During a hilarious cross-examination he achieved a certain immortality. 'No, sir, I don't know what "incestuous" means. I think there is a suggestion of indecency about it.' When asked if he was familiar with the injunction, 'Stick it!' he replied that he had heard it used in the rough and tumble of criminal investigation but never by a member of the police force.[9]

3

As the bastions of moral censorship fell during the 1960s and 1970s, Labour or Conservative governments seemed more willing to prosecute those whose motives were political. Protection of press freedom against the Official Secrets Act was often the work of jurors. A jury upheld the right of Jonathan Aitken and the *Sunday Telegraph* to inform the nation and the House of Commons that they had been lied to by Harold Wilson as prime minister in 1971, when British arms were supplied to a corrupt regime in Nigeria to destroy the breakaway province of Biafra. A jury in 1985 acquitted a civil servant, in the face of instructions by the trial judge. Clive Ponting had revealed to a parliamentary committee what he regarded as deceit by the Ministry of Defence over the sinking of the Argentine cruiser *General Belgrano* in the Falklands War. The jury appeared to believe that Parliament and the public had a right to know of the allegation.

The new millennium and the years immediately preceding it saw a systematic introduction of political censorship by both parties in power. The Labour government of 1997 was credited with creating a society in which ordinary people began to confide to one another, 'You've got to be careful what you say', as if under occupation by a foreign power. Yet the Public Order Act was first put in place by a Conservative government in 1986. The aim of such legislation seemed twofold. In a new age of terrorism, there must be laws of public safety. In parallel, religious or racial groups, as well as sexual minorities, must be protected from offence.

Public safety encouraged such concepts as a Prevention of Terrorism Act or, indeed, a Serious Organized Crimes and Police Act. In practice, these secured the arrest of Walter Wolfgang for accusing the Foreign Secretary of lying. They also facilitated the arrest and conviction of Maya Evans for reading out the names of the British war dead in Iraq; a police record for a man who asked people to sign a petition against identity cards, and yet another for a man whose T-shirt denounced the actions of Bush and Blair in Iraq.

Within such legislation also lay the curious offence of 'glorifying' terrorism. Attacked as unworkable by parliamentary opponents, the provision left courts to decide who is and who is not a terrorist or what constitutes 'glorification' or 'incitement'. As Justice Oliver Wendell Holmes explained in 1925, 'Every idea is an incitement . . . The only difference between an expression of an opinion and an incitement . . . is the speaker's enthusiasm for the result.'[10]

One reader's terrorist is another reader's patriot or martyr, as the history of Ireland or the Middle East makes clear. Are Palestinian suicide bombers in Israel to be seen as patriots or terrorists in the British courts? Is it a crime to express admiration of those former IRA gunmen with whom the British government itself now does business? The very language of the new law makes the ancient courtroom arguments over such formulae as 'deprave and corrupt' in obscenity legislation seem uncontentious by comparison.

To all such laws there are practical objections. A trial is a public event and what was alleged to have been said by way of glorification must be spread through every newspaper and newscast. There may also be an acquittal. A final stumbling block to such provisions in the modern world is that those who are determined to glorify terrorism may do so easily from beyond the jurisdiction of the British courts by broadcast or Internet, even by the printed word.

The second object of the new laws, the protection of religious, racial or sexual minorities in the cause of equality or diversity, was to be accomplished in the first place under the Public Order Act. It was more likely to affect people in their daily lives than any form of anti-terrorist legislation. Words were to be criminal when they might cause 'harassment', 'alarm' or 'distress'. Whether a 'racist' or 'homophobic' comment warranted prosecution was at first for the police to decide. Penalties might then be imposed on the spot, without troubling a court of law. It was not necessary to show that anyone had been offended so long as offence was possible, had such a person been present. It was certainly not expected that people might have stood their ground and answered back. 'We must all be alike,' says Captain Beatty, the chief book-burner in Ray Bradbury's futuristic nightmare *Fahrenheit 451* (1954). 'Our civilization is so vast we can't have our minorities upset and stirred.'[11]

The objections to such proposals, so far as they proscribed religious hatred, came mostly from religious groups. Some 1,000 congregations from Christian denominations petitioned the Prime Minister. Jews, Christians and Muslims supported this. The National Secular Society, the British Humanist Association, the Christian Institute, the Evangelical Alliance and the Muslim Forum called on MPs to defeat the Religious Hatred Bill of 2005 in favour of freedom to debate, criticize and even to ridicule religious belief.[12]

Among individual protests was one from a pastor who had quoted the Koran while addressing a seminar on Islam in Australia during March 2002. On the basis of a complaint by the Islamic Council of Victoria, he was ordered by an Australian court to apologize and to pay some £30,000 to advertise the verdict. In default, he would go to prison for six months. The maximum prison sentence in Britain under the new legislation was to be seven years.

New laws, whether against terrorism or religious, racial and sexual intolerance, were to be implemented by a police force with good reason to feel demoralized and politicized. In the past half-century, too many of its officers had proved corrupt, to the point where the Metropolitan Police Commissioner, Sir Robert Mark, wryly described a good police force as one that catches more crooks than it employs. Ultimately it became a target of those who resented its treatment of racial and sexual minorities. Following the murder of the black teenager Stephen Lawrence in 1993, it was alleged that racist attitudes endemic in the force had led to the acquittals of those widely believed to be his murderers.

In 1999, the Macpherson inquiry found the police in this case to be 'institutionally racist'. This term seemed to be the Calvinism of so-called political correctness. Every policeman, however well-meaning, was tarnished by bigotry. Training in racial awareness and gender studies followed. Community Safety Units stood ready to enforce laws which gave priority to any suspected incident of racism, homophobia or domestic strife. Should the police fail to respond satisfactorily, they might themselves be guilty of secondary victimization. A 2005 report by the Commission for Racial Equality regretted that community and race relations training had still not made a sufficient impact on the nation's police but acknowledged that such courses were now 'politicized' and sensitive. It would not have been surprising if many officers and their commanders lived in apprehension of not being sensitive enough. However defective the new laws might be, the zeal with which they were enforced must never be in doubt.

Police forces were left by the new legislation to balance freedom from offence against freedom of speech. There was a right to freedom of speech but also a right not to be offended. There was therefore freedom for Ulster Protestants to stand outside Belfast City Hall on 19 December 2005 with placards reading 'Sodomy is Sin', a statement which the Bible surely obliged them to believe. Yet there must somehow be freedom from feeling harassed or distressed for the two lesbians who entered the hall to contract a 'marriage' under the Civil Partnership Act 2004. It was a precarious and short-lived coexistence.

The expression of religious belief became a target under the Public Order Act. On 26 October 2005, for example, John Banda of the United Church of Zambia was stopped by the police near London Bridge. He was threatened with arrest and prosecution for displaying 'abusive or insulting' material, intended to stir up religious hatred. In other words, he carried a placard with two messages, 'Jesus Christ is Lord' and 'Repent, therefore, and be converted that your sins may be blotted out'. No one had complained about him.

An evangelist with his placard was a common sight in the nation's past, in streets, fairgrounds or on holiday beaches. If open-air preaching to the unconverted, the unbelieving and downright heathen had been illegal, where would this have left such towering figures of the English tradition as John and Charles Wesley or the 'tinker theologians' of the seventeenth century? The love of Jesus was usually balanced in their preaching against warnings to sinners of hellfire, which the Public Order Act 1986 might now call 'harassment, alarm or distress'. Indeed, they were said to have caused faintings and fits as the hardened sinner was set on the path to salvation. Were Salvation Army missions or Corpus Christi processions now illegal?

The Wesleys might well have antagonized York magistrates sitting on 25 April 1997 as they had, for example, Staffordshire magistrates in October 1743. Two open-air evangelists, Alan and Alison Redmond-Bate, were convicted of obstructing the police by preaching to a crowd in the city centre. The police dismissed their gospel as 'religious hype and highly charged twaddle'. Their predecessors denounced the Wesleys as 'disorderly persons, styling themselves Methodist Preachers'. Since then, free speech had been particularly protective of hype and twaddle, even in the form of defeatist Communist propaganda during 1940. By 1997, however, it was possible to curb unwelcome views quietly without the publicity of a further prosecution, by orders banning the speakers from specific areas. Mr Redmond-Bate claimed that he preached because he believed 'This nation is in great trouble.' It seemed he was not alone.

As for Mr Banda, how he might stir up distress or hatred with his placard was not explained. 'When I came to Britain, I thought I was coming to a Christian country,' he said sadly. 'I did not realize that to advertise my faith would make me a criminal.' He vowed to continue his campaign and take the consequences. At least it was open to a jury to ignore the law and agree with him.[13]

Conflict was inevitable, for example, between religious belief and the endorsement of homosexual conduct which fifty years earlier would itself have been criminal. On 6 September 2006, Christian Voice handed out leaflets at a Mardi Gras rally in Cardiff: 'Same-sex love – Same-sex sex. What does the Bible say?' Their leader, Stephen Green, was arrested under the Public Order Act and charged with using words or behaviour 'likely to cause harassment or distress'. The charge cited such texts as 'Thou shalt not lie with mankind as with womankind. It is an abomination.' After Mr Green had spent several hours in a cell, the South Wales Police and the Crown Prosecution Service decided to bring the case to Cardiff Magistrates Court on 28 September. Then it was revealed that a reviewing lawyer had overruled a prosecution based on quotations from the Bible, presumably because a jury might hesitate to criminalize them. It seemed, after all, only a step away from convicting an evangelist who distributed the Ten Commandments because their contents might cause distress to those in breach of them.

The cases of Lynette Burrows, author of *Fight for the Family*, and Sir Iqbal Sacranie, of the Muslim Council of Great Britain, were in a different category. In December 2005 in a Radio Five Live discussion, Mrs Burrows suggested that to allow two homosexuals to adopt a boy was equal in risk to two heterosexual men adopting a girl. It was not necessary to agree with this to see it as a rational argument and an issue of public interest in the debate which the BBC had facilitated. It was open to anyone to prove, if they could, that Mrs Burrows was talking nonsense, as it was to her supporters to justify her view. Instead, the Community Safety Unit of Fulham police interviewed her on the following day over this alleged 'homophobic incident', as her words became, reported by a member of the public. There were insufficient grounds for a prosecution but it was the duty of the unit to record and note such incidents. Mrs Burrows found the police action and explanation sinister and unacceptable.

On BBC Radio 4 in January 2006, Sir Iqbal Sacranie remarked that homosexual practices incurred health risks and were morally harmful. As with the South Wales evangelists, if he believed the precepts of his religion and the text of the Koran, it was impossible that he should think otherwise. Once more, the truth or falsity of his warning was a matter of public interest and yet it appeared to be the very thing with which the investigation was not concerned. Without the issue being argued, the homosexual community had most to lose by rumour and innuendo; next weekend, the press carried reports of members of that community who deliberately engaged in 'unprotected' sex with others known to have Aids, as a form of 'Russian Roulette'. The police investigated Sir Iqbal. Again they took no action. What they appeared to want was not justification of his views but silence. Had they charged him, he would no doubt have stood by the truth of his words and brought evidence to justify them. Most people wanted the truth in such matters. A public debate, unimpeded by censorship, might have given them that.

The first case to offer a possibility of conviction for homophobia was at Oxford in May 2005. An undergraduate celebrating the end of his exams approached a mounted policeman in the High Street. He said, 'Excuse me, do you realize your horse is gay?' Thames Valley Police afterwards claimed he was drunk and disorderly. The Crown Prosecution Service later admitted there was no evidence that he had been disorderly. Yet his alleged crime was now a homophobic offence under the Public Order Act. Thames Valley Police insisted he had made 'homophobic comments . . . deemed offensive to people passing by'. Since no other passer-by had complained, there were facetious suggestions that the horse had protested at the remark.

Those passing by had not been questioned: they were deemed to have been offended. Two squad cars arrived and the young man was arrested. After a night in the cells, he was subjected to on-the-spot justice and a fine of £80. This would give him a police record and would presumably affect his chances of employment. He refused to pay. Before the magistrates on 12 January 2006 the Crown Prosecution Service conceded that they lacked evidence to support a case. It seemed a delicate balance of the farcical and the sinister.

The past, as well as the present, was at issue. In 2004 a play which had held the London stage for four centuries was cut by the National Theatre to avoid offence. Christopher Marlowe's *Tamburlaine the Great* had been written in 1587 and published three years later. Though the Muslim Council discouraged any cuts, they could not speak for those Islamic fundamentalists who might stage a riot. The production was 'smoothed' over, as the management described it, to omit such boasts of Tamburlaine's in the second part of the play as:

> Where's the Turkish Alcoran,
> And all the heaps of superstitious books
> Found in the temples of that Mahomet
> Whom I have thought a god? They shall be burnt.

Tamburlaine goes on to taunt Muhammad inviting him, if he has any power, to come down from heaven and work a miracle. No miracle occurs and copies of the Koran are burnt on stage. The long speech with its references to the Koran and Muhammad was cut and the burning became merely an incineration of what the theatre called 'a load of books'. In the play, Tamburlaine shows equal contempt for both Christianity and Islam. Ironically, Marlowe illustrates Christian perfidy towards Islam. King Sigismund of Hungary and his allies put aside religious differences to form a pact with the Turks against Tamburlaine. In an act of fourteenth-century *realpolitik*, Sigismund waits until the Turks disarm, then attacks them, repudiating his oath sworn 'by He who made the world and saved my soul'. A further irony was that the play should have been licensed for performance and publication by the political censorship of Elizabeth I, only to fall foul of multiculturalism four centuries later.

Though *The Merchant of Venice* was a Shakespearean classic, Arnold Wesker doubted that Shylock the Jew could still be safely portrayed. Historically, however, the part of Shylock was a gift to a great actor with the power to personify a beleaguered hero. William Hazlitt saw Edmund Kean's first night on 26 January 1814. Kean's 'terrible energy' drew 'a thunder of applause . . . our sympathies are much oftener with him than with his enemies.' In 1879, Sir Henry Irving showed 'a firm front to the last . . . a fine curl of withering scorn upon his lips', as he walked away 'to die in silence and alone'. Now it seemed Shylock belonged 'inescapably to the literature of anti-Semitism', as John Gross put it when the play was filmed for schools in 1996. It was debatable whether children should be exposed to it. In the end, Shylock was allowed out on licence but with a teacher guiding pupils to a proper understanding of the play. Even such guidance was not always sufficient. By February 2006, the Welsh Assembly was concerned that Shakespeare might lead to child abuse. Its guidelines advised drama teachers to cut or adapt plays to prevent kisses between characters like Romeo and Juliet being any more than a peck on the cheek and not to be influenced by concerns for the 'artistic integrity of the text'.[14]

Those who thought the National Theatre had overreacted in the case of

Tamburlaine the Great were less certain two months later. The Birmingham Repertory Theatre staged *Behzti* ('Dishonour') by Gurpreet Kaur Bhatti. It included an incident of rape and murder in a Sikh temple. On 18 December, a crowd of more than 1,000 Sikhs attacked the theatre with stones and eggs, forcing their way in and halting the performance. On Monday, the director of the theatre deplored the denial of free speech but took the play off as a matter of public safety. His opponents approved. 'Free speech can go so far,' said one of them warningly. To yield to protests had been rare in the theatre since *Perdition* was taken off by the Royal Court in 1987 because of objections to its portrayal of Zionist leaders as wartime allies of Germany. There had been no riot, however.

Within a month of *Behzti*, the BBC televised *Jerry Springer the Opera*, depicting what the Christian Alliance called a 'perverted nappy-wearing Jesus, swearing and ranting'. Despite protests and demonstrations, the BBC went ahead. A number of theatres followed suit. A spokesman for the Global Gospel Fellowship, which forwarded 50,000 objections, suggested that the BBC would not have dared to transmit the play had the protesters been Muslims or Sikhs. Indeed, both the Sikhs of Birmingham and the Muslim Council of Great Britain supported the Christians against the BBC. At a time when censorship on religious grounds still seemed an antique notion, Christianity had been an easy target, most famously in the film *The Life of Brian* in 1979 and in Martin Scorsese's *Last Temptation of Christ*, passed by the Board of Film Censors in 1988 and shown on television in 1995. Thereafter, the adage that debunking Judaism is Fascist, debunking Islam is racist, but debunking Christianity is free speech acquired a certain plausibility.

Theatres, cinemas, writers and the press might seem to have more to fear from mob violence than from legislation. Yet in their attempt to outlaw religious hatred it was futile for government ministers, including a prime minister, to make promises that a new law would never interfere with art or literature. In 1857, for example, Lord Chief Justice Campbell swore that he had not 'the most distant contemplation' of his Obscene Publications Act being applied to true literature, not even to Dumas' *La Dame aux camélias*, whose morality he deplored. By the end of the reign, those condemned included the Protestant Electoral Union; what *The Times* called two 'well-intentioned' philanthropists who had issued a fifty-year-old tract on birth control, and Henry Vizetelly who went to prison for publishing Maupassant and Zola.[15]

Once a law is passed it is no longer the property of Parliament but is liable to interpretation by the courts and by judges with the eyes of government ministers upon them. Parliamentary good intentions are of little value. Meantime its likely and insidious effect is one of self-censorship, imposed on theatrical producers, publishers or authors who cannot predict the law's verdict on their works and are encouraged to play safe.

4

In the implementation of censorship political nightmares like *Fahrenheit 451* or *Nineteen Eighty-four* identify two powers necessary to the control of truth. The first is a manipulation of language, of which Orwell's Newspeak was the famous example. The second is power over the historical past. In *Nineteen Eighty-four* it is a required belief that the past belongs to the Party. Under torture, Winston Smith is taught that who controls the present controls the future and who controls the past controls the present. When he discovers history which contradicts official 'truth' he must learn to believe it false. His torture intensifies until he not only learns but believes that '4' equals '5' if the Party decrees it.

The new millennium offered nothing as extreme as Newspeak but showed how it might be implemented by governments. *The Equal Treatment Bench Book* of 2006, for example, issued by the Lord Chancellor's department, included terms henceforth unacceptable for use by the judiciary. They included 'man and wife', perhaps offensive or prejudicial to unmarried couples; 'Asian', which might offend Asians; 'immigrant', which might cause prejudice against immigrants; 'asylum seeker', which might discriminate against asylum seekers, and 'homosexual', which might distress homosexuals. Before the purge was over, it was not entirely surprising that the term 'common sense' was banished. The Metropolitan Police supplemented the list by outlawing the Victorian term 'yob' to describe the antisocial young, for fear it might alienate them. It had once been backward slang – in this case 'boy' spelt backwards. Embarrassingly, it was then noted that 'yob' had been sanctioned both by the Prime Minister in the House of Commons and by the Labour party election manifesto of 2005.[16]

Control of courtroom language was seen as a further politicization of the judiciary. To many, the judiciary had been increasingly a protector of individual liberties against government, at least since Lord Denning famously informed a cabinet minister in his court in 1977, 'Be you never so high, the law is above you.' Lord Ackner in October 2005 reasserted the duty of judges to ensure that governments act lawfully. 'If we take that away from the judiciary we are really apeing what happened in Nazi Germany.'

16

In the establishment of control over language, words with a long history were not exempt from attention. The Welsh Development Agency, five hundred of whose employees had been trained in 'equality and diversity issues', laid down that the term 'nit-picking' was unacceptable under the Racial Equality Act. The word had referred to searching the heads of slaves for lice. In the real world, nits also believed in equality and searching had extended over all races and classes.

Curiously, neither the Welsh Development Agency nor the Lord Chancellor's office and other connoisseurs of the unacceptable attempted to exterminate 'gay' when describing homosexuals. 'Homosexual' was objected to because Krafft-Ebing first used it in 1886 to describe a medical condition. Yet it was preferable to 'gay', universally used in the Victorian period, and within living memory, as a gentle synonym for 'prostitute' or 'whore'. 'I ain't gay,' says Kitty to Walter in the diary of *My Secret Life* (1888). 'What do you call gay?' 'Why, the gals that come out regular of a night, dressed up, and get their livings by it.' 'Gay' had the potential to cause distress and was surely a candidate for oblivion in the Welsh Development Agency or a Lord Chancellor's list.[17]

Cool Britannia's careless vocabulary also adopted the term 'feisty'. It became both compliment and cliché, used to flatter a young woman of spirit and 'attitude', as in 'feisty young chick'. Had she known its true meaning, she might have considered an action for damages. A feist was a small and snappy dog of evil odour. It was kept in the southern United States by poor families in the nineteenth century to disguise their own unwashed state. Its derivation was located by Chambers Dictionary in medieval English as 'fisten', meaning to break wind.

Sometimes there was a hint of Newspeak in official terminology, as in the word 'diversity'. It might seem to welcome the dissident, provocative and rebellious, but it did nothing of the kind. 'Diversity' was the subject of compulsory training not only at the Welsh Development Agency but in universities, public services and business corporations. It sought to ensure that employees thought and acted alike in relations with colleagues and consumers, of whatever race or sex. It denoted obligatory, not diverse, institutional values. It did not mean, for example, that Muslim women were welcome to wear veils or Christian women their crucifixes but that both were liable to be banned for fear of offending.

At St Andrews University in 2004 the student newspaper was closed and its student staff required to attend 'diversity awareness training'. Three Welsh evangelists had protested against a sacrilegious play. In a light-hearted aside, the paper's editor suspected the Welsh of 'evil doings, ever since they spawned the caterwauling Charlotte Church'. Charlotte Church and the people of Wales had more important things to do than be offended by a student joke. They might, however, resent being described as a 'minority group' rather than a 'nation', of which the university's 'diversity awareness' directorate seemed ignorant.

Diversity of opinion was certainly not encouraged on sensitive topics. In March 2006, a senior lecturer at the University of Leeds alleged that available evidence would show black people to be genetically less intelligent than whites. He was not invited to defend his view in Milton's 'free and open encounter' but told to leave work, go home and keep his mouth shut. This gave the impression that the entire university could not produce a debater to confute him and it short-changed the black community in failing to do so. By the 1980s, many institutions had embraced 'assertiveness', and even assertiveness training, depending on it as an alternative to the powers of argument.

The Leeds incident was a depressing contrast to the American response to a similar thesis in *The Bell Curve* (1994), when the next issue of the *New Republic* contained a digest of the book and eighteen replies dealing with defects of evidence, systemization and argument. This storm in a plastic teacup also left unresolved such questions as whether it is an offence against racial equality laws for a white person to cite tests showing American Asians to have a higher average IQ than whites, as *The Bell Curve* had done, or for a gentile to show that Jews have a higher average. Is it illegal to make a comparison unfavourable to one's own race? The official response seemed to echo the Brighton bouncers, 'Be quiet. No more noise.'

Almost daily there appeared some example of what was now called 'political correctness gone mad' similar to what Orwell categorized as 'smelly little orthodoxies'. They ranged from a ban on advertising a Passion play for fear of promoting one religious group above another to demands that Scotland Yard's Black Museum be renamed to avoid racist language; from a Somerset vicar whose resignation was suggested by the Racial Equality Council for joking in his parish magazine about a 'nip in the air' and possibly offending the Japanese to a Scottish branch of Matalan which excluded England football shirts in order not to offend Scots.

Christmas-time became enlivened by self-parody. In 2005 the Department of Education warned against terrifying young children with the figure of Santa Claus or alarming them by pantomimes, while it encouraged electronic Christmas cards to save paper and the replacing of presents by breakfast in bed. The Hindu Forum of Britain deplored an Asian 'Madonna and Child' on Royal Mail Christmas stamps as insulting to its religion. Birmingham abolished 'Christmas' in favour of 'Winterval'.

For more than two centuries, censors had remained sensitive to any suggestion that they were acting as censors. The British Board of Film Censors in 1988 had renamed itself a board of 'classification' so as not to seem to be doing what it actually was doing. In 2005 'Equality Essentials' for staff of Kirklees Metropolitan Borough outlawed sexist words like 'chairman' or 'policeman', and denounced phrases like 'political correctness' or 'political correctness gone mad'. 'Political correctness gone mad' was 'a direct physical attack'. Yet it was gentler than the prophecy of its ancestor: 'Quis deus vult perdere, prius dementat – Whom the god wishes to destroy, he first makes mad.'[18]

5

Altering history to suit the present is an ancient craft, more effective when images accompany words. After Dan Brown's novel *The Da Vinci Code* had run its course in 2006, an Opinion Research Business poll found that 60 per cent of those who had read it now believed that Christ fathered a child on Mary Magdalene. The film *Enigma* in 2000 showed the crew of a US submarine capturing the German code machine which, in reality, had been captured in 1942 by the crew of the destroyer HMS *Petard*, two of whom died in the process. *Colditz Story*, dominated by American actors, attracted scorn since there were seldom any American prisoners in the castle. Of nineteen escapes, eleven were British, the rest being French, Polish and Canadian. Without American escapers, however, it was said that box office takings would suffer.

Even documentary television was susceptible of such treatment. In 1997 *The Traitor King* portrayed Edward VIII, Duke of Windsor, as a British staff officer in 1940. He was described leaving Paris, for Spain, to sun himself while others fought and died. It must have been so: he was shown on film in a bathing suit propelling a pedalo through sunlit shallows. Most viewers might not recognize this as a home movie shot by Mrs Simpson on the Dalmatian coast in 1936. The real Duke of Windsor, whatever his faults, was making a rather dangerous and disagreeable trek to Spain in the consul-general's party from Nice.

To punish unwelcome views of history in Britain would seem incompatible with freedom of opinion. It was certainly true that two centuries earlier Jonathan Swift's account of the end of the Stuart dynasty in 1710–14, *The Four Last Years of the Queen*, was so unpopular with governments that it was considered unsafe to publish the book until 1758, thirteen years after its author's death. Yet there had seemed no place for the censorship of history in modern Britain, as opposed to its alteration.

Some European states, particularly those like Austria, France and Germany, which had taken part in the Holocaust of 1933–45, had made it a criminal offence to deny that the crime took place. In Germany, even a comparison between Hitler's 'Final Solution' and the firestorms caused in German cities by Allied bombing brought criminal charges in April 2005. In Britain, on 29 January 1997, Tony Blair as leader of the opposition promised: 'There is a very strong case that denial of the Holocaust should be a specific offence. We are giving active consideration to how this should be achieved.' The promise was unenthusiastically received by most historians and campaigners for freedom of speech who believed that demonstration of the truth was more telling than the punishment of falsehood. The promise did not long survive the election victory, perhaps because anything that might be presented as an official version of the past, however finely spun, had inevitable Orwellian overtones.

The origin of the German law of 1994 was in the *Historikerstreit* quarrels of the 1980s, when conservative historians like Joachim Fest were attacked for suggesting that, repulsive though the Nazis may have been, their evil was not unique. Comparative evil is a contradiction. Yet the tyranny of Stalin or the fall in population of German territories during the horrors of the Thirty Years War, from 21,000,000 to 13,000,000, suggested that there was no monopoly in wickedness on a grand scale.

Criminalization of Holocaust denial would not be without some precedent in Britain. The great constitutional event between Magna Carta and the Reform Bill of 1832 was the Glorious Revolution of 1689, when constitutional government replaced absolute monarchy. For a century it was criminal to insult its glory, a charge tacked on in almost every seditious libel case. In 1792 Thomas Paine was charged with seditious libel after denouncing 'the farce of monarchy and aristocracy' in his *Rights of Man*. He was convicted additionally of 'vilifying the Glorious Revolution'. By the new millennium, vilifying was no longer a problem since so few people had ever heard of the Glorious Revolution.[19]

However deserving the cause, censorship of history is easily tainted. Article 301 of the Turkish Penal Code, for example, makes 'insulting Turkishness' a crime. It is illegal to affirm Turkey's slaughter of over a million Armenians by 1915, or sully the memory of Ataturk or even criticize a court ban on such subjects. Several journalists were prosecuted in 2006 for attacking a ban. Turkey's Nobel prizewinner, Orhan Pamuk, was tried, though acquitted, for telling a Swiss journalist that massacres of Armenians and Kurds were forbidden topics.

Such censorship is also open to political exploitation by enemies. In revenge against Turkey, the French National Assembly on 12 October 2006 made it criminal in France to deny the Armenian massacres, which it was a crime to affirm in Turkey. The assembly majority was immediately accused of hostility to Islam and of trawling for the large Armenian vote in France. The European Commission compounded confusion by adding that it was not for the law to write history, which would presumably invalidate bans on Holocaust denial.

On 11 December 2006, in an impressive gesture of spite, the Iranian government chose to reinforce its hostility to the state of Israel by hosting a conference of Holocaust deniers, 'Review of the Holocaust: Global Vision'. Among its topics was the alleged faking of the gas chambers at Auschwitz. Sixty delegates would be received by President Mahmoud Ahmadinejad, who had already described the Holocaust as 'a myth'. The conference was to conclude that it had been 'one of the most important propaganda tools to politically justify the support for the Jewish people in the twentieth century'.

The Labour government's proposal to ban Holocaust denial had been aimed principally against the British historian David Irving, later imprisoned for three years in Austria in 2006 for seeking to 'diminish, deny or justify' the Holocaust. This charge related to speeches in Austria sixteen years earlier that included such passages as, 'It makes no sense to transport people from Vienna, Amsterdam and Brussels, 500 kilometres to Auschwitz, simply to liquidate them, when it can be more easily done 8 kilometres from the city where they live.' Irving could only admit that his words denied the Holocaust. Further papers of Hitler had now persuaded him that the Holocaust had occurred. Even so he was sent to prison for three years, raised to martyrdom by a claim to have suffered for free speech.

In the matter of Holocaust denial, the true encounter of John Milton's Truth and Falsehood was to be vindicated, not in the Viennese court, where the result was preordained and savoured of a nation ill at ease with its own past, but in the High Court in London in 2000, where Irving brought a libel action against Penguin Books and Deborah Lipstadt. Professor Lipstadt had denounced him as a Holocaust denier, and therefore a liar. Irving maintained that the story of millions of victims gassed and cremated at Auschwitz must be false; and if such things did not happen at Auschwitz, the most notorious of the camps, surely the

Holocaust was called into question. He claimed incontrovertible proof in RAF reconnaissance photographs of Auschwitz, which showed fuel dumps of coke. The amount of coke was inadequate for the cremation of so many bodies. The coke available for each body would fit into a small mineral water bottle. No one could hope to burn a human body with so little. There was therefore no Holocaust at Auschwitz, and if not there, it was nowhere.

Richard Rampton QC cross-examined patiently but persistently, rather like an Oxford don with a difficult pupil. He too had evidence on the matter of the cremations. His figures showed the difference between a hopeless attempt to burn a single body with so little fuel and the cremating of bodies in the mass, where fat from one would serve to ignite the next. The figures and the science proved that there was, after all, enough fuel at Auschwitz for this terrible purpose – there had been a Holocaust.[20]

Truth had vanquished Falsehood. A television record of the exchanges went round the world. No law against historical denial could have had the impact of quiet argument. What good, if any, came of the Austrian trial was questionable. One of the first volumes Irving found in the prison library was a German translation of his book *Hitler's War*. There was no reason to ban it in Austria or anywhere else. As its author describes it, the war is seen from Hitler's side of his desk. The Holocaust is not denied but disposed of by simply omitting it where necessary. He autographed the prison copy, in tribute to his hosts.

Even Orwell was too optimistic in believing that the records of the past must be altered to suit the present. In reality, governments need only allow the tides of oblivion to drown the past except for certain topics, perhaps including the Holocaust and the slave trade, which may be politically useful. In the new millennium, a majority of people told pollsters that Oliver Cromwell fought at the Battle of Hastings, as some schoolchildren three years earlier named him a Battle of Britain pilot. The 'Glorious Revolution', once protected so zealously, meant nothing. Those who sought to preserve the memory of the Holocaust had less to fear from David Irving than from an educational system which, on the basis of a poll in 2001, produced 200,000 British schoolchildren between eleven and eighteen who believed the nation's prime minister in the Second World War had been Adolf Hitler. Three years later, 20 per cent of Britons named the wartime prime minister as Harold Wilson, while 10 per cent now thought Adolf Hitler was a fictional character.[21]

6

As the first government of the millennium drew to its end, those who felt grudgingly that 'Nowadays you've got to be careful what you say' had a brief moment of glee. The teeth of correctness-gone-mad sank into the ankle of Cool Britannia.

In 1999 there had been elections to a newly created Welsh Assembly. Wales seemed to care little about this body, promised by the government in 1997. Asked if they would like an assembly, half the electorate did not bother to vote; of those who did, the majority in favour was less than one per cent. On this shaky foundation elections were held, the Labour party expecting outright victory. Those who had not wanted an assembly now seemed to take revenge on the party that had saddled them with it. Labour did not win a majority.

A former Downing Street aide, Lance Price, published his memoirs, *The Spin Doctor's Diary*, six years later. He recalled the Prime Minister watching the poll results on television and allegedly heard him shout several times, 'F—— Welsh!' This item was removed from the book before publication at government request but became news in the press. Someone complained of a racist incident to the North Wales Police. The law now required the force to investigate every such complaint or face charges of 'secondary victimization'. The North Wales Chief Constable confirmed that the Prime Minister's alleged remarks might be incitement under the Public Order Act.

In the New Year, there was a public row. Lord Mackenzie of Framwellgate, a former senior police officer, called the investigation a waste of money; the Crown Prosecution Service advised dropping it. Lord Mackenzie was warned by North Wales Police of the consequences to him of such comments. He, in turn, suggested they might find themselves in trouble if they tried to intimidate a member of Parliament; he would not bow to conduct 'befitting the Stasi secret police of East Germany'. It was as inevitable as a well-aimed custard pie that the press should now nickname the North Wales force 'the Welsh Stasi'.

North Wales Police, also dubbed the 'Keystone Cops' for acting seven years late, sent officers to Downing Street on 2 May 2006. Afterwards, the government said that what had been discussed was a matter for the North Wales Police. The North Wales Police made no comment. Yet those oppressed by the need to be careful of what they said might reflect that the Prime Minister at his 1997 victory had vowed to 'hit the ground running' and now appeared to have done exactly that.

Major cases under the new laws were few, though ministers had insisted on the laws because they could not fight twenty-first-century crime with nineteenth-century methods. Yet in redefining free speech, it seemed they chose to fight twenty-first-century crime with eighteenth-century methods. The purpose appeared to be not so much prosecution as intimidation.

A case in open court involved publicizing objectionable material. Two hundred years earlier this was avoided by such devices as the Attorney-General's 'ex-officio information'. The troublemaker was not brought before a magistrate but charged directly by a political appointee and required to pay ruinous sureties pending trial. Without sureties there was no bail. The trial was delayed and a culprit effectively served a term of imprisonment. The charges could then be dropped – and new ones brought as necessary. Not until 1819 was the trial delay limited to a year. In court, the only proof needed of guilt was whether the defendant had published the opinions complained of.

Even more adroitly, the new millennium might deny troublemakers their 'day in court'. An arrest and a Section 44 stop-and-search notice plus an identification video ensured a police record. Punishment, if necessary, might be dealt out quietly in a prosecutor's office on the evidence of a policeman. Like ex-officio informations the proceedings could be brought repeatedly, until dissidents learnt obedience. They need only think of the effect of a police record on families or livelihoods. The artistic director of the National Theatre rightly concluded in 2005, 'I'm proud of this play – but I'm not prepared to do seven years in jail for it.' It was a state of mind any censor would approve, as might rioters at the Birmingham Repertory Theatre or any Islamic fundamentalists offended by *Tamburlaine the Great*.[22]

History had often been a chronicle of liberty lost or gained. In the twenty-first century many people felt that in the right to speak, to argue, to offend, the past had been better than the present. Folklore, if not nostalgia, evoked a perfect day when Britons were not slaves; when freeborn Englishmen and women inherited liberty as a birthright and not by courtesy of a government; when freedom of opinion and the power of argument were common property. It was a time to which reformers two centuries ago had looked forward, as others now looked back. Where had that perfect day come from, where had it gone – and had it gone for ever?

2

In Retrospect: 'The Perfect Day'

IN THE SUMMER of 1884, William Stubbs set out from Oxford to become Bishop of Chester. As Regius Professor of History in the University for eighteen years, he left behind him a four-volume *Constitutional History of England*, published in 1874–8. In writing it he felt 'little desire for literary fame', protesting that much of the work was 'dull reading', that it was 'tiring my eyes out'. Yet he woke to find his *Constitutional History* hailed as a monument and a masterpiece. It was coupled with Edward Gibbon as English historical writing at its best.[1]

Yet Stubbs' *History* was a curious book, ending with the coming of the Tudors. For him, what had happened by then determined the course of the next four centuries. His explanation occurs in a striking image at the end of his final volume. In 1485 England stood at the division of the Middle Ages and the modern world. In Stubbs' view, a single change carried history irreversibly from one era to the next. It was not a war, nor a rebellion, not even a revolution in belief, but the introduction of moveable type into England by William Caxton in 1476. Two centuries later, when William of Orange landed in England to accomplish the Glorious Revolution, the first weapon unloaded from his ship was his printing press. To Stubbs, the press was the 'apt emblem or embodiment' of a future in which 'every man becomes a reader and a thinker; the Bible comes to every family, and each man is priest in his own household. The light is not so brilliant but it is everywhere, and it shines more and more unto the perfect day.'[2]

There was nothing to suggest the imprisonment, torture, disfigurement and execution which were the rewards of some English publishers and authors in the next three centuries; nothing to suggest more subtle methods of suppression by political and financial coercion. These still controlled the press until five years before Stubbs was born. He looked over and beyond such aberrations towards his own middle years in the 1870s. By then the light which fell everywhere was shed by popular history and fiction, and by poetry more widely read than poetry had ever been. It shone by courtesy of publishers like Moxon or Bentley and family magazines appearing at weekly or monthly intervals. The new enlightenment of Carlyle, Ruskin or Mill could be borrowed or bought from the lending libraries of Charles Mudie or, after 1851, from the railway bookstalls of W. H. Smith. In the pilgrimage of human progress, for Stubbs and his contemporaries, the perfect day unto which the light of freedom shone was Victorian England. This progress had been as much a crusade as any in the course of history, the earthly equivalent of many an evangelical hymn and hope: 'Lift your eyes, ye sons of light: Zion's city is in sight!'

Some disappointment was inevitable. Freedom will not benefit those who are unfit to use it, though it may be meaningless if restricted only to those who are. Nor was the new enlightenment universal. The liberty of the press which the later Victorians enjoyed was a recent and very rapid development in England. Outside the English-speaking world it was a rarity. Russia remained an unenlightened despotism. Prussia under Bismarck was subject to the Press Decree of 1851, banning all publications calculated to bring the crown, the state or the church into disrepute. As late as 30 October 1902, *The Times* reported the cases of two newspaper editors who had recently been led in chains through the streets of Dortmund and Beuthen, following their convictions. In France, freedoms lost by the press law of 1835 were briefly regained by the revolution of 1848, only to be lost again under the Second Empire of 1851–70.

The brightest beacon of freedom, in that part of the world which had a press of any kind, shone from the First Amendment to the Constitution of the United States: 'Congress shall make no law respecting an establishment of religion, or prohibiting the free exercise thereof; or abridging the freedom of speech, or of the press; or the right of the people peaceably to assemble, and to petition the government for a redress of grievances.' In Britain, those who held such freedoms were conscious of how recently that prerogative had been acquired.

2

William Stubbs was born in 1825. In the previous ten years, the government and its supporters had launched over a hundred political press prosecutions important enough to reach Westminster Hall and the Court of King's Bench. While Stubbs was a boy these continued, dwindling after the radicals gained a measure of electoral reform in 1832. Until then, publishers, authors and booksellers faced fines and imprisonment, as well as demands for sureties on a scale intended to bankrupt them. Their crimes were the publication of sedition, blasphemy or obscenity, and criminal defamation of important individuals.

During the Napoleonic Wars a few defendants, after criticizing the personal habits of the Prince of Wales, had been fastened in the pillory at Charing Cross or the Royal Exchange to be pelted for an hour or two by a hostile mob. In some earlier cases, the pillory had been fatal, a licence for the mob to stone to death an unpopular culprit. All this was on the rim of collective memory as Stubbs published his *History*.

When his contemporaries looked back at the fight for democracy and political justice, free expression was in the foreground of the struggle. Until 1695 each printed publication was subject to a licence from bodies empowered by the crown. Macaulay, whose *History of England* pre-dated Stubbs by a decade, described the abolition of licensing as having done more for liberty and civilization than either Magna Carta or the Bill of Rights. It was a large claim, but it was echoed across the field of historical writing. H. T. Buckle, in his *History of Civilization in England* (1857–61), described the free press of the 1850s as having 'diffused among the people a knowledge of their power and . . . to an almost incredible extent, aided the progress of English civilization'.[3]

This sense of liberal jubilation was almost like the end of a great war or the fall of a loathsome dictatorship. The truly remarkable feature was the speed with which the change had come. Among authors, books or publishers facing the judges of King's Bench in the century before Victoria came to the throne were William Congreve, Jonathan Swift, Henry Fielding, William Shakespeare posthumously, John Cleland's *Fanny Hill*, John Wilkes, Thomas Paine's *Rights of Man* and his *Age of Reason*, William Cobbett, Leigh Hunt, Percy Bysshe Shelley, Lord Byron and the Marquis de Sade's *Juliette*.[4]

The defendants had been a distinguished, not to say varied, company. Shakespeare was declared seditious because Fielding had quoted him in such a way as to mock the Walpole government in 1737. Most of these crimes were described as seditious libel or blasphemous libel. However, this had nothing to do with defamation. 'Libel' was merely lawyers' Latin for a book or publication. The journeymen of the obscenity trade also appeared dutifully in court from time to time on charges of obscene libel, served their time, and went back to business.

The most remarkable statistic was not so much that five hundred major press prosecutions had been brought in the century before Victoria's accession. One hundred and sixty were brought in less than twenty years before she came to the throne – and one hundred and twenty of these were political prosecutions. The times had seemed to be getting worse, or at any rate more revolutionary.

Nineteenth-century punishments of opinion were far less severe than in the old prerogative courts of the Tudors and Stuarts, notably Star Chamber, but readers were regularly reminded of such atrocities by popular historians. Prerogative courts were abolished in 1641 but under them there was no legal restraint on the way in which a sovereign dealt with dissident authors or publishers. A monarch and his ministers in Star Chamber were not dependent on judge or jury. Protestants and Catholics went to the rack and then to their deaths under the Tudors for expressing unwelcome opinions. Under the Stuarts, disfigurement became a deterrent.

Three Puritans were held up to Victorian readers as martyrs for a free press. William Prynne a barrister, John Bastwick a physician, and Henry Burton a clergyman, were condemned in 1637 for their writings. All had previous convictions. Prynne's *Histriomastix: Women Actors Notorious Whores* made an ill-timed appearance in 1633, just as Charles I's queen, Henrietta Maria, acquired a taste for amateur theatricals. In 1633, Star Chamber had ordered Prynne's ears to be cut off while he was in the pillory and fined him £5,000. He bribed the executioner five shillings not to cut off his ears at the base. At his later appearance, the Lord Chief Justice ordered his hair to be turned up and said peevishly, 'I had thought Mr Prynne had no ears, but methinks he hath ears.' This was soon remedied. The defendants were also fined, sent to prison for life and, while in the pillory, were branded on each side of the face with 'SL' for 'Schismatical Libeller'.

During their public ordeal they behaved with such dauntless courage that their example won far more converts than their pamphlets might ever have done. They continued to smuggle out attacks from their remote prisons, Burton denouncing the bishops picturesquely as 'anti-Christian mushrumps' and Bastwick, on being invited to recant, replying that he would do so on Doomsday – in the afternoon. Their fortunes changed under Cromwell, though Prynne was never at ease with authority and found himself gaoled again by his own side. He survived the royalist restoration and, in 1662, a fellow guest at dinner in Trinity House reported him showing 'out of his pocket' examples of 'the lust and wicked lives of the nuns heretofore in England'. It was a salutary reminder not to confuse 'puritan' with 'prude'.[5]

Such well-known martyrdoms and examples were used repeatedly to remind Victorian England of what it had escaped. Yet still the rapidity with which the resistance to a free press had collapsed caught most contemporaries by surprise. Governments who appeared invincible proved no more than frightened and incompetent in the face of a sustained challenge by liberals and radicals.

The astonishment in the tone of Victorian voices is unmistakable. During the election of 1834, Sir John Campbell, the Attorney-General, was a Tory candidate for the city of Edinburgh. He was also a future Lord Chief Justice and Lord Chancellor. In the election campaign he had been reproached with being 'not sufficiently liberal' in his opinions. 'I said truly, that, although Attorney-General to the Crown, I had uttered sentiments for which, forty years before, I should have been sent to Botany Bay.' In the wake of this, H. T. Buckle rejoiced at 'the rapid progress of democratic opinions' and the novelist Mrs Gaskell marvelled at how 'rapid have been the changes for the better'.[6]

Victoria's youth and open-mindedness had much to do with this. Leigh Hunt saluted her readiness 'to fall in with every great and liberal measure'. He had spent 1812–14 in prison for debunking a court eulogy of the Prince Regent as 'an exciter of desire' and 'an Adonis in loveliness'. In reality, wrote Hunt, this 'corpulent man of fifty' was 'a violator of his word, a libertine over head and ears in disgrace and debt, a despiser of domestic ties, the companion of gamblers and demi-reps'. In Victoria's England, Hunt denied ever being a republican 'though I have lived during a period of history when kings themselves tried hard to make honest men republicans by their unteachableness'.[7]

The change also seemed irreversible. In 1844, Benjamin Disraeli proclaimed the permanence of democracy and a free press. He wondered only how the weak and frightened ministers of George IV could have imposed themselves on the country for so long: how impossible it would be 'to us, with our "Times" newspaper every morning on our breakfast table, bringing, on every subject which can interest the public mind, a degree of information and intelligence which must form a security against any prolonged public misconception'.[8]

Politics alone did not explain the change. Victorian England was also the first great age of technology. The press had grown beyond the power of a government to control it by traditional means. Until 1855 every copy of every newspaper was required to bear a government stamp. As early as 1712, a Stamp Act had greeted the first newspapers, though there was also an illegal underground press which published its papers unstamped. The tax had been increased to fourpence a copy in 1815 to curb radicalism and subversion. The price of The Times also rose, reaching six and a half pence, four pence of which was tax. When this 'tax on knowledge' was abolished in 1855, the cost of the same paper fell from seven pence to three pence.

In the face of new technology and a massive demand for newspapers, the censors of thirty or forty years earlier would have seemed like figures of medieval chivalry charging the latest armament of the Industrial Revolution. *The Times*, with a circulation of 7,000 after the Napoleonic Wars, sold 70,000 a day by 1861. The *Daily Telegraph*, founded in 1855, had a daily circulation of 150,000 and *Reynolds News* reached 350,000. The *News of the World* had begun as a popular Victorian newspaper on 1 October 1843 with a rape, a seduction and a chronicle of violent crime in its first issue, soon supplemented by divorce court scandals. By mid-century, a web printing machine, producing continuous rolls rather than separate pages, was capable of turning out 7,000 copies an hour and could be bought for £600. How could such an industry be policed by an office of conscientious drudges stamping every page?

Yet even as the echoes of national self-congratulation faded, other voices began to debate how free a free press could expect to be.

3

Mainstream liberal England took its creed from John Stuart Mill, a belief which fifty years earlier – or later – would have sounded like the lunacy of a political fringe. Mankind was no more justified in silencing one man's opinion than he would be justified in silencing mankind. What if the one person expressed a view that the world would be a better place when a particular religious or racial group had been exterminated? What if the one person, during a war in which the nation was fighting for its life against an odious tyranny, believed soldiers should desert or civilian workers walk out of the munition factories?

Mill believed that every opinion should be allowed somewhere, probably in the press, but not everywhere, certainly not where it might immediately incite crime. However, the incitement must produce immediate action, not merely a predisposition to act in a certain way later on. As James Fitzjames Stephen put it in his *History of the English Criminal Law* (1883), 'nothing less than a censure which has an immediate tendency to produce such a breach of the peace, ought to be regarded as criminal.' Similarly in the United States, the incitement to violence must come 'dangerously near success' to be criminal.[9]

Underlying such beliefs was a Miltonic faith that truth, in a fair fight, would defeat falsehood. The proposition was as simple as a paragraph from Homer, in which two champions fought and one fell. 'When truth and error have fair play,' said Benjamin Franklin in his *Apology for Printers* (1731), 'the former is always an overmatch for the latter.' This liberal faith died hard.[10]

The Victorian legislature and judiciary moved quickly to extend political freedom of the press. The Parliamentary Papers Act 1840 threw open official papers and made it a complete defence for a publisher to repeat something already published by order of Parliament. In 1888 the Newspaper Libel Act indemnified editors against libel actions in reporting parliamentary and judicial proceedings as well as bona fide public meetings. The Quarter Sessions Act of 1842 deprived magistrates of the right to try cases of seditious, blasphemous or defamatory libel, removing a fear of petty and vexatious prosecutions.

Politicians, legislators and administrators were answerable to the people or its press as they had never been in the reigns of George III or George IV. In an 1877 judgment, Sir James Fitzjames Stephen, one of the most eminent of Victorian jurists, ruled, 'Every person who takes a part in public affairs submits his conduct therein to criticism.' The law was no more to protect a politician or a civil servant than an author or a painter from the hostile judgments of critics. This was not a new statement of principle but a recognition of what had been established in the previous thirty years. In the 1850s, for example, the newly founded *Daily Telegraph* had attacked with impunity the House of Lords as 'the chartered lords of misrule ogling in the ancient face of bigotry'. It then went on to denounce the royal family for 'seeking pensions *in forma pauperis* for their daughters whom it should be their pride and pleasure to support'.[11]

Press law — notably the laws of seditious libel and of criminal libel — existed to prevent a breach of the peace. This was no mere figure of speech. When a man of rank had been 'calumniated' in the press, as the seventh Earl of Cardigan termed it, the wholesome remedy was to visit the newspaper office and horsewhip its editor: a journalist was below the level of honour at which a gentleman would call him out on the duelling ground. Cardigan, a short-tempered regimental commander, threatened to flog the editor of the Liberal *Morning Chronicle* for comments on scandals in the 11th (Prince Albert's Own) Hussars. 'After so unbecoming a threat,' wrote the editor nervously on 16 August 1839, 'were his lordship to forget himself further, we should have no hesitation in handing him over, with the least possible ceremony, to a police officer.' The nervousness was not misplaced. Several years earlier, Cardigan had waylaid and horsewhipped John Drakard, editor of the *Stamford News*, before a large and enthusiastic crowd on Northampton racecourse, after comments on quarrels in the 8th Hussars.

Necessary political censorship was built upon existing common law. The object was no longer to stifle criticism but to prevent personal violence or general insurrection. There were two methods. The first was a prosecution for criminal libel, where an individual was the target. Unlike civil libel, this was a criminal prosecution, where defamation was so gross as to threaten a breach of the peace. Until the Libel Act of 1843 it was not even a justification to show that what had been published was true, since truth might just as easily cause public disorder. Hence, 'The greater the truth, the greater the libel.'

It was one thing for the press to make general criticisms of the royal family and its associates, quite another to impute criminal conduct to them. Before the arrival of Prince Albert, one of those who caught the young Queen's eye was her cousin, Charles, Duke of Brunswick. Though others thought him entirely unsuitable, she found him 'very good-looking' as her dancing partner when they first met in 1836. The truth was that he had been expelled from his own country as unfit to rule and was suspected of what the English common law called uncharitably 'the abominable crime of buggery'. Indeed, seeing him later, driving four-in-hand down Oxford Street, 'wild and odd' with a friend at his side, or 'pale and haggard' at a charity ball, it seemed plain to Victoria that he was not the right choice after all.[12]

Three periodicals, the *Age*, the *Satirist* and the *Weekly Despatch*, thereupon sought to administer the *coup de grâce* and were prosecuted for imputing unnatural conduct to him. A sporting journal and gossip sheet, the *Age* was first to print an epigram. Brunswick had made matters even worse for himself by swapping insults with the journalists over his alleged proclivities, as the *Age* now informed its readers.

> To do so he courage or prudence must lack
> Yet it sometimes *is* the case
> That men will do behind your back
> What they will not do to your face.

This appeared on 6 February 1842, followed by more attacks in April and July. The editor and the publisher were convicted of criminal libel on the Queen's cousin, the former going to prison for a year, the latter for three months.[13]

In politics, the sword of criminal libel glinted over the heads of the impetuous. One of those convicted was the future prime minister, Benjamin Disraeli. Following the Maidstone by-election of 1837 in which he had been the successful Conservative candidate, there had been a petition against him. Counsel for the petitioners, Charles Austin, alleged that Disraeli offered bribes to the voters and afterwards refused to pay. Austin's remarks in court were privileged. Disraeli sought satisfaction by a letter in the *Morning Post* on 5 June 1838. He denounced Austin's 'impertinent calumnies', describing him as a member of a profession 'the first principles of whose practice appears to be that they may say anything provided they be paid for it . . . the privilege of circulating falsehoods with impunity'. Disraeli might have got away with general comments but he then set about Austin, accusing him of 'the blustering artifice of a rhetorical hireling, availing himself of the vile licence of a loose-tongued lawyer, not only to make a statement which was false, but to make it with a consciousness of its falsehood'. At least Disraeli had his money's worth. The youthful politician only escaped imprisonment by an eloquent apology to the court.[14]

Even the Victorian Church was not exempt from the rancour of criminal libel. During the anti-Catholic hysteria of the 1850s, the palm for criminal abuse went to the improbable figure of the future cardinal and saint, John Henry Newman, one of the greatest minds and supreme stylists of the age. The Protestant Electoral Union had recruited Father Achilli, a former Dominican friar, to address public meetings on the fraud and hypocrisy of Rome. In 1851, Newman published his *Lectures on the Present Position of Catholics in England*. Either Father Achilli's sponsors had no idea of his past or had hoped no one else knew.

Newman acknowledged Achilli as the triumph of Protestants and the confusion of Catholics. Then came chapter and verse, as if in the voice of the ex-Dominican. 'I have been a Roman priest and a hypocrite; I have been a profligate under a cowl; I am that Father Achilli, who, as early as 1826 was deprived of my faculty to lecture, for an offence which my superiors did their best to conceal.' At Viterbo in 1831 Achilli had 'robbed of her honour' a girl of eighteen; a crime repeated in 1833 and in 1834. He was convicted of 'sins similar or worse' throughout the area, at Capua in 1834 and 1835, at Naples in 1840 with a girl of fifteen. He had chosen the sacristy of the church for one crime and Good Friday for another. 'Look upon me, ye mothers of England, a confessor against Popery, for ye "ne'er may look upon my like again".'

It was the death of Achilli the platform orator. A prosecution for criminal libel was brought against Newman's publishers, Burns & Lambert. He asked that his own name should be substituted in the indictment. Witnesses and documents justified his accusations. The Libel Act of 1843 now allowed a defence that publication was for the public good. In the unhappy circumstances of 1851, it did not seem to be so. The outcome of the trial pleased no one, since some of the accusations against Achilli were found to be proved and others not. Newman was convicted and fined £100 with the alternative of imprisonment. The fine was paid. For many years afterwards, editions of Newman's *Lectures* appeared with asterisks where the offending passage had been.[15]

4

In the prosecution of political publications, the pretext was usually the safety of the realm. In the early years of the reign some authors and editors felt their causes could only succeed through force, while governments remained determined to silence them. The Reform Bill of 1832 did too little to head off the creation of a Chartist movement and its 'People's Charter', demanding annual elections, voting by ballot and universal male suffrage. By 1839, it had 1,200,000 signatures. A new charter of 1842 bore 3,000,000. Both were rejected by Parliament.

Men like Henry Hetherington were tired of waiting for improvement. His *Poor Man's Guardian* was part of the illegal underground press which ignored the Stamp Act. On 25 May 1833 he published advice to the working-class radical on how to protect himself against his enemies, particularly police or mounted troops who tried to break up demonstrations. The man should take bread and cheese with him. In order to eat it, he would need a knife with a long blade and a stout handle, 'for it is a pity he should run the risk of being starved'. This was regarded as advocating violence, for which Hetherington went to prison.[16]

In 1839, Feargus O'Connor, Irish barrister and Chartist leader, editor of the radical Leeds newspaper, the *Northern Star*, also went to prison for eighteen months. He had been convicted for a seditious libel in his paper on 13 July. The article reported his speech attacking the government for attempting to 'put down the cause of the people by physical force' and urging his followers to give a 'warm reception' to any repetition. For good measure, 'let the whole country strike on a given day and never return to their callings till they have worked out their political and social salvations.' The charge made clear that he was not being prosecuted for his opinions. He had urged his readers 'to overturn and change the Laws and institutions of the Realm and to make insurrections, riots, and tumultuous and illegal assemblies, and to arm themselves for the purpose of more effectually obstructing and resisting the Laws and Government of the Realm'.[17]

By 1848, Chartism gave way to Irish Nationalism and new charges of

34

incitement to political violence. Two men who overstepped the bounds of tolerance were John Mitchel and Charles Gavin Duffy with articles in the *United Irishman* and the *Nation* on the technique of vitriol-throwing, as well as sympathizing with an insurrection in 1848. By a stroke of good fortune for them, both prosecutions failed. Duffy made his way to Australia, became Prime Minister of Victoria and received a knighthood. Mitchel, after being convicted as an Irish rebel, escaped to the United States, where by some quirk of personality he became an advocate for the retention of slavery.

When agitators stood trial it was usually for advocating violence. By mid-century this was associated with Anarchists or Nihilists, their aims wider and their territory the whole world. If they applauded the assassination of English officials in Ireland, they approved of the assassination of 'tyrants' everywhere. The Paris bomb plot of 1858 in which the Italian conspirator, Felice Orsini, and his accomplices attempted to assassinate Napoleon III, killing ten people and wounding more than 150, had been matured in England. When much of the English criminal law was codified by the Offences Against the Person Act 1861, murder and incitement to murder became punishable in England even if the target was overseas.

By the 1880s, extremist movements seemed all the more sinister because the country appeared at risk from foreign terrorists in its midst. A clandestine foreign-language press was also at work in London. The German-language *Freiheit* – or *Freedom* – involved three men in prosecutions for advocating murder. In 1881 Johann Most was convicted for an article congratulating the assassins of Tsar Alexander II, murdered on 13 March. He praised 'the most energetic of all tyrant-haters, the Russian Nihilists' and deplored the fact that 'here and there even Socialists . . . abominate regicide'. In conclusion, 'what one might in any case complain of is only the rarity of so-called tyrannicide. If only a single crowned wretch were disposed of every month, in a short time it should afford no one gratification henceforward still to play the monarch.'

Prosecutions were also brought against William Mertens and Frederick Schwelm for articles in the magazine on 13 and 27 May 1882. The first congratulated the assassins of Lord Frederick Cavendish, Chief Secretary to the Lord Lieutenant of Ireland, and Thomas Burke, the Permanent Under-Secretary. The two men had been stabbed to death in Phoenix Park, Dublin, murders denounced at once by Parnell and the Irish Nationalists. *Freiheit* thereupon advocated the murder of Parnell as well. Most transferred his activities to the United States, where he was convicted in 1891 and 1901 of advocating assassination.

The paper was an international publication and on 27 May 1881 supporters of *Freiheit* who had escaped arrest struck back. 'The international gang of monarchs has made a great mistake imagining to close the mouths of the London Social Revolutionists by prosecuting the *Freiheit.*' Before the reign was over, David Nicholl's more blandly titled paper, the *Commonweal*, was in trouble. This was the paper of the Socialist League, founded and first edited by William Morris; his *Dream of John Ball* (1886–7) and *News from Nowhere* (1890) first appeared in its pages. In 1892 it attacked the trials and the sentences passed on the so-called 'Walsall Anarchists'. The police raided the paper's offices and Nicholl was sent to prison for eighteen months. Small wonder that it was seventy years after the first publication of Shelley's *Hellas* (1822) before editors felt it safe to include his comment on 'those ringleaders of the privileged gangs of murderers and swindlers, called Sovereigns'.[18]

5

As it happened, Shelley's poetry was dealt with by another law, little used in the Victorian period but always available. No one so far thought it necessary to repeal the Blasphemy Act 1698 or to abolish the common law offence of blasphemous libel. Under the Act blasphemy involved anyone brought up as a Christian or a convert (other than Unitarians) denying any one of the three Persons of the Holy Trinity to be God; asserting or maintaining that there are more Gods than one; denying the Christian religion to be true or the New and Old Testament to be of Divine Authority. The common law was more flexible and punished whatever offences seemed to be in need of it.

In the 1820s an increasing number of non-Christian Deists had gone to prison during a campaign by the Society for the Suppression of Vice, more often associated with attacks on pornography. One of the offenders, William Clark, went to prison in 1821 for publishing Shelley's *Queen Mab*. Another was sued by Byron's publisher, John Murray, in 1822 to prevent the publication of Byron's poem *Cain*, which Lord Chancellor Eldon ruled was blasphemous and therefore not worthy of copyright protection. It seemed unthinkable that the giants of the Romantic Revival would be troubled again.

The complete *Poetical Works of P. B. Shelley* was eventually published by Edward Moxon in 1840, in consultation with the poet's widow. At her request, certain deleted passages were restored. Moxon was a distinguished publisher, son-in-law of Charles Lamb, his authors including Wordsworth and Tennyson. A year later he was astonished to hear that he was being prosecuted for blasphemy. An information had been laid against him by Henry Hetherington, recently imprisoned for attacking the morality of the Bible. At his trial, Hetherington had asked whether there was 'one law for the "low booksellers of the Strand" and another for the aristocratic booksellers of Dover Street'. There was not.

The Attorney-General read *Queen Mab* in the new edition of the *Poetical Works* and saw that, thanks to Hetherington, he had no alternative but to prosecute Edward Moxon, bookseller to the carriage trade. Moxon appeared alone in the Court of Queen's Bench on 23 June 1841, taking all responsibility on himself. The four passages in the indictment were radiant with the intensity of Shelley's atheism. God is denounced as 'A vengeful, pitiless and almighty fiend', Christian believers are 'slaves' and Bible narratives are 'childish mummeries'. The defence argued that the words were no worse than speeches put into the mouths of the fallen angels by Milton in *Paradise Lost*.

Counsel for the Crown dealt gently with the case, admitting the 'greatness of Shelley' and the 'respectability of the defendant'. Moxon could hardly escape conviction but unlike Hetherington, who had now finished four months in prison, he was merely bound over to keep the peace in his own recognisances. Counsel for the Crown added the hope that the case might 'establish that no publication on religion should be a subject for prosecution'.[19]

The Commissioners of Criminal Law thereupon distinguished irreligion and scepticism, which were not to be criminal, from blasphemy, which was. Blasphemy was 'a mischievous design to wound the feelings of others, or to injure the authority of Christianity with the vulgar and unthinking by improper means'. Next year the common law judges agreed that a decent denial of the truths of the Christian religion was not criminal. So, for example, Charles Southwell still went to prison that year after his *Oracle of Reason* called the Bible's heroines 'assassinating Jezebels, the tale of whose lewdness and infamy would put Fanny Hill or Harriet Wilson to the blush'. Were it not called the Bible, 'no modest woman would suffer it to be read in her house.'[20]

Yet despite the new leniency, the old laws were not dead but sleeping. Forty years later, there was a similarity to Southwell's ribaldry in the *Freethinker's* 'Comic Bible Sketches', which earned G. W. Foote a year in prison and his co-editor William Ramsay nine months. The cartoons included a 'Comic Life of Christ' and 'A Father's Love', portraying the rich man roasting in hell. Lazarus with God at his side sits among bottles of champagne and thumbs his nose at the victim, refusing him so much as a drop during his torment.

The challenge to Christianity in the *Freethinker*'s 'Comic Bible Sketches' of 1882 was stronger than any insult to Islam in the so-called 'Danish Cartoons' of 2005. Yet the battles of Faith and Doubt in the Victorian period had left Christianity more self-confident. It did not need the protection of the law for its doctrines, and even the scurrility of the cartoons was no occasion for threats and mob violence. The government declined to prosecute. It took a private prosecution, brought by a member of Parliament with leave of the Attorney-General, to get the *Freethinker* to court at all.

At the first trial, the jurors could not agree and the prosecution was dropped. A second case, with new material from the 'Christmas number' of the *Freethinker* for 1882, was more strictly tried. Mr Justice North interpreted the law with a severity that the common law judges had repudiated forty years earlier. He assured the jurors that even to deny the existence of God was blasphemous. All the same, a first jury was divided. The case was sent for retrial and only at a third attempt were the defendants convicted and sent to prison in 1883. The proceedings did not suggest that convictions for blasphemy would be easily obtained in future.[21]

Throughout the Victorian period there were private acts of religious censorship, not so much court cases as additional background to *Barchester Towers*. J. A. Froude's novel, *The Nemesis of Faith*, was burnt in the hall of Exeter College, Oxford, in 1849 on the orders of the senior tutor. Newman's *Tract XC*, in which he asserted the Catholic nature of the Thirty-Nine Articles of the Church of England, was condemned by Heads of Houses at Oxford in 1841. Two years later, Dr Pusey, Regius Professor of Hebrew, was suspended from preaching for two years by the Vice-Chancellor for seeming to approve the Roman doctrine of transubstantiation. Two contributors to *Essays and Reviews* (1860) were convicted of heresy by the Court of Arches, to which they were answerable as clergy; the decision was reversed by the Privy Council. Benjamin Jowett, future Master of Balliol, was prosecuted by Dr Pusey in the Vice-Chancellor's court for an essay, 'On the Interpretation of Scripture', but the case was dropped. In the end, no one suffered a criminal conviction, much less several disagreeable months in Horsemonger Lane gaol.

6

In the following century, whenever Victorian censorship was mentioned, the minds of most people flew to pornography, a word that was not even in general use at the time. Yet the censorship itself was more a matter of chance than judgment.

In the House of Lords on a Monday afternoon, 13 May 1857, their lordships were debating a bill on the sale of poisons. This was a tribute to the career of Dr William Palmer, 'The Rugeley Poisoner', who had been unlucky with his third victim and was hanged in 1856. The Lord Chief Justice, Baron Campbell, rose to intervene. 'I am happy to say that I believe the administration of poison by design has received a check. But, from a trial which took place before me on Saturday, I have learnt with horror and alarm that a sale of poison more deadly than prussic acid, strychnine or arsenic – the sale of obscene publications and indecent books – is openly going on.'

For many years, until 1727, the judiciary had felt no alarm or horror. Books later to be condemned as obscene were licensed by the authorities before 1695 without the least misgiving. Three cases in 1707–9 confirmed that there was no such offence at common law. The defendant who changed the common law was that rare creature, a rogue publisher disliked by everyone. After his downfall in 1727, Edmund Curll made a famous appearance in Pope's satire *The Dunciad* (1728) racing among his rivals in unholy competition, slipping and slithering in excrement. The two books for which he was condemned, *Venus in the Cloister* and Meibomius' *Treatise of the Use of Flogging in Venereal Affairs*, had been published for many years, the former officially licensed in the Term Catalogue for Easter 1683. Now they offered a means of dealing with him. He was convicted of publishing two obscene books and the memoirs of John Ker, a government spy whom he had met in prison in the reign of Queen Anne.

Curll was fined and 'set in the pillory' at Charing Cross, to face grievous bodily harm. But being, as the official report says, 'an artful, cunning, though wicked fellow', he was 'not pelted nor used ill'. He had had pamphlets passed round the crowd, claiming he stood in the pillory for defending the memory of good Queen Anne, whose posthumous popularity had risen as that of George II had sunk. The mob was on his side and 'it would have been dangerous even to have spoken against him'. When his time in the pillory ended, his well-wishers 'carried him off, as it were in triumph, to a neighbouring tavern'.

The eighteenth century was the time of William Hogarth and *Tom Jones* but it was also the age of John Wesley and William Wilberforce. Wilberforce and his Proclamation Society, followed by the Society for the Suppression of Vice in 1802, pursued the pornographers of the Napoleonic Wars and the Regency. John Cleland's *Fanny Hill*, Sade's *Juliette*, *The History of Dom B——, Harris's List of Covent Garden Ladies*, as well as a host of erotic prints and periodicals like the *Town* or the *New Rambler's Magazine*, put their publishers in prison.

A major problem for Victorian censors was that pornography shared the new technology of printing, making it far easier to produce material and in much greater quantities. There was also the use, or abuse, of the new art of photography. Ten years before Lord Campbell made his speech, the photographic nude was gracing the bookstalls of Paris, London and Vienna.

Two days before the debate, Campbell had presided over the trial of two booksellers from the little streets north of the Strand. William Dugdale was a familiar figure, who spent as much time in prison as out of it and was almost seventy. His companion was William Strange. They were charged with selling two periodicals, *Paul Pry* and *Women of London*. The second contained what a later age would call bathing beauties or pin-ups, though as steel engravings rather than photographs.

Paul Pry was started in 1856 by Robert Martin, now in prison. It contained steel-engraved models, and stories like the seduction of Susan in the bedroom of the Right Honourable Filthy Lucre. It also advertised Stereoscopic Gems 'Just received from Paris' and 'depicting some of the fastest and richest scenes in the Bagnios of the French capital, all taken from life'. These photographs had in all probability been taken in a back room near the Strand and the talk of gendarmes, censorship and the difficulty of importing such treasures was a standard method of talking up the price.

As always, there were products of a kind known to later ages as the 'sucker trap'. The most famous was *The Dreadful Disclosures of Maria Monk*. In the new millennium, 170 years later, this was still being sold shrunk-wrapped to the unwary, its cover suggesting the wildest shores of lesbianism or sexual sadism. When the purchaser opened the treasure, the sad truth appeared. With the same title, this book had been in print since a pious anti-Catholic reaction of 1833. It was a publication of the Presbyterian Tract Society.

In May 1857, Lord Campbell proposed a bill to deal with such material. The legislation had to pass through all its stages by the end of the parliamentary session, hardly two months away. To his exasperation, at its second reading in June, some members of the House of Lords opposed it. Lord Brougham, former Lord Chancellor and survivor of the Regency, treated the proposals as humbug and tosh. Lord Lyndhurst, a Regency realist with a well-bred contempt for popular sanctimoniousness, saw no difference between a bookshop print of a couple making love and the same subject on view in Correggio's *Jupiter and Antiope* at the Louvre. Were the London police to start rounding up Correggio prints?

The House of Commons seemed unenthusiastic. John Roebuck, who had brought down Lord Aberdeen's government two years earlier by moving for an inquiry into the conduct of the Crimean War, denounced the bill as a doomed attempt to make people virtuous by Act of Parliament. Those who wanted pornography would find a way of getting it, no matter what laws were passed.

Fortunately for Lord Campbell, many parliamentarians hesitated to be seen opposing the control of corrupting material. There was a sufficient majority to carry the legislation, though a former Lord Chancellor advised him that 'no legislation is necessary' and warned him that he had far better leave the law 'as it stands'. This was not what Campbell and his supporters wanted to hear. The proposals became law in July as the Obscene Publications Act 1857. It was to be the law on obscenity for the next 102 years.

At first, the Society for the Suppression of Vice was jubilant. Thanks to the new law, it had been able to seize thousands of indecent prints, hundreds of books and copperplate engravings, and hundredweights of letterpress. Yet, within a period of eleven years, something had gone badly wrong. The society's annual report for 1868 admitted as much, deploring 'a new phase developed in the history of vice' by the use of photography and the stereoscope, as well as the facilities for 'secret trading' offered by an improved postal service.

The new law had at least simplified procedure, in allowing for 'destruction orders'. The police might seize material and bring it before a magistrate; the magistrate could then grant an order for the material to be destroyed. Only rarely was this refused. The retailer might sign a form relinquishing ownership and would be released without fine or imprisonment, unless there was other material not covered by the order. It made the question of obscenity akin to that of a public nuisance rather than a major crime.

Elsewhere, the Act showed the marks of all hasty and ill-considered legislation. During the report stage of the bill, Lord Campbell had produced Dumas' novel *La Dame aux camélias*. He assured the house that he had not 'the most distant contemplation' of interfering with great art or serious literature, even where he disapproved of it, as he did of this novel. His target was 'works written for the single purpose of corrupting the morals of youth, and of a nature calculated to shock the common feelings of decency in any well-regulated mind'.

Unfortunately, such assurances were not worth the breath needed to carry them across the floor of the house. Once a new law ceased to be the property of Parliament it became what the judiciary chose to make of it. This one was so badly drafted that they needed to make a great deal. Nowhere did it give a definition of obscenity. Even Campbell's reference to books which deliberately corrupted the morals of youth or shocked feelings of decency was nowhere in the statute and was a questionable definition anyway. Some of the most notorious novels, like Sade's *Juliette* condemned by King's Bench in 1830, had certainly not been written with the sole purpose of corrupting youth. Moreover, shocking the feelings of decency in a well-regulated mind was question-begging to say the least.

With this unhappy leave-taking, the law passed from Parliament. Its first major test was in 1867–8. Ironically, the prosecution was of a man who would never have thought of himself as a pornographer: a pious Wolverhampton bookseller who had sold a publication by the Protestant Electoral Union. This body existed neither to corrupt youth nor to shock decency but to 'restore and maintain the Protestant Constitution of the Empire as established by the Revolution of 1688'. In other words, it abhorred all things Catholic.

The Confessional Unmasked was not an original publication. It was an anthology of advice from Roman Catholic theologians, revealing the abuse of the confessional by wayward priests. It described how errant confessors allegedly persuaded female penitents to reveal secret desires and specific experiences. Whatever its pretext, the book crossed a contemporary frontier between the indelicate and the indecent. In an act of extraordinary naivety the Protestant Electoral Union had bought the printing plates for their edition, including remarkable illustrations, from the same William Strange whom Lord Campbell had sent to prison for selling *Women of London*, two days before his House of Lords intervention on obscenity. It seemed a small world.

In a further case, a Protestant activist, George Mackay, had given a series of lectures drawn from *The Confessional Unmasked* and had been gaoled for fifteen months. In 1871, the secretary of the Protestant Electoral Union was also to be convicted for publishing an account of Mackay's trial, complete with quotations. On 18 March 1867, copies of the book had first been seized from H. Scott of Wolverhampton and an order granted for destruction. Scott took his appeal all the way to the Court of Queen's Bench. The case became famous on appeal as *Regina v. Hicklin*. Scott lost his appeal but, giving judgment in April 1868, Sir Alexander Cockburn framed a definition of obscenity that has endured ever since:[22]

The test of obscenity is whether the tendency of the matter charged as obscenity is to deprave and corrupt those whose minds are open to such immoral influences and into whose hands a publication of this sort might fall.[22]

This bequeathed a legacy of ambiguities and uncertainties but it survived, like other Victorian legal definitions, because no one could think of a better one. As if shackled together at the ankles, the Hicklin judgment and Lord Campbell's Act limped on together for another century.

For the time being, Victorian pornographers were dealt with by destruction orders and loss of their stock or summary sentences at magistrates courts. Those waiting for a literary trial of obscenity were further disappointed by the next major case. In 1877 Charles Bradlaugh, a crusading MP and the first atheist to sit in Parliament, and the philanthropist Annie Besant, friend of the East End match-girls, found themselves brought before the Central Criminal Court. Whoever Lord Campbell's 'distant contemplation' foresaw, it can hardly have been what *The Times* report called 'this well-intentioned pair'. Their crime was to reissue Charles Knowlton's somewhat unreliable guide to birth control for the working class, *The Fruits of Philosophy*. The book had been available since 1834 and had never run into trouble before. The defendants' Freethought Publishing Company issued it, though they felt it contained 'philosophical mistakes' and they could not endorse its 'medical views' because they were not doctors. 'But since progress can only be made through discussion, we claim the right to publish all opinions so that the public may have the material for forming a sound judgment.'

Unfortunately, the Lord Chief Justice and the Solicitor-General Sir Hardinge Giffard, later Lord Halsbury, had already formed their opinions. The judge warned the jury that the question was not whether the book was obscene 'in the coarser sense of the term but whether its tendency is to vitiate public morality'. Sir Hardinge Giffard answered that question. It was a book 'tending to create morbid feelings and leading to unlawful practices'. In other words, if its readers believed contraception worked, they would be less likely to control their sexual instincts. Far worse, it was clearly aimed at the lower orders. In its present form it was to be 'sold in the streets at sixpence a copy'.

Charles Bradlaugh and Annie Besant were convicted of publishing an obscene libel. Yet their reputations and obvious benevolence were such that the jury added, 'We find that the book is calculated to deprave public morals but we entirely exonerate the defendants from any corrupt motives in publishing it.' They were fined £200 each and sent to prison for six months, but immediately released on promising not to circulate further copies of the book. By contrast, in 1880 Edward Truelove suffered both imprisonment and confiscation of his stock for selling books with a similar theme, including Robert Dale Owen's *Moral Physiology* and J. J. Palmer's *Individual, Family, and National Poverty*. A further 1,400 copies were destroyed on the court's orders.[23]

The case for which Lord Campbell's critics might have been waiting did not come until 1888. Henry Vizetelly was a reputable and long-established London publisher. He had issued the Mermaid Series of Elizabethan and Jacobean dramatists, each volume with an introduction by authors including Swinburne, Edmund Gosse, John Addington Symonds and Havelock Ellis. He introduced English readers to a range of European fiction, including the novels of Dostoevsky, George Sand, Maupassant, Daudet and Zola. Among authors in his own country, he was the publisher of Richard Jefferies and George Moore.

Vizetelly's problems came with Zola, Maupassant, and the French Catholic novelist Paul Bourget. A new vigilante organization, the National Vigilance Association and Travellers' Aid Society, had sprung up in the wake of the white slave scandals of 1885. In 1888 it first undertook a prosecution of Vizetelly for publishing what it called 'three of Zola's grossest novels', *Nana*, *Soil* and *Piping Hot*, a case which was then helpfully taken over by the Crown. Though he was seventy and in poor health, Vizetelly was determined to fight for his reputation and his books. The Crown employed a young lawyer eager for hack work in the Long Vacation. The future prime minister H. H. Asquith spent a fortnight, 'with scissors and a pot of paste at hand, in a diligent quest for the most objectionable passages in M. Zola's voluminous works'.[24]

Vizetelly might have thought he had avoided trouble by publishing such 'realistic' novels as Zola's at six shillings, equivalent to £80 or £90 in terms of modern wages. Prosecutors were quicker to drop on cheap material sold to the 'unthinking working class'. The downfall of Charles Grieves in 1870, for example, had been the illustrated cover of his weekly, *The Ferret*, displayed by newsboys in streets and outside railway stations. It cost a penny and its cover lured the passer-by with 'In a Music-Hall Canteen', where bare-legged dancing girls ogled a silk-hatted swell. Grieves went to prison with hard labour for a year.[25]

In Vizetelly's case *La Terre*, translated as *Soil*, was a realistic account of the bestiality of peasant life. It had already caused protests in France. When the trial came on in November, the jurors listened to a few passages and asked to be spared the rest. Vizetelly's counsel advised him to change his plea to guilty. He was fined £100. 'In future,' wrote The Times, 'anyone who publishes translations of Zola's novels and works of similar character will do so at his peril, and must not expect to escape so easily as Mr Vizetelly.' The complete text of La Terre was not published again in England until 1954.

His enemies in the National Vigilance Association had not done with him. He was at once prosecuted for a further half-dozen novels, published long before the first case. Three were by Zola, two by Maupassant, and one by Paul Bourget. Vizetelly was treated as if he had published them after his conviction, in defiance of the verdict. Six months later he was in court again, branded by the Solicitor-General as one who specialized in French novels and unexpurgated editions. The Recorder remarked that there was no point in fining him, since he had no money to pay, and sent him to prison for three months.

The moral flexibility of governments in matters of censorship is not confined to the Victorian period. However, Zola fled from France to England in 1898, as a supporter of Colonel Dreyfus in the famous espionage scandal. Anglo-French hostility made it convenient for British leaders to lionize this celebrated exile. The elderly publisher who brought to readers the Elizabethan and Jacobean dramatists, the 'realistic' fiction of Dostoevsky or Zola, and, to the innocent young, Daudet and 'French fiction of an unobjectionable character' for a shilling, had ended as a gaolbird. At the end of his autobiography, he acknowledged wearily what he called the irony of fate:

> After having been prosecuted for issuing Monsieur Zola's novels by the solicitor-general of one administration, I read in the newspapers at the very moment I am penning these concluding lines, of the enthusiastic reception of Monsieur Zola at the Institute of Journalists, with Sir Charles Russell, the attorney-general of another administration, giving the signal for the rounds of ringing cheers with which the representatives of British Journalism welcomed the great French novelist.[26]

3

Testing the Limits

A NEW CENTURY was now to test the limits of Victorian censorship and to determine whether freedom of opinion could be as free as Mill demanded and whether, perhaps, the frontiers of obscenity could not be pushed back. Prosecutions involving political freedom of speech were to be rare but memorable. The bulk of censorship – even the word itself – was now associated with literature or plays regarded as erotic, pornographic or obscene. Such literature had evolved even since Henry Vizetelly went to prison. A new science of psychopathology, in the hands of Richard von Krafft-Ebing and Havelock Ellis, illustrated sexual eccentricities whose very mention might seem obscene to the few who knew what was being talked about. This last proviso was important. A word like 'lesbian', for example, had simply meant an inhabitant of the island of Lesbos until Krafft-Ebing in his *Psychopathia Sexualis* (1886) substituted it for the Victorian term 'sapphic'.

A far greater threat to morality appeared in the large number of English novels and magazines now produced in Paris and elsewhere beyond the reach of the English law. Most were slim, plain-covered and paper-bound, and slipped conveniently into an Edwardian overcoat pocket to be smuggled into the country. A parliamentary committee was to consider this problem in 1908.

In parallel, censorship of the stage by the Lord Chamberlain was to continue until 1968. In 1912 it also became necessary to censor before exhibition that novelty of the 1890s, the bioscope or mutoscope – what Americans called 'movies' and the British described as 'films', 'moving pictures' or just 'the pictures'.

Political censorship between the death of Queen Victoria and the First World War was dominated by two prosecutions. The first, in 1909, combined fear of sedition or rebellion with the new cause of anti-colonialism. Guy Aldred, who described himself as a 'Communist Anarchist', was sent to prison for a year as the publisher of the *Indian Sociologist*. He produced the magazine in Shepherd's Bush at his Bakunin Press, named after the Russian Anarchist. The printer of the magazine was gaoled for four months.

The circumstances of publication laid Aldred open to accusations of inciting murder. A Hindu Nationalist, Madan Lal Dhingra, a student at the University of London, went one night to the Imperial Institute and shot dead both Sir W. Curzon Wylie and his companion Dr Cowas Lalcaca. Dhingra, a self-professed martyr for Indian freedom from colonial rule, was convicted and hanged. The *Indian Sociologist* reprinted the condemned man's last words from the Old Bailey dock: 'I am proud to have the honour of humbly laying down my humble life for the cause of my country.' Aldred then denounced 'the sword of Imperialism' by which Dhingra's life was taken and its apologists, 'Cromer, Curzon, Morley & Co.', as criminals. 'Murder, which they would represent to us as a horrible crime, when the murdered is a Government flunkey, we see practised by them without repugnance or remorse, when the murdered is a working man, a nationalist patriot, an Egyptian fellaheen, or a half-starved victim of society's blood-lust.' The law of seditious libel applied as surely to Guy Aldred as it had last done in 1842. Mr Justice Coleridge reminded the jury that all incitement to 'rebellion, insurrections, outrages, assassinations' was automatically a crime of seditious libel.[1]

Far more dramatic in the second case were allegations at the time of his 1911 coronation that George V had contracted a secret marriage as a young man and that his subsequent marriage to Queen Mary was bigamous. There had been no such prosecution for a criminal libel on the monarch since the conviction of the printer and publisher of the *Sunday Times* for 9 February 1823, which claimed that George IV was as mad as his father and under restraint at the Brighton Royal Pavilion. An offence which was thought to have lapsed in an age of stagecoaches was now revived in a world of aeroplanes, cinemas and mass circulation newspapers.

Shortly before the coronation of 1911, it was plain to his ministers that the rumours about the King must be dealt with immediately or left to fester for ever. It had been whispered from time to time that his marriage in 1893 to Princess May of Teck, who was now Queen Mary, was not his first. George V was certainly no hermit as a youth. As a naval officer, he had kept a girl in Portsmouth. With his elder brother, the Duke of Clarence, he had shared another in St John's Wood. To his diary he confided, 'She is a ripper', a term which had not yet acquired the sinister connotation that came with the Whitechapel murders four years later.

So deeply rooted in national folklore was the belief of a 'first marriage' that the gossip still circulated at the time of the death of his son George VI in 1952. The first marriage was alleged to have taken place in 1890 when, as Duke of York, George seemed an unlikely heir to the throne. His grandmother Queen Victoria was still alive, his father was Prince of Wales and would become Edward VII. He had an elder brother, the Duke of Clarence, who would presumably succeed Edward VII. George, as Duke of York, would spend his life as a ceremonial officer in the Royal Navy. It was the sudden death of Clarence in 1892 which changed all that.

As early as April 1893, when the Duke of York's betrothal to Princess May of Teck was about to be announced, he wrote to his father's private secretary that a story of his being already married to an American woman in Plymouth was 'really very amusing'. It became far less amusing as time went on. After his betrothal was announced, the *Star* newspaper published a more specific account of a first marriage, said to have taken place in Malta to the daughter of a British naval officer. No action was taken against the paper. Years went by and rumours persisted with no chance for George as Duke of York or, after 1901, as Prince of Wales to disprove them. Yet a prosecution would merely stir up further gossip.

Between the death of Edward VII in 1910 and the coronation of George V in the following year, the rumours took on more substantial form and were repeated in the press, including *Reynolds News* and the *Brisbane Telegraph*. Despite denials by the King's private secretary and the Dean of Norwich, the account became common currency. Then a republican magazine, the *Liberator*, produced what sounded like chapter and verse. This monthly was edited in Paris by Edward Holton James, nephew of the novelist Henry James, who disinherited him after the scandal. Edward worked with an English assistant editor, Edward Mylius. James was beyond the sanction of the English law but Mylius remained within the jurisdiction.

In its issue for November 1910, the *Liberator* described the new King as having been an officer in the Royal Navy in 1890, which was true. He had commanded the gunboat HMS *Thrush* on a voyage from Plymouth to North America, via Gibraltar, which was also true. Though Mylius made this sound like a sinister diversion, the truth was that *Thrush* had been ordered to tow a torpedo boat from England to Gibraltar before her Atlantic crossing. The gunboat remained at Gibraltar for just over a fortnight while her engines were serviced. During this time, according to Mylius, the future King had visited Malta, where the Commander-in-Chief of the Mediterranean Fleet was Admiral Sir Michael

Culme-Seymour. The admiral had two daughters. The younger, Laura Grace, had died in 1895. The elder, Mary Culme-Seymour, was alleged to have been the bride of the future King. By him she had two or possibly three children. Under the Royal Marriages Act 1772, the marriage would have been unconstitutional without the consent of monarch or Parliament and the children would have had no claim to inherit the crown. Mylius suggested, however, that they were 'the only rightful heirs to the English throne'.

In his article 'Sanctified Bigamy', he pulled no punches. 'It is now that we are offered the spectacle of the immorality of the Monarchy in all its sickening beastly monstrosity. In order to obtain the woman of Royal blood for his pretended wife, George Frederick foully abandoned his true wife, the daughter of Sir Michael Culme-Seymour of the British Navy, and entered into a sham and shameful marriage with the daughter of the Duke of Teck in 1893.' As for the Established Church, which must have connived at the imposture, 'The Anglican Church, with its crew of emasculated, canting priests, presents little more resemblance to Christianity than if it were some idol fetish of a tribe of South Sea Cannibals.' George V had 'a plurality of wives just like any Mohammedan Sultan, and they are sanctified by the English Church'. Nor was this the end of the *Liberator's* interest. In its December number, Mylius inquired, 'The *Daily News* of London informs us that the King plans to visit India with his wife. Would the newspaper kindly tell us which wife?'

A prosecution was a calculated risk. Yet the rumours had persisted for eighteen years and the amount of detail in the present version made it possible to examine and discredit it. The principal witnesses, Sir Michael Culme-Seymour and his daughter Mary, were still alive. Of course, the fact that there was no entry of the marriage in the church registers of Malta would not convince those who believed the authorities would take care to leave no traces.

The law officers and Winston Churchill, as Home Secretary, moved swiftly. Mylius was arrested on 26 December 1910 and charged ex officio by Sir Rufus Isaacs, the Attorney-General, which avoided the publicity of a magistrates' hearing. Bail was set at £10,000, far more than £1,000,000 a century later. The defendant had no option but to remain in prison. Since he chose to defend himself, he was also incommunicado. The case was heard speedily before Lord Chief Justice Alverstone on 1 February and a jury was chosen from the special jurors list. Against Sir Rufus Isaacs, Mylius had been unwise to dispense with counsel. His one hope of cutting short proceedings or staging a show trial was to have a subpoena served on the King, requiring him to attend as a witness and be cross-examined. This 'impudent buffoonery', as Churchill called it, failed when the application was rejected by the Lord Chief Justice. The monarch, as the constitutional source of law, could not be summoned to give evidence in his own court.

Thereafter, the prosecution had matters its own way. Sir Michael Culme-Seymour established that he with his wife and daughters had lived in Malta during his command of the Mediterranean Fleet in 1893. They, their surviving daughter and three sons confirmed this. The future King had not visited the island between 1888 and 1901. The younger daughter died in 1895 and never met the King. Mary Culme-Seymour had not met him between 1879 and 1898. In 1899, she married a naval officer who was now Vice-Admiral Sir Trevelyan Napier.

Marriage registers from Malta were produced in court. They contained no record of the alleged marriage. The King's engagements at Gibraltar for sixteen days while HMS *Thrush* was in dock would have made it impossible for him to visit the island. The jurors were left to decide whether Mylius and Edward Holton James had put together a fabrication or whether there had been a conspiracy between the King, the government and the Culme-Seymour family to cover up a constitutional crime. In that case, where were the children of the first marriage? Unsurprisingly, the jury found the defendant guilty.

Mylius went to prison for a year. In New York, beyond the reach of the English law, he then published his story as *The Morganatic Marriage of George V*. It included information which he had not brought forward at the trial, perhaps because he had not found it in time. For example, Mary Culme-Seymour had sworn she did not meet the King between 1879 and 1898, when she was eight and twenty-seven years old respectively. Mylius or one of his sympathizers had found an entry in the *Hampshire Telegraph and Sussex Chronicle* describing a ball at Portsmouth Town Hall on 21 August 1891. The dancing had been opened by the Duke of York with Mary Culme-Seymour as his partner.

Whether or not this was vital additional evidence was questionable. Supporters of the King would feel that Mary Culme-Seymour might make an error in forgetting something that had happened twenty years before the trial. She had opened a number of balls and had met the King on several occasions since then. Sympathizers of Edward Mylius might point out that she had been positive about not meeting the future King from the time she was eight until she was twenty-seven. In all that time, if there had been one occasion when she had met him and had been his partner at a ball, it would surely have been a memorable moment, worthy of an entry in her diary –

let alone her memory. Yet even if Mylius was right, an attempt to cover up the truth as he alleged it would have required a considerable conspiracy by the Crown at his trial, with catastrophic results for the monarchy if it went wrong. Better, surely, to have left his accusations well alone. But this one inconsistency was, to say the least, odd.[2]

2

If political censorship, in such cases as Guy Aldred or Edward Mylius, was rare, blasphemy was a one-man campaign in the early twentieth century before disappearing almost entirely for fifty years. The law remained as stated by the Blasphemy Act of 1698 and its amendments, which seemed in every sense a dead letter. To the twentieth century, as indeed to much of the nineteenth, it was evident that a religion must depend for its survival on an ability to do without the assistance of Crown lawyers. The only limit to tolerance was where the offensiveness of blasphemy made it likely that violence would result.

In 1917 the House of Lords reiterated the Victorian opinion that the propagation of anti-Christian doctrines was not criminal, 'apart from scurrility and profanity'. The last such case was the prosecution of William Gott in 1921–2. Gott, a Bradford haberdasher, was a bizarre figure with a number of previous convictions for blasphemous libel, offences under the Defence of the Realm Act, and sending obscene books through the post. He was fifty-five years old, described euphemistically as not well-educated – or less euphemistically by his own counsel as 'ignorant'.

In November 1921 Gott, surrounded by a large crowd, was selling various publications in Stratford Broadway. They included his own twopenny pamphlets, *God and Gott* and *Rib-Ticklers: or, Questions for Parsons*. His style was knock-down abuse rather than argument, as in his description of Christ entering Jerusalem, 'like a circus clown on the back of two donkeys'. This style earned him few converts, offending Christians and secularists alike. The crowd became restive, shouting 'Disgusting! Disgusting!' and 'You ought to be ashamed of yourself!' There was a danger of violence. The police moved in and arrested Gott, at first for his own protection, then for blasphemy.

At the Central Criminal Court in December, Gott was described by a police officer as 'a Socialist and Atheist of the worst type'. The jury convicted him but recommended clemency. Mr Justice Avory interpreted this as nine months' hard labour. There was some dissent and a voice from the back of the court appealed to the judge's sense of Christian charity. 'Love

51

thy neighbour and forgive him seventy times seven!' 'You have been guilty of a gross contempt of court in making that remark,' said Avory to the voice, adding, 'and I fine you £5 for it.' Gott appealed against his conviction in January 1922 but the Lord Chief Justice upheld it. The publications were such that it did not require 'a strongly religious person' to be outraged by them.

This was the fourth time that Gott's *Rib-Ticklers* had put him in prison and his chances were not much helped by the way in which he tried to turn each public appearance into a music-hall performance. He had been sent to prison at Leeds Assizes in 1911, after he and his friends had performed an open-air comedy involving the characters of Dr Nikola, an unbeliever who supported Gott; the recently executed wife-murderer, Dr Crippen, and God. The dialogue was reported by Police Officer George Kirman before Leeds magistrates on 9 August. On the Day of Judgment, the virtuous Dr Nikola would be called to answer.

> 'Good morning, Dr Nikola, do you believe the Creation story?' 'No.' 'Do you believe the Flood Story?' 'No' . . . 'To hell with him over Heaven's battlements . . . Call Dr Crippen.' 'How do, God.' 'Do you believe the Creation Story?' 'It's a walk over.' 'Do you believe the Flood Story?' 'That's easy.' 'Did you leave your brother, sister, wife and child to follow Jesus?' 'Yes. I killed the wife first, thinking you would look after her . . .' 'Give him a harp.'

There was also yet another *Freethinker* cartoon with an elaborate caption: 'Great Prize Fight for the Championship of the World between G. Hovah, the Celestial Crusher, and B. L. Zebub, the Pet of Pandemonium'.[3]

Gott went his way and the laws against blasphemy remained undisturbed for the next half-century. For the future, it seemed that it would take a man of extreme persistence to get himself prosecuted under their provisions.

3

The censorship of political and religious views became such a rarity that it presented few problems in the opening years of the twentieth century. The greater and growing concern was over what the law still called obscenity in literature and what ordinary people began to call pornography. It was no longer a question of preventing the publication in England of such authors as Maupassant or Zola, indeed they had now appeared in expurgated form. In addition to books over which there might be a debate, there was also the well-organized trade in material which seemed to pride itself on its illegality. Long before the First World War, smut had gone global.

In May 1908, a joint select committee of Parliament sat to consider 'Lotteries and Indecent Advertisements'. At first sight the subject might seem to have little to do with literature of any kind. Yet when the report was published on 29 July, the evidence of two most important witnesses showed otherwise. Chief Inspector Edward Drew, representing what would later be called Scotland Yard's Obscene Publications Squad, began by saying that he was 'dealing with the indecent part of this Inquiry'. In the far corner, Robert Standish Siever appeared as a champion of bawdy humour. Siever was a sporting gentleman and rogue, so little trusted by his rivals at the racecourse and on the hunting field that under no circumstances was he ever allowed to hold the stakes in a wager.

A portly and moustached figure in cap and gaiters, Siever was also editor of the *Winning Post*, which had endured prosecution for obscenity. Like most sporting papers it regarded itself as reading matter for the smoking room and for those who liked a bit of 'fun'. It advertised glamour pictures and retailed gossip. On 22 June, Siever entered the parliamentary committee room unabashed, having asked for a chance to defend his paper against what he might have called nonconformist cant. When Viscount Llandaff pointed out an indecent picture in one number, Siever with his sportsman's bounce replied, 'That is only a blot . . . That is what I have had to suffer sometimes.' When asked about a paragraph for which his paper had been prosecuted, he replied that it had been written by a clergyman.

Herbert Craig tried to corner him by inquiring if he was prepared to defend everything in the paper's 'Summer Annual'. Siever said he was. '*That* for instance?' Siever looked at it and read it out, ensuring its immortality in the parliamentary papers.

> There was a young lady of France,
> Who decided to give it a chance,
> In the arms of her beau she let herself go,
> And now all her sisters are aunts.

Siever then added, 'If you wish to say she let herself go, and did something wrong, I say there is a vulgarity there, but it does not suggest that. It suggests that she let herself go, that she was married and did what she liked.' The joint select committee decided that it could get no further with Mr Siever.[4]

Far more significant was an earlier hearing on 21 May, when Chief

Inspector Drew treated the members of the committee to an illustrated lecture on the problems of censoring indecent or obscene literature. Warned by the sight of a reputable publisher like Henry Vizetelly being sent to prison, the black sheep of the profession migrated to Paris or Brussels and set up English publishing houses there. If anyone faced the penalties of the English law, it would be the customer returning home or receiving material through the post, or possibly a bookseller in the Charing Cross Road who took a chance on selling such items.

A retailer might suffer the fate of Edward Avery, a Greek Street bookseller, in 1900. He was induced by what Inspector Drew called 'a certain ruse' to sell a book of a 'grossly obscene nature'. In other words, a persuasive plain-clothes officer had pretended to be an interested member of the public. Avery was arrested and his premises searched. The search revealed a large number of similar books and printed sheets ready for the binder. There were also 'beautifully carved ivory models showing persons in the act of coition'. Avery went to prison for four months at North London Sessions.

The French authorities showed little interest in trying to suppress books in any language other than their own. While English publishers moved to Paris, French publishers of similar material, like Jules Gay and Auguste Poulet-Malassis, left for Brussels, Geneva, Bordighera and San Remo. Poulet-Malassis had been Baudelaire's publisher and had endured prosecution for *Les Fleurs du mal*. Jules Gay, a publisher and bibliographer on the run, solved the problem of supply by bribing the guard of the Brussels–Paris night express to see his illegal parcels safely to their destination in France.

Among the first émigrés from London in the 1890s was Paul Ferdinando, Portuguese-born, a London van driver and errand boy who turned to publishing as Charles Carrington. His ostensible purpose in going to Paris was to publish editions of Aristophanes without having to expurgate the text of the comedies. Even in the 1950s the precise implications of lines from such comedies as the *Lysistrata* were left prudently vague. From his premises in the Faubourg Montmartre and another in the rue de Châteaudun, convenient for the ferry trains from the Gare Saint-Lazare to England, Carrington issued literature banned for a variety of reasons. After Oscar Wilde's disgrace and imprisonment in 1895, he took over such titles as *The Picture of Dorian Gray*, which Methuen were reluctant to keep in print, and issued new editions of such erotic classics as *Fanny Hill* or *The Autobiography of a Flea* and pedantic oddities like the *Manual of Classical Erotology*.

Carrington remained in business until the First World War, thanks largely to official French indifference to protests by Scotland Yard and the Home Office. Much of his output consisted of elegantly written fiction both in English and a milder French version. Other publications were principally remarkable for their labyrinthine titles. *Raped on the Railway: A True Story of a Lady Who Was First Ravished and then Chastised upon the Scotch Express* contrived to outrage the New Woman and to appal Scots the world over by making the pride of the London and North-Western Railway sound like a whisky dray. Among enduring titles of the 1890s was *Two Flappers in Paris* with their 'Uncle Jack'.

By 1900, as Inspector Drew explained, Carrington had competitors. H. S. Nichols had been in partnership with a former Sheffield solicitor, Leonard Smithers. They had produced a twelve-volume edition of Sir Richard Burton's translation of *The Arabian Nights* with a further volume of plates, including as much Eastern eroticism from the first privately printed edition as they thought safe. Nichols was raided by the police in 1895 and two tons of material of 'the worst description', as Drew described it, was seized from his shop in the Charing Cross Road. Smithers seemed to know when police raids were pending. On these occasions he would pack the stock from his Old Bond Street shop into Gladstone bags and deposit them in railway station cloakrooms all over London until the danger passed.

Nichols fled bail, reached Paris and set up in business. Twelve years passed before Scotland Yard realized this, and only then from a complaint by a man in London who had received an unsolicited pamphlet in which Nichols offered bound volumes of a pornographic magazine, 'which I beg to offer to you at a bargain price'. Scotland Yard alerted the French authorities that England 'was being flooded with pamphlets of a similar nature'. The French replied that there was nothing they could do: French law did not permit the prosecution of a man 'for offences committed abroad'. In the end, they agreed to serve Nichols with an expulsion order, whereupon he left for New York.

The Metropolitan Police rented rooms in various London lodgings in order to see what they could buy from Paris by post. There was a brisk trade in photographs. Dolly Ashford, the widow of a Paris entrepreneur, had taken on the business. She had sent her advertisements wrapped in copies of a daily newspaper, *Le Matin*. It was impossible for British Customs to dismember every one of thousands of newspapers arriving from France. In 1904, Mrs Ashford was offering 'some real hot photos at 21s. per dozen'. She also offered breezy advice on what to do if they were intercepted, though she sent parcels by registered post and 'no book sent in this way has ever been seized in the post'. If the worst happened, the recipient should flatly deny ownership and insist that there had been a dreadful mistake, or perhaps a malicious prank.

The French authorities were even less interested in photographs than they were in books. Inspector Drew regaled the joint select committee with the case of C. Keary, trading from the rue du Maubeuge and the publisher of 'a book named *Illustrated Artistic Encyclopedia*', for which he had sent out a catalogue in November 1907. Inspector Drew became technical.

> I would like to furnish your Lordships and the Committee with a specimen of the catalogue. It contains photographs which the police consider are of an indecent nature and I would like at this point to inform your Lordships' Committee, what in the opinion of the police is the difference between a photograph of an obscene nude person, and one which might be considered indecent, although not obscene, and that is where the hair is clearly shown on the private parts. That we should consider in this country an obscene photograph on which we could institute proceedings under the Obscene Libels Publication Act (*handing in a book*). You will see on the front page a representation of what we would consider an obscene picture.

As the members of Parliament passed the catalogue round, Inspector Drew broke bad news. On 7 December 1907, the Assistant Commissioner at Scotland Yard had written to the Chef du Sûreté in Paris, pointing out the photographs with hair and emphasizing the urgency of preventing them reaching England. The Chef du Sûreté had considered the matter and replied on 29 January 1908. 'In returning you the enclosed papers, I have the honour to inform you that the photographs forwarded are not considered as obscene in France.' However, the French had warned Keary that dealing in books containing such photographs was prohibited in England. 'I venture to say that will not have a very salutary effect upon him,' said Inspector Drew gloomily.[5]

There was a surreal moment during his evidence, when Drew introduced the moral scourge of 'trick cards', which were 'in themselves of a perfectly innocent character, but when certain parts of the photograph are covered up with a finger, it discloses what is certainly a very obscene photograph'. Copies of the cards were passed round but the committee members failed to work out how to place a finger over part of each image so that an obscene result was produced. With the assistance of Chief Inspector Drew they got the hang of it.

His appearance before the joint select committee was not the high point of Edward Drew's career. Two years later, as Chief Inspector of the Criminal Investigation Department at Scotland Yard, he was appointed to the newly formed Secret Service Bureau, the forerunner of MI5. He was to be its general factotum in countering peacetime German espionage. Scotland Yard had evidently put its best brains on to the obscenity problem. Also at the committee hearing in 1908 was Chief Inspector Walter Dew who was to be even more famous in 1912, when he brought the wanted murderer Dr Crippen back from Canada.

4

By no means all police attention was directed to professional pornography produced at home or imported from abroad. Since the trial of Charles Bradlaugh and Annie Besant in 1877 for publishing *The Fruits of Philosophy* it was not at all clear where the law stood on the literature of birth control, let alone on such subjects as psychopathology. A revolution in the categorization of terms employed in psychopathology had been carried out by the Professor of Psychiatry at Vienna, the Baron Richard von Krafft-Ebing. English translations of his *Psychopathia Sexualis* were published in 1892 and in 1894, by a firm of medical publishers in Philadelphia. No attempt was made at suppression, though the original had gone through nine editions in six years. Lord Alfred Douglas recalled that Oscar Wilde was reading the book in 1893, while writing *Salome*. 'He showed me the book in his room. He was continually reading it and talking about it.'[6]

The book was influential yet apparently innocuous, in the sense that it came into the hands of very few people. However, it introduced a new vocabulary, coining the terms 'sadism' and 'masochism', the latter from an author still alive. It established 'lesbian' in a new meaning and acquired the useful term 'fetishism', suggested by the philologist Max Müller, of Christ Church, Oxford. It used 'paedophilia' in a modern sense, not simply to mean love of children.

In Krafft-Ebing's pages, all these symptoms were illustrated by case histories of patients, though his accounts were brief and dispassionate. It was not offered to the public gaze in libraries and was not, like *The Fruits of Philosophy*, 'sold in the streets at 6d. a copy'. Similarly, an unexpurgated translation of Aristophanes on a railway station bookstall might attract the police but there was nothing to stop a schoolboy with sufficient classical Greek from reading both the original text and the speculations of its editors on the lewder passages. An underground novel like *Teleny: or the Reverse of the Medal*, the best-known homosexual pornography of the

57

1890s, was a target for prosecution. Yet the Latin text of the second satire of Juvenal, its sardonic surgeon grinning with satisfaction as he lances the haemorrhoids of a 'catamite', was untouched by prosecution and required only the key of classical learning to unlock.

Havelock Ellis was a more popular author than Krafft-Ebing and, indeed, had edited the plays of Christopher Marlowe for Vizetelly's Mermaid Series. His *Studies in the Psychology of Sex* extended to seven volumes and his accounts of individual cases were far longer and more elaborate than most of Krafft-Ebing's had been, some of them having the tone of short stories. Their style was more accessible to the general reader. The book which brought him to the attention of the law in 1898 was *Sexual Inversion*, whose eight chapters were followed by appendices on 'Homosexuality Among Tramps' and 'The School Friendships of Girls'.

Among enthusiasts for his work were George Bedborough and the Legitimation League, whose aim was the legitimation of illegitimate children. Bedborough and his wife described themselves as freethinkers, communists, feminists, neo-Malthusians, vegetarians and abstainers from alcohol. They occupied separate bedrooms in order that each should have a free choice of sexual partners. None of this need have involved Ellis or the police, had not Bedborough also sold *Sexual Inversion* from the front room of his house in John Street, Bedford Row.

Ellis was little more than a sympathetic onlooker at the meetings of the Legitimation League. Yet *Sexual Inversion* remained in danger. Despite the thirty years between them its case histories were more specific than anything in a banned post-war novel like *The Well of Loneliness* (1928). Indeed, Ellis had misgivings about the book's suitability as a choice for the first volume of *Studies in the Psychology of Sex*. 'It was not my intention to publish an abnormal manifestation of the sexual instinct before discussing its normal manifestations . . . It may even be that I was inclined to slur it over as an unpleasant subject, and one that it was not wise to enlarge on.'[7]

It had been most unwise to draw attention to such a subject. Unknown to its organizers, the Legitimation League already included two plainclothes Scotland Yard officers, keeping surveillance on anarchists. One of them was John Sweeney, a former royal bodyguard and officer of the Special Branch. The official attitude was tolerant to men and women of the world who attended. The objection, according to Sweeney, was that 'lads of eighteen or nineteen, and well-dressed, thoughtful-looking girls of the same age attended the meetings.' The tableau of Ellis' supporters was completed by George Ferdinand Springmuhl von Weissenfeld, alias de Villiers-Singer, alias the Brandy Distillers Company, alias Dr Sinclair

Roland MD of Cambridge. Unsurprisingly, he was a swindler with convictions for fraud.[8]

Sweeney arrested Bedborough, who was charged at Bow Street on 13 June 1898 with selling 'a certain lewd wicked bawdy scandalous and obscene libel entitled *Studies in the Psychology of Sex: Sexual Inversion*'. He was convicted at the Central Criminal Court on 11 October. His counsel had unsuccessfully applied for a writ by which the case could be transferred to the High Court and the scientific value of the book argued. Under the Obscene Publications Act this was otherwise irrelevant.

To the dismay of his followers, Bedborough admitted selling the book but claimed he had done so in good faith and now disowned its contents. He revealed the true villain as 'Dr de Villiers' of the University Press, Watford, who published the book and received the money. 'My lord,' said counsel for the Crown, 'Dr de Villiers has absconded.' He was thought to have fled abroad. A warrant had been granted for his arrest, should he ever return. The printing works at Watford had been raided. Thousands of copies of the book were found as well as six new linotype machines which had been working at full capacity.

There was no university at Watford but there was a long trail of fraud left by the first English publisher of Havelock Ellis. He now had thirty bank accounts and a score of pseudonyms. His most spectacular fraud was the Brandy Distillers Company Limited of 1891, for which he sent out a prospectus showing extensive vineyards, none of which were his. He gathered in £60,000. To impress visitors, his female servants would change into expensive costumes and sit about his drawing room, posing as wives and daughters of foreign ambassadors, statesmen and celebrities.

The University Press at Watford was a more modest deception inspired by a view, which Weissenfeld shared with the trial judge, that Ellis could be marketed as a salacious author to make his backers rich. More than three years after the case, Scotland Yard grew suspicious of 'Dr Sinclair Roland MD' and his wife, living in a large house on the outskirts of Cambridge. The house was entered by Detective Inspector Arrow and Detective Sergeant Badcock from Scotland Yard. There was no sign of the fugitive. After a thorough search, a secret panel was found. Behind it lay a passageway, large enough for one man to pass through. Sergeant Badcock entered and emerged dragging Weissenfeld, whose loaded revolver was knocked out of his hand in the struggle.

Weissenfeld became agitated and called for water. He drank a few drops, began to choke and dropped dead. The coroner's jury suspected apoplexy. John Sweeney took another view. 'Dr de Villiers, a doctor, chemist, and scientist, used to have in his possession a gold seal ring; in that ring was hidden behind the seal a few grains of a poison which de Villiers boasted years ago would kill a man and leave no trace behind. On his arrest the ring was on his hand.'[9]

5

In the wake of Bedborough's conviction a new resistance to literary censorship emerged. There had been protests at the prison sentence on Vizetelly but no public outcry on behalf of Zola's fiction. There was sympathy for Charles Bradlaugh and Annie Besant but no campaign for Charles Knowlton and his *Fruits of Philosophy*. After Bedborough had been charged his Anarchist friend, Henry Seymour, set up a Free Press Defence Committee to fight for the right of literature to be published rather than to secure the welfare of the publisher. His committee included Bernard Shaw, Frank Harris and George Moore.

This committee was not a libertarian vanguard determined to throw off existing restraints but a fight against further restraints that were now threatened. Before the joint select committee in 1908 witnesses had demanded stricter censorship of indecency in novels, magazines and of all crime magazines in the 'Police News' group. A 'small prohibitory board' at the Home Office was suggested, to which publications 'of any description' might be taken and banned, if thought improper, 'without the need of legal process'.

As for fiction, there were now novels 'about as bad as can be'. Those cited included Elinor Glyn's *Three Weeks*, published the previous year, and two others, Hubert Wales's *Cynthia in the Wilderness* and Filson Young's *The Sands of Pleasure*. These were 'far more outspoken, more gross in expression' than any French fiction. 'That I think is allowed on all hands.' It was certainly not allowed by a magistrate who ordered the destruction of Balzac's *Contes drolatiques* in the following year.

One problem was that when W. H. Smith banned a novel from their bookstalls or the Times Book Club refused to take it, the news spread rapidly and seemed to increase its sale elsewhere. However, it would be possible to 'terminate the existence or the possibility of such novels being published in the future' by use of the 'prohibitory board' to enforce a ban. The most scandalous of the novels mentioned was *Three Weeks*, a best-seller by any standards, its notoriety heightened by a scene in which the hero and heroine made love on a tiger skin. A popular music-hall verse of the day commemorated it.

> Would you rather sin
> With Elinor Glyn
> On a tiger skin?
> Or would you prefer
> To err with her
> On some other fur?

Even in 1915, during a civil action, Mr Justice Younger still suggested that it was not too late to bring a prosecution against the book. Happily for Elinor Glyn, she had a powerful protector. She was the mistress of Lord Curzon, Viceroy of India in his thirties, future Foreign Secretary, who since his days as an undergraduate had encouraged a cult of 'effortless superiority' over lesser mortals and colleagues alike.[10]

A moral distrust of fiction in all its forms lay deep in the English puritan tradition. Homer's *Iliad* had seemed to Daniel Defoe nothing but 'the rescue of a whore'. The evangelical poet Robert Montgomery had addressed nineteenth-century fiction writers in verses 'On the Effects of Indiscriminate Novel Reading':

> In thy lewd leaves how many pens have taught
> The filth of fancy and the lust of thought?

Twenty years before Elinor Glyn, Ruddock's *Lady's Manual of Homoeopathic Treatment* listed the causes of early sexual maturity in girls as spiced food, bad ventilation, late hours, dancing and 'novel reading'. For the adult male, John Thompson in *Man and His Sexual Relations* advises the patient that 'Nearly all the novels that deluge our bookstalls are seasoned with exciting references to the exercise of amativeness.' Sylvanus Stall in the Anglo-American best-seller of 1897, *What a Young Boy Ought to Know*, has the last word. 'Read histories and biographies. Read about the sciences and arts. Read of travels and explorations. Read about morals and religion, but do not read story books and trash.' What hope could there be for sex on a tiger-skin rug?[11]

The classic as well as the commercial, the past as well as the present, was under fire. Summing up at London Sessions in 1900, in the trial of a bookseller who had sold the sixteenth-century *Heptameron of Queen Margaret of Navarre*, the Common Serjeant instructed the jury: 'In the Middle Ages things were discussed which if put forward now for the reading of the general public would never be tolerated. In towns buried from the corrupt times of the Roman Empire . . . there are discovered pictures of the most lewd and filthy character. Nobody would think of destroying those pictures, but to sell photographs of them in the streets of London would be an indictable offence.'[12]

Vizetelly himself had tried to anticipate the prosecution against him by sending to the Treasury Solicitor *Extracts Principally from English Classics: Showing that the Legal Suppression of M. Zola's Novels would Logically Involve the Bowdlerizing of some of the Greatest Works in English Literature*. The extracts ranged from Shakespeare to Dante Gabriel Rossetti, from Henry Fielding to Swinburne, supported by acknowledgements of the greatness of Zola's Rougon-Macquart series of novels from critics like Henry James and Andrew Lang.

Vizetelly ended his polemic with a question to the Treasury Solicitor. 'I ask for my own and other publishers' guidance, whether if Zola's novels are to be interdicted, "Tom Jones" and "Roderick Random", "Moll Flanders" and "The Country Wife", "The Maid's Tragedy" and "The Relapse", in all of which the grossest passages are to be met with, will still be allowed to circulate without risk of legal proceedings.' He received no answer.[13]

He misjudged his situation. The court was concerned only as to whether Henry Vizetelly had broken the law, not whether someone else had done so. Far worse, the National Vigilance Association was headed by John Kensit, for whom the idea of a classic warranted a sneer. In the association's Third Annual Report for 1888 he had attacked the acquittal of Boccaccio's *Decameron* at the Guildhall. 'Some literary persons were shocked at the idea of prohibiting a standard classic four hundred years old . . . The worthy Alderman who boasted that he had read the original both in Italian and French seems to have been afraid to deal with a classic, and declined either to interfere or to give any reason for not interfering.'[14]

By 1896 Kensit and his followers had put classics, especially when foreign, in their place. 'Although it has been charged upon us by English *littérateurs*, when we first attempted to prevent the importation of foreign filth into the English markets, that we were striking a blow at classical literature we dared to go steadily forward, and today there is a healthy consensus of opinion against free trade in obscenity.' A feather in the association's cap was that it might 'congratulate itself' on being chosen by Lady Burton to destroy books and papers of her late husband, Sir Richard Burton, 'which, in her opinion, could not judiciously be read by an indiscriminate public, and in this connection it was our privilege to burn, on one occasion, books to the value of £1,000'.

Against such onslaughts, the civilized reservations of Vizetelly could have little effect. Yet a new generation of novelists had a champion in one of his younger authors, George Moore. Moore had made a name for himself with *A Modern Lover* and *A Mummer's Tale* before he published *Literature at Nurse: or, Circulating Novels* under Vizetelly's imprint. Like all formulaic novels, whether Marxist, feminist or paperback romance, the danger which lay in wait for the library favourites of the day was puerility. Moore seized upon it. 'Instead of being allowed to fight, with and amid, the thoughts and aspirations of men, literature is now rocked to an ignoble rest in the motherly arms of the librarian . . . in and out of his voluminous skirts run a motley and monstrous progeny, a callow, a whining, a puking brood of bastard bantlings, a race of Aztecs that disgrace the intelligence of the English nation.'

It was a battle-call to writers suffering under a correctness of taste imposed by Charles Mudie, W. H. Smith and their kind. In 1883, Mudie had withdrawn Moore's novel *A Modern Lover* because 'two ladies in the country had written to him to say that they disapproved of the book'. The novelist's freedom was curtailed by a literary philosophy which first decided what type of novel must be written and then worked backwards from that. As Moore described it, 'if the right to probe and comment on humanity's frailties be granted, what becomes of the pretty schoolroom, with its piano tinkling away at the "Maiden's Prayer", and the water-colour drawings representing mill-wheels and Welsh castles?' The writers of the new century, including H. G. Wells and D. H. Lawrence, wrote for an audience beyond that of Charles Mudie or W. H. Smith. As Moore insisted, there could be no compromise over the portrayal of the adult world and the issues of public life. 'We must write as our poems, our histories, our biographies are written, and give up once and for ever asking that most silly of all silly questions, "Can my daughter of eighteen read this book?" Let us renounce the effort to reconcile those two irreconcilable things – art and young girls.'[15]

In October 1907, the *Spectator* struck at the root of such arguments in an editorial on 'Socialism and Sex Relations', aimed at the sexual morality of H. G. Wells and his novels. Its complaint was that Socialism in its current form, despite its shared values with Christianity and though many of its adherents were Christian, used propaganda to undermine the values of marriage. In *In the Days of the Comet* Wells had made free love 'the dominant principle for the regulations of sexual ties in his regenerated state. The romantic difficulty as to which of the two lovers of the heroine is to be the happy man is solved by their both being accepted.' Wells had dutifully published a letter in the *Clarion* on 18 October insisting that he had never advocated free love or the destruction of the family. To the *Spectator*, however, both things were inevitable under Socialism, 'wives in common and husbands in common will follow goods in common.'[16]

On the publication of H. G. Wells' *Ann Veronica* in 1909, the magazine headed its review 'A Poisonous Book'. The problem was not coarse words nor 'suggestive' passages but 'a book capable of poisoning the minds of those who read it' by its ideology. The plot of the book, in which Ann Veronica leaves her father's home at twenty-one, lives independently in London as a biology student at Imperial College and associates with Fabians and suffragettes, is not described in any detail by the review. She serves a short prison sentence for her political activities but the book ends more decorously than it began, its heroine married to her lover, pregnant by him, and the family reconciled.[17]

Readers of the *Spectator* needed no persuasion that something must be done to save the English novel. Next week the solution was introduced by the familiar words of the censor, 'We hate a censorship . . . however . . .' No one, after all, was likely to admit to an enthusiasm for censorship, especially if they felt it. Herbert Bull, a clergyman of Westcliff-on-Sea, took up where Inspector Drew had left off the year before. He proposed a government committee to whom objectionable books could be referred by readers. He had tried to persuade the Home Office to prosecute a book the year before but was told this would 'do more harm than good' by giving publicity to a novel which might be acquitted.

The *Spectator* adopted his proposal for an independent organization of 'men of the world, the kind of men who get returned to Parliament by the best type of constituency'. They would pass judgment on books sent to them. Such a plan would suppress the modern tendencies in literature which Herbert Bull had denounced. Those who could afford to do so would guarantee a sum of money, if needed, towards the costs of prosecuting a publisher, distributor or author. At a lower level, individual readers would protest to publishers over a book which 'any average clean-minded man would not like to see his women-folk reading'. There should be a boycott of all those 'who continue to sell bad books and magazines, &c., after one warning'.

This proposal was more threatening than anything suggested by the National Vigilance Association. The *Spectator* was a literary weekly with a distinguished pedigree. It promised that books would not be censored merely for being 'coarse' or 'suggestive'. Each decision would be made by reasonable men and women and would therefore be unanswerable. Nor was it before time. Herbert Bull had a list of ninety-eight books 'which a single firm has placed under ban', a firm presumably of librarians or booksellers.

On the heels of this came a demand by Dr William Barry in the *Bookman* in January 1910 for 'The Cleansing of Fiction'. He declined to cite titles, for fear of promoting them. However, they rivalled the bawdiest dramatists of the Restoration, 'Wycherley, Congreve, and other offenders against morals in literature'. Recently, fifty novels had been withdrawn by Mudie's library under pressure from their readers. 'It would be ridiculous in their advocates to maintain that by an *auto da fé* of all of them literature would suffer loss.' Once again, H. G. Wells was among the 'trash' for burning.

If proof was needed that the new censors were not philistine fanatics, it was to come five years later when an essayist and distinguished man of letters, Robert Lynd, reviewed D. H. Lawrence's novel *The Rainbow* in the *Daily News* on 5 October 1915. Lynd called the book 'a monstrous wilderness of phallicism'. Had Lawrence written the *Iliad*, Paris and Helen would have been 'simply a pair of furious animals'. Yet Lynd does not condemn the book for its animalism; such a novel may still be fine literature 'by reason of its humanity'. The true crime of *The Rainbow* is its lack of 'the marks of great literature'.

Gentle, reasonable, sophisticated such a reviewer might be, yet behind him stood policemen and magistrates. Soon the limits of fiction would be tested in earnest.

6

In parallel with fiction, the new century still exercised moral vigilance over the stage and had yet to devise a policy of pre-censorship for the emerging entertainment of 'moving pictures'. Since 1737, under the Licensing Act, any performance on the English stage had first to be approved by a member of the Royal Household, the Lord Chamberlain, or more often his 'Reader of Plays' deputizing for him as censor. This lasted until 1968, when it was abolished by Act of Parliament and the theatre, like publishing, became liable only to the law of the land.

In the 1890s several well-known plays had been refused a licence. Subject to the law, it was still possible to perform them without a licence in a theatre club, for a small audience of members. This happened when Oscar Wilde's *Salome* was banned in 1892 and *Mrs Warren's Profession* by Bernard Shaw was refused a licence two years later. The reason for banning *Salome* was its biblical subject, while Shaw's play was the story of a woman who has begun as a prostitute and gone on to become the proprietress of brothels. The plot of the play was its downfall and Shaw's restrained but moralistic style failed to redeem it. Similarly, Henrik Ibsen's *Ghosts* with its associated subject of venereal disease had failed to pass the censorship in

1891. Maurice Maeterlinck's *Monna Vanna* proved too sexually suggestive in its dialogue for the censor in 1902, while plays by Frank Wedekind and Arthur Schnitzler would wait until the second half of the new century for a production.

It was also open to the Lord Chamberlain to introduce a temporary ban. On 19 August 1909, Sir William Gilbert complained to a joint select committee of the two houses of Parliament about the suppression of *The Mikado* during a Japanese state visit. He was informed indirectly that the Lord Chamberlain believed the operetta 'might give offence to our Japanese allies'. In fact, his music was so far from offending them that it was played on their warships moored in the Medway. Offence was caused only to Gilbert, who claimed he had lost £10,000 by the removal of *The Mikado* from the London stage.

Between 1900 and 1912, almost 6,500 plays were submitted to the Lord Chamberlain's office. Of these only forty were refused a licence. The objection to pre-censorship was a matter of principle rather than of the number of plays being banned. If a performance was licensed, any deviation from the approved script was a criminal offence. If infringement of this rule was suspected, a member of the Lord Chamberlain's staff attended a performance incognito to check. Portrayal of the Deity or members of the royal family, living or dead, was forbidden in any case, as was the portrayal of the head of a friendly foreign state. Prosecutions were brought as late as the spring of 1939 against those who mocked Hitler on the stage and even in 1962 sketches portraying John F. Kennedy were banned, though the White House let it be known that he had no objection to them.

As Sir William Gilbert had discovered to his cost, operas were not exempt from the censorship. In 1905, Oscar Wilde's banned play *Salome* was adapted as a German libretto for the opera by Richard Strauss. Five years later Thomas Beecham attempted to stage it at Covent Garden. He argued that other 'biblical' operas, notably Saint-Saëns' *Samson et Dalila*, had been performed for thirty years. The Lord Chamberlain replied that Samson and Delilah was an Old Testament story, John the Baptist and Salome belonged to the more sensitive New Testament.

Beecham's family, rich from the sales of Beecham's Pills, knew the Prime Minister. Asquith listened attentively to Beecham's assurance that Britain would look ridiculous if a famous opera in German were banned. Consent was given, subject to 'modifications'. John the Baptist must only be called 'The Prophet'. Salome's passion was to be a plea for spiritual guidance. The Prophet's severed head, sung to by Salome for almost twenty minutes at the end of the opera, must be covered with a cloth and must not be shaped like a head. Beecham replied that it could hardly be shaped as an arm or a leg.

Officials from St James's Palace filled the Lord Chamberlain's box on the first night. After half an hour of the expurgated version, Salome made a slip and reverted to the banned libretto. The other singers followed suit. At the first performance in Germany, Richard Strauss had famously exhorted the orchestra, 'Louder, louder! I can still hear the singers.' Beecham urged the Covent Garden orchestra to maximum volume to drown the voices. It was impossible during Salome's long and ghastly solo to the severed head. As the curtain fell, Beecham saw the party from the Lord Chamberlain's box advancing. It was merely to congratulate him. None of them knew German nor had understood a word of the opera anyway.[18]

Of far greater concern was the new and unregulated entertainment of the cinema. A film that was seditious, blasphemous or obscene might be prosecuted after it had been shown but by then the damage was done. By 1907 it was evident to the police that indecency and the art of the moving picture or 'mutoscope' were as inseparable as photography and obscenity had been fifty years before. It was not even necessary to visit a cinema to sample the result. Proprietors of mutoscope machines installed them in fairgrounds, on seaside piers and in places of amusement generally.

The mutoscope consisted of 'two eye-pieces with lenses of a stereoscopic nature, and a photograph or series of photographs behind it. When you put a penny into it or in some cases when you turn a handle, a series of scenes presents itself.' The rapidly flickering cards gave the illusion of moving figures, in such brief dramas as 'The Artist's Model' or 'The First Night'. In some cases a viewing cost a penny and in others only a halfpenny. However, the handle of the machine would only turn forward so that it was impossible for the connoisseur to go back to a particularly rewarding moment.

The nature of the entertainment varied little, according to the police. 'Some of the exhibitions that are to be seen in the mutoscopes, such as the exhibitions of almost, if not entirely, nude women, bed-room scenes, undressing scenes and so on, without which no mutoscope exhibition is complete nowadays, are very demoralizing to the young boys and girls who congregate about them.' They flourished in London districts like Southwark, where large shops were 'completely gutted' to accommodate rows of machines. Similar premises had been gutted in the 1850s to provide 'penny gaffs' for scantily clad dancers. By 1907, they offered moving pictures of 'women undressing, showing their underclothing, and sitting in certain postures in a highly suggestive manner'. The images were 'highly demoralizing . . . when exposed to young persons of either sex'. Each machine also had a title on it, among which were 'How shocking!', 'Naughty! Naughty! Naughty!', 'Very spicy' and 'Don't miss this!'

Some magistrates had taken action under the Vagrancy Act 1837–8, imposing a £25 fine, but this was hardly a deterrent. On a Sunday night Chief Inspector Edward Drew had visited an exhibition at the Elephant and Castle, whose owner was prosecuted. 'At the least estimate', the inspector had found more than three hundred boys and girls who had seen the displays and were now themselves 'indulging in all sorts of indecent acts'.[19]

The morals of the mutoscopes were only one cause for concern. The new celluloid films were highly inflammable in more senses than one. This fire risk led to the Cinematograph Act of 1909 under which they could only be exhibited in premises licensed by a county council or other competent authority. After that, censorship was inevitable but film-makers had learnt from the experience of the theatre. They preferred to impose a control of their own. In 1912, the new industry created a voluntary body, the British Board of Film Censors. As a pledge of good faith, all members were vetted and approved by the Home Office. The scheme would be financed by the applicants, who would pay by the foot for each film they submitted for approval.

The BBFC held sway until film censorship withered in the 1970s – only to return when the government took power to ban or cut films under the Video Recordings Act of 1984. Under the voluntary code, films were to be classified as 'U' for universal exhibition, 'A' when children under sixteen were not admitted unless accompanied by an adult and, in 1933, 'H'. This last category was a recognition of the new 'horror' film, represented by *Frankenstein* and *Dracula*, banned to all those under eighteen.

The film censors had no legal jurisdiction but local authorities might refuse a licence to a cinema. Private performances were not exempt, since the physical safety of the audience was still an issue. This opened the way to political censorship. The Salford Watch Committee in the 1920s banned private showings of Soviet films at the Salford Workers' Film Society, while Manchester permitted them. A general ban on Eisenstein's *Battleship Potemkin* was imposed in 1926 and remained in place until 1954. However, it was open to an individual local authority to ignore the board and license the showing of a film in its area, though this was not common.

Among films forbidden by the BBFC, a social worker's film on the evils of white slavery, *Night Patrol*, was banned because all mention of white slavery was forbidden on the British screen. Bernard Shaw thereupon suggested that public opinion should sweep away the censor and his powers and his department into the dustbin. Ivor Montagu's short film *Free Thalmann*, demanding the release of the Communist leader in the Reichstag from a Nazi prison, where he had been held without trial for three years, was banned in 1936 under the category of films 'likely to wound the just susceptibilities of Friendly Nations'. Thalmann was held until 1944 and then shot in Buchenwald. The *March of Time* newsreel on Mussolini's invasion of Abyssinia was cut to omit the statement that units of the British fleet had gone to Alexandria, a fact that was common knowledge anyhow.

Even films in the making were censored. A life of Judge Jeffreys was abandoned when the Board advised that no reflection on the administration of British justice at any period of history could be permitted and that the phrase 'The Bloody Assizes' would be forbidden. The bland and uncontroversial nature of British cinema led to J. B. Priestley's appeal to producers in 1936: 'I wish one of them would come out with something hot and strong on the radical side (if he wants any assistance he can have it), so that we could make a test case of it with the Censor.' The time when that might happen was still more than twenty years ahead.[20]

To Edwardian England, censorship was apparent in the infrequent prosecution of those who attempted to market Havelock Ellis or *The Decameron*; of opportunists who opened arcades of mutoscopes and fell foul of the law, or who staged plays forbidden at the command of St James's Palace. Sex was what seemed to catch the censor's eye. In the summer of 1912, few people paid much attention to a parliamentary bill which passed through the House of Commons in a single day. Only a handful of MPs opposed it. Its title was the Official Secrets Act. The first decade of the century with its love of more or less innocent titillation, voyeurism and scandal had gone into the dark. The new law was the prelude to a war in which the publication of political subversion and treason would be the target of retribution. Sometimes it drew a prison sentence and, in one case at least, a sentence of death.

4

The Defence of the Realm

I

ON 22 AUGUST 1911, the Commons were summoned to the bar of the House of Lords to hear the new Official Secrets Act receive the royal assent. It was to remain in force during two world wars, the uneasy peace between them, and the Cold War that followed. It would be used against defendants as diverse as the novelist Compton Mackenzie, the Governor of Pentonville Prison, the editor of Roger Casement's diaries, the auctioneers Sotheby's, two contributors to the Oxford undergraduate magazine *Isis*, whom it sent to prison, two well-known Conservative politicians, Duncan Sandys and Jonathan Aitken, as well as campaigners against capital punishment, or in favour of nuclear disarmament, and a good many more.

The 1911 Act was amended in 1920 to incorporate wartime experience, and again in 1939 to protect those who sought to alert Parliament and the voters to deficiencies in the nation's defences. There was a further Act in 1989 to limit the class of information covered by the provisions. Hitherto, it had been regarded as 'prejudicial to the interests of the State' to divulge information on matters as varied as the staff holiday rota at Broadmoor Criminal Lunatic Asylum or the contents of catalogues in the British Museum, listing the Private Case of pornographic literature and the even more strictly controlled collection of Suppressed Books which the museum did not admit to possessing.

The progress of the 1911 bill was rapid. It was introduced in the House of Lords by Lord Haldane as Minister of Defence and read a first time on 17 July. Almost all discussion took place in the Lords. The Commons were asked to pass it through all three stages on 18 August. Though the country was at peace, 'in the opinion of the government it is of an urgent nature.' The debate began at 12.30 p.m. and ended by 1.00, in time for a bill to provide Old Age Pensions.

In this brief debate, one member objected to the attempt to 'rush through' such a law. Another opposed the bill's provisions. 'It upsets Magna Carta altogether.' (The press recorded 'laughter' at this.) A further objection was to the 'unusual and extraordinary powers' given to the police. An 'ordinary constable' might now arrest and search suspects without a warrant. The requirement that a warrant must be granted by a Justice of the Peace was abolished; it could henceforth be authorized by a police superintendent. Nor would it be necessary to prove a defendant guilty of any particular act against the interests of the state. On conviction, the maximum sentence was imprisonment for fourteen years. The Under-Secretary of State for War promised that the new bill was only 'a small amendment' of existing law, while the Attorney-General added reassuringly that 'the principle of the Bill is nothing new.' In any case 'with the safeguards in the administration of justice in this country there is no danger to innocent persons.' The government got its way by 107 votes to 10.

There were two powerful reasons for pushing the law through in the last hours of a parliamentary session. In April, the Sultan of Morocco had been threatened by a rival claimant. France, who with Spain had been given authority to police the territory by the 1906 Algeciras Conference, sent troops. Germany thereupon accused her of abusing her powers and despatched the torpedo gunboat *Panther* to the Moroccan harbour of Agadir, effectively seizing the port. Threats were exchanged, Germany demanding compensation by the concession of rights in the French Congo. On 21 July, Lloyd George, as Chancellor of the Exchequer, made a Mansion House speech, promising that Britain would stand by France. After several days of what seemed like pre-war tension, Germany climbed down.

There was also an underlying cause which seemed to justify the new law. The 1904 *Entente Cordiale* between Britain and France marked the end of a natural Victorian alliance with Germany. Combined with naval rivalry, this set the stage for a 'German invasion' phobia followed by a 'German spy' hysteria in 1910–14. Official secrets were the currency of an age of espionage. Sensitive information might travel hundreds of miles in minutes or seconds. In 1815, it had taken four days for the news of Waterloo to appear in *The Times*; ten years earlier, it had taken that of Trafalgar a fortnight. The telegraph had revolutionized reporting, even by the time of the Crimean War in 1854–6, when Lord Raglan, as Commander-in-Chief of the British army in the Crimea, had complained vigorously to the War Office about press correspondents, notably William Howard Russell of *The Times*.

On 13 November 1854, from his camp before Sebastopol, Raglan wrote in some distress to the Minister of War. Russell's despatch in *The Times* of 23 October had contained a mass of intelligence which Raglan thought 'invaluable to the Russians'. This included figures for British losses from cholera; the accuracy of Russian shells falling on the Light Cavalry Division; the location of forty pieces of British artillery; the total of British and French heavy guns, and the location of a powder mill with twelve tons of gunpowder, which the Russians had targeted ever since the paper had been published. Newspaper despatches reached the enemy in Sebastopol, via neutral capitals, before they could be read by British commanders in Balaclava. The War Office itself was so insecure that Raglan was reduced to sending sensitive information by the longest route, rather than by telegraph, so that it should be of no value to the enemy by the time it reached Whitehall – and unfortunately not much use in Whitehall either.[1]

As late as 28 April 1915, J. L. Strachan-Davidson, Master of Balliol, informed the *Morning Post* that Field Marshal Helmut von Moltke had sent one of his officers to London during the Franco-Prussian War of 1870–71. The man was to 'study each morning every line coming from France in the correspondence columns of the British newspapers'. He would do more for his country in this way than by any act of gallantry on the field of battle. Yet by the 1880s censorship still seemed more applicable to guarding diplomatic or military papers in government offices. It was a world described by Sir Arthur Conan Doyle in Sherlock Holmes stories like 'The Naval Treaty' or 'The Bruce-Partington Plans', shrewdly exploiting his readers' curiosity over secret alliances and plans for new weapons.

Secret treaties were a crucial function of diplomacy. They could be made without parliamentary approval, as an exercise of the royal prerogative. The Congress of Berlin in 1878 had been preceded by 'secret conventions' between European powers. Britain signed three, with Russia, Austria-Hungary and Turkey. Bismarck's secret alliance with Austria-Hungary in 1879 became a Triple Alliance with the inclusion of Italy in 1882. A secret *Dreikaiserbund* of June 1881 secretly bound Germany, Austria-Hungary and Russia to observe benevolent neutrality towards any member at war with an outside power.

At the time of the Congress of Berlin, on 27 June 1878, Charles Marvin, a part-time copying clerk in the Treaty Department of the Foreign Office, appeared at Bow Street Magistrates Court. Those who charged him could find no better legislation than Section 30 of the Larceny Act 1861, and he was tried for 'stealing, copying and appropriating certain documents connected with the negotiations pending between the governments of England and Russia'. Marvin was a man with a grudge: as a temporary clerk, he was paid even less than the messenger who carried the documents.

With the *projet de memorandum* of the treaty in his hands, he made a copy on 30 May 1878 and passed it to the *Globe*, the oldest evening newspaper in London. The paper published a special edition at once and gave details next day.

On 9 July, the Bow Street magistrate decided that passing information to a newspaper did not support a charge of larceny. Marvin was discharged. Responsibility for the treaty lay with Lord Salisbury as the Foreign Secretary who accompanied Disraeli to Berlin. When a Conservative government next took office, Salisbury was Prime Minister. He had been embarrassed by Charles Marvin seven years earlier and now ensured it would not happen again.

An Official Secrets Act, making it criminal to divulge information contrary to the interests of the state, wound its way through Parliament in the summer of 1889. An almost identical statute became law in India soon afterwards. There was no urgency. The law was exclusively a deterrent to those in positions of trust tempted to betray information to the press. It stopped at 'wrongfully obtaining and disclosing information' rather than spying.

Had there been a foreign enemy in view, it would have been France rather than Germany. Yet Germany's victory in the Franco-Prussian War prompted one accurate glimpse of the true threat three decades ahead. Colonel Sir George Chesney wrote a story for *Blackwood's Magazine* in 1871, 'The Battle of Dorking', in which a Prussian army invades England, defeating the British near this Surrey town.

A far greater impetus to secrecy and censorship came with the German Navy Law of 1898, providing for twelve battleships, ten large cruisers and twenty-three light cruisers to be launched by 1903, the year in which Britain's alliance switched to France. Literature once again anticipated life in that year as Erskine Childers described German preparations for an invasion of Eastern England. It was to be launched from the creeks, rivers and islands of the German North Sea coast between Wilhelmshaven and Emden. *The Riddle of the Sands* was the first and one of the best espionage novels. In 1906, assisted by Field Marshal Lord Roberts and backed by a £3,000 advance from the *Daily Mail*, William Le Queux described a future attack in *The Invasion of England in 1910*. By this time, Roberts and Colonel Charles à Court Repington, former head of army intelligence, led the National Defence Association. The association demanded the introduction of conscription and Repington, as military correspondent of *The Times* for the next ten years, was well placed to support it.

The theme of Le Queux's novel is England's unpreparedness in the face of obvious danger. The German army lands first in Norfolk and then in north-east England, captures East Anglia and industrial Yorkshire but is overwhelmed at last in a protracted battle to take London. The success of the novel was ensured by the *Daily Mail*'s serialization, during which its newsboys appeared on the London streets in Prussian military uniform.

The scare ended in laughter with an illustrated novella, *The Swoop: or, How Clarence Saved England* (1908), by the young P. G. Wodehouse. England is invaded simultaneously by a variety of nations including the Swiss, whose navy bombards Lyme Regis and captures the bathing machines, the principality of Monaco, and Moroccan tribesmen mistaken for Negro minstrels by bank holiday crowds at Margate. Invasions have been made so boring by Le Queux and his kind that the news appears only as one line in the Stop Press of the evening papers between cricket scores and racing results as, 'The German army landed in Essex this afternoon.' The first Germans are thought to be refugees from a fancy-dress party. When the truth is discovered, they are set upon by wily bungalow-dwellers, cruelly intent upon selling them life insurance.

The invasion scare also reached the stage. One of the West End successes of 1909 was Guy du Maurier's play *An Englishman's Home*, whose plot included a German invasion of Britain, and which was duly revived on the outbreak of the Second World War thirty years later. Throughout its run in 1909, an army recruiting booth stood in the theatre's foyer.

2

The form of censorship in the Official Secrets Act was determined at the Committee of Imperial Defence, whose members included both Admiral Sir John Fisher and the King's Private Secretary, Lord Esher. It accompanied the creation of a military intelligence service which, by the outbreak of war in 1914, included MI5 for domestic purposes and MI6 overseas.

The use of legislation to control information seemed justified, even though the first prosecutions to combat espionage were a fuss about very little. In September 1910, a German engineer officer, Lieutenant Siegfried Helm, was arrested at Portsmouth. His sketchbook contained drawings of Southsea Castle and the Spithead forts done from outside the structures 'For my own study'. Helm had gone to Portsmouth at the invitation of a young woman, Gertrude Wodehouse, with whom a brother officer had had an affair. Before long Siegfried Helm was also having an affair with her. When Miss Wodehouse discovered his sketches, she informed the orderly officer at the Royal Marine barracks. The amateur spy had sketched nothing that anyone else might not have drawn. He pleaded guilty at Winchester Assizes, was bound over and set free.[2]

The professional spies of 1910 were usually British, operating in Germany. Lieutenant Vivian Brandon of the Royal Navy and Captain Bernard Trench of the Royal Marines appeared in the Imperial Court at Leipzig in December, charged with 'betrayal of military secrets'. They were denounced as agents of British Admiralty intelligence. On the stretch of coast where Erskine Childers had set *The Riddle of the Sands*, they compiled information on fortifications, guns, searchlights and depths of water. There was laughter in court when counsel held up a copy of Childers' novel. Trench said he knew the book, Brandon had read it three times.

Unlike Siegfried Helm's sketches of a public view, the Borkum spies had scaled a fence to enter a prohibited site. They had sent the information to 'Reggie', whom they refused to identify and who was presumed to be the Intelligence Department of the British Admiralty. Their purpose was the updating of a 'Naval Baedeker', kept by the British as a record of German military installations. 'The English press,' said the prosecutor, 'always asserts that Germany is planning an attack on England.' His facts would prove that 'England is planning an attack on Germany.' Captain Taegert, a naval representative, showed that information obtained about the pier at Sylt and its coastline could be useful only for putting troops ashore. Brandon and Trench were convicted and sentenced to four years in a military fortress, not an onerous form of confinement.

The *Cologne Gazette*, whose chauvinism Bismarck once praised as worth an army corps on the Rhine, warned that British strategists were planning an invasion. The Berlin *Lokalanzeiger* and the Catholic *Germania* added that any landing would be without declaration of war. As it happened, Admiral Sir John Fisher, an intimate of Edward VII, had horrified the King by recommending that the Royal Navy should 'Copenhagen' the High Seas Fleet at Kiel without declaring war, in the manner of Nelson with the Danes. It must be done while Britain had seven dreadnoughts in commission and Admiral Tirpitz had none and could not use any without rebuilding the Kiel Canal. By July 1911 Tirpitz had dreadnoughts and his Baltic Squadron passed through the canal.[3]

Within a week of the Official Secrets Act becoming law, Oberleutnant Max Schultz was detained at Plymouth and charged with attempting to procure a solicitor, Samuel Hugh Duff, to obtain military and naval intelligence for him. Schultz posed as a correspondent for 'an important German newspaper' and would pay for information. Mr Duff became a double agent. Schultz telegraphed information to Ostend, or posted it via the address of a German waiter in London. He wanted Royal Navy views on the Agadir crisis, as well as figures for mobilization and manning in the 3rd and 4th Squadrons of the Home Fleet. He went to prison for twenty-one months at Exeter Assizes.[4]

In November, Heinrich Grosse, alias Hugh Grant, was charged with espionage at Portsmouth, a coded letter being found in his pocket. His interest was in coal supplies, without which much of the Royal Navy could not put to sea. A loaded revolver was found at his lodgings and a curious disc, suggesting that his cipher was a primitive form of the Enigma Code utilized in the Second World War. He went to prison for three years.[5]

A spy mania stirred the country with absurd results. A Frenchman with a small Kodak box camera approached a policeman near Woolwich Arsenal. He asked to be directed to lodgings because he had missed the last train to London. As the policeman showed him the way, two men from Woolwich Arsenal saw the camera. 'You are a foreigner,' they said. 'You have no right here.' They accused him of spying and told the policeman that he could not take the man to the lodging house because he was carrying a camera. They, not the 'spy', were arrested. Elsewhere, rumours ran through South Wales in December about a man called Stein who spoke Danish fluently. He had asked questions about forts in the Bristol Channel. He examined one at Lavernock Point, near Cardiff, and said, 'if they are all like that it would be child's play to take them.' He proved as elusive as the Scarlet Pimpernel.

The first traitor under the new Act appeared in 1912. George Charles Parrott, a former naval gunner, was convicted of passing information to a German contact, whom he met on visits to Ostend, and went to penal servitude for four years. There was the stuff of spy fiction in such questions from Germany as, 'Where is the Second Destroyer Flotilla now? Have there been mobilizing tests of the flotillas and coast defences in the Firth of Forth? What number of Royal Fleet Reserve Class "A" men are called in now for the yearly exercise?'[6]

3

Such was the background to press censorship in the last days of peace. Yet critics of the Official Secrets Act pointed out that it did not impose a direct control on the press. A far more contentious restriction appeared in 1912. Defence Notices – or D-Notices – were to be issued by a committee representing the government, the military and the press itself. Involving the press would make it harder for editors or publishers to break ranks. D-Notices were addressed to editors, informing them of a story or piece of information which might come their way and telling them, in the national interest, not to publish it. No penalties were provided in advance but a prosecution might follow under official secrets legislation. The D-Notice system was found too useful ever to be abolished.

Lord Haldane, Secretary of State for War, the hawk who had carried the 1911 legislation through Parliament, tempered this by a visit to Germany six months later. He dined with the Kaiser, discussed differences with Bethmann Hollweg as Imperial Chancellor, also with Grand Admiral Tirpitz and the Prussian Minister of War. As he left for home, the German press described its people as ready for friendship with England 'on the basis of mutual respect and good will'. War might yet be averted. As late as 23 July 1914, Lloyd George was still assuring the House of Commons that the future of 'two great Empires' lay in cooperation for mutual bene-fit. The points of such cooperation were far more numerous than those of 'possible controversy'.

Within a fortnight the two nations were at war. Before it ended, cen-sorship had struggled against a determined opposition. The Union of Democratic Control, supported by Bertrand Russell, E. D. Morel and sev-eral Radical or Independent Labour members of Parliament, was not to be silenced. Its supporters claimed that such speeches as Lloyd George had made were cynically calculated to deceive the people while the govern-ment prepared to fight.

The attitude of some wartime governments made the Official Secrets Act seem almost libertarian. Throughout the French press on 26 January 1916, a statement to journalists by Prime Minister Aristide Briand warned protesters, 'It is in vain that you talk only of the principles of liberty. Liberty! But do you not know what is the true way to defend it? Never forget, gentlemen, that if victory should not be ours, Liberty will be dead for us and for the world.'

In 1914, as in 1939, the British cabinet prepared for war by a single statute under which delegated regulations could be issued from time to time. This was the Defence of the Realm Act 1914, known for conveni-ence as DORA. Two regulations, updated from time to time, dealt with the press and publication. The first controlled information, as the Official Secrets Act already did in part. The second sought to control the expres-sion of opinion. The expression of opinion might also fall into the category of treason, if the accompanying circumstances warranted it.

Regulation 18 prohibited the collection of any information relating to the armed forces of Britain or her Allies 'without lawful authority', or more vaguely the collection of any such information 'as is calculated to be or might be directly or indirectly useful to the enemy'. More contentious was Regulation 27, which applied to 'any newspaper, periodical, book, circular, or other printed publication'. It was to be an offence to 'spread false reports or make false statements'. It was also criminal 'to cause disaffection to His Majesty, or to interfere with the success of His Majesty's forces . . . or to prejudice His Majesty's relations with foreign powers'. It was even criminal to commit such offences in respect of His Majesty's allies.

Pacifism was taken care of under Regulation 27 by banning reports or statements 'intended or likely to prejudice the recruiting of persons to serve in any of His Majesty's forces', including the police force or fire brigade. It was also criminal to spread reports or statements 'intended or likely to undermine public confidence in any bank or currency notes which are legal tender in the United Kingdom or any part thereof'. For good measure, this would include attempting to 'prejudice the success of any financial measures taken or arrangements made by His Majesty's Government with a view to the prosecution of the war'.

Common sense supported a ban on the unauthorized export of newspapers to neutral countries – where they might be bought by an enemy. Cables sent by foreign journalists from Britain were also strictly vetted. On the outbreak of war, under the International Telegraph Convention, 'all telegraphic and radio-telegraphic services throughout the Empire would be suspended'. The extent of disruption was daunting. As 'an act of grace', however, services would still operate for the time being. Messages must be in French or English, in 'plain language', and would be 'subject to censorship by the British authorities'.

There was dismay among press and publishers at the provision that any offence would be dealt with by 'competent naval or military authority'. Did this mean martial law being used to control information and opinion? Apparently so. In the House of Commons on 22 November 1914, Sir Stanley Buckmaster, Director of the Press Bureau, told questioners irritably that the regulations meant what they said. 'They are perfectly plain. If orders that are given for the safety of the State are broken, the punishment is punishment by court-martial – anything up to imprisonment for life.'

Fleet Street and Bloomsbury were alike appalled at the threat of editors or publishers having their liberty decided by a court of army or naval officers with no appeal to a jury. The government relented next summer. A new Regulation 56 transferred cases to the Director of Public Prosecutions.

The last Director of the Press Bureau, Sir Edward Cook, recorded that in practice during the rest of the war, offences against the regulations were dealt with summarily before magistrates or on appeal to Quarter Sessions. Maximum sentences imposed were six months' hard labour or a fine of £100 – or both.

The government kept further powers in reserve. It could not allow the press to publish subversive material first and punish culprits when the damage had been done. Under Regulation 51, military authority would seize the printing presses used, to ensure that a publication did not appear again. It would also order police to enter the printer's premises and seize the type, if it suspected that an illegal publication was to be produced. To avoid such a confrontation, it set up an official Press Bureau three days after the outbreak of war. On 7 August 1914 its existence was announced by the First Lord of the Admiralty, Winston Churchill. The bureau would see to it that 'a steady stream of trustworthy information supplied both by the War Office and the Admiralty can be given to the Press'. The press, in turn, must submit to the bureau any stories that had come its way and obtain permission to publish them.

The Press Bureau was installed in Whitehall, in the Royal United Service Institution. By managing news it would manage the press. Its first director, a close friend of Churchill's, was the maverick Conservative politician and barrister, F. E. Smith, a great courtroom performer of his day. Smith took up residence on the Western Front. By sending back what news he chose, he might avoid press correspondents arriving in France and interfering with the war. It was not until 2 December 1914 that the government offered 'necessarily limited numbers' of correspondents access to the front. Smith's principal complaint was that the weekly box of cigars posted by his wife was routinely stolen by dishonest soldiery. All future packages must be labelled 'Army Temperance Society Publications Series 9'. He never lost another cigar.[7]

Such management of news was easily justified. At Bolton on 9 December 1914, Sir John Simon, as Attorney-General, argued that only a 'bold use of censorship' had ensured the safe passage of the British Expeditionary Force across the Channel. It was 'established on the other side without the slightest risk of attack on the way'. Secrecy later enabled a transfer of the BEF from the centre of the Allied line to the left wing, blocking a German advance on Calais. Sir Edward Cook, an experienced journalist who later rose to be director of the Press Bureau, congratulated it on having kept details of the mobilization of the Royal Navy from the pages of the papers in 1914.

Some censorship was, to say the least, opaque. A quotation from Kipling, 'The captains and the kings depart', was cut from a press despatch to London. The King of the Belgians, through whose country the front line ran, might have been visiting his troops. No reference to the King was intended and he was not with his troops anyway. Yet the censors held that, had he been, the report might have made him a target. It was 'a matter of special importance to keep His Majesty's movements secret'.[8]

After F. E. Smith, Sir Stanley Buckmaster took over the bureau, only to resign in 1915 on becoming Lord Chancellor. Until the end of the war the post was held by Sir Edward Cook, who had made his career with W. T. Stead and the *Pall Mall Gazette*. He was also author of a famous biography, *Delane of 'The Times'*. Cook presented himself as a friend of the press: without him there could be no news. He was the dispenser of good things, and sometimes a cautionary voice, warning editors not to publish information they had come by in other ways.

Though the Press Bureau was wound up with the coming of peace, DORA outlived the war and kept in check some of the highest in the land. Lord Fisher, as the patron of the dreadnought had become by 1919, recalled in his memoirs the inertia of his colleagues during his years as First Sea Lord. 'At that time I was "Pooh-Bah" at the Admiralty; the First Lord was in a trance, and the Financial Secretary had Locomotor ataxy.' Fisher unilaterally took over their powers of decision. 'I referred, as First Sea Lord, a matter to the Financial Secretary for his urgent and favourable consideration, and he favourably commended it to the First Lord, who invariably cordially approved. It was all over in about a minute. *Business buzzed!*' Fisher added, however, 'I'm doubtful whether this ought to come out before Dora's abolished. That's why I wanted these papers to be edited in the United States . . .'[9]

4

These forms of censorship were at least open to a form of scrutiny. The existence of others was itself an official secret. Scotland Yard, through its Special Branch, was entrusted with the task of preventing the circulation of publications which were not in themselves illegal. So, for example, in October 1915 it went to considerable lengths to prevent the appearance in England of Jefferson Jones' *The Fall of Tsingtau*, published in the United States by Houghton Mifflin. Japan was now one of Britain's allies. Jefferson Jones took an anti-British view of a government which had gone to war in defence of Belgian neutrality, but was happy to see Chinese neutrality violated by its Japanese ally in order to deny the Germans use of a port. It was 'the very thing that had seemingly so shocked her in Belgium'.

Belgium's colonial record was an embarrassment to those who now came to her aid. The British government sought to suppress wartime publications – and indeed memories – relating to Belgian atrocities in the Congo in the period to 1903, when Leopold II and his appointees administered the Congo Free State. So, for example, *The Truth About Civilization in Congoland* (1903) had now been 'locked up and withheld from Readers' in the British Museum library. *The Curse of Central Africa* was to be 'removed from general circulation'.

To protect the image of 'gallant little Belgium', the trustees of the British Museum agreed on 15 December 1915 to comply with the terms of a letter from the Metropolitan Police Criminal Investigation Division, written on 13 November. This requested that 'in view of its hostile attitude towards the Allies', *The Fall of Tsingtau* by Jefferson Jones should not be made available to readers, 'till after the war'. Even the minutes of the meeting which agreed to this would remain an official secret for the next fifty years. By transferring the Jefferson Jones title to the Suppressed Books section, there would be no public record whatever of the library possessing it.[10]

5

Public embarrassment for the government often came from the battlefield in France. Yet few anticipated that the source would be Sir John French, the Commander-in-Chief, nor that his target would be the nation's warrior-hero, Field Marshal Lord Kitchener, now Secretary of State for War. The occasion of the ill-feeling was the Battle of Aubers Ridge on 9 May 1915. This was a British infantry attack on German trenches, preceded by an artillery bombardment. During the attack, the British sustained 11,500 casualties, discovering too late that the German defences were still largely intact. The artillery bombardment had failed, as it seemed, because the gunners ran out of shells. Such was the origin of the 'shell shortage' scandal.

Field Marshal French turned to Lloyd George and Lord Northcliffe of *The Times* and the *Daily Mail*. Whatever their differences, they were united in hostility to Kitchener. The military correspondent of *The Times* was the same Colonel Repington who had allied himself with Lord Roberts and conscription in 1906. His despatch appeared in *The Times* on 14 May: 'British soldiers died in vain on Aubers Ridge on Sunday because more shells are needed. The Government, who have so seriously failed to organ-ize adequately our national resources, must bear their share of grave responsibility.' This was a prelude to the collapse of the pre-war Liberal government, under Asquith's premiership, which had remained in power during ten months of the conflict.

On 19 May, Northcliffe contributed an editorial to his paper: 'Men died in heaps upon the Aubers Ridge ten days ago . . . Lord Kitchener must bear his share of the responsibility.' Northcliffe also knew what the public did not. The shell scandal had been preceded by a cabinet quarrel, between Churchill as First Lord of the Admiralty and Fisher as First Sea Lord, as to how the ill-fated Gallipoli campaign was to be supported by the navy. It was unlikely that Fisher could remain in office and rumours to this effect had been circulating since 14 May. In the House of Commons, Conservatives seemed ready to break the wartime truce. On 17 May Asquith advised the King that the government should be 'reconstructed' as a coalition.

Yet shells held the headlines. On 21 May, Northcliffe let the *Daily Mail* off the leash with front-page banners: THE SHELLS SCANDAL. LORD KITCHENER'S TRAGIC BLUNDER. OUR TERRIBLE CASU-ALTY LISTS. CAUSE OF THE CABINET CRISIS. Fisher and Churchill had already caused a cabinet crisis with no assistance from Repington or the Harmsworth press. In the newsroom on the evening before publication, however, Tom Clarke showed a proof of the morning edition to a colleague. 'Have you read the leader? We are going to break some windows tomorrow.'

It was far too late for anything the Press Bureau could do. Section 27 of DORA made it a criminal offence to cause disaffection to His Majesty – did this mean to His Majesty's government? Perhaps the matter was best left to public opinion. A placard appeared that day outside the *Daily Mail* offices at Carmelite House, 'The Allies of the Hun'. That night a special police guard was put on the building. Copies of both the *Daily Mail* and *The Times* were ceremonially burnt at the Stock Exchange and Field Marshal Haig wrote privately of 'the reptile Harmsworth press'. In the aftermath, the *Daily Mail* lost 300,000 of its circulation.[11]

On 25 May the Press Bureau moved at last. Northcliffe had received several stories from officers at the front supporting his account of the shell shortage. When these were refused clearance by the Press Bureau, he gave orders that no more were to be submitted for censorship. 'Send all these censored proofs to Lloyd George and Curzon. They know the truth and it will let them see how the Press Bureau is keeping it back.' Curzon was a

Conservative member of the coalition cabinet; Lloyd George was Minister of Munitions.

The scandal passed but not the problems of Kitchener as Secretary for War. By November 1915, the threat of having to rescue the British invasion force from Gallipoli, to which he was opposed, took him to the Dardanelles. On 6 November, *The Times* revealed that in his absence 'Lord Kitchener's name was the subject of many rumours yesterday afternoon. One of these was that he had resigned.' Stories were already circulating that Kitchener had resigned and gone to the Mediterranean to assume command of British forces. The Press Bureau had denied this at 5.30 p.m., describing him as 'temporarily absent on public duty'.

It was a London evening paper, the *Globe*, which first announced his resignation, implying that his cabinet colleagues were not sorry to see him go. Despite official denials, this was repeated in the paper on the following day as 'The Truth About Lord Kitchener – Reassertion of the *Globe* Statement – His Resignation Tendered – What the Country Thinks and Wants'. The last of these was crucial. The country wanted its hero as Secretary for War. A lively response to the 'resignation' story persuaded Asquith that he must keep him. Kitchener had feared he might be dismissed during his Dardanelles visit.

The following afternoon, a detachment of police officers led by Chief Inspector Fowler of Scotland Yard arrived at the offices of the *Globe* in the Strand with a pantechnicon van. Yet this was a military operation ordered by Major-General Sir Francis Lloyd as the 'competent military authority' under DORA. They seized all copies of the newspaper for the past two days, as well as files, private and personal correspondence, and essential parts of the printing presses.

Further publication of the *Globe* was prohibited, or 'suspended', and a debate on press freedom began in the House of Lords. The specific offence was not one of publishing the original resignation story but repeating it after a denial by the Press Bureau. Northcliffe came to its aid in *The Times* on 9 November: 'Freedom of speech, tempered by patriotic discretion, is the best safeguard of the State and of the people against the errors in policy and in execution to which all Governments are subject, and of which we have confessedly had a plentiful and disastrous harvest during the course of the war.' There was no room for 'half-truths nicely doled out to create false impressions or to save imperilled reputations'. The nation's rulers must display to the people 'an alacrity, a vigour, a foresight, and a resolution which have been conspicuously lacking until now'.

If this had been the first trial of strength between Fleet Street and the

Press Bureau, it seemed uncertain where victory lay. On Friday 5 November, the evening of the *Globe*'s indiscretion, the *Daily Chronicle* submitted an article on the Kitchener rumours and was told it could not publish. Yet what its editor called almost identical stories had been passed for publication next morning in *The Times*, the *Daily Mail* and the *Morning Post*. On Monday, the *Morning Post* printed a letter from William Joynson-Hicks, a Conservative MP, 'practically reaffirming what the *Globe* said about Lord Kitchener and accusing the Prime Minister and the Press Bureau of lying into the bargain'. If the purpose of wartime censorship was to rally opinion behind the government, it had failed lamentably.

Three days after the police raid, negotiations between the *Globe* and the government began. There was an interview at the Home Office and a formal letter from solicitors of the paper, which withdrew its story 'that there were grounds of dissension between Lord Kitchener and his colleagues, such as to affect their future ministerial cooperation'. The proprietors asked for the return of their printing plant. Major-General Lloyd agreed to a 'conditional return'. The paper appeared on 22 November with a new editor. Kitchener died in office on 5 June 1916, when the cruiser HMS *Hampshire* struck a mine off the Orkneys on her way to Russia.

6

When a comparable case occurred in 1917, it was Kitchener's adversary Lloyd George who complained most vehemently and Colonel Repington who was the cause of the trouble. With the entry of the United States into the war in April 1917 and the end of German hostilities with Russia in December, German strategy was predictable. There must be a spring offensive in the west before the bulk of American forces could arrive.

In the face of this threat, on 1 February 1918, the Supreme War Council of Allied leaders met at Versailles. At Clemenceau's suggestion, it resolved to create a general reserve of troops on the Western Front to meet an attack, wherever it should come; the reserve was to be responsible to the War Council and its advisers, rather than to military commanders elsewhere. No one was more offended by this than Field Marshal Sir William Robertson, Chief of the Imperial General Staff. He would tolerate a general reserve only under his command and able to act at once in an emergency. It had not been made clear who was to be the commander of such a reserve.

The proposal seemed an attempt to transfer power from the Chief of the

Imperial General Staff in London to an ill-defined alliance of political leaders and advisers in Versailles. It confirmed a hostility between military leaders and politicians like Lloyd George, who criticized generals prepared to sacrifice thousands of lives for paltry territorial gains. This in turn provoked a sector of the press, which felt that generals were being obstructed by dishonest politicians. In December the *Globe's* 'Hands off the Army' campaign had been supported by the *Morning Post* and the *Daily News*. The *Spectator* denounced Lloyd George for his levity, irresponsibility, recklessness and injustice, a man 'not fit to be the Prime Minister of this country'. The *Nation* followed by suggesting an alternative government under Lord Lansdowne, an advocate of ending the war by a negotiated peace.

In February, it seemed that Sir William Robertson or an officer of the General Staff had betrayed the secret Versailles decision on the general reserve to Colonel Repington, now Military Correspondent of the *Morning Post*. Lloyd George insisted that it must be so, but the Director of Public Prosecutions pointed out to him that he could hardly indict the whole of the General Staff. Repington's first article of 8 February 1918 insisted that 'The decisions of the recent Inter-Allied War Council regarding the control of British troops in the field are of such a strange character that Parliament should demand the fullest details.' That evening, the *Globe* reprinted Repington's 'disquieting telegram'. It also described the plan for a new command structure and inquired, 'Is there or is there not a Generalissimo?'

Lord Milner wrote to Lloyd George that evening, enclosing a cutting from the *Globe* and suggesting that Field Marshal Haig would now resist having any divisions transferred to the proposed 'secret' reserve. On 11 February, the *Morning Post* published a further article by Repington in which, as Lloyd George reported, he quoted the English text of the secret minutes of the War Council meeting. 'He uses my own words as recorded then. I know nothing comparable to this betrayal in the whole of our history.' Worse, in the German magazine *Prussische Jahrbuch* on 24 February a German military strategist, Professor Delbrück, thanked the *Morning Post* and Repington for supplying such useful information. Even if the information proved of little use, the Germans had enjoyed this display of British incompetence.[12]

The War Cabinet considered the 'treachery of the *Morning Post*', its ministers judging that the paper had given 'valuable military information to the enemy'. Sir Edward Cook explained that the article had been submitted to the Press Bureau: 'He had endeavoured to censor it, but its whole character was such that amendment was practically impossible.' He had returned it to the editor, warning him that it infringed Section 18 of the Defence of the Realm Act. The editor made a few small alterations and published it. 'Anyhow,' said Repington next day, 'it is something for us not to be in prison after our indiscipline this morning.'[13]

There was still no proof that Repington had got his information from the embittered Chief of the Imperial General Staff, but Sir William Robertson was not to hold that command much longer. On 18 February he read in a newspaper that he had resigned. He was already reported as saying that he and Repington 'could no more afford to be seen together just now than we could afford to be seen walking down Regent Street with a whore'. Repington returned from a lunch party on 13 February to hear that the police had called on H. A. Gwynne, editor of the *Morning Post*. Shortly afterwards he was also served with two summonses to appear at Bow Street to answer charges under the Defence of the Realm Act. He was gratified to find that the crowds and cameramen were more numerous than any since Dr Crippen, the best-known murderer of recent times, had appeared there six years earlier.[14]

The case went ahead with the Solicitor-General, Sir Gordon Hewart, appearing for the Crown. However, the only charge that could be realistically proved against Repington and the *Morning Post* was one of breaching the Defence of the Realm provisions by publishing without authority 'plans and conduct of military operations' and 'military dispositions', for which the penalty was a fine of £100. Lloyd George noted that it had been difficult to frame charges without 'the actual plans agreed upon at Versailles' getting further publicity. Any implication that the article was accurate would merely 'aggravate the mischief'. None the less, he pointed out to Lord Derby as Secretary for War that an ordinary soldier who betrayed such information as Repington had done 'would have been shot without any compunction'.[15]

7

Wartime subversion came in many forms. At one extreme were supporters of the government's aims who disliked its methods. At the other was a variety of opponents who either wanted the war stopped at all costs or hoped that Germany might win.

Treasonable publication was the crime of Sir Roger Casement, former British Consul in the Congo, who died on the gallows in 1915 for Irish nationalism and independence. He had been arrested soon after landing in Ireland from a German submarine with the intent of organizing rebellion to British rule in his homeland. Though Casement pleaded not guilty, he claimed that his was a Sinn Fein rebellion. 'My going to Germany was only to get guns and such help as was possible to allow of Irishmen at home fighting, instead of talking.' Bernard Shaw advised him to insist on being treated as a prisoner of war rather than a traitor and to tell his accusers, 'I am an Irishman captured in a fair attempt to achieve the independence of my country.'

In the event, Casement did not give evidence but read a statement from the dock, in which he told the court that he had never asked Irishmen to fight for Germany but only to fight for Ireland against England. Yet one of the six nails in his coffin, as the counts in the indictment were to prove, was the publication and circulating of a recruiting pamphlet to Irish prisoners of war in Limburg Lahn Camp.

> Irishmen, here is your chance to fight for Ireland. You have fought for England, your country's hereditary enemy. You have fought for Belgium in England's interest, though it was no more to you than the Fiji Islands. Are you willing to fight for your own country with a view to securing the national freedom of Ireland? With the moral and material assistance of the German Government an Irish Brigade is being formed.

The pamphlet promised that the brigade would fight 'solely for Ireland' and 'under the Irish flag alone', with its own officers and its own distinctive uniform. What else Casement had done might be debatable but not only did he admit the authorship of the pamphlet, he was proud of it. The law had its way with him. The argument that his allegiance was to Ireland rather than Britain counted for nothing. At his appeal, it was argued that the Statute of Treasons 1351 did not apply to acts committed outside the King's realm, in this case in the 'German Empire', and that the indictment was invalid. The appeal was dismissed and leave to appeal to the House of Lords was refused. Casement was hanged at Pentonville prison on 3 August, 'the bravest man it fell to my unhappy lot to execute', according to Ellis, the hangman.[16]

Among petitions on Casement's behalf was one to the Prime Minister from Sir Arthur Conan Doyle. He appealed for Casement's life because his execution might turn opinion against Britain in the United States and neutral countries. A reprieve might win friends. Yet certain people, including neutrals, were being shown typescripts made by Scotland Yard of Casement's diaries, kept while he was Consul in the French Congo and Consul-General in Rio de Janeiro. On 10 June, after his trial, the *Daily Express* called him 'an extremely degenerate traitor'. The *Weekly Despatch* on 16 July referred to his diary and wondered whether Mr Clement Shorter who was organizing a reprieve petition had read this 'remarkable document' or if Conan Doyle was 'aware of its contents'.

The diaries were found among his clothes when the locked trunks at his London lodgings were opened. It was alleged they contained accounts of Casement's sexual encounters with young boys and men in the Congo and South America. The first question was whether they were genuine. Secondly, whether genuine or not, were Scotland Yard and its masters making grossly improper use of them? By the time this was asked, the harm had been done. To many who read them, including some Irishmen, Casement was a hero no more.

The first typescript was headed, 'Scotland Yard. August 1916. REX v CASEMENT', and described as 'Copies of entries in Lett's diary for the year 1903 and part of the year 1904'. However, the 1911 volume was the most explicit with accounts of youths and boys he had seen in the street and in some cases picked up. They make sad reading and it seems certain that had a private individual circulated them, there would have been a prosecution under the Obscene Publications Act.

There was controversy for the next fifty years as to whether these were government forgeries. Some who knew Casement were permitted to read pages of the original and reluctantly agreed it was his handwriting. It was suggested that the earlier diary was not his own but was copied out by him as part of a report. Unfortunately, the 1911 diary made this quite untenable. As to the use made of the diaries, the American Ambassador, Dr Page, reported an after-dinner exchange with the Prime Minister, two days before Casement's execution. Asquith asked the ambassador whether he had heard about the typescript. Dr Page had. 'And what is more I have been given photographs of some of it.' 'Excellent,' said Asquith, 'and you need not be particular about keeping it to yourself.' On the following day, the cabinet decided that Casement should die next morning.[17]

Having made use of the diaries, those who had done so sought to cover their tracks. In May 1922, the journalist Peter Singleton-Gates was given a bundle of papers with the assurance that they would make 'a book of unusual interest'. They included a copy of the typescripts and a *procès-verbal* of the interrogation of Casement at Scotland Yard by Basil Thomson, Assistant Commissioner and Head of the Special Branch, and by Captain Reginald Hall, Director of Naval Intelligence.

Singleton-Gates proposed to publish the diaries and to reveal the government's actions in his book, *The Secret Diaries of Roger Casement*. On 10 January 1925, the *Evening Standard* announced this title, adding that it had been necessary to edit this diary very carefully before publication. The martyr's halo was likely to be a little dimmed. Next day Singleton-Gates was summoned to the Home Office and confronted by the Home Secretary, Sir William Joynson-Hicks, with his Chief Legal Adviser, Sir Ernley Blackwell. The first question was 'Where did the documents come from and who gave them to you?' Singleton-Gates reminded them that journalists 'do not under any circumstances, or under whatever pressure, reveal the names of those who place confidence in us'.

Blackwell warned him that under the Official Secrets Act anyone who refused to give information to a police officer above the rank of inspector 'relating to an offence or suspected offence' was liable to imprisonment for two years. On 26 January, Singleton-Gates handed over the secret *procès-verbal*. The Home Office 'emasculated' the text of the proposed book and, for good measure, Lord Birkenhead, Attorney-General at Casement's trial, went the rounds of London publishers warning them not to touch it. On 30 January, Blackwell wrote to Singleton-Gates at the *Evening Standard*, reminding him that the Home Secretary 'will be glad to receive from you, as promised, the extracts dealing with Casement's diary and Sir Basil Thomson's interrogation of Casement together with your undertaking not to publish the book in question'. Singleton-Gates reluctantly observed the undertaking but kept his copy of the typed diaries for publication in 1959.[18]

8

By 1917, the immensity of losses on the Western Front had become a powerful argument for ending the war, among pacifists and non-pacifists alike. The most influential body of its kind, the Union of Democratic Control, had been founded in September 1915 and was now concerned with the duplicity of those who had started the war. Its target was 'secret diplomacy', which had led the nation into catastrophe. The UDC's interest was in foreign affairs and its secretary, E. D. Morel, became known as 'the Foreign Minister of Dissent'.

Morel, who was to serve a prison term in 1917–18 for communicating unauthorized printed matter to a neutral state, denounced the Foreign Secretary of 1914, Sir Edward Grey, as a weakling who was the 'puppet' of his permanent officials. '"British Policy" WAS the policy not of Britain, but of the handful of Liberal cabinet ministers who with their accomplices in the world of Foreign Office and embassy officialdom, journalism and finance, were running the country on to the rocks.' Morel's list included Grey, Asquith, Churchill, Haldane, Crewe and Fisher. He cites Fisher's advice to the late King to 'Copenhagen' the German fleet without declaration of war.

Despite the cheering crowds in London and Berlin, there had been a strong undercurrent of opposition to war. Wilfrid Scawen Blunt, poet, traveller and friend of the famous, listed Britain's allies on the second day of hostilities. They included Serbia, a nest of 'murderous swine'; Russia, the tyrant of Poland; France, who was Britain's 'fellow brigand' in North Africa, and Belgium, whose atrocities against the native population of the Congo had outraged the House of Commons in 1903. A good many people in England still recalled the music-hall verse about King Leopold II, following reports of natives who had their hands cut off for returning at evening with an unsatisfactory harvest of rubber.

> Listen to the cries of Leopold's ghost,
> Burning in hell for his hand-maimed host;
> Hark as the demons cackle and yell,
> Cutting his hands off down in hell.

No one was better qualified to deal with the Belgian myth of 1914 than Morel, a friend of Britain's previous consul in the Congo, Sir Roger Casement. Both men had taken up the cause of the subjugated Congolese. As for the outbreak of war H. N. Brailsford, an MP who joined the UDC, told the House of Commons on 3 August 1914 that, by comparison with Belgium, 'When we go to war with Germany, we go to war against a people who, after all, hold largely the ideals that we hold.'[19]

With Morel as its secretary, the UDC attracted support from the Independent Labour Party, trades unions and well-known individuals, including Bertrand Russell and Bernard Shaw. Among MPs was Arthur Ponsonby, whose father had been a courtier and confidant of Queen Victoria. Arthur Ponsonby shared the view of John Bright at the time of the Crimean campaign: 'Wars are supported by a class of arguments which, after the war is over, people find were arguments they should never have listened to.'[20]

An anti-war meeting of the UDC in November 1915 was secretly monitored for the War Office by Major R. M. Mackay, Assistant Provost Marshal. It was broken up by soldiers, who had entered with forged tickets. Mackay's report was the subject of debate in the House of Commons on 7 December. It was alleged that trouble was caused by one of the leaders of the Independent Labour Party, Ramsay MacDonald, sending a message to have the soldiers ejected. This was not true. Mackay also reported that someone 'whose name I could not ascertain' caused disorder by provocative language. The stewardesses 'not only appeared to be Teutonic but could be classified as such from their accents'. Ponsonby protested there was no Teuton nor a Teutonic accent anywhere in the building. The government spokesman later acknowledged his errors in his report to the Commons. The attribution to Ramsay MacDonald of words he had never used and of Teutonic accents to the stewardesses were 'read hurriedly from a report made to him'.

In 1917, Assistant Provost Marshal Mackay was charged with wrongful arrest and in 1918 was dismissed the service for misemployment of military personnel and misuse of public funds. It was then revealed that he had been deaf for many years and by 1915 would have had great difficulty in hearing what was said at the UDC meeting, in Teutonic accents or not.[21]

Breaking up meetings was memorably described by Bertrand Russell, following an attempt to hold one in support of the Kerensky revolution in Russia in 1916. Held at the Brotherhood Church in Southgate, it was attacked by 'colonial' troops and 'drunken viragos' brandishing boards with nails projecting from them. The police did nothing on being told that Russell was a famous philosopher. Only when they were assured that he was the brother of an earl did they hurry forward to rescue him.[22]

Morel was not prosecuted for his views published in such books as *Truth and the War* (1916), if only for fear of publicizing his account of 'The Betrayal of the Nation, 1906–11' and 'The Betrayal of the Nation, 1912–14', in which he described how Grey had committed the country to war with Germany before a German foot touched Belgian soil. Moreover, it carried a foreword by a leading parliamentarian, Philip Snowden, who was to be Chancellor of the Exchequer in the post-war Labour government. Morel's downfall was more complex. He was to go to prison for sending a book to Switzerland which he could have sent to France, Italy or Russia without difficulty.

Romain Rolland, author of such novels as *Jean-Christophe*, as well as poetry and biography, had won the 1915 Nobel Prize for Literature. From Switzerland, he asked intellectuals in every country to work for an end to the war. He was an admirer of Morel's work. On hearing this, though assuming that Rolland was living in his native France, Morel asked a friend, Miss Sidgwick, who was going to France to take an autographed copy of *Africa and the Peace of Europe*, 'the least controversial book, I think, I have ever written', and of a new pamphlet, *Tsardom's Part in the War*. It had not occurred to him that he was doing anything illegal. What he did not know was that there had been an addition to DORA. Though it was possible to send such material to an allied country, it was an offence to send it to a neutral. Neutral countries were a means of communicating information to the enemy or, at least, damaging Britain's reputation in neutral eyes. By the time he realized that Rolland was living in Switzerland it was too late.

There followed what he described in a pamphlet as *The Persecution of E. D. Morel: The Story of his Trial and Imprisonment.* 'I was sent to prison for six months as a common felon in the company of housebreakers, receivers of stolen goods, forgers, and so on. The occupant of the cell on my right was a thief; on my left a man who had raped a child of tender years.' Morel came out of prison to launch an attack on Lloyd George, the Prime Minister whom he denounced as having spurned peace with Germany in 1917.[23]

In 1917 a Committee for a Negotiated Peace had been set up, led by the Conservative statesman Lord Lansdowne. It was subsequently argued that a negotiated peace had been offered by Germany but rejected by the Allies. President Wilson then put forward his 'Fourteen Points' upon which peace might be agreed. Lloyd George, in his 'Message to the Music Halls', accused the Germans of responding to Wilson with a massive military offensive. Casting the Prime Minister as a liar, Morel detailed two months of German responses to the proposal before that offensive began. Wilson's proposals were discussed by the German Chancellor and the Austro-Hungarian Minister for Foreign Affairs in public speeches: 'Most of them were accepted . . . none of them were rejected.' Lloyd George, however, had no intention of making peace; his was 'a political device to tide over a temporary difficulty'.[24]

Even when the war was over, Morel clung to his adversaries like a terrier with its teeth in the leg of a burglar. In August 1920, he revealed what the press and the government preferred to keep silent. *The Horror on the Rhine* is his account of Allied depravity in the occupied Rhineland. Not only were brothels set up in German towns for the French occupation forces, local people had their houses confiscated for the purpose and municipalities were obliged to pay both for the brothels and for 'the weekly examination of the prostitutes'. In Landau the community charge was 10,835 marks, in Wiesbaden 41,000 marks with a further sum for a house requisitioned as a brothel for African troops. Morel quotes Prince Max von Baden: 'The wrong done to the black troops is not less than the wrong done to the German people.' At Mainz the charge rose to 70,000 marks and at Saarbrucken winter coal for the population had been purloined to heat the brothels. There were also eighty documented cases of rape. 'Such is the hell created west of the Rhine by French militarism.' Also created, though Morel would not live to see its consequences, was a

German hatred and resentment whose harvest would be gathered not far in the future.[25]

Another member of the UDC, Bertrand Russell, had also been in trouble. In 1916, as conscription was introduced, he had written a leaflet on behalf of the No Conscription Fellowship. It cited the case of a school-teacher sentenced by court martial to two years' hard labour for refusing to fight, despite the 'conscience clause' in the legislation. Thirty-seven conscientious objectors were sentenced to be shot, though the sentences were commuted after protests to the Prime Minister.

Russell heard that some of those distributing his leaflet had been sent to prison. He wrote to *The Times* on 17 May acknowledging authorship. He was tried at the Mansion House court and fined £100. He refused to pay. Bailiffs took sufficient of his possessions at Cambridge to cover the sum. On 11 July, he was deprived of his Fellowship at Trinity and the government refused him a passport to teach at Harvard. Yet Russell, writing an explanatory letter to Professor James H. Wood at Harvard on 30 July, spoke of a new spirit abroad. He also wrote an open letter to President Woodrow Wilson, appealing to him to intervene on the side of peace. Though it was illegal to send such a letter to a neutral country by post, there was nothing to stop an American friend taking it back with her. It appeared in almost every American newspaper.

Following the entry of the United States into the war, Russell wrote a further article in the *Tribunal*, issued by the No Conscription Fellowship. He forecast that American troops would be used for strike-breaking in Britain, as they had been at home. For this, he went to prison for six months in May 1918. When he came out it was already evident, as he said, that the war was ending.

9

As the German offensive in the early months of 1918 threatened last-minute defeat rather than negotiation, the public now heard from those in the opposite camp to the pacifists. It was possible, in that camp, to believe that the war was not being fought hard enough. It was particularly easy to believe this if one also believed that the country had been secretly penetrated by German agents carrying a list of 47,000 leading citizens of Britain who were sexual perverts. The indulgence of their perversions evidently left them neither the time nor the energy to fight a world war.

As the German army captured Soissons and Rheims in the spring of 1918, its advance units only forty miles from Paris, the Central Criminal

Court echoed to an unusual vocabulary. Instead of recriminations about shell shortages or resignations from the General Staff or the formation of strategic reserves, newspaper readers now became acquainted with such terms as 'clitoris' and 'orgasm', 'fetishism' and the 'Count de Sade'. The ringmaster of this rhetoric was of course a German: Professor Richard von Krafft-Ebing.

The defendant, Noel Pemberton Billing, Independent member of Parliament for East Hertfordshire, was a patriot. He was distressed by the retreat of the Allies in the face of the current German onslaught and he was able to put his finger on the cause. As editor and proprietor of the *Imperialist*, his views were seldom in doubt. On 26 January 1918, he informed his readers that a 'Black Book' existed in 'the *cabinet noir* of a certain German prince'. It contained the names of 47,000 English men and women and had been compiled by 'German Agents who have infested this country for the past twenty years'. While infesting it, they had also made time to seduce those who crossed their paths, 'spreading debauchery of such a lasciviousness as only German minds could conceive and only German bodies execute'.

In case his readers might still be in doubt, Pemberton Billing's newspaper specified 'the propagation of evils which all decent men thought had perished in Sodom and Lesbia'. The names gathered by these conscientious German agents included 'Privy Councillors, youths of the chorus, wives of Cabinet Ministers, dancing girls, even Cabinet Ministers themselves, while diplomats, poets, bankers, editors, newspaper proprietors, and members of His Majesty's household follow each other with no order of precedence'. With the sales of his next issue in mind, Pemberton Billing added, 'The matter must not rest.'

On 9 February, the *Imperialist* acquired a more exciting name: the *Vigilante*. The previous year, Pemberton Billing had founded 'The Vigilante Society' to promote purity in public life, with the novelist Marie Corelli as one of its patrons. On the day following the debut of the *Vigilante*, the *Sunday Times* advertised two performances at a London theatre club of Oscar Wilde's *Salome*. Though still banned by the Lord Chamberlain, *Salome* did not require a licence for a private performance. This gave Pemberton Billing the opening he needed.

On 16 February, his paper carried a startling headline, 'The Cult of the Clitoris', taking up where the *Imperialist* had left off. The title had been recommended by a local doctor as an oblique reference to lesbianism. Reminding readers that a club was to produce Wilde's play, Pemberton Billing added, 'If Scotland Yard were to seize a list of these members I have no doubt they would secure the names of several thousand of the first 47,000.'

Wilde's play required the heroine to address John the Baptist in languorous and honeyed tones, to strip herself in the dance of the seven veils in order to accomplish his murder and then to possess his severed head as her amorous plaything. Maud Allan, who was to play Salome, was not denounced as being one of the 47,000 names in the Black Book. However, she had pandered to them, which was possibly worse.

Maud Allan and J. T. Grein, who was putting on the two performances, sought legal advice. By leave of a judge in chambers, the injured parties were able to prosecute Pemberton Billing for both criminal libel and obscene libel. It was entirely possible that criminal libel might be shown, though it must be so gross as to threaten a breach of the peace.

The trial at the Central Criminal Court opened on 29 May 1918. Pemberton Billing could only be tried on one indictment at a time, so the alleged criminal libel on Maud Allan was proceeded with. He conducted his own case and tried unsuccessfully to make Mr Justice Darling stand down because, in Parliament and in the press, Pemberton Billing had attacked his lordship's administration of justice. Throughout the case, he treated the judge with a mixture of impatience and contempt.

Pemberton Billing argued that Wilde's play was 'an evil and mischievous travesty of a biblical story'. The author endowed Salome with a sadistic, even cannibalistic, sexual passion for John the Baptist. There had already been a discussion of the Marquis de Sade at the magistrates' hearing. Certainly Salome's address to the severed and bleeding head was hardly the girl-meets-boy attraction which Maud Allan made it sound in the witness box when she suggested the play was no worse than the current West End hit *A Little Bit of Fluff*. 'Ah! thou wouldst not suffer me to kiss thy mouth, Jokanaan. Well! I will kiss it now. I will bite it with my teeth as one bites a ripe fruit.'[26]

As one of his witnesses, Pemberton Billing produced Mrs Eileen Villiers-Stuart, who described being taken by two army officers to the Hut Hotel in Surrey and shown the Black Book. Both men had since been killed in Palestine. Pemberton Billing asked quickly whether Mr Justice Darling's name was in the Black Book. 'It is,' said Mrs Villiers-Stuart before anyone could stop her. The judge demanded whether the book could be produced. Mrs Villiers-Stuart said it could but, since it was in Germany, that would have to wait until after the war. Pemberton Billing asked hastily, 'Is Mrs Asquith's name in the book?' 'It is in the book.' 'Is Mr Asquith's name in the book?' 'It is.' 'Is Lord Haldane's name in the book?'

'It is.' This was what the press gallery had been waiting for. 'Leave the box!' said Mr Justice Darling. 'You dare not hear me!' she replied.

Pemberton Billing produced a copy of a letter from Mrs Villiers-Stuart, confirming the existence of the Black Book at an earlier date. As he only had a copy of the letter, it could not be evidence. However, she was able to give evidence of brothels in London 'practising criminal and unnatural vices'. She was followed in the witness box by Captain Harold Spencer, formerly of Admiralty Intelligence and now on the staff of the *Vigilante*. He claimed to have seen the Black Book while in Serbia. As he gave evidence, he was applauded by soldiers in the public gallery. The judge threatened to have the gallery cleared but by now Pemberton Billing was turning the trial into both a political demonstration and a public entertainment. When Spencer, under cross-examination, was asked whether the article had referred to the production of sensations in the clitoris 'by improper methods', he agreed. He then added that an exaggerated clitoris 'might even drive a woman to an elephant'. This time the howls of laughter from the public gallery were on such a scale that Mr Justice Darling let them pass.[27]

Dr Serrell Cooke gave expert evidence on sadism, Krafft-Ebing, Sacher Masoch, and clothes fetishism. 'Cannot we leave out the fetishism?' asked Mr Justice Darling wearily. In case the interest of the spectators was wandering, however, Ellis Hume-Williams for the prosecution rallied them when he examined Dr Serrell Cooke on the manias of the 'Count de Sade'.[28]

The fourth day of the hearing produced a star performer, Lord Alfred Douglas, reformed victim of Oscar Wilde's passion, who now abominated homosexuality and everything to do with it. Wilde had written *Salome* in French and Lord Alfred had translated it into English. He also revealed that Wilde's inspiration while writing it had been Krafft-Ebing's *Psychopathia Sexualis*. Wilde had intended Salome to bite through the lips of the severed head and wanted her to work herself up into 'a sort of orgasm'. The reformed Lord Alfred thought the play 'a horrible thing'. In cross-examination he was taunted with such questions as 'When did you cease to approve of sodomy?' which he rejected as unfair, like 'When did you leave off beating your wife?'[29]

Pemberton Billing's other witness was Father Bernard Vaughan SJ of Farm Street, who denounced the play as an abomination, as 'constructive treason' against God. He described any woman who played the part of Salome as 'a perverted creature'. Such sentiments were again applauded by the spectators. On occasion the prosecuting counsel and even the judge were discreetly hissed. Pemberton Billing appeared to the soldiers and the public as the only true patriot on either side.

Before the jury retired, Mr Justice Darling informed them that the passage in the *Vigilante* asserting that a membership list of the theatre club would contain several thousand of the 47,000 was not libellous in respect of Maud Allan; they could forget the Black Book. This left a very large gap in the prosecution case and it was no surprise when the jurors returned in half an hour to acquit the defendant. The other two indictments were not proceeded with.

Crowds round the Old Bailey roared their cheers for Pemberton Billing and for all those who despised the men and women responsible for bringing the nation to its knees by moral weakness. Both men and women were involved in the German plot, as Lord Alfred had indicated in several lines on the Asquiths from 'All's Well With England'. 'Margot' and 'Squiffy', as he called them, were Downing Street friends of Wilde's surviving companion, Robert Ross. While the earth of Flanders is red with English blood and the nation's children are sacrificed to Moloch as the god of war, Lord Alfred depicts the Asquiths sitting comfortably at home. Margot is decorated with 'Lesbian fillets', while with front of brass 'Old Squiffy' hands the purse to Robert Ross.

10

In wartime, the reasons for official secrecy had been sometimes good, sometimes dishonourable and sometimes ludicrous. Two days after the end of hostilities, the Admiralty announced the loss of HMS *Audacious*. The ship had sunk four years earlier 'after striking a mine off the North Irish coast on the 27th October 1914'. It had long been common knowledge that *Audacious* had sunk; indeed, hundreds of passengers on a passing liner, *Olympic*, had watched it happen. A letter signed 'Audax' had appeared in *The Times* as early as 4 December 1914, demanding an announcement. Yet so many of the Royal Navy's ships had developed serious defects that Admiral Lord Jellicoe felt the least said about this one, the better.[30]

Wartime censorship in many areas survived the coming of peace, lingering for twenty years until it was reprieved by the next world conflict in 1939. Its urgency and importance were frequently replaced by farce. The Official Secrets Act reached its nadir in 1935, when Sotheby's proposed to auction letters written by Wellington and Nelson. The most recent dated from 1815. On 3 July, the Foreign Office warned the auctioneers and the purchasers that anyone buying papers written by serving officers would be liable to prosecution. The auctioneers withdrew the letters and they passed to the government.

Among similar instances, Sir Compton Mackenzie was fined £100 at the Central Criminal Court on 12 July 1933 for his book *Greek Memories*. He had mentioned in it the names of several Secret Service officers who had served with him in the war. Most of the information was already available in *The Allied Secret Service in Greece* (1931) by the Director of Intelligence, Sir Basil Thomson, whom it seemed the authorities had not troubled. Of Mackenzie's 'names', one was dead, another had never been in the Secret Service and the third had already published the information without interference in his *Who's Who* entry.

Official Secrets legislation extended to every area of life, not least miscarriages of justice and the legal process. Major F. W. Blake, retired Governor of Pentonville Prison, was fined £250 in December 1926 for writing articles for the *Evening News* about a death-cell confession by Frederick Bywaters in 1923. The trial of Frederick Bywaters and Edith Thompson for murder in 1922 had caused much controversy. The stabbing of Percy Thompson by Bywaters, the lover of his wife Edith Thompson, was performed in front of witnesses. Yet the letters of Edith Thompson, in which she spoke to her lover of poison and ground glass, seemed on the evidence a mere attempt to make him believe she was trying to get rid of her husband. At the autopsy, for example, there were no traces of internal injuries which the passage of ground glass would have left. Bywaters swore to her innocence in court. She was an extremely foolish woman but not a killer and her last courtroom cry, 'I am not guilty! Oh, God, I am not guilty!' had a terrible probability. However, the revelation of a final attempt by Bywaters to save her from the gallows a few moments before his own execution was less than welcome to a Home Secretary who had hoped to hear no more of the case.[31]

Similarly, at Bow Street on 26 March 1943, a leading campaigner against capital punishment, Mrs Van der Elst, was to be fined for contravening the Official Secrets Act. A prisoner at Wandsworth had been told to burn hospital case sheets relating to men hanged for murder. He kept them and sold them to Mrs Van der Elst for £12. She made copies for the Home Secretary. 'They are reports by the doctor of the prison on the condition of men who had been condemned to be hanged and I must say that they are most ghastly reading. They also tell one that when men are hanged they still live over fifteen minutes. I feel these facts have always been suppressed from the Home Secretary.' She refused to tell the court how she obtained the information. 'If you give me ten years, I won't tell you. I have a right to photograph them when they are evidence of the very thing I want.'

Another 'temporary' wartime measure, the Defence of the Realm Act 1914, also proved embarrassingly resilient. Herbert Metcalfe, a London magistrate, was dismayed to find himself applying its zanier provisions in 1931. A shopkeeper was charged with selling a packet of biscuits. There was no reason to make this criminal, except that DORA's wartime provisions still required the shop to be 'closed' for biscuits when it might be open for the sale of cooked meat. While a quarter of a pound of cooked meat could be sold, a quarter of a pound of raw meat would also be illegal.

What had this to do with the defence of the realm in 1931? Metcalfe's courtroom response deserves quotation. 'What lunatics there are in the world! The person or persons responsible for DORA ought to be taken out and publicly hanged. It is these fatuous fools who seized upon the war to put across the people restrictions of all kinds.' He had, as the obituary writers conceded, 'a reputation for straight and plain speaking'. History certainly suggests that governments who restrict freedom, with assurances that this power is temporary but necessary in a present emergency, ought never to be believed.[32]

Ironically the most famous post-war case of political censorship related to the annual Mutiny Act and showed how easily a government may destroy itself by the very instrument it attempts to employ. The first Labour administration, under Ramsay MacDonald, walked a parliamentary tightrope in 1924. With 191 seats, only the support of 178 Liberals enabled it to hold off 258 Conservatives. It was also beset by fears of a Bolshevik threat from the new Soviet Union and suggestions that some of its supporters were part of that threat.

On 25 July, during 'Anti-War Week', a Communist newspaper, *Workers' Weekly*, addressed an open letter to British troops. It invited them, if ordered to act against strikers, to 'use your arms on the side of your own class'. In a literal sense, this was an incitement to mutiny. Some of MacDonald's colleagues thought so. The Attorney-General, Sir Patrick Hastings, consulted the Director of Public Prosecutions. John Ross Campbell of *Workers' Weekly* was arrested for offences under the Mutiny Act.

Opinion and events then turned against the government. There was hostility in the Labour party and the trade union movement. John Ross Campbell proved to be no work-shy agitator but a hero of the war. Moreover, he had only been acting editor of the paper when the article was published. Worse still, MacDonald knew almost nothing of the case until told by a junior minister that Campbell had been arrested. Even then, he only learnt of the decision to prosecute from reading a newspaper. Too late, he called the prosecution 'ill-advised from the beginning'.

However ill-judged the case and even if conviction seemed unlikely, MacDonald refused to give way under political pressure. Indeed, when Hastings told him that 'the whole matter could be dropped', the Prime Minister replied that once it had been started the government must stick to its guns. Then it was confirmed that Campbell was merely acting editor. On 6 August, MacDonald gave way after all.

The unhappy government faced Parliament on 30 September. MacDonald first insisted that it was not for politicians to interfere with the judicial process and complained that he had not been consulted 'regarding either the institution or the subsequent withdrawal' of the proceedings. This was, wrote the Cabinet Secretary, Maurice Hankey, 'a bloody lie'. On 2 October, Asquith as leader of the Liberals moved for a select committee to inquire into the Campbell affair. It could hardly avoid turning up the 'bloody lie'. Worse still, MacDonald was warned by his law officers that his denial of being involved was inaccurate. On 8 October, he was obliged to apologize for misleading the House of Commons.[33]

He might still have avoided defeat, had not the 258 Conservatives, contrary to expectations, supported the Liberal motion for an inquiry into the attempted suppression of *Workers' Weekly*. The Conservatives cared nothing for Campbell or his paper but the government's fumbling with the apparatus of political censorship had delivered it into the hands of its opponents. Late on the evening of his apology, MacDonald's government was crushed by 359 votes to 198 and Labour's first experiment in power ended after nine months. Those who sniped at the Prime Minister as 'The Loon from Lossiemouth' were jubilant. A few weeks later, the electorate returned Baldwin's Conservatives to power with a majority of 413 to 191. The itch to suppress dissent had far better have been ignored.

5

Between Two Wars

I

IN MATTERS OF taste and propriety, no less than in the extremes of politics, post-war society of the 1920s was divided into two tribes. The hopes and intentions that sustained their opposing beliefs were not in doubt. Much was said, on one side, of a new world, where the waste and slaughter of the recent past was never to be repeated. This contended against a contrary hope, born of nostalgia and images of a pre-war security. Its believers spoke of 'getting back to normal'. Most famously, at Boston in June 1920, the future President of the United States, Warren Gamaliel Harding, coined a term for it, 'normalcy'. The alternatives were never more clearly put: the present age needed 'not heroics but healing; not nostrums but normalcy; not revolution but restoration.'

If 'normalcy' had ended in Britain with the coming of the war, some of its last acts had been directed against the moral peril detected in such fiction as the novels of H. G. Wells and D. H. Lawrence. Was that the point from which the post-war debate should continue or had the war changed the world to such an extent that the attacks on Wells and Lawrence belonged to another order of existence?

In wartime, the values of sexual morality are apt to be put into storage, in reality and in imagination. From the reminiscences of Sir Maurice Bowra, as a young officer serving in the First World War, it seemed that the French-published English pornography which had so exercised Inspector Drew and his parliamentary committee in 1908 had become the stuff to give the troops on the Western Front. Bowra recalled that when the German bombardments began, his commanding officer would summon the regiment round him. Like a father with his children, he would then read in a stentorian voice, audible above the detonations, from Charles Carrington's edition of *The New Lady's Tickler: or, The Adventures of Lady Lovesport and the Audacious Harry* and other Victorian frolics of the kind.[1]

It remained to be seen whether the easy-going literary morality of the trenches was a wartime aberration or an influence on the future. Similarly, Pemberton Billing's public revelations of Maud Allan and the 'Cult of the Clitoris' had the justification of rooting out perverts and traitors who were leading the nation to military defeat. In the Edwardian world, such a public display by Krafft-Ebing's troupe of sexual acrobats would have been unthinkable. Was this a necessary moral sacrifice in time of war or the shape of things to come?

The only wartime prosecution of a novel for obscenity had been that of *The Rainbow* in 1915 and it was merely an application by the police for a destruction order. *The Times'* reviewer warned his readers on 1 October that 'Mr Lawrence is a realist to the point of brutality.' 'Realist' had been useful shorthand since the conviction of Vizetelly. *The Rainbow* was then reviewed by Robert Lynd, in the *Daily News* on 5 October. It was 'a prolix account of three generations of sexual crises in the Brangwen family' of Marsh Farm. 'If the author of the book is like any kind of surgeon, it is a veterinary surgeon.' Lynd made it sound like a cross between Zola and Galsworthy, though containing the pessimism of Strindberg and the sensuality of Pierre Louÿs. Its characteristic was 'animalism', a complaint against Zola repeated in the present case.

On 14 November, the Bow Street magistrate granted the police a destruction order. The prosecution called the book 'a mass of obscenity' and could not understand how a firm like Methuen had published it. The magistrate fined them ten guineas, adding that they had been 'soiled by the publication of this work'. The prosecution quoted James Douglas in the *Star* on 22 October, insisting that 'a thing like *The Rainbow* has no right to exist in the wind of war.' An expurgated edition followed in 1926. The complete text appeared in America and in a 1949 Penguin paperback.

Lawrence's work was in a tradition leading back to Galsworthy and Zola, even to George Eliot and the mid-Victorians. By the 1920s, influences of a different kind were at work. From France, the name that rang loudest was no longer that of Zola or Maupassant, but Marcel Proust and *Remembrance of Things Past*. The seven parts appeared in English at intervals. It was no disparagement to say of the fine translation by C. K. Scott Moncrieff that Proust wrote a style of French which seemed almost English in structure and design. But curiously the dogs of censorship did not bark or even growl at the advent of Proust. In *Swann's Way*, published in England in 1922, the first subtle analysis of sexual deviation appears in the lesbian and sado-masochistic relationship of the daughter of the composer Vinteuil and her visitor. This was followed by the grosser conduct of the

Baron de Charlus and the passionate jealousy characterizing the narrator's love for the sexually ambivalent Albertine.

It would be unjust to compare the more modest talents of Radclyffe Hall with those of a work which may claim to be the most innovative novel of its century. That the censor who overlooked the skilfully suggested lesbian depravities which form an important theme of Proust's story, yet found what James Douglas called 'a phial of prussic acid' in the sincerity and the homely setting of *The Well of Loneliness* (1928) was an oddity.

While Proust escaped, another novel embodying modernism of a different kind was less fortunate. James Joyce had already published *Dubliners* (1914) and *Portrait of the Artist as a Young Man* (1916). Twenty-two publishers read the manuscript of *Dubliners* before it was accepted. When it was published, some 'very kind person' bought the entire edition and had it burnt in Dublin. It had appeared through the enthusiasm of Harriet Shaw Weaver of the Egoist Press.

For much of the war, Joyce lived in Zurich and worked at the novel by which he remains best known, *Ulysses*. It was completed in Paris in 1921. Its subject, the minutely detailed actions and uncensored thoughts of two middle-class Dubliners, Stephen Dedalus and Leopold Bloom, on a single day in 1903, set it apart from any other fiction. Incomplete phrases or ideas, ellipses of words and absence of punctuation gave it the reputation of being difficult. The famous monologue of Molly Bloom, which occupies forty-four pages of the book, is written in eight sentences and confirmed its reputation for obscenity. The first of these sentences, some 2,500 words, is longer than many complete short stories. A realistic frankness of language throughout the novel and such episodes as this sexual self-revelation of Molly Bloom put *Ulysses* into the contemporary classification of obscene publications.

In England, Harriet Shaw Weaver began serialization in her literary review, the *Egoist*. Five episodes were published in 1919 before the printers declined to go any further. T. S. Eliot, a friend of Joyce and an admirer of *Ulysses*, later revealed that the novel could not be printed in book form because printers in England feared the legal consequences. At the Hogarth Press, Leonard and Virginia Woolf regarded the text as 'reeling with obscenity' but thought in any case it would take two years to set the type for more than a thousand pages of Joyce's prose.

The novel was saved by Sylvia Beach of Shakespeare and Company, a Left Bank bookshop in Paris. In 1920, she asked Joyce if she might have the 'honour' of publishing it. A numbered edition of 1,000 copies was issued in February 1922. Among the few reviews in Britain, James Douglas, who had denounced *The Rainbow*, spoke for the *Sunday Express*. *Ulysses* was 'the most obscene book in ancient or modern literature'. Within a paragraph, Douglas invoked sewers, leprosy, blasphemy, orgies, satanism and the Black Mass. Joyce was not without admirers. Middleton Murry, Arnold Bennett and J. B. Priestley saluted his genius. Sisley Huddleston in the *Observer* on 5 March, commenting on Molly Bloom's monologue, thought it 'the vilest according to ordinary standards in all literature. And yet its very obscenity is somehow beautiful and wrings the soul to pity. Is that not high art?'

In the moral climate of 1922 there could be little doubt which view would prevail. T. S. Eliot was scandalized when all but one copy of a third edition of 500 copies, printed in France for the Egoist Press in London, was seized by customs officers at Folkestone and burnt. The sole survivor was sent by post. No inventory was kept and it was rumoured that many of the missing copies had been purloined as curiosities by officers entrusted with the burning. A second edition of 2,000 copies had been printed and 500 of those were burnt by the New York Post Office administration on arrival there. Of 3,500 copies printed in the first year of the novel's life, 1,500 had gone to the flames.

In 1920, a prosecution was brought against the *Little Review*, which began to serialize the novel in New York. At the end of the year, with the publication of the thirteenth episode, it was convicted under obscenity laws and fined $100. Because the law does not protect that which is illegal, it seemed Joyce had lost United States copyright in his novel. Samuel Roth of the magazines *Two Worlds Monthly* and *Two Worlds Quarterly* produced an expurgated edition. An international protest, signed by more than 150 famous names, urged the people of America to oppose Mr Roth and his 'enterprise'. The signatories included Benedetto Croce, Robert Bridges, T. S. Eliot, Havelock Ellis, E. M. Forster, John Galsworthy, André Gide, Ernest Hemingway, D. H. Lawrence, Wyndham Lewis, Thomas Mann, John Masefield, Somerset Maugham, André Maurois, Middleton Murry, Sean O'Casey, Virgil Thomson, Paul Valéry, Hugh Walpole, H. G. Wells, Rebecca West, Thornton Wilder, Virginia Woolf and W. B. Yeats.

Not all of these were admirers of *Ulysses* but they presented a daunting array against the philistinism of a censorship prepared to cast such a book to the sharks of commercial publishing. There had been no protest on this scale before. Vizetelly fought a lonely battle on behalf of Zola and Maupassant. Methuen had not even told Lawrence that *The Rainbow* was to be taken to court. Support for *Ulysses* began to have its effect. Samuel Roth found himself the defendant in the New York Supreme Court on 27 December 1928, where an injunction was issued restraining him from using the name of James Joyce in any of his publications. It was a partial success.

The battle for *Ulysses* was to be won in the United States. The British government had gone on the offensive against indecency in literature under a new Home Secretary. Sir William Joynson-Hicks, a Conservative traditionalist known as 'Jix', saw pornography and night clubs as twin evils of the post-war world. He was the inspiration behind the customs officer searching the hero's books in Evelyn Waugh's *Vile Bodies* (1930), praising a Home Secretary who believes that 'If we can't stamp out literature in the country, we can at least stop its being brought in from outside.'[2]

Beyond the Atlantic, there was a more liberal interpretation of obscenity. In 1917 there been an acquittal of a New York bookseller who sold Théophile Gautier's *Mademoiselle de Maupin*. In 1929, Radclyffe Hall's novel of lesbianism, *The Well of Loneliness*, was acquitted. While in 1924 it was held that there was a triable case against Arthur Schnitzler's *Casanova's Homecoming*, six years later the new firm of Simon & Schuster issued it and were acquitted. In 1933 Random House planned to publish *Ulysses*. They began by ordering a copy from Paris, so that it might be confiscated and open the way to a test case. US Customs slipped up and the book arrived unmolested. Random House returned it to the authorities and the firm, though not any individual, was indicted under the Tariff Law of 1930.

The trial which followed was one of the most dramatic and absorbing of American test cases, comparable in its way to the famous 1925 Scopes 'Monkey Trial' over the teaching of Darwinian evolution in Tennessee. Counsel for the defence of *Ulysses* was Morris L. Ernst, a civil rights and anti-censorship advocate. He was a lucid and compelling courtroom speaker, a gentle but devastating cross-examiner. His gifts had made him one of Roosevelt's 'bright young men' in 1932, addressing public meetings on the New Deal, the president's Banking Act, and the crisis which had required the closure of the banks.

Before Judge John M. Woolsey, Ernst attacked head-on the two supports of the prosecution case: the use of the word 'fuck' or its companions and the sexual frankness of Molly Bloom's monologue. To have veiled the most infamous word in such cases would have been to concede the prosecution argument. Ernst used it bluntly. 'Judge, as to the word "fuck", one etymological dictionary gives its derivation as from *facere* – to make – the farmer fucked the seed into the soil. This, your honor, has more integrity than a euphemism used every day in every modern novel to describe precisely the same event.' That euphemism, he explained, was 'They slept together.'

Molly Bloom's monologue was more difficult. Ernst chose to base his argument on Joyce as an innovator. The monologue was explicable only in terms of 'the double stream of consciousness' used to open the minds of the characters to the reader. Judges dislike what they do not understand. 'Stream of consciousness' was soon a cliché of academic criticism but in 1933 it might not be clear to the judge without assistance. The exchange between Ernst and Woolsey was one of the most illuminating in courtroom proceedings or, indeed, literary debate. Woolsey asked if Ernst had 'really read this entire book'. Ernst said he had, the previous summer in preparation for the case. 'And while lecturing in the Unitarian Church in Nantucket on the bank holiday . . .' Woolsey interrupted him. 'What has that to do with my question – have you read it?' Ernst replied:

> Will your honor let me explain how I was able to plough through it? While talking in that Church I recalled after my lecture was finished that while I was thinking only about the banks and the banking laws, I was in fact at that same time, musing about the clock at the back of the Church, the old woman in the front row, the tall shutters at the sides. Just as now, Judge, I have thought I was involved only in the defense of the book, this one cause – I must admit at the same time I was thinking of the gold ring round your tie, the picture of George Washington behind your bench and the fact that your black judicial robe is slipping off your shoulder. This double stream of the mind is the contribution of *Ulysses*.

He did not know it at that moment but he had won his case. The literary technique which was to spawn so many volumes and theses had been defined by Ernst in a single minute. Woolsey rapped the bench before him.

> Now for the first time I understand the significance of this book. I have listened to you as intently as I know how. I am disturbed by the dream scenes at the end of the book, and still I must confess, that while listening to you I have been thinking at the same time about the Hepplewhite furniture behind you.

Woolsey was a collector of furniture from the Colonial period. His judgment in the District Court, New York, in *United States v. One Book Called 'Ulysses'* elegantly balances literary appreciation and jurisprudence. If the novel is pornographic, 'that is the end of the inquiry and forfeiture must follow. But in "Ulysses", in spite of its unusual frankness, I do not detect anywhere the leer of the sensualist. I hold, therefore, that it is not pornographic.'

As to the problem of 'dirty' words, they are 'known to almost all men, and I venture, to many women, and are such words as would be naturally and habitually used, I believe, by the types of folk whose life, physical and mental, Joyce is seeking to describe'. As for the 'stream of consciousness with its ever-shifting kaleidoscopic impressions', Joyce had displayed its movements with 'astonishing success'. He had been 'loyal to his technique' with the result that '"Ulysses" is a sincere and honest book . . .' Finally, 'In respect of the recurrent emergence of the theme of sex in the minds of his characters, it must always be remembered that his locale was Celtic and his season spring . . . "Ulysses" may, therefore, be admitted into the United States.'[3]

The word 'milestone' was apt to be overused in such cases. Yet the attitudes and perceptions of Judge Woolsey belonged to a new age, by comparison with those who had judged not merely Henry Vizetelly in 1888 or *The Rainbow* in 1915 but almost every censorship case in England and many in the United States until the 1960s. For the time being, those in England who were concerned to ban *The Well of Loneliness* or *The Satyricon* of Petronius, minor French classics by Pierre Louÿs and J-K. Huysmans or a work of general medical interest like Edward Charles' *The Sexual Impulse*, had been caught on the wrong foot by the Woolsey judgment. Customs officers might ferret diligently for copies of *Ulysses* from Paris or, indeed, New York. Yet for how much longer would the walls stand against the flood?

The answer came three years later. In 1936, John Lane of the Bodley Head proposed to imitate Bennett Cerf of Random House by having a copy of *Ulysses* posted from Paris and informing the Attorney-General of what he intended to do. The Attorney, Sir Donald Somervell, made no response. In October, the Bodley Head published the first London edition of *Ulysses*, consisting of 1,000 copies, of which 100 were signed by the author. If no action were taken, it would be only a matter of months before a very much larger edition followed.

On 4 November, Sir Donald Somervell summoned the Director of Public Prosecutions and gave him his instructions. Rather surprisingly, he laid down that the definition of obscenity in *Regina v. Hicklin* was 'inadequate'. Instead, 'the question of intention has to be taken into account.' For more than thirty years after this pronouncement, however, courts trying cases of obscenity were routinely told that the author's intention was irrelevant. The test was the liability of the material to deprave and corrupt.

The Attorney went on: 'No one today would, he thought, be found to hold that such books as those of Havelock Ellis on sexual matters were obscene, nor any medical books dealing with sexual abberations [*sic*].' Only the year before, Edward Charles' *The Sexual Impulse* had been condemned, to be followed two years later by Stekel on *Sadism and Masochism*. In the *Evening Standard* on 27 July 1939, W. R. Inge, the 'Gloomy Dean' of St Paul's, confessed that he had works in Latin and Greek on his shelves which might be seized by the police if they were in English. None the less he had burnt his copy of Havelock Ellis' *Studies in the Psychology of Sex*.[4]

In the case of *Ulysses*, the Attorney-General also noted that 'Standards in these matters were constantly changing' – an argument which was dismissed by both Lord Chief Justice Goddard and the Recorder of London in the 1950s. Finally, if challenged in the House of Commons over *Ulysses*, Sir Donald Somervell proposed to demonstrate 'its established place now in literature'. Yet that was the very defence which the Obscene Publications Act of 1857 denied.

Ulysses and John Lane were lucky. Sir Donald Somervell talked less like a libertarian than a man with more important things in mind. As Attorney-General at that moment he was the still centre of a political earthquake, capable of bringing down the government and the British monarchy. One week earlier, the divorce petition of Mrs Wallis Simpson had passed discreetly through a district court in Ipswich. Sir Donald Somervell was involved in ensuring that there was no injudicious visit to the town by Edward VIII to prevent the decree nisi being made absolute. It was plain to the government, though the nation knew nothing of the matter, that if the King insisted upon marrying Mrs Simpson his abdication must follow. As the government's chief legal adviser, the Attorney-General had more important business to attend to than *Ulysses*.

2

Compared with the international drama of *Ulysses*, censorship of other 'obscene publications' drew fewer headlines. In 1928, D. H. Lawrence published *Lady Chatterley's Lover* in Florence, through a Florentine bookseller, Orioli. A further edition was issued in 1928 by Pegasus Books in Paris. In this form it made its way privately to London or New York. English magazines or newspapers which noticed it, responded with more or less vitriolic abuse.

Because the novel was obscene by both British and American standards, it enjoyed no protection from the courts. In the United States, it was impossible to protect it from pirates who issued an expurgated text as the real thing but thereby avoided prosecution. As Lawrence said, their coyly suggestive asterisks made his work seem truly obscene. In London, his publisher Heinemann put out an expurgated edition to combat piracy. Not until 1960 was the fate of the unexpurgated *Lady Chatterley* to be decided.

In 1929, while Lawrence was still living abroad, his manuscript volume of poems, *Pansies*, and an introduction to his paintings were seized by the Post Office while on their way to his London publisher. They were forwarded to the Director of Public Prosecutions, who in turn sent them to the publisher with a recommendation that fourteen of the poems should not be published. These were removed from the book.

On 8 August, the owners of the Warren Gallery, Maddox Street, appeared at Marlborough Street Magistrates Court. 'As a result of a complaint being made', the police had raided the gallery on 5 July and 13 July. On the first occasion they seized illustrated books, including *Ecce Homo* by George Grosz, and Lawrence's paintings on the second. The case was adjourned *sine die*, on condition that the gallery did not in future exhibit any of the pictures or any watercolours by Lawrence, nor exhibit reproductions. Pictures already sold could be sent to the purchasers and the remainder returned to Lawrence.

The only prosecution in London to rival in its significance that of *Ulysses* in New York was to prove an exercise in irony. Marguerite Radclyffe Hall (1886–1943) was a successful novelist who had won the James Tait Black Memorial Prize in 1926 with *Adam's Breed*. Those who knew her knew also that she was a lesbian and that this was the subject of *The Well of Loneliness* (1928). The novel had not a remotely obscene word from start to finish. Indeed, it was far more open to accusations of bogus gentility. Its setting, among the minor post-war gentry of Gloucestershire with their rituals of hunting and killing, had an echo of Mary Webb's *Precious Bane* or *Gone to Earth*. Many of those who were to rally to the book's defence as to a battle-flag of sexual politics, might be simultaneously repelled by the country sports and the elitist lifestyle in which their martyr indulged. Moreover, though her father, Sir Philip Gordon, had wanted a son, this heroine was 'Daddy's little girl', if ever there was one. Unlike her admirers from humbler backgrounds, the decision to 'send her to Oxford' or not was the privilege of the family, rather than of the university.[5]

In many respects, the novel was a superior version of the fiction gracing such socially ambitious magazines as *Woman's Journal* between the wars. Its child's-eye observation of the artefacts and hidden corners of manor house life had something in common with Emily Brontë's loving detail in *Wuthering Heights* or, for that matter, the shrewder observations in Carson McCullers' classic *The Member of the Wedding*. Above all, whereas *Ulysses* appeared from beyond the reach of the English law, this novel was to be issued by a respected London publisher, Jonathan Cape of Bedford Square. The only trap for a publisher of *The Well of Loneliness* was that its heroine, called Stephen because her father so much hoped for a son, was a lesbian.

Certainly, this was no laughing matter. Lytton Strachey's unpublished *Ermyntrude and Esmeralda* and the romps of Victorian pornography belonged to another world. The earnestness of Radclyffe Hall's novel was as marked as its lesbianism. Stephen Gordon follows a meticulously described progress from a fox-hunting tomboy's crush on the maidservant Collins to a physical passion for Angela Crosby with her look of a medieval page. This runs parallel to her devotion to her father and her bewildered response to a proposal of marriage from a friend she had regarded as a brother. Even when the first lesbian affair ends, Angela remarks that it was never more than 'a few rather schoolgirlish kisses'.[6]

The rest of the novel offers less than it should. Stephen becomes a successful novelist but, on the basis of the evidence, the reader accepts this on trust, rather than feeling it to be true. A prosecutor trawling the book in hope, as Asquith had done with Zola, would have drawn in meagre returns. The lives of female ambulance crews in the war and the affair with Mary, who eventually decamps with Stephen's male friend, leads again to passionate avowals and kisses. The inexplicit conclusion is 'and that night they were not divided . . .' with a later reference to Mary lying in Stephen's arms. In this respect, the characters hardly exist from the waist down and the book ends with ringing piety: 'Acknowledge us, oh God, before the whole world. Give us also the right to our existence!'[7]

The novel seemed almost top-heavy with earnestness, honesty and decency. Eight years later Sir Donald Somervell, who as Attorney-General set *Ulysses* free, remarked to the DPP that 'No one today would be found to hold that such books as those of Havelock Ellis on sexual matters were obscene.' In one respect, *The Well of Loneliness* might almost be taken for an extended reminiscence from *Studies in the Psychology of Sex*. Ellis includes 'Homosexuality Among Tramps' by the pseudonymous 'Josiah Flint' with such episodes as the rape of 'a coloured boy' by the occupants of a freight car, far more shocking and brutal than anything in Radclyffe Hall. 'The School Friendships of Girls' is a compilation by Ellis of letters from his informants on this topic. In 'The Development of the Sexual Instinct' or 'Histories of Sexual Development' he had included autobiographies of 10,000 to 12,000 words. Indeed, 'The History of Florrie and the Mechanism of Sexual Deviation' would occupy about half of *The Well of Loneliness*. It was not surprising that the author whose commentary prefaced the first edition of the novel, praising its presentation 'in a faithful and uncompromising form' of 'one particular aspect of sexual life as it exists among us today', was Havelock Ellis himself.

Unlike a novelist of male homosexuality, Radclyffe Hall was not depicting criminal behaviour. Lesbianism had never been formally criminalized, though some of its practitioners had been punished by justices of the peace before whom they appeared in the seventeenth and eighteenth centuries. Male homosexuals had been liable under common law for the 'abominable crime of buggery'. When the Criminal Law Amendment Act 1885 was passed, in response to the white slave panic, indecency between male persons became criminal by statute, with a sentence of two years' imprisonment. No provision was made for women. This was said to be because Queen Victoria could not believe in the possibility of such conduct between members of her sex, while her outgoing Prime Minister, W. E. Gladstone, had not the courage to argue the point.

Such was the situation when Jonathan Cape was offered The *Well of Loneliness* by Radclyffe Hall's agent, Audrey Heath. The author explained that she had written the book from a deep sense of duty to defend those who were themselves defenceless in the present state of society. In May 1928 a contract was drawn up and review copies were sent out. The subject of the book was a cause for some unease but the author's purpose and integrity could scarcely be questioned.

The first reviews confirmed Cape's judgment. The *Times Literary Supplement* on 28 July found it 'sincere, courageous, high-minded and often beautifully expressed'. On 7 August the *Daily Telegraph* – not a harbinger of sexual innovation – called it 'finely conceived and finely written'. The review acknowledged the 'unreserved frankness' and 'burning sincerity' with which the author had described 'an aspect of abnormal life seldom or never presented in English fiction'. It was not until Friday 17 August that James Douglas, scourge of *The Rainbow* and reviewer for the *Sunday Express*, warned Cape that his weekend article would denounce *The Well of Loneliness*. The book had almost sold its first printing of 1,500 copies and a reprint of 2,000 copies was ordered. There had been no move against it by the Attorney-General or the DPP.

Douglas attacked the 'increasing effrontery' and 'insolently provocative bravado' with which the post-war horrors of sexual perversion flaunted themselves. 'Normalcy' it seemed was not winning the battle. Yet there was one sentence in the review which, with its populist appeal, doomed the novel. Across seventy-two years it echoed the sentiment of Lord Campbell's speech on the Obscene Publications Bill with almost complete accuracy: 'I would rather put a phial of prussic acid in the hands of a healthy girl or boy than the book in question.' Douglas appealed to the Home Secretary to 'instruct the Director of Public Prosecutions'.

This marked such a change from the earlier reviews that it was not surprising if Jonathan Cape was shaken. He wrote to the Home Secretary and asked advice. Sir William Joynson-Hicks consulted the DPP, Sir Archibald Bodkin, whose deputy replied on 20 August that among other things 'the authoress herself is what is known as a homo-sexualist.' Joynson-Hicks advised Cape to withdraw the book at once. Though most of the 3,500 copies had been sold, the second reprint was cancelled.

There was no reason, other than advice received and perhaps common sense, why the book should not still be sold. H. G. Wells and Arnold Bennett came to its defence, while Bernard Shaw in the *Daily Herald* of 6 October denounced the publisher's decision to withdraw it. As a compromise, Jonathan Cape licensed the Pegasus Press, Paris, to publish an edition which might be ordered by individuals in England. The moulded type was flown to France for printing.

Orders were received in Paris but when the first consignment arrived at Dover it was seized by customs and a destruction order applied for. Legally, Cape's defence was weaker than it might have been. The Obscene Publications Act required that a book should be shown to be obscene; the Customs Consolidation Act 1876 required only that it should be deemed indecent.

On 9 November, before Sir Chartres Biron at Bow Street Magistrates Court, the application was heard. Norman Birkett, the great defender in murder cases between the wars and the most impressive advocate of his day, appeared for Cape. Herbert Metcalfe, who as Old Street magistrate had wanted the proponents of DORA publicly hanged, appeared for Leopold Hill, the importer.

Chief Inspector Prothero of Scotland Yard agreed with Herbert Metcalfe that the subject of the book was treated with frankness and sincerity. He did not agree with a reviewer who thought it 'high-minded and beautiful'. For the defence, Birkett argued that 'it is not for the magistrate to act upon his own personal view, but upon the views of reasonable people generally.' This category hardly included Sir Chartres Biron, who had informed Joynson-Hicks that if the book came before him, he would commit it for trial. When Sir Chartres asked Birkett if he was saying the book did not deal with sexual perversion, Birkett said it did not. 'Nowhere is there an obscene word, a lascivious passage.'

Birkett called his first witness, Desmond MacCarthy, perhaps the most widely read critic of the day. He asked whether the novel was obscene. Sir Chartres intervened at once and said the question was for the court alone to decide; the opinion of witnesses was not admissible. Birkett tendered the evidence of thirty-nine further witnesses that the book was not obscene. They included Leonard and Virginia Woolf, E. M. Forster, Rose Macaulay A. P. Herbert, Victoria Sackville-West, Laurence Housman and Julian Huxley.

'I reject them all,' said Sir Chartres. He found *The Well of Loneliness* obscene, remarking that 'there is not one word which suggests that anyone with the horrible tendencies described is in the least blameworthy' and that 'certain acts are described in alluring terms.' Though Jonathan Cape appealed to Quarter Sessions on 14 December, the appeal was dismissed. This second court described the book as 'most dangerous and corrupting', accepting the view of the Attorney-General, Sir Thomas Inskip, that 'The whole book as to ninety-nine hundredths of it may be beyond criticism, yet one passage may make it a work which ought to be destroyed as obscene.'[8]

So far as the law was concerned, the case had two important implications. The first was the legal exclusion of evidence as to the quality of the book on trial, while the second confirmed that a book might be destroyed because of a single objectionable passage.

If there was consolation anywhere on earth, it was in New York. In the following year, Morris Ernst won another remarkable victory when he secured the acquittal of Donald Friede for possessing and selling Radclyffe Hall's novel. Ernst produced statements by Sherwood Anderson, Sinclair Lewis and Ernest Hemingway in the book's favour and argued that it 'deals with a delicate social problem which in itself cannot be said to be a violation of the law, unless it is written in such a manner as to make it obscene'.

3

Not until the 1950s was there to be a case of such fame as *The Well of Loneliness*, nor a single outlaw in Paris as controversial as *Ulysses* or *Lady Chatterley's Lover*. Most cases in the 1930s involved publishers who issued a run-of-the-mill novel or others who repeatedly tested the law.

The only major firm to be prosecuted were Heinemann, publishers of the English edition of Wallace Smith's novel of life in an American brothel, *Bessie Cotter*, in 1935. Reviewers' opinions ranged from that of the *Manchester Evening News*, which thought it a 'brilliant and appalling novel' for those who did not wish to 'condemn by taboo', to the *Daily Sketch* which thought it 'should never have been printed'. Sir Patrick Hastings, briefed for the defence, pleaded that if the publishers had been warned the book was considered objectionable they would have withdrawn it at once. Heinemann pleaded guilty and were fined £100 with £105 costs at Bow Street on 10 April 1935.

Without evidence as to literary merit, most seizures were dealt with by a simple application to a magistrate for a destruction order, even where reputable publishers were concerned. On 4 March 1929, Norah James' *The Sleeveless Errand* was condemned by the Bow Street magistrate. This study of a group of dissolute bohemians had been recommended to Eric Partridge of the Scholartis Press by the critic Edward Garnett. When his premises were searched, Partridge asked the police, 'Whoever says this is an indecent book? I never heard such a thing. I don't deal in such stuff.' Jack Kahane, who later published the book in Paris, thought it much the sort of thing Ernest Hemingway had written in *The Sun Also Rises*, 'but what passed my comprehension was why it had been banned'.

For the prosecution, Perceval Clarke answered this. The story covered two days of conversation between 'persons entirely devoid of decency and morality, who for the most part are under the influence of drink . . . Filthy language and indecent situations appear to be the keynote of the book.' Particular exception was taken to the way that 'the name of God or Christ was taken in vain', as in 'For Christ's sake give me a drink.' It was the duty of the law to protect 'decent-minded people' from 'such foul stuff as this'. The magistrate agreed. 'The book in question would suggest in the minds of the young of either sex, or even to persons of more advanced years, thoughts of a most impure character.' The destruction order was granted with costs.

A small firm, Boriswood of South Kensington, was taken to court in 1935 to face destruction orders in respect of books found on its premises during a police search. They included Edward Charles' *The Sexual Impulse*, for which Julian Huxley had written a preface. As a work of non-fiction, evidence as to the book's value was admitted. Dr Maude Royden of Eccleston Square Church and Julian Huxley appeared, Huxley confirming the book's 'scholarly and educational value'. The Westminster magistrate made short work of this, remarking that the book was not 'fit and decent for people of the working class to read'. He also assured Professor Huxley, 'I call it rubbish.'

Boriswood then faced criminal prosecutions for *Boy*, by a distinguished novelist James Hanley. It described the fate of a boy who runs away to sea to escape brutal treatment at home. He is sexually assaulted and murdered.

Though the book had been published in 1931, no action was taken against it for four years and no one had suggested that it belonged to the pornographic underworld. The *New Statesman* called it harrowing but certainly not obscene. Boriswood was fined £250 at Manchester Assizes and a further £50 at London Sessions on 10 December. In the publishers' favour, the magistrate remarked on 24 October, 'I remember that they took some pains in sending round the manuscript to various people before the book was published.' At their appeal, the judge was none other than Perceval Clarke who had been prosecutor of *The Sleeveless Errand*.

Not all defendants took such pains as Boriswood. William Henry Waldo Sabine's satire on sexual hypocrisy, *Guido and the Girls* (1932), targeted Lord Halifax, a devout High Churchman who had been Viceroy of India, was soon to be the Foreign Secretary who accompanied Chamberlain to Munich, and narrowly missed succeeding Chamberlain as prime minister in 1940. Sabine was fined £500 for publishing an obscene and criminal libel.[9]

In the bohemian underworld of the 1930s, whose denizens regarded censors as enemies to be defied and defeated, by far the most colourful rebel was 'Count Geoffrey Wladislas Potocki de Montalk', who maintained a claim to the thrones of Poland, Hungary and Bohemia, as well as to the titles of Grand Duke of Lithuania, Silesia and the Ukraine, Hospodar of Moldavia and High Priest of the Sun. During the Second World War, Herbert Morrison as Minister of Home Security assured the House of Commons that this 'extravagant' and 'preposterous' person and his forebears 'appear to have had no association with Poland for several generations'.

Born in New Zealand and author of an autobiography, *Blue Blood in the Butter Republic*, Potocki was a distinctive figure, remembered for wine-coloured robes and sandals, shoulder-length hair and an engaging habit of standing halves of bitter in Soho pubs. He was naturally a monarchist, editor of the *Right Review*, as well as translator of the poet Charles Maurras of Action Française. Five of his own collections of poems had been published. In 1932 he was ready with a sixth: *Here Lies John Penis*.

> Here lies John Penis
> Buried in the Mount of Venus.
> He died in tranquil faith
> That having vanquished death
> HE SHALL RISE up again
> And in Joy's Kingdom reign.

What might have seemed innocuous thirty or forty years later was as explosive in 1932 as it would have been a century before. No publisher would touch Potocki's lightly disrespectful English renderings of Rabelais and Verlaine. He decided to have the booklet printed and issue it himself. In company with a friend and carrying his poems, he approached a policeman on duty outside the Law Courts in the Strand. He showed this officer the poems and asked if he knew of a typesetter not averse to setting 'spicy' poetry. The policeman, perhaps surprisingly, gave him directions. At the typesetters, a few minutes of conversation indicated that there was something amiss. Only then did the two visitors see a notice, 'Printers of the *Methodist Recorder*'.

Leslie de Lozay of Comps Ltd in Hatton Garden looked at the poems and agreed to let Potocki set them in type. He quoted a price and his visitors left. 'I then phoned the police.' The claimant to three European thrones and a fistful of titles was arrested and lodged in Brixton prison. Technically, to show a piece of writing was to 'publish' it. Indeed, in *Martin et Uxor v. The Trustees of the British Museum and E. M. Thomson* it appeared that the Trustees might be liable if they allowed a reader access to a book containing defamatory material.

Potocki was tried before the Recorder of London, Sir Ernest Wild, who was disinclined to see the matter as a joke. The jury convicted without leaving their box. Richard Du Cann pleaded that his client had intended only to print a few copies 'for a small circle of poets and literary experimenters to test certain words'. 'A man must not say he is a poet and be filthy,' said Sir Ernest sternly. 'He has to obey the law just the same as ordinary citizens and the sooner the highbrow school learns that, the better for the morality of the country.'

There was little meeting of minds. Sir Ernest turned to the defendant and asked a question which, in the case of a claimant to European royalty, was probably an unwise one, though not as unwise as the answer. 'Can't you suggest what punishment you think you deserve?' 'Yes, my lord. I think I deserve to be sentenced to several years in Buckingham Palace.' What he got was six months in Wormwood Scrubs, reflecting the personal antipathy of the judge rather than the magnitude of the crime. Potocki's experience of the penal system was recorded in a booklet, *Snobbery with Violence*. He left England for the more sympathetic climate of Draguignan, in southern France.[10]

One publisher in the literary underworld of the 1930s provided the legal profession with more employment than any other in the 1930s. The Fortune Press was the creation of Reginald Ashley Caton and, astonishingly, it survived from 1924 until 1969. Caton had his fingers in other pies, including slum property in Brighton and ticket-touting at Wimbledon.

From the firm's premises in Buckingham Palace Road, he issued learned editions of Restoration dramatists, Gothick novels of the eighteenth and nineteenth centuries, fiction and non-fiction dealing with what he liked to call 'amatory unorthodoxy' and poets as yet unknown, including Cecil Day-Lewis, Dylan Thomas, John Wain, Kingsley Amis, Lawrence Durrell, Thom Gunn, Philip Larkin, Sylvia Plath and Wallace Stevens. Before their business relationships ended, most wished they had never heard of him.

Caton's sources were varied. Charles Carrington was by then dead and buried but the Fortune Press acquired such titles of his as Brantôme's *Lives of Fair and Gallant Ladies* and the spurious Byron poems in *Don Leon*, praising homosexual and heterosexual sodomy. There were also translations of Huysmans' *Là-bas* and Baudelaire. The *éminence grise* of Caton's world was the shadowy figure of 'Father' Montague Summers, scholar of the Restoration, the Gothick novel and the more saleable subjects of witchcraft, demonology and the Marquis de Sade. Apart from his poets, Caton published whatever novels would miss being censored by the narrowest possible margin, with titles like *Feathers in the Bed*. His novels about boys for those who were no longer boys themselves were a success, as were such titles as J. A. Park's *Strange Occupation* with a dash of narcotics and a scene of the heroine being spanked in a taxi as it drove in circles round Hyde Park.

Caton managed his business with skill except on such occasions as the collective appearance of his books in court on 10 October 1934. The trouble was caused by a police raid on a nearby bookshop, Sequana, where a large number of his titles happened to be in stock. It was a busy day in court.

Among those condemned to the flames by the Westminster magistrate were Huysmans' *Down There*, a translation of *Là-bas* published four years earlier; *The Confessions of Madeleine Bavent*, a Montague Summers translation of satanic practices among nuns; *Strato's Boyish Muse*, extracted from *The Greek Anthology*; the *Satyricon* of Petronius; Montague Summers' translation of Ludovico Maria Sinistrari's *Demoniality*; translations of Pierre Louÿs' *Aphrodite* and his lesbian poems *Les Chansons de Bilitis*, and a collection of drawings by Beresford Egan, *The Marquis de Sade*. The last title was spared after an agreement between the publisher and the court to redraw one picture so that female genitalia were obscured. Two novels were freed and also J. Downes' *Roscius Anglicanus*, whose title had suggested to the police some rare sexual perversion but which was actually a study of the Restoration theatre.

In the background lurked Father Montague Summers, the plump unhealthily pale face, the black biretta and cassock, the ordination which was said to have been 'irregular but valid' because those who would have advised the Catholic Church against it had been kept in the dark. Summers was at work upon the poems of the Earl of Rochester, including the five-act farce of King Bolloxinion and his court, *Sodom: or, The Quintessence of Debauchery*, first prosecuted in 1689. 'My laws shall act more pleasure than command / And with my prick I'll govern all the land.' The elderly Sir Edmund Gosse was delighted. 'But be discreet!' he cried. It was hard to see how. Arthur Bullen suggested publishing *Sodom* as a separate appendix to Rochester's poems, in very small type. As Summers pointed out, everyone would write in for the appendix and ignore the main work. Lord Rochester, as the author of *Sodom*, waited another thirty years for fame.[11]

Caton and the Fortune Press executed a deft minuet with the powers of the law. Others were prepared to take English writing abroad and publish it there – not merely pornography but anything of value that was banned at home. The leader of this movement was a Manchester businessman, Jack Kahane, who believed as he said that the sex book will die when sex dies. Kahane chose Paris and found premises in the Place Vendôme. Here he set up the Obelisk Press, to be followed twenty years later by his son Maurice Girodias and the Olympia Press. By 1938, the father had established a considerable list, padded out by two novels of his own, written as 'Cecil Barr', *Daffodil* and *Suzy Falls Off*.[12]

In the first place, Kahane published books condemned by the English courts or not in print because they might be condemned. He rescued three important casualties: Norah James' *The Sleeveless Errand*, Wallace Smith's *Bessie Cotter* and James Hanley's *Boy*. Those which would never have survived in London included Frank Harris' *My Life and Loves* and Sheila Cousins' *To Beg I Am Ashamed: The Story of a London Prostitute*. Though there was greater freedom in America, a number of writers were effectively banned. The Obelisk list contained two titles by Henry Miller, *Tropic of Cancer* and *Black Spring*. While expatriate publishing was dormant during the coming war, it revived quickly in the years that followed. For fifteen years after the war, few London or New York publishers would have thought it sensible to market the fiction of Henry Miller or the unexpurgated memoirs of Frank Harris.

4

It did not seem to censors in the 1930s that they had overstepped the limit of necessary restriction. On 21 October 1936, the Director of Public Prosecutions, Sir Edward Tindal Atkinson, warned the nation that it had 'gone a little too far' in tolerating a good many publications since the last war. Even 'books and photographs of a grossly indecent character, produced mainly on the Continent', met with no difficulty.

Those who imported material wholesale ran an occupational risk of being caught. A man whose consignments were stopped several times was George Gerald Swan, brought before Clerkenwell Magistrates Court in 1938 for importing 'indecent and obscene books' from France. Two earlier consignments had been stopped by customs in January and February 1936. On the first occasions, Swan expressed surprise at the nature of the books and vowed never to order such material again. The vow was short-lived. Next time he said plaintively, 'I don't want to handle this sort of stuff but if I don't the others do, and then they get all my trade.' His speciality, for which he was duly convicted, was magazines of a size more difficult for an individual traveller to smuggle.[13]

It was rare for the police to find the producers, as opposed to the retailers, of material when it originated in England. One such case was heard at Brighton Magistrates Court on 16 April 1937. The producer in this instance was a retired Deputy Superintendent Registrar of Births and Deaths at Lambeth, now living in Lancaster Road, Brighton. His supply consisted of 750 photographs and prints, described by Detective Superintendent Arthur Pelling as 'grossly obscene', thirty books and fifty 'typewritten manuscripts', some of which he may have written to order or obtained from those who had written them, and ten photographic plates for printing. The complexities of typesetting and binding meant that most underground pornography was typewritten for the next thirty years. It seemed that this defendant had volunteered useful information to the police, in return for the lenient sentence of being bound over for twelve months in the sum of £100.

A more alarming aspect of the underworld of pornography in the 1930s was the extent to which it was spreading beyond central London to outlying areas like West Ham, where one such shop was being run by Elizabeth Fenton. On 22 February 1938 a concerned citizen, 'Madame X', saw a copy of *Life's Sweet Sin* in the window. Inside the shop, she was offered a selection of books which came, literally, from under the counter. She returned four days later, followed by Detective Sergeant O'Sullivan, who first asked for *Stolen Sweets* from the window and was then told, 'If you want to read a few spicy stories, I have a book that will suit you.' There were 470 books in all: what the sentencing magistrate called 'an awful sink of filth'. The defendant was fined £5 with £5 costs and sent to prison for a month.[14]

Cinema opened up another lucrative area with the 'Blue Film' show.

By the end of September 1936, police were warning the public that films of 'an obnoxious character' were being smuggled from France on cross-Channel steamers through the smaller ports where customs officers were fewer. Some were even brought in by plane. They were not for sale but for exhibition, usually in the provinces, at certain hotels and in buildings like garages which could accommodate an audience of twenty or more people. 'But each one has paid highly for the privilege of seeing the pictures.'[15]

As both theatre and cinema tested their freedom, censorship became news. It ranged from the ludicrous to the ominous. At one extreme, a trained chimpanzee in the film *Girl of the Jungle* was discovered by the censors to have bald patches on its hindquarters, in common with other chimpanzees. It was a defect which the censorship found harmful to children. The bewildered animal was led away to the Max Factor wig department to be fitted with a pair of 'real hair panties'. He appeared in the film, wearing the panties and a puzzled expression. In May that year, Alfred Hitchcock was required to alter the ending of *The Secret Agent* so that Peter Lorre did not shoot his opponent. 'There must not be the suggestion that the Secret Service employed killers to shoot men in such a manner.'[16]

Rather more sinister was the deference shown by the Lord Chamberlain and his officials to Adolf Hitler, because a foreign head of state must not be offended by portrayal on the English stage. In *Spread it Abroad* at the Saville Theatre in April 1936, after the Wehrmacht's seizure of the Rhineland, a sketch was banned because it showed a Hitler lookalike sneezing his moustache off in the middle of a blustering speech. Another sketch was banned in *To and Fro* at the Duke of York's Theatre in November. It showed an auction in which the world was put up for sale and an actor dressed as Hitler offered to buy it.[17]

In the New Year of 1937, the pantomime *Robinson Crusoe* at the King's Theatre, Hammersmith, incurred criminal prosecution by showing Hitler on stage. At the West London Magistrates Court on 2 February, one of the cast and the manager faced charges of 'unlawfully acting' thirty seconds of uncensored material. The scene, approved by the censor, showed Crusoe and his white companions in a stockade, defending themselves against black islanders. The criminal addition depicted an actor made up as a frightened Adolf Hitler, running on with a white flag and taking shelter in the stockade. The prosecution accepted that it was 'humanly impossible for a comedian not to put in impromptu "gags"'. However, impersonating a distinguished head of state was a serious matter. The actor was fined £10 and the theatre manager £15, equivalent to some £400 and £600 in modern terms.

The moral character of a head of state was not an issue. March 1939 was the month of 'the rape of Czechoslovakia' and also when Hitler revoked his non-aggression pact with Poland, preparatory to invasion, and annexed Memel from Lithuania. Mussolini closed in on Abyssinia. On 31 March, the Lord Chamberlain ordered the removal of a song potentially offensive to the Führer and the Duce, from the revue *Nine Sharp* by Herbert Farjeon at the Little Theatre. 'Even Hitler had a mother, even Mussolini had a ma . . .'

The coming of war made no difference to the regulations. A fortnight after Dunkirk, in the revue *We'll Be There* at the Aldershot Hippodrome, an actor playing a devil in hell who sang 'Adolf's Here At Last' added an 'unauthorized' line of his own and made an allegedly indecent upward gesture with a pitchfork. He was fined £20, or £800 in modern terms. The producer, the business manager, the licensee of the theatre, even the man who had submitted the script to St James's Palace – none of whom had any immediate control over the actor – were each fined £10, or £400 by modern values.[18]

The Lord Chamberlain had no veto over the output of the BBC. However, Hitler need not have been concerned. As late as 1937 the corporation banned a broadcast by Colonel J. C. Wedgwood MP shortly before it went on air on 24 February on the grounds that it was offensive. The passage objected to was 'What Hitler wants is Austria, Czechoslovakia, Lithuania, Latvia, Estonia, some of Poland and the Ukraine, and I hope the South Tyrol, not to mention Switzerland, Alsace-Lorraine, Schleswig-Holstein and Malmedy.' Other references objected to included Mussolini requiring Majorca, Malta, Cilicia, Palestine, Egypt, Arabia, Tunis, and the control of Spain. As for Ireland: 'De Valera might want Ulster first and Liverpool next.'

Hitler was not the only figure whose stage portrayal invited censorship. The political drama *Parnell*, a hit on Broadway, was banned outright by the Lord Chamberlain in 1936 'because it brings in famous political figures and it is thought that some dishonour might be done to the dead and hurt to the living'. Parnell had then been dead forty-five years. Though Queen Victoria had been dead for thirty-six years, Laurence Housman's innocuous portrayal of her in *Victoria Regina* was still banned from the London stage in 1937.[19]

Even more sensitive was the portrayal of God. Marc Connelly's *Green Pastures* was refused a stage licence in 1931 because of 'the portrayal of God as a Negro' who smoked ten-cent cigars in a Negro heaven and whose angels wore paper wings. The film version was given a certificate in November 1936 after a five-month delay. Sir Charles Taylor protested in the House of Commons on 12 November but the Home Secretary replied that he had no power to ban the film once it had a certificate. Three days later, the Provost of Chelmsford deplored films for adults only as 'a serious menace to the morals of our society'. A film that was unsuitable for children should not be shown at all.

Where performers or managements chose to ignore theatre censorship, prosecution followed. At West London Police Court on 10 August 1937 Freddie Forbes, Angela Barrie and a theatre manager appeared. They had deviated from the licensed script in a sketch called 'Just in Fun'. They were unlucky because, on the night of 15 June, Shepherd's Bush Empire, one of the Stoll chain, was visited by Mr Albert Titman, the Lord Chamberlain's secretary, incognito. There was a bedroom scene in which the bedtime drink Horlicks was mentioned. Angela Barrie said, 'Sounds like a rude word', which was not in the script. A line, too indelicate to be read aloud in court, followed. There was a chase in which Freddie Forbes pursued Angela Barrie. She was supposed to fall over the bed. He was licensed to aim a smack at her bottom and miss. As Mr Titman looked on, Forbes did not miss. The cast and the manager were arrested. Forbes was fined £20 with ten guineas costs, a month's salary, and the theatre manager £10 with costs. Sir Oswald Stoll, one of the country's foremost impresarios, was let off on the grounds that he could not know what was going on in all of his theatres all of the time.

5

Throughout the 1930s the threat of prosecution for civil or criminal libel could weigh heavily on freedom of criticism and debate. The greatest sensation of this kind in the cinema had nothing to do with the censor but everything to do with a film review by a famous novelist, Graham Greene, and the reputation of an even more famous child star, Shirley Temple. Greene was a contributor to the prestigious magazine *Night and Day*, which began life in 1937 as a counterpart to the *New Yorker*. Contributors were among the most distinguished of their day: Evelyn Waugh, Anthony Powell, John Betjeman, Herbert Read, Cyril Connolly, Malcolm Muggeridge and Elizabeth Bowen.

Graham Greene had made his name as the author of *Stamboul Train*, *A Gun for Sale* and had written but not published *Brighton Rock*. Prior to the issue of *Night and Day* for 28 October 1937, he had reviewed films for *Night and Day* and the *Spectator*, including three of Shirley Temple's. The winsome child who sang 'The Good Ship Lollipop' was the ideal child of mothers of the decade. In retrospect, all Greene's reviews carried an implication that her portrayals were not so much a promotion of childhood innocence as a feast for dirty old men. His criticism was directed not at the child actress but at the Hollywood moguls whom he alleged exploited her and knew exactly what they were doing.

The film which caused trouble was *Wee Willie Winkie*. Greene commended the nine-year-old actress's 'well-developed rump', described as being as voluptuous in its trousered agility as Marlene Dietrich's. From her audience of middle-aged men and clergymen, Greene caught a 'gasp of excited expectation' as she swaggered across the barrack square in her kilt to confront the sergeant's raised palm. There was much more but this was enough to ensure trouble.

W. H. Smith, wisely as it proved, refused to stock this issue of the magazine. However, the publisher of *Night and Day* took counsel's opinion and was assured by D. N. Pritt KC that the review, though robust criticism, was not libellous. The magazine went on sale with placards promising 'Sex and Shirley Temple'. It sold well but Pritt was proved wrong. *Night and Day* as well as its publishers, printers and Graham Greene were sued by Shirley Temple and both American and English branches of Twentieth Century-Fox Film Corporation.

There was virtually no defence, certainly none likely to get past the irascible figure of Lord Chief Justice Hewart who presided in the High Court on 22 March 1938. Sir Patrick Hastings for Miss Temple and her film company called the libel 'one of the most horrible that could be imagined'. He understood his client to be 'a child who has a world-wide reputation in films'. As for Greene's review: 'It is such a beastly thing to have written that if it had been a question of money it is difficult to say what would have been a proper sum for damages.' The magazine agreed to pay Shirley Temple £2,000 and Twentieth Century-Fox £1,500.

The magazine apologized, the publishers apologized, the printers apologized. The only person who did not apologize was Graham Greene because he was in Mexico collecting material for *The Lawless Roads* and correcting proofs of *Brighton Rock*. Lord Justice Hewart asked grimly, 'Who is the author referred to?' Valentine Holmes for the defence replied, 'Mr Graham Greene.' 'Is he within the jurisdiction?' asked Lord Hewart. 'I do not know where he is.' Presently the Lord Chief Justice interrupted him again. 'Can you tell me where Mr Graham Greene is?' 'I have no information.' Lord Hewart had heard enough. 'This libel is simply a gross outrage, and I will take care to see that suitable attention is drawn to it.' He had in mind charges of criminal libel. Papers in the case were sent to the Director of Public Prosecutions and Greene was warned by his correspondents to stay out of the country until the fuss died down. He returned soon afterwards and heard no more of the matter.

In the world of the arts there had been an astonishing case the year before, involving the Tate Gallery and a dead painter, Maurice Utrillo. The gallery put on an exhibition of his works and produced a catalogue to go with it. This explained that 'Utrillo became a confirmed dipsomaniac and at intervals throughout his life was placed under restraint.' From 1919 until his death in 1934 he was 'almost continually under supervision'.

In *Regina v. Ensor* (1877), a South Wales libel case, Mr Justice Stephen had ruled that the dead have no rights and cannot be libelled in civil law. The author of the Tate catalogue therefore let rip with the uncensored truth. Utrillo had 'indulged a taste for alcohol' while still a boy and in 1900 his mother had taken him to a lunatic asylum. When painting, it was his habit 'to keep a bottle by his side which he constantly replenished'. By 1910 he was 'a confirmed drunkard' and in the following year his riotous and disorderly conduct brought him into violent conflict with the police. He was also convicted of indecent exposure. By 1913 he was 'saturated with alcohol' and when he had no money to buy liquor 'used to consume lamp spirit, methylated spirit, petroleum, benzine, eau de cologne, and ether'.

Utrillo was also a fraud who would 'sign the canvases of other and inferior artists in return for a few francs with which he obtained drink'. He attacked a man, stuck a woman with a pin and was arrested as 'a menace to women and small girls'; it took five policemen to restrain him. For good measure, he 'smoked opium and hashish' and had fallen down incapable in the Champs Elysées. In 1921, 'following a drunken orgy, M. Utrillo was certified to be a dangerous lunatic and inebriate'.

It had been a remarkable career. The Tate went ahead with its exhibition and published its catalogue containing this chronicle of moral depravity. It then heard from solicitors representing Maurice Utrillo who had not died in 1934 but was still alive and remained so until 1955. Indeed, in 1935 he had married the woman who helped to rehabilitate him. He had conquered his drinking habit as far back as 1928. The man who died in 1934 was a Spanish writer, Miguel Utrillo. So many people had expected Maurice to die that even part of the French press had muddled the identity. The Tate's catalogue was indefensible, however accurate.

The gallery and its director, as defendants, owed their salvation to the generous nature of the man they had libelled and who was now restored to health. Utrillo wanted a public apology and his good name vindicated. It must be made clear that he was rehabilitated and that this had been stated in a book published in 1928, *La Légende et la vie d'Utrillo*. He wanted no damages.[20]

The civil courts of the pre-war years were a busy place for litigants trying to maintain a healthy tone in public life by suppressing one another's publications. The causes once again ranged from the entertaining to the sinister. One of the more sensational was *Windsor v. William Heinemann and Geoffrey Dennis* (1937). Subsequent accounts of the abdication of Edward VIII in order to marry the American divorcee Mrs Wallis Simpson were apt to make it sound like a long-fought battle by the King against his government. As a private feud this was true but for most people the crisis had come and gone in a couple of weeks, from the moment the press broke its silence to the abdication on 10 December 1936.

In one of the most successful censorships of all time, the government had persuaded the British press to say nothing for several months of the growing conflict between monarch and government over Mrs Simpson. By December the barrage of foreign press coverage with such New York headlines as 'KING WILL WED WALLY' made the agreement pointless. Having been kept in the dark, the public was all the more eager for the full story.

One of those who supplied an answer was Geoffrey Dennis in *Coronation Commentary*. He was sympathetic to the newly created Duke of Windsor and his Duchess. However, his book sought to counter certain rumours. The first was that Wallis Simpson had been the King's mistress before the abdication. This not only upset the couple but threatened the decree nisi of divorce which Mrs Simpson had gained by arrangement with her husband. Though the book's approach was to deny the truth of the rumours, it laid them before the public.

Rumour alleged that the government thought Edward VIII unsuited to be king and were delighted at the crisis. 'Until the marriage was mooted, they had no notion how to get rid of him. She whom they pretended was a disaster was in fact a godsend.' Among examples of royal incompetence were, 'Things left undone . . . duty neglected . . . papers held up . . . muddling . . . fuddling . . . meddling.' Under pressure, King Edward drank heavily. A long-standing engagement to open Aberdeen Royal Infirmary was avoided by sending his brother the Duke of York instead, so that the King could meet Mrs Simpson from her train and escort her to Balmoral.

At the abdication, 'Edward himself was prolonging the crisis, holding out for more money.'

From his exile in France, the Duke of Windsor sued both the author and the publisher. His legal adviser, Sir Walter Monckton, was dismayed. Mrs Simpson's divorce was not yet absolute. Two people had already sworn affidavits alleging collusion. A skilful cross-examiner would have little difficulty in showing that she had been the plaintiff's mistress before the abdication, thus putting the divorce in peril. As Prince of Wales, the Duke's conduct with companions like Mrs Freda Dudley Ward was also an open secret. His character was vulnerable to reports of his indiscretions in official files.

During his visit to Japan in 1922, for example, the Ambassador Sir Charles Eliot had reported to Lord Curzon as Foreign Secretary that the Japanese were cooperating in providing the Prince with professional 'female companions' along his route. However, since professionals carried a risk of infection, these companions were first inspected and disinfected. There had almost been what the ambassador called 'a terrible scandal' when two lady missionaries tried to present him with a Bible in Japanese. The Japanese took no chances and the well-meaning ladies were rescued just in time as they were being taken for inspection and disinfecting.

Coronation Commentary was withdrawn from sale on 26 April 1937. Yet the Duke still intended to sue, a course supported by his friend Winston Churchill. Exception was taken to two chapters, 'Edward VIII' and 'Abdication'. Fortunately, by the time the case came to court on 22 November 1937, reason had prevailed. Sir William Jowitt was briefed for the plaintiff. On his advice damages were agreed and an apology by the author and publishers was accepted. The apology was made in court before Lord Chief Justice Hewart.

As with Graham Greene and Shirley Temple, Hewart was plainly dissatisfied. When Sir William Jowitt asked that the record be withdrawn, he agreed 'with some hesitation'. He spoke wistfully of a criminal prosecution. 'It appears to be forgotten that the writing and publication of a libel may be a crime because it is calculated to provoke a breach of the peace. These particular libels, the jury might think, appear almost to invite a thoroughly efficient horse-whipping.'[21]

6

Unlike the coming of war in 1914, the outbreak of hostilities in 1939 surprised almost no one. For several years beforehand, the issue of free speech

was interwoven with the challenge of Fascism. The autumn of the abdication in 1936 was also the autumn of such attacks on the Jews of the East
End as the so-called 'Battle of Cable Street' on 4 October. By that
summer, the literature of Fascism was vicious enough for the government
to invoke the common law of seditious libel, which had gathered dust for
a century. The occasion was an issue of the *Fascist*, whose proprietor
Arnold Leese had refused cooperation with Sir Oswald Mosley, believing
that Mosley was in the pay of the Jews because he was less anti-Semitic
than Leese.

This proprietor of the *Fascist* was a retired vet whose Fascist Legions
consisted of three dozen members. He subsequently became secretary of
the Imperial Fascist League, still convinced that Mosley's British Union of
Fascists was 'pro-Jew'. Given the size of Leese's organization and the
unhinged rant of soap-box oratory which was his politics, the issue was
whether the viciousness of his views warranted publicizing them to the
entire country in legal proceedings, rather than to the handful of readers of
the *Fascist*, the tenor of which was represented by such proclamations as: 'It
is well established, in spite of many shameless denials, that Jews practise a
ritual murder of Christians in order to obtain fresh blood to mix in their
ceremonial bread.'

Seditious libels usually libelled the sovereign, the government or the
constitution with a view to causing their overthrow or alteration 'other
than by lawful means'. To that extent, the prosecution of Arnold Leese
might seem like swatting a gnat with a mallet. Yet the common law offence
of seditious libel might, more rarely, apply to a publication calculated 'to
promote feelings of ill-will and hostility between different classes of [His
Majesty's] subjects'.

Once charged, the behaviour of the defendant grew increasingly bizarre.
He asked that the Director of Public Prosecutions should take similar
action against publishers of the New Testament which said 'practically the
same thing' as he. His newspaper had said that the 'alternatives' were to kill,
or to sterilize, or to segregate his racial enemies, 'and our policy is the last
one'. He fought a losing battle and clung to a single argument over the
law's inconsistency, as he saw it: 'I allege that there is a certain absurdity in
this charge. The very Book on which witnesses for the prosecution swore,
and which the Court uses as a symbol of truth, charges the Jews with being
hereditary murderers.' There was a distant echo in these words of martyrs
for atheism in the 1830s and 1840s who credited the Bible with strumpet
heroines worse than Fanny Hill and Harriet Wilson in their depravity.
Ironically, Charles Southwell's *Oracle of Reason* in 1842 did not denounce

the Bible as condoning ill-treatment of Jews but, on the contrary, as 'The Jew Book' itself.

On 21 September, Leese was convicted at the Central Criminal Court of 'a seditious libel on the Jews' and sent to prison for six months. The printer of his newspaper was fined £50. Elsewhere, the authorities were in no mood to tolerate anti-Semitic outbursts. On 28 August, John Penfold, who had addressed a crowd of 250 in Finsbury Square, was fined for advocating the expulsion of Jews from England, 'headed by Belisha with a beacon on his head and one in each hand'. Penfold was charged with using insulting words and behaviour. When convicted, he protested, 'There is a fundamental principle at stake – freedom of speech.' 'Freedom of speech is one thing,' said the Old Street magistrate, 'and liberty or licence is another.'

Fascist opinion did not do well in court. A test of opinion was the case against the principal Fascist newspaper *Action* and its regular contributor John Beckett, who was to quit the British Union of Fascists in favour of William Joyce's National Socialist League. The break with Mosley came in the course of this suit, when Beckett and *Action* were sued by Lord Camrose and his paper, the *Daily Telegraph*. In the attack on Camrose, Beckett had written that the two greatest insults were to tell a man that he was Jewish and that 'his financial interests are far greater outside the country than in it.' As it happened, Lord Camrose was Welsh but he was not Jewish, though the libel was no less malicious towards those who were.

This was a jury trial and the jurors, having found for Lord Camrose and his newspaper in the High Court on 15 October 1937, were invited to fix the damages. Their aim seemed rather to punish Beckett and what he stood for than to compensate Camrose. They awarded him the astonishing sum of £12,500 and £7,500 to his newspaper. Beckett himself was unrepentant about his statements. He had the facts from people 'on whom rightly or wrongly I placed great reliance' and his was not 'the weak, cooing, inoffensive article' that Gerald Gardiner for the defence had suggested.

Not all such actions were provoked by anti-Semitism. On 9 November 1936, John Beckett had again been a defendant in the High Court, in company with the British Union of Fascists. This time, the attacks were made in a pamphlet and in *Fascist Quarterly* against the Amalgamated Engineering Union and its officers. In the King's Bench Division, the judge ruled that it was not libellous to say of the AEU executive that there is 'no reasonable limit to the comfort that they may enjoy or the expenses they may incur'. The libel was in what followed.

If on top of all this an opponent looks like defeating a good member of the executive, well, the executive appoints the paid organizers, and many a rebel has discovered that a paid organizership is preferable to a probably hopeless attack upon an executive position. Members of the executive of the AEU are rarely defeated. When they are it is more often the revenge of a fellow executive member because they have been 'obstructive' than the ventilation of the righteous wrath of the membership.

Mr Justice Singleton held that the words in the passage meant that officials broke union rules, were 'dishonst and corrupt', indifferent to the interests of their members and 'corruptly suppressed opposition to themselves'.

By now, however, Fascism had lost what appeal it might once have held for all but a perverse band of stragglers. Sir Oswald Mosley said, even if he was not believed, that he would fight first for his country and not for his political creed. By 1938 the case of censorship which held public attention was not anti-Semitic harangue, nor the escapades of the Fortune Press, but that of Duncan Sandys, a young member of Parliament. As a Territorial Army officer in anti-aircraft defence, he had defied threats of prosecution under the Official Secrets Act 1911 to force a change in the law. The Official Secrets Act 1939 enabled members of Parliament who knew the truth to warn the country that it was largely defenceless in the face of a rearmed Germany with universal military conscription and a brutal tyranny at its head.

6

Total War: The Home Front

I

BY 1939 A good deal of censorship and press control still remained in place from the war of 1914–18. The Official Secrets Acts pre-dated the earlier conflict as did the Admiralty, War Office and Press Committee of 1912, responsible for issuing D-Notices and requesting the press not to report a particular item. That the D-Notice system lagged behind the speed of modern communications was embarrassingly evident even during the last months of peace in 1939.

After Hitler's occupation of the independent remainder of Czechoslovakia, the British government and most people were resigned to war. On 4 April, Lord Stanhope as First Lord of the Admiralty was to play host to the Duke of Kent at a film show, in a hangar of the aircraft-carrier *Ark Royal* at Portsmouth Dockyard. At the last moment, the Duke was unable to attend because of laryngitis. However, the hangar was crowded by a thousand guests, including senior officers, journalists, film chiefs and naval ratings. The show went ahead.

Lord Stanhope explained to the audience that the Duke was unavoidably absent. He then made a statement which caused dismay. 'Unfortunately there are others who are not with us tonight, because shortly before I left the Admiralty, it became necessary to give orders to man the anti-aircraft guns of the Fleet.' There was near-disbelief, not least among the journalists. Stanhope appeared to mean that a surprise attack by the Luftwaffe without declaration of war was anticipated, in which *Ark Royal* was a likely target. He added: 'Long before guests came aboard this ship, sixteen anti-aircraft guns could have given a warm welcome to anyone who happened to come this way.'

Reporters scrambled for the ship's telephone. They were met by Captain Lord Louis Mountbatten who said, 'The First Lord has asked me to say that he has no objection whatever to his remarks being published.' Louis Wulff of the Press Association telephoned to the wire service an account of what had happened. After the film had been shown, he cornered Stanhope who confirmed that the anti-aircraft gunners had not yet been stood down and that *Ark Royal* was ready for the worst. Was this war at last? Wulff read his note back to the First Lord, who gave him permission to publish it.

Later that night the secretary of the D-Notice Committee, on orders from Downing Street, told newspaper editors not to publish Lord Stanhope's comments. By then the story was on the wires across the world. Returning to London, Wulff met Stanhope on the platform of Portsmouth Central railway station. The First Lord advised him to obey the secretary's D-Notice, which had been approved by the Prime Minister. Wulff could only tell him that it was too late. Next day in the House of Commons, Neville Chamberlain remarked wistfully that the First Lord's words at the film show 'gave a wrong impression'.

The details had long since reached the German press, which headlined them on 6 April in such terms as 'British Secret Mobilization Revealed' and 'English Minister Unmasked as Warmonger'. The *Völkischer Beobachter*, the paper of the Nazi party, once again denounced the habitual 'flood of lies' which passed for information from the British government. The *Localanzeiger* described the incident as 'like something out of a madhouse . . . a game as dangerous as it is unscrupulous and which is now being deliberately played with the peace of the world'. The *Berliner Zeitung am Mittag* accused Chamberlain's government of deliberately trying to panic the small nations of Europe into an alliance for the encirclement of Germany. In the history of the D-Notice system, it had never handed quite such a propaganda victory to its adversaries. The time had come for the handling of sensitive information on a more reliable basis.

2

In June 1939, a secret course of instruction was held for about forty press censors. With Vice-Admiral C. V. Usborne as director, they included retired officers and a number of civilians. None had much practical idea of censorship in a modern war. The retired officers, barristers, solicitors, publishers, journalists, teachers, art critics and advertising agents were described by a future director as 'The blind leading the blind'. There had previously been a trial run by a group of retired officers during the Munich crisis but the results had not been good.

On 26 August, eight days before war began, the trainees were called up. A new Censorship Division of the Ministry of Information was housed with the ministry in the requisitioned Senate House of London University. A few hours after the declaration of war, a U-boat sank the liner *Athenia*. The censorship was overwhelmed by cables and telegrams awaiting clearance.

Immediately on the outbreak of war the press came under the control of the newly passed Emergency Powers (Defence) Act 1939 and the Defence Regulations implemented from time to time. Every London newspaper and every provincial newspaper with a London office, as well as every press agency, had a representative with a teleprinter or telephone at the censorship division. They attended press briefings and negotiated approval for stories in their newspapers. There were three rooms for the censors: one for photographs, a second for articles in the British press, and a third for press mails to be distributed overseas. The stamp 'Passed by the Censor' was a guarantee of immunity. Thirty-eight censors of letters and telegrams had also been appointed throughout the country by November 1939. By 31 March 1943, the numbers were 1,588 men and 5,640 women.

Admiral Usborne regarded the press as a burden he had to bear. 'No, I don't know anything about the British Expeditionary Force,' he was heard saying to one editor, 'and if I did I wouldn't tell you.' His deputy and eventual successor, Admiral Pirie Thomson, was more relaxed. An *Evening Standard* request to publish a photograph of gas-masks being issued at a Holborn school had been refused for fear that the Germans might locate the school and bomb it. But gas-masks were being issued at every school in the country. Thomson told the *Standard* to publish, though its rival the *Star* had already been refused.[1]

Censorship had no consistent frontier. One official banned the *Daily Express* from publishing a list of Britain's capital ships. A retired naval officer pointed out that German intelligence would certainly have a copy of the latest edition of *Jane's Fighting Ships*, in which the ships were already listed. There were queries over a ban on locating gas or electricity supplies. How did one report amateur matches played by a football team from Battersea Power Station?

News might be delayed rather than banned. Reports in 1939 of the sinking by a U-boat of the battleship *Royal Oak* in Scapa Flow were withheld until they were of no further use to the Germans. The courage of the crew who brought home the crippled submarine *Triumph* was kept secret from 1939 until 1941. The Admiralty was vigilant for any mention of a ship's name which might indicate 'the whereabouts of warships or merchant ships'. Under the rules governing disclosure, censors removed sarcastic references to both the *Marie Celeste* and HMS *Pinafore*.[2]

News bulletins were not allowed to give details of German air raids, for fear that these might aid the attackers next time. So, for example, the first 'Baedeker raid' on a holiday resort in June 1942 was referred to only as an attack on a coastal town in the West Country, rather than on Weston-super-Mare. Editors of school magazines, who regularly recorded the present careers of former pupils, were warned not to specify which unit of the armed forces any of their alumni had joined.

Weather forecasts were banned for fear of assisting the Luftwaffe. However, after Dunkirk, the censors allowed forecasts to be given for the Straits of Dover. Since the Germans were already there and could see the weather for themselves, there was no point in withholding the information from the people of Britain. Sometimes censorship seemed downright counter-productive. In 1942, the military historian Major-General J. F. C. Fuller had been writing for the *Sunday Pictorial*, urging the Allies to invade North Africa. When they decided to do this, he was told to stop writing about it. 'If I suddenly stop saying so now,' he complained, 'what are the Germans going to think?'[3]

More difficult to sustain was secrecy over such public setbacks as the Bethnal Green shelter disaster of 1943. The air-raid shelter, used to accommodate local people and their bedding, was also Bethnal Green underground station. On 8 March 178 men, women and children were suffocated in what was variously described as an accident or a stampede. It occurred when some of those hurrying down the stairs after the air-raid siren had sounded lost their footing and fell upon those below. Though the drama was reported, the name of the tube station was at first withheld on the Home Secretary's orders. Its location was given away in an *Evening Standard* report a few days later.

The *Standard* described the mayor of Bethnal Green trying to calm a large crowd outside the coroner's court, as they protested about the 'red tape' in which the truth had become concealed. After that there could be little doubt in the minds of the enemy which station was involved. Yet when the official inquiry was over, Herbert Morrison told the House of Commons on 8 April that the government felt bound to keep its conclusions secret, 'since publication would convey information to the enemy'. The name and location of the tube station, as well as the nature of the accident, were withheld from Parliament.

Violations of censorship were rare, though a correspondent of the *New York Times* smuggled out a report that the cruiser *Belfast* had been torpedoed in the Firth of Forth on 21 November 1939. Seven one-line cables were sent from London on a single evening, all unexceptionable, including

'Please tell Harvard I want my son entered.' When the last word of each cable was read in succession, the result was 'Submarines entered Forth, attacked, damaged Belfast, escaped.' As it happened, there were no submarines. *Belfast* had struck a mine and the damage kept her out of service for three years.

The censors might fall foul of the War Office as well as the press. A 1939 story about the British Expeditionary Force arriving in France was authorized at 9 p.m. on 12 September. The War Office had second thoughts and at 11.30 p.m. informed the Ministry of Information that permission was withdrawn. Police were sent to newspaper offices to stop the printing presses, and to railway stations to ensure that papers already there were unloaded from trains. After three hours of chaos – and the realization that the BEF's arrival had already been announced twice on French radio and cabled to New York – the War Office relented.

On 7 July 1943, Winston Churchill countermanded a release of information about the new 'Z-type' rocket-firing anti-aircraft batteries. By this time, late afternoon, the *Daily Mirror* had already printed its Scottish and Irish editions. To reprint them would mean missing the trains. The Air Ministry was called in by Pirie Thomson and a new edition for 8 July was flown to its destinations from an RAF station.

The Press and Censorship Bureau remained under the Ministry of Information except for a brief period of independence from October 1939 to May 1940 with Sir Walter Monckton as Director-General. From December 1940 until the end of the war, the director was Admiral Pirie Thomson. He was known affectionately in Fleet Street as 'Uncle'. The Deputy Assistant Director, who decided when an article must be scrutinized, was predictably known as 'DAD'.

The most graphic means of spreading information was on the cinema screen, and more stringent film censorship followed the outbreak of war. All cinemas were closed as an air-raid precaution on 3 September but most were allowed to open again on 9 September. The British Board of Film Censors was no longer the sole censorship. On 30 September, the Air Ministry banned *An Englishman's Home*, passed by the board and due to open at the London Pavilion on 2 October. 'It cannot be publicly exhibited without a modification.'

This film was based on the play by Guy du Maurier, written before the 1914 war and depicting an attempted invasion of Britain. In September 1939, it had been passed by the Ministry of Information, which was to formalize its own Film Censorship Division at the time of Dunkirk. However, the Air Ministry had lent Blenheim and Wellington bombers for the filming, when war was by no means certain. If a print of the film now came into enemy hands, perhaps through a neutral capital, it would enable German intelligence officers to study the design and performance of Britain's latest bombers at leisure. It was not unreasonable to demand that scenes in which they appeared should be cut.

A month later there was a similar difficulty over an Alexander Korda film, *The Lion Has Wings*, starring Ralph Richardson and Merle Oberon. It included footage of the departure and return of planes involved in a make-believe raid on the docks and canal at Kiel. However, after the film was viewed by service chiefs the ban proved to be temporary. In less than a fortnight it was being screened again at the Leicester Square Theatre.

The censorship worked because film-makers and exhibitors, the press and its editors, were cooperative and patriotic. On 23 January 1940 Arnold Maplesden, on behalf of the *Evening Standard*, saluted the official press censor as 'the editor's friend and not his enemy', the man who could shield him from legal proceedings. The ultimate safeguard against an abuse of censorship lay in the hands of 'an incorruptible British judge' and a jury, 'with all the traditions of liberty since Magna Carta residing in their hands'.

3

If the wartime censorship of information was uncontentious, the suppression of opinions which the government believed might hearten the enemy or endanger the confidence of the people in their leaders was another matter. On 2 May 1940, eight days before Hitler's attack on Western Europe, the Home Secretary, Sir John Anderson, was asked if he would censor subversive publications and organizations, specifically those who might damage the Allied cause by writing 'in terms approximating to Nazi hatred and mendacity'. He replied that action against immoderate or inaccurate language 'would involve a very extreme interference with the liberty of the press'. He would only consider it 'in serious cases of propaganda deliberately designed to impede the national war effort'.

The written or spoken word was at its most repulsive when broadcast by a traitor from enemy territory to the people he had betrayed. Yet censorship of enemy material was not absolute. The full translated text of Hitler's *Mein Kampf* had been published by Hurst & Blackett in March 1939 with provision for royalties to be paid to the German propaganda bureau in Berlin. The outbreak of war had not led to the book being banned.

The Oxford and Cambridge Schools Examination Board had set *Das*

Neue Deutschland, or *The New Germany*, as general reading for eighteen-year-old pupils sitting papers for their Higher School Certificate in German, later to be replaced by A-level. Not until 3 July 1941 did this come to the attention of MPs. They were informed that the book contained a photograph of Hitler 'and described his genius in great detail and in emphatic terms, and elaborated the drawbacks of democracy'. Moreover, 'much of the information in the book was supplied by the Junkers aircraft firm', whose planes were currently bombing British cities, and by other armament manufacturers in Germany.

A fortnight to the day after this, Geoffrey Mander, Liberal member for Wolverhampton who had discovered the use of *Das Neue Deutschland*, unearthed a second outrage. A different examination board had set a German propaganda text for its Higher Certificate candidates. *Adolf Hitler*, published under the Nazi regime in 1935, was prescribed as background reading for the history of modern Germany. The parliamentary Secretary to the Board of Education, Chuter Ede, explained that he was 'no German scholar' but was 'taking steps to have it read to me'. In the end common sense prevailed with an acceptance that the history of contemporary Germany could hardly be understood without some grasp of the appeal of Hitler for his countrymen. The Liberal *Manchester Guardian* even thought it healthy to include a regular column of news as reported in the German press.

For most people propaganda was synonymous with radio. As early as 21 October 1939, France had indicted her first citizen who had broadcast for the Germans. However, Paul Ferdonnet, whose programme went out from Stuttgart, could only be tried in his absence. He was already known in the British press as the French 'Lord Haw-Haw'. Though William Joyce had not yet been identified as the most frequent voice to broadcast from Berlin to Britain, the famous nickname had established his reputation. This war was also the first in which captured servicemen might be induced to spread enemy propaganda from radio stations. All ranks of the British Expeditionary Force in France and the RAF were warned on 26 March 1940 that, if captured, they must not agree to broadcast any material in any form whatever.

During the winter of the 1939–40 phoney war, William Joyce's principal contact in London was Anna Wolkoff, a Russian émigrée whose father had been naval attaché at the Imperial Russian Embassy before the Communist revolution of 1917 and whose family subsequently managed the Russian Tea Rooms in Kensington. She and Joyce had been members of the Right Club, founded before the war by the member of Parliament for Peebles, Captain Archibald Ramsay, interned after Dunkirk as a security risk under Section 18B of the Defence Regulations.

Such zealots were active during the first wartime winter. However, MI5 had its agents in the Right Club from the start. Early in 1940 Anna Wolkoff was in touch with neutral embassies sympathetic to Germany and her messages to Joyce in Berlin went through the Roumanian Embassy. They were carried to the embassy by a female courier, a fellow member of the Right Club who had, unknown to Miss Wolkoff, been planted there some years before by MI5.

On 10 April 1940, an envelope addressed to Herr W. B. Joyce at the Rundfunkhaus, Berlin, was opened by MI5 officers on its way to the Roumanian Embassy. The message was read and allowed to pass. It advised Joyce of the effect in England of his broadcasts from Germany, suggesting how best to engage his audience. He should avoid praising the IRA or attacking the King. 'Churchill not popular – keep on at him as Baruch tool and war-theatre extender, sacrificer Gallipoli etc. Stress his repeated failures with expense, lives and prestige . . . Butter ration doubled because poor can't buy . . . bacon same. Cost living steeply mounting. Shopkeepers suffering. Acknowledge this by Carlyle reference radio. Reply same channel, same cypher.' A few days later, over the airwaves from Berlin, Joyce remarked, 'We thank the French for nothing. Where is their Shakespeare? Where is their Carlyle?'

Anna Wolkoff also passed to Berlin the contents of messages between Churchill and Roosevelt, stolen by a cipher clerk at the United States Embassy in London, Tyler Kent. She went to prison for ten years and he for seven. Among other activities, under cover of the blackout, she and her supporters advertised their views by adhesive messages, and used greasepaint to deface directions to ARP centres, medical posts or shelters. There was also a Right Club 'sticky-back' campaign. Sticky-backs with pro-Hitler slogans were pasted on Belisha beacons at pedestrian crossings, lamp-posts, phone kiosks, hoardings, or bus stops – but not on walls because the glue was not strong enough to adhere to rough surfaces.

The messages were predictable. 'This is a Jews' war . . . Lend to defend the rights of British manhood to die in a foreign war every twenty-five years . . . Don't be selfish. Save for shells and slaughter . . . Just remember your savings are much more wisely spent in the noble cause of death and destruction. Come on the first million pounds.'[4]

Ironically, those closest to hand in the dark were not the police or MI5 but Communists, slapping their own anti-war propaganda on retentive surfaces. These pro-Soviet messages might be few but they alarmed

London Transport which, early in 1941, banned the distribution of all leaflets at tube shelters, for fear of 'the passing on of subversive propaganda'. It was no secret that the Communist Party of Great Britain leafleted shelterers from the blitz and endeavoured to get its own members appointed as shelter marshals.

4

Sooner or later, there were bound to be confrontations between the government and Fleet Street. In the nineteenth and twentieth centuries, there had been wartime prosecutions but nothing equivalent to closing down a major newspaper. Even in 1915, the *Globe* was suspended for only a fortnight after its mischievous announcement that Lord Kitchener had resigned as Secretary for War.

In 1939–40, the government faced Fascist denunciations. After Dunkirk, it was challenged more effectively by Communist agitation, until the German invasion of the Soviet Union in June 1941. Until then, both the *Daily Worker* and the *Week* remained loyal to the principles of the German-Soviet pact formed in August 1939. From this viewpoint Britain and France, as both the *Daily Worker* and William Joyce would have agreed, represented capitalism and plutocracy against the peoples of the world. J. B. S. Haldane was chairman of the newspaper's editorial board and Sean O'Casey one of its members.

A few newspapers were prosecuted for publishing items which the Ministry of Information deemed of possible use to the enemy. The rap across the knuckles was scarcely severe, little more than bureaucratic muscle-flexing. For example, under the Defence Regulations the Sunday paper *Reynolds News* was fined £15 at Bow Street on 11 December 1940, for including facts which, as the prosecution had admitted on 14 November, might have been 'useful to an enemy' but had already been passed for inclusion on a previous occasion. It was conceded the case was 'not serious'. In truth, it was a waste of the court's time.

Under Regulation 2D of the Defence General Regulations 1939, the government was empowered not merely to prosecute but to suppress without legal proceedings any newspaper which it deemed guilty of 'systematic publication of matter calculated to foment opposition to the prosecution of the war to a successful issue'. In July 1940 the *Daily Worker* was warned that its editorial policy was in breach of this. The warning had little effect.

The moment of decision came in January 1941, when the British Communist party sponsored in London a 'People's Convention', whose

2,000 delegates demanded a 'People's Government' and a 'People's Peace' with Germany. On 1 January 1941, the *Daily Worker* celebrated the new year by proclaiming that 'The legend of an anti-Fascist war is dying.' As Douglas Hyde, the circulation manager, had put it when arrested after Dunkirk, British soldiers were not defending democracy so much as defending the profits of the bosses in armaments and other industries.[5]

The last straw for the Churchill cabinet was the *Daily Worker* of 20 January 1941, praising both the People's Convention and a Communist Congress in London. Of the Communists it wrote, 'They proclaimed their solidarity with the rest of the world's workers, whether in Berlin, Turin, Paris, or Shanghai. All were equal victims of the capitalist system.' As plainly as William Joyce, the *Worker's* message appeared to be, 'Lay down your arms. Resistance is useless.' In a further insult, this issue of the paper included a cartoon, 'Their Gallant Allies', ridiculing the present allies of the British government. They included the Free French and the Polish leader General Sikorski, who appeared with a banner reading, 'War on the USSR – Peace with Italy'.

Next day, as the Home Office announced that the paper had been suspended under Defence Regulation 2D, officers of Scotland Yard's Special Branch raided its premises. Seized in the raids was the Communist magazine, the *Week*, a cyclostyled production edited by Claud Cockburn, whose last issue appeared on 15 January. The *Week* had drawn a parallel between Ernest Bevin as Minister of Labour and Dr Ley of the German Labour Front, his opposite Nazi number in Berlin. 'The German government – like the British government – has of course been making the most strenuous efforts to prevent the rise of working-class earnings.' Such comparisons were not what the government wanted to hear, certainly not what it wanted the population to read. Far worse, the article went on to discuss the forms of agitation used by workers in Germany, in the hope that their British counterparts might copy them.

Yet, as so often, censorship did not work as the censors imagined it would. Until the surreptitious use of a printing press could be arranged, 'underground' issues of the paper took the form of cyclostyled sheets printed off in a private house. They were carried through the night in large bundles, often as the bombs fell, by tram and bus to their secret distribution points. Workers, housewives and sympathetic journalists in Fleet Street helped the enterprise. In order that its best stories should be widely read, the *Daily Worker* gave them to interested reporters on other papers.

The ban on the *Daily Worker* ended more than a year after the Soviet Union became Britain's ally. Meantime, protests grew in number and strength. Members of Parliament, including the former prime minister and veteran Liberal leader, David Lloyd George, and the Labour Party Conference in May 1942 demanded that the ban should be lifted. Lloyd George described it as 'an act of stupid and wanton partisan spite', which compromised the Anglo-Russian partnership.[6]

January 1941 was also the month that saw an escalation of hostilities between the government and the *Daily Mirror*, the most successful populist paper of the day which now had a masthead slogan of 'Forward With The People'. The dispute began on 1 January, when William O'Connor, writing as the columnist 'Cassandra', copied a paragraph from *Life* magazine. According to this, Churchill had returned a long-winded memorandum to Anthony Eden with the note, 'As far as I can see, you have used every cliché except "God is Love" and "Please adjust your dress before leaving".'

Though the rebuke had a Churchillian ring, the personal private secretary to the Prime Minister wrote to the paper's owner, Cecil King, on 23 January enclosing two cuttings to which Churchill had taken exception. The first concerned the rebuke to Eden, which Churchill denied; the second was an editorial by Cassandra. This described a reshuffle of the cabinet which ended with the same old faces in different jobs. 'Keep it in the family!' wrote Cassandra. 'Scratch my back and I'll scratch yours! Talk about musical chairs! The trouble is that this particular game is being played to a funeral march. Ours.'

King sent a conciliatory reply but a further letter from Churchill on 25 January accused the *Daily Mirror* and its sister paper the *Sunday Pictorial* of acting like a Fifth Column by opening the way to defeatism and demands for a negotiated peace. This was plainly not the papers' intention. It was the *Mirror* which had celebrated the successful 'little ships' rescue of 334,000 troops from the beaches of Dunkirk with the banner headline, 'BLOODY MARVELLOUS!' It was the most widely read newspaper among servicemen and in the course of the war its circulation more than tripled to 3,000,000. As a daily enticement it featured the strip-cartoon heroine Jane, who compensated for military setbacks by stripping closer to total nudity as the news got worse. It was many times more effective as the voice of the ordinary soldier or factory hand than the *Daily Worker* could ever hope to be.

Churchill was not the *Mirror*'s prime target. 'Churchill *is* wartime England,' wrote King in his diary. However, its patience was not endless and certainly did not extend to the lesser members of the cabinet. When Singapore fell to the Japanese on 15 February 1942, the *Mirror* demanded 'Who Is To Blame?' suggesting that it was now time to ask not whether the country had the right government but whether it had the right leader.

The final collision between the paper and the cabinet came on 6 March 1942. The Ministry of Fuel had authorized a one-penny rise in the price of a gallon of petrol. The *Mirror*'s cartoonist, Philip Zec, drew a page-wide dramatic seascape, in which a lone sailor lay face down and dying on a life-raft in a stormy but empty ocean, a survivor of one of many oil-tankers sunk by U-boats. The picture was strongly drawn and unexceptionable but the caption was explosive. '"The price of petrol has been increased by one penny." – Official.'

Nor was that all. Herbert Morrison, Home Secretary, pointed out a leading article in the same issue, which he read to the House of Commons. Its subject was Britain's military leadership. 'The accepted tip for Army leadership would, in plain truth, be this: All who aspire to mislead others in war should be brass-buttoned boneheads, socially prejudiced, arrogant and fussy. A tendency to heart disease, apoplexy, diabetes and high blood-pressure is desirable in the highest places.' It was not hard to imagine the satisfaction or the amusement which this piece had given to the other ranks of His Majesty's forces.

The *Mirror* explained that the innocent purpose of the cartoon was to warn its readers not to waste petrol. The government, through Morrison, insisted that it was an attack on the petrol combines for profiteering and on the government for allowing them to do so. As Morrison told the Commons on 19 March, 'The cartoon is only one example, but a particularly evil one, of the policy and methods of a newspaper which, intent on exploiting an appetite for sensation and with a reckless indifference to the national interest and to the prejudicial effect on the war effort, has repeatedly published scurrilous misrepresentations, distorted and exaggerated statements and irresponsible generalizations.' He promised that action would be taken under Regulation 2D, enabling the government to close down the paper if it chose, but agreed that at this stage a warning of closure might be sufficient.

That warning had already been given just before the debate, when Morrison summoned to the Home Office the editor of the *Mirror*, Cecil Thomas, and the Vice-Chairman of the company, Harry Bartholomew. With a long experience of Labour politics behind him, the Home Secretary was a formidable adversary. To his officials and his visitors he denounced the cartoon as 'worthy of Goebbels at his best' and recalled that he had closed one national newspaper, the *Daily Worker*, the year before. 'If you are closed, it will be for a long time. We shall act with a speed that will surprise you.'[7]

There were enough reservations in Parliament over this threat to press freedom for a full debate to follow. Meantime, the *Mirror* took up cudgels against Morrison, reminding him publicly that as a Labour politician he had been a contributor to its columns and had benefited from its support. This was a newspaper which had stood against the appeasement of Hitler at Munich in 1938, when others caved in, and had celebrated the miracle of Dunkirk in more vigorous language than its rivals. Moreover, Morrison had misled the House of Commons in his quotation from the 'brass-hats' article. This had actually welcomed an Army Council initiative to instil 'physical fitness and mental alertness' among higher ranks. As for the Zec cartoon, both sides had now had their say.

The debate in the Commons was not particularly instructive. In the House of Lords the Lord Chancellor, Lord Simon, quoted Milton's *Areopagitica* on the freedom of the press, while remarking of Cassandra that the same person in Greek tragedy 'came to a sticky end'. In the Commons, speakers who believed in freedom of the press added that, of course, it could not be unbounded. Others who distanced themselves from the *Daily Mirror* none the less believed in press freedom. From the Labour benches, Fred Bellenger quoted at length an article which was fully as deserving of suppression as anything in the *Mirror*, a deliberate subversion of the war effort. Its conclusion alone was proof of that.

> Go forth, little soldier. Though you know not what you fight for – go forth. Though you have no grievance against your German brother – go forth and kill him. Though you may know he has a wife and family dependent upon him – go forth and slay him; he is only a German dog. Will he now kill you if he gets the chance? Of course he will.
> He is being told the same story!
> His King and Country need him.

The article might well have applied to the present war but had been written to debunk Kitchener's 1915 recruiting poster, 'Your King and Country Need You!' Bellenger pointed out that, embarrassing though it might be, the author of the article was sitting in his place during the current debate. He was, of course, the same Herbert Morrison who had just threatened to close down the *Daily Mirror* but who, as a pacifist, had actively opposed the earlier war.

Morrison remained a target in the press and at public meetings. On 29 March 1942, the National Council for Civil Liberties demanded an outright repeal of Regulation 2D. On 11 April 1942, a public meeting called by the council condemned the continued suppression of the *Daily Worker*, nine months after Britain had become an ally of the Soviet Union.

Aneurin Bevan announced that he had 'never met a less judicially minded man than Morrison'.

The meeting also condemned the way in which a famous and free-spirited tabloid, *Picture Post*, had been punished by withdrawal of a subsidy which had enabled copies to go to servicemen in the Middle East. The NCCL then attacked British censorship of news in Palestine, and censorship of cables which carried journalists' opinions. On the same day, a former Labour MP, W. J. Brown, announced his candidature in the Rugby by-election as an Independent, standing on a platform of press freedom and with a commitment to reversing the decisions in the cases of the *Daily Mirror* and the *Daily Worker*.

Even as the threat to the *Mirror* receded and the *Worker* was allowed to reappear, there was a further form of subversion, involving politics of a different colour. Britain's alliance with the Soviet Union was, for many people, a matter of convenience at best. The Ribbentrop–Molotov pact of August 1939 and the material aid given by Germany to Russia until June 1941 were cited as evidence of Stalin's treachery. The dictator's crimes against Poles and Catholics might seem comparable to those of Hitler. With such opinions in the air, it could only be a question of time before the nation's Eastern ally came under attack from sections of the press.

In the House of Commons on 16 June 1942, the *Review of World Affairs* was accused of having cast doubt on the loyalty and the effectiveness of Russia in an article included in its issue of 1 June. Osbert Peake, Under-Secretary at the Foreign Office, insisted that a ban on such opinions would be an unwarrantable interference with freedom of expression in political matters.

By the autumn a far more influential paper was singled out for criticism. Once again, Herbert Morrison was asked to deal with the matter. On 8 October, the Labour MP Tom Driberg cited an article in the *Catholic Herald* for 25 September, 'Stalingrad – and After'. The occasion had been the visit of the Soviet Foreign Minister, Vyacheslav Mikhailovich Molotov, to London to sign a twenty-year treaty of Anglo-Soviet alliance. Despite the valiant defence of Stalingrad, the reputation of the Soviet Union was for many people that of Molotov and his kind. He appeared the spokesman for an uncompromising and bloodthirsty tyranny, cynical enough to have signed a similar treaty with Nazi Germany three years earlier.

Molotov had espoused the policy of exporting revolution and became the man whom Nikita Khrushchev later described as 'a saboteur of peace'. None the less, Driberg wanted 'to discourage further publication of such defeatist propaganda' as the *Catholic Herald* had disseminated. He demanded action against the paper in the form of a warning under Defence Regulation 2D. As in the case of the *Daily Mirror*, this would serve notice on the national newspaper of British Catholics that it faced closure for any further error of judgment.

Morrison's position was unenviable. He appeared to have the choice either of offending Catholics to whom the Soviet Union was an atheist tyranny or of alienating a swathe of left-wing opinion, some of it pro-Soviet and much of it optimistic about future 'changes for the better' in that tyrannical regime. He walked the tightrope as gracefully as he could. 'While a large body of opinion will share the view as to the objectionable nature of these references to an Ally, I feel sure that the majority of people will support the view of the Government that the special powers vested in the executive in wartime should not be used to suppress expression of opinion which, however objectionable, is not calculated to have any appreciable effect on the war effort.'

A good many people – non-Catholics among them – failed to see anything objectionable in such home truths. By the following year the battleground had changed but not fundamentally. On one side it was occupied by attacks from the reopened *Daily Worker* on the non-Communist Polish government in exile in London. On the other it consisted of denunciations of the Soviet Union by the Polish-language press in England, which served those Poles who had escaped the fall of their country to fight Germany from the West.

Stirring up discord was now a sufficient reason for censoring cables sent by foreign journalists. In March 1942, a new Minister of Information, Brendan Bracken, told the House of Commons that in future censorship would not be restricted to information that might help the enemy. It would prohibit any despatches 'calculated to create ill-feeling between the United Nations or between them and a neutral country'. Polish demands in London for a Red Cross inquiry into the newly discovered graves of 4,000 Polish officers murdered by the Russians at Katyn in 1940 were of just this nature.

On 20 May 1943 Brendan Bracken also promised to look into the 'activities of some newspapers'. In June he issued a warning to the London-based Polish press of the 'consequences of failing to observe proper restraint' in their comments on Soviet policy. On a number of occasions in the following six months, the chief offender, the editor of *Wiadomoski Polski – Polish News*, was warned that his remarks were 'calculated to stir up discord among the United Nations'.

This was a curious offence which had no specific regard to whether comments were true or false. In February 1944, Bracken closed the paper by the simple means of refusing it any further allocation of paper. There were strong protests in the House of Commons on 17 February and a protest from the Polish Union of Journalists in London, which pointed out that 'the existence of the Polish press in Great Britain is one of the principal means by which the Polish nation defends her rights and ideals against totalitarianism.'

That was certainly true but unanimity among wartime allies once again took precedence over the truth. Unanimity counted for little in July 1944, however, when the Russians recognized the Lublin Committee of Polish Liberation in Moscow as the authority for a liberated Poland and ignored those who had escaped from their country to fight on in the West against their Fascist and Communist oppressors. There was nothing the Western Allies could do.

5

Apart from government regulation of the press, action against publications thought to be defamatory to a political or public figure created major wartime scandal. Some had profound significance for the conduct of the war. Between its two encounters with Herbert Morrison, the *Daily Mirror* was involved in a drama of this kind.

As the German armies attacked neutral Holland and Belgium on 10 May 1940, Admiral Sir Roger Keyes flew to Brussels to act as special liaison officer to King Leopold III, on behalf of the British government. Keyes had been a national hero of the First World War, commander of the Dover Patrol and leader of the famous Zeebrugge Raid on St George's Day 1918. This naval assault on the German-held port had sunk blockships in the Bruges canal and landed a force of Royal Marines on the harbour mole with explosive charges to put the entire installation out of action for the rest of the war. In the course of the night, eight of the attackers won the Victoria Cross.

Twenty-two years later, in May 1940 and after more than two weeks of fighting, British troops who had entered Belgium were in danger of losing contact with the main formation of the French army. They were ordered to fight their way south-west. Unless the Belgians could move as well, there was bound to be a breach between the two armies. Leopold asked Sir Roger to inform the British government and Lord Gort, commander of the British Expeditionary Force, that the Belgian army had neither tanks nor planes to support it. It was merely a defence force and could not hold out against Panzer tank divisions and Stuka dive-bombers. The King did not feel it right for the British to jeopardize the existence of their army by maintaining contact with Belgian troops. However, if the Germans drove a wedge between the allies, Belgium would have no alternative but to ask Germany for an armistice.

As the situation deteriorated, the Belgians assisted a French and British withdrawal to more strongly fortified positions. In consequence, the Germans drove the anticipated wedge between Belgians and British. By 27 May, the small area of Belgium still in Leopold's hands was crowded with refugees who were being machine-gunned systematically by low-flying German planes. Keyes had remained with the King. At 5 p.m. on 27 May, Leopold warned him that he must ask the Germans for an armistice from midnight.

In London next day, Keyes reported on the situation. The news that Belgium had surrendered was not well received. Queen Wilhelmina of the Netherlands and her government had withdrawn to England to continue the war from exile. By now, moreover, the BEF was seen to be fighting for its life. As a matter of fair-mindedness, Keyes asked the nation to suspend judgment on Leopold, whom he described as 'a very gallant soldier', until the facts were known.

The *Daily Mirror* passed judgment two days later. It described Leopold III as 'a skunk' and the 'Rat King'. As for Sir Roger Keyes, hero of Zeebrugge and the Dover Patrol, 'What were you up to in Brussels?' Demanding to know whether he had lost his sense of smell as well as his guts, bootscraping and bowing in the Rat King's palace, the paper informed him that until he took back such descriptions of Leopold as 'gallant soldier', it would revise its view of his own previous gallantry and suspend judgment on him.

The attack was indefensible, nor did the *Mirror's* prospects improve when Keyes' son received a posthumous VC for a daring attack on Rommel's North African headquarters. The paper pleaded fair comment. Yet as blitzkrieg, particularly massacres of refugees by aerial attack, became more familiar, this sounded unconvincing. In court, there was no defence but to admit that 'the dignified and fair-minded attitude of Sir Roger Keyes had been abundantly justified and the Daily Mirror tendered to him a sincere apology.'[8]

A second libel case of the year was brought against the *New York Times*, by Captain A. H. Ramsay, the member of Parliament for Peebles who was interned in May 1940 under the Defence Regulations. In August that year, the paper called him a Fifth Columnist, pro-Hitler and a traitor. It was not likely that his action would succeed. He admitted his Fascist sympathies; he had been a founder of the pre-war Right Club, whose members included William Joyce, Anna Wolkoff, now serving ten years for passing information to Joyce in Berlin, and Tyler Kent of the US Embassy who had stolen telegrams exchanged by Churchill and Roosevelt. When Captain Ramsay was asked whether he knew that Kent was betraying the trust of his employers at the American Embassy, he could only reply, 'I did not look at it in that light.'

Nor was the case dependent upon guilt by association. When Special Branch officers raided Captain Ramsay's house at the time of his arrest, they found a supply of the posters and sticky-backs which had been appearing on the walls of London, including an 'Alphabet'.

> A stands for the Army, conscripted for France,
> that, even when it got there, couldn't advance.
> B for Belisha, who waved it good-bye, with a smile
> on his face as the lads went to die . . .
> G for the Germans . . .
> H for Hitler, their saviour and guide, who broke
> down Versailles and restored them their pride . . .
> T for the 'Traitors' all working for peace,
> Mosley, Lord Tavistock, Ramsay and Leese . . .

There was even a hymn, which Captain Ramsay and his followers in 1940 left on London buses and trams, or anywhere from which copies might be picked up by the susceptible. It was sung to the tune of 'Land of Hope and Glory'.

> Poorer still and poorer grow thy true-born sons,
> Faster still and faster, they're sent to feed the guns . . .

As a technicality, Ramsay won his case for he had been called a traitor without ever being convicted of treason. The judge confessed he did not know what being a Fifth Columnist meant. However, Ramsay's reward was a farthing damages and a bill for the defendant's costs as well as his own. In summing up, Mr Justice Atkinson said, 'Captain Ramsay has also expressed a belief that the war is a Jewish "ramp". I do not believe that any man outside a lunatic asylum could persuade himself of that. I am convinced Hitler would call Captain Ramsay a friend. He is disloyal in heart and soul to our King and our government and our people – a people fighting and dying, not for appeasement or the preservation of Nazism, but for victory and the destruction of Nazism.' This case, in most respects, was the last stand of pre-war Fascism.[9]

Among civil actions in 1942 was a libel suit brought by the Duke of Hamilton in the High Court on 18 February. The defendants were two leading members of the Communist party, Harry Pollitt and Ted Bramley, as well as the publishers of their pamphlet, *World News and Views*, and the author, Ivor Montagu. On 10 May 1941, the Duke was a serving officer of the RAF on duty in the operations room of a radar site near Glasgow. An enemy plane was picked up over the North Sea and later crashed in flames south of Glasgow. The Duke was woken at about 2 a.m. and told that the plane had been a Messerschmitt 110 fighter and that the pilot, who had baled out, had been captured. He had given his name as Alfred Horn and insisted that he must see the Duke of Hamilton, whom he knew personally.

When they met, the Duke knew he had never seen the prisoner before. Once they were alone the man said in English, 'I do not know if you recognize me, but I am Rudolf Hess.' Though the Duke had attended the Berlin Olympics in 1936, he had never met Hitler's deputy. After reporting the conversation to Churchill in London, the Duke was present at a conversation in German between Hess and a Foreign Office official who identified him. He never saw Hess again.

On the basis that Hess was a long-standing friend trying to negotiate a peace with Britain, so that the two countries might unite against the Soviet Union, the Communist *World News and Views* denounced the Duke as an admirer of the prisoner, who approved the part Hess had taken 'in persecuting, torturing and murdering members of the working class'. It added that the Duke remained sympathetic to countries with whom Britain was now at war. He and his friends aimed to 'smash the working-classes and destroy democratic rights' and 'ought to be thrown into prison'.

There was not a word of truth in this. The defendants pleaded that they had drawn their impressions from the Ministry of Information and the BBC, the latter having said that the Duke had known Hess and had continued to correspond with him after the outbreak of war. They gave an unreserved apology and the action was withdrawn.

The downfall of *World News and Views* followed a similar case on 6 May 1940 when Sir Walter Citrine, General Secretary of the Trades Union Congress, and six members of the General Council recovered damages against the *Daily Worker* – not yet banned – which, in its issue of 13 December 1939, had accused them all of criminal dishonesty without, as the judge put it, a scintilla of evidence. At this time, Communists and non-Communists were rivals for leadership of the trade union movement.

The most remarkable aspect of the case, almost a plea on behalf of the generally despised views of the *Daily Worker*, was a passage from Mr Justice Stable's judgment. Because it was delivered in a time of war and emergency, when the very existence or survival of the nation was uncertain, it deserves to stand with John Stuart Mill or John Milton. Sir Wintringham Stable reiterated the principles of free speech and stressed the particular importance of the law in protecting 'those views which are held only by a few, which are unpopular and which run counter to the views of the great majority of mankind, particularly in time of emotional national crisis such as wars'. It was these views that 'the Court should be particularly jealous to protect'.

6

In the lives of ordinary people, failing to talk optimistically about the nation's prospects was sometimes enough in itself to constitute an offence. On 25 July 1940, it was revealed in Parliament that there had so far been almost a hundred cases of penalties for 'silly talk'.

Before the fall of France in June 1940, it was felt better that Fascists should remain where they could be seen and heard. On 6 November 1939, for example, Mrs Margaret Griggs, Chairman of the Women's Organization of the BUF, was merely bound over for twelve months after speaking in Limehouse from behind the safety of a police cordon. 'If ever a country wants a revolution now it is Great Britain,' she shouted, while the East End crowd jeered her with cries of 'Dirty spies!', 'Dirty Germans!' and 'Go home to Hitler!'[10]

In a similar case, two girls of sixteen and seventeen, arrested while selling the Fascist paper *Action* in Shoreditch High Street on 4 January 1940, were charged with using insulting words. They too had been rescued by the police from 'a crowd of hostile men'. Though the younger girl shouted 'Hail Mosley!' at the magistrate and gave the Fascist salute, they were merely bound over for two years and released on the unenforceable condition that they ceased selling the paper.[11]

Fascists were not the only targets of such prosecutions and before long pacifists also found themselves in court. At Marlborough Street on 4 March 1940, for example, it was those who had tried to sell *Peace News* on the pavement at Marble Arch who faced police charges of obstruction. They were not deterred and appeared before the court again on 6 May, having once more been selling *Peace News* on the pavement. The magistrate, Sir Gervase Rentoul, fined them only five shillings each. 'I suppose there is no other country in Europe where five men selling literature of this kind would merely have to answer a charge of obstruction.' That, at least, seemed true. When, on 5 September 1941, the Deputy Chief Constable of Leicester stopped the street sale of pacifist leaflets by delegates to a Jehovah's Witnesses' conference, this was rare enough to be newsworthy and, in any case, followed a street demonstration against the sellers. There was no question of banning the sale on private premises.

For Fascist publications, there was no future under the Emergency Powers (Defence) Act. This was passed on 22 May 1940, as British troops evacuated Arras and the 1st and 2nd Armoured Divisions of the Wehrmacht came within striking distance of Calais and Boulogne. Next day, Special Branch and CID officers raided the headquarters of the BUF in Smith Street, Westminster. Seven officials were arrested and vanloads of documents were taken away.

Those arrested and interned without trial included Sir Oswald and Lady Mosley, and Captain Archibald Ramsay. During the following week-end, as Boulogne and Calais fell and the Dunkirk evacuation began, the CID began to round up Fascist and Communist open-air activists. A man selling *Action* in Croydon town centre on Saturday was arrested after several people threatened him. A woman snatched the papers, tore them up, and threw them at him. 'When the Germans get here, they will show you how to run Croydon,' he said.

At Ealing, Inspector Carter arrested the speaker Douglas Hyde, circula-tion manager of the *Daily Worker*, and was cheered by the crowd. 'I have never been cheered before when making an arrest,' he said modestly. A Communist speaker at Edgware was rescued from angry servicemen and gaoled for three months. Another, at Hyde Park Corner, was led away among shouts of 'People like you are Quislings!'

As the prospect of victory grew dimmer, sentences became longer. By contrast with the Fascists of 1939–40 Elsie Orrin, a schoolteacher, was severely dealt with. On 25 June 1941, Mr Justice Humphreys sent her to penal servitude for five years for saying to soldiers in a public house, 'Hitler is a good ruler, a better man than Mr Churchill.' She also denounced the Jews, attacked the Churchill government, and criticized the soldiers for not being men enough to 'kick it out'. The soldiers reported her to the police. When they raided her home, they found a portrait of Sir Oswald Mosley. She said, 'I am proud to belong to the British Union.'

Five years was by no means the longest sentence. In April 1943 a twenty-eight-year-old farm labourer from Gloucestershire, a former member of the now defunct British Union of Fascists, was accused of attempting to communicate with a person whom he had 'reasonable cause to believe was assisting the enemy'. As the 'person' was the German Minister in Dublin, it was hard to see how he could believe otherwise. The labourer had been twice interned but released in April 1941 on condition of good behaviour.

In December 1942 he wrote to the Home Secretary that Mussolini's biography had reconverted him to Fascism. Then he wrote his letter to the German Minister in Dublin offering his services, a letter whose address absolutely guaranteed that it would be opened by the postal censorship. He had previously written to the War Ministry in Berlin in 1938 making the same offer to 'place my services and my life at the disposal of the Reich and to eventually earn the honour of becoming a German citizen'.

To complete his postal hat-trick, the defendant added a letter to Winston Churchill. 'I demand that you immediately make way for the one man who is really fit for the position you hold. Oswald Mosley can and will save the British Empire.' He might as well have named Adolf Hitler. For this bizarre round of correspondence, the young man was sentenced to penal servitude for life. His appeal against sentence was dismissed.[12]

For spreading 'alarm and despondency', under the Defence Regulations in force since June 1940, offenders were liable to imprisonment and a fine of £50, or £2,000 in modern terms. Careless talkers were also subject to prosecution or reprimand. In February 1940, Ealing Studios were commissioned to make short 'anti-gossip' films, starring John Mills and other famous faces, under such titles as *Miss Nobody Spoke in a Café*. In April 1941, a government scientist, Dr Richard Beatty, was so efficiently advised about his careless talking by a sergeant of the Special Branch that he was found dead the next day.

Careless talk combined easily with 'despondency'. In May 1943 Edward Ryan, inventor of anti-submarine devices used by the Admiralty, was sent to prison for a month. He had told other fire-watchers in Liverpool of his uncensored letters to the British Embassy in Madrid, revealing that the last five convoys from Liverpool had lost two hundred ships between them. To this he added, 'The last shots in this war will be fired in 1949. Germany will form a government similar to Russia and the two of them will overrun this country.' The statement was said to have caused great distress to those who heard it.[13]

Some offenders had no political allegiance. Mrs Dorothy Rycraft of Wood Green was accused in April 1941 of 'deliberately and persistently publishing statements with the object of stirring up trouble and causing despondency and alarm among women'. She had said to a Wood Green housewives' club, 'We will never win the war. We are going to be invaded. If the women meet a poor German they're not going to be hard on him. We are going to starve, not the Germans.' She added that food rations were insufficient and 'the poorer classes are going short while people with money can get what they want'. That was a general belief. She urged the club to march on the town hall and demand better rations. She then incited further 'discontent', by asking why the government had not built deep shelters to protect the general population from air attacks.[14]

Truth or falsehood was not an issue. There was ample evidence of inequality of sacrifice between rich and poor. The belief that Britain was not going to win the war was widespread across the world. The successes of U-boat packs threatened starvation. That month, the Germans occupied Yugoslavia. The British army evacuated the Greek mainland to avoid 'another Dunkirk'. On the day Mrs Rycraft was fined £50, Rommel seized the Halfaya Pass and opened a way to Egypt. Yet such talk was resented and fists flew. A Londoner that month heard defeatism spoken behind him. He turned round and punched the culprit to the ground, only to find that he had hit the wrong man. He was fined ten shillings and ordered to pay £5 compensation.[15]

The law against spreading despondency applied equally to neutrals. On 20 November 1941 an American citizen once married to a German, Elizabeth Marion Hayward, went into a Brighton store. There she was guilty of 'publishing to Grace Richardson and Reginald Chapple a statement relating to matters . . . likely to cause despondency'. In conversation with a shop assistant, she said, 'We do not get true news in the newspapers because journalists are all crooks, whereas in Germany the press is under the control of one person, and the German press is always true. You always get true news from the German wireless.' She believed Germany would win and that Russia was finished; the German army could enter Moscow when it chose. The manager joined the discussion and she told him, 'You should listen to Lord Haw-Haw.'

When arrested, Mrs Hayward said, 'I am very sorry I allowed myself to be drawn into this little discussion with my friend here. Everybody talked about the war a little, but perhaps I talked a little more. Americans are apt to give their opinion more freely than English people. They consider themselves free, free country, free speech, and of course one forgets there's a war on.' Brighton Borough Bench fined her £25. The facts of her case were placed before the Regional Commissioner with a view to having her interned.

On 23 March 1942, by which time America had entered the war, she was in court again at Hove. Restrictions had been put on her movements but on 21 February she had got into conversation with an army officer in a café. She told him it was Britain's fault the country was at war. Then she expressed admiration for Hitler and his regime, adding that Germany would defeat Russia in the spring and then invade England, which would have little chance of survival. She was fined £50 with a month's hard labour.

There was continuing disaffection among those who, as late as 1943, still advocated a negotiated peace. The Communists, who had wanted a negotiated peace in 1940–41, now wanted to extend the war in Europe in order to take pressure off the Soviet Union. That could only be done by a full-scale invasion of France. 'Second front now!' said the graffiti simply.

For the disaffected, Churchill and his government were fair game. A middle-aged civil servant was fined in June 1943 after chalking graffiti on the blinds of Southern Railway trains. 'Durable peace can be obtained only by negotiation,' he wrote. 'Ask the King to call an armistice now. W.C.M.G.' – W.C.M.G. was subversive shorthand for 'Winston Churchill Must Go'. By then, however, the great fear of 'despondency' had passed and Oliver Ward was merely fined £2 for defacing the property of the Southern Railway.[16]

By the war's end, the people in general were deeply suspicious of government propaganda and increasingly attached to the notion of free speech. 'Speakers' Corner' at Hyde Park was still cherished as a symbol of freedom, the place where a man with a soapbox could go on a Sunday afternoon and preach to the unconverted that, for example, the world was flat, that the Pope was Antichrist, that Communism or even Fascism alone could save mankind, or demand insinuatingly, as others had demanded for more than a century past, why the bishops still refused to open Joanna Southcott's box and reveal her predictions of the world's fate.

Yet the public was in a fury – or was encouraged to believe so – at the wartime activities of traitors who took free speech to its limit. Their voices came through the whoops and gurgles of the airwaves from Berlin; their writings circulated among prisoners of war. In what might sound like a situation comedy, a group of them had created a British division of Hitler's SS, 'The Legion of St George', with swastika uniforms and Union Jack lapel flashes. It was no comedy when the war ended. For the first time in

Britain since a young printer, John Matthews, was hanged in 1719 for a leaflet favouring the Jacobite pretender to the English throne rather than George I who sat upon it, men like John Amery and William Joyce would die on the gallows of Wandsworth prison solely for the opinions they had expressed.

7

Total War: A Sort of Traitors

I

WITH THE COMING of liberation and victory, there were scores to be settled with authors and broadcasters who had taken the side of the enemy. It was exceptional in a modern democracy for men to be put to death for the opinions they had expressed but these were exceptional times. Sometimes there was unease about the procedures and even sotto voce questions as to the credentials of some of the prosecutors who now demanded the blood of their adversaries. John Dryden, a favourite author of one of those who went to the gallows, had observed three centuries earlier:

> How easy still it proves in fractious times
> With public zeal to cancel private crimes.

If Britain needed an example of post-war justice, a good many liberated territories offered it even before the war was over. The French Communist party, loyal to the German–Soviet pact until the invasion of Russia in 1941, set the pace, conveniently forgetting its own posters of 1940. These had urged French workers to welcome the invading Germans as brothers and to support the new regime of Marshal Pétain. On 17 June 1940, the party newspaper, *Humanité*, gave its support to the military surrender and armistice negotiations with the Third Reich. Its editorial refused to permit 'England with its 40 million people to exploit 400 million'.[1]

The pipers of peace now played another tune. Among those whose lives were sought in liberated France was the novelist Louis-Ferdinand Céline, known internationally as the author of *Voyage au bout de la nuit* (1932). Céline had been a Fascist before the war and so a natural supporter of Pétain's Vichy regime. With the liberation, he fled to Germany in 1944 and then to Denmark. A warrant for his arrest on charges of treason was issued in France on 19 April 1945. In Copenhagen extradition proceedings began. Yet under the liberal Danish constitution and despite the country's wartime sufferings, he could not be extradited for a political crime. He remained in Denmark. When the French at length tried him in his absence in 1949, the demands for blood had abated. Instead of death for his treason, Céline was sentenced to imprisonment, a fine, and the confiscation of all his property. He kept clear until 1954 and then returned to benefit from an amnesty for all Frenchmen who had fought in the First World War.

French journalists who supported the Vichy regime were less fortunate and definitions of treason were sometimes imprecise. The Anglophobe Henri Béraud of the pro-Vichy *Gringoire* was sentenced to death but reprieved, after protests that he had merely denounced de Gaulle and the English. The seventy-seven-year-old Charles Maurras of the monarchist Action Française, on trial in Lyon in 1945, remained unrepentant and attacked his prosecutors as the true traitors to France. As a reprisal, he was sentenced to hard labour for life and held till just before his death at the age of eighty-six.

In January 1945, Robert Brasillach, editor-in-chief of the weekly paper *Je suis partout* since 1938, was condemned to death, along with two assistants; a third assistant was sentenced to hard labour for life. Brasillach, like Béraud, had denounced England and 'Gaullist traitors'. The greater offence was that he had 'glorified Germany and reminded France of her conquered condition'.[2]

Found guilty, Brasillach was taken to the courtyard of Fort de Montrouge, where he was shot by a firing squad, crying, 'Courage! Vive la France!' From 1939 until the surrender of 1940, he had been a soldier. His last words to the government commissioner had the air of a martyr, 'You have done your duty, I have fought for my country.' The government commuted the other two death sentences to imprisonment with hard labour for life. The last was passed on Claude Jeantet. Whatever his opinions about de Gaulle and the English, he had sheltered French Jews from their hunters during the occupation.[3]

More important trials were pending. Marshal Pétain, now eighty-nine, hero of Verdun in 1916 and head of the Vichy state from 1940 to 1944, as well as his prime minister, Pierre Laval, were sentenced to death. Laval was shot but Pétain's sentence was commuted to life imprisonment on the Île d'Yeu. In October 1944 an IFOP poll had asked the people of France whether Pétain should be punished for requesting an armistice from Hitler in 1940 and subsequently acting as leader of the Vichy regime, where 'Work, Family and Nation' replaced 'Liberty, Equality and Fraternity'. In their replies, 58 per cent thought he should not be punished, 10 per cent had no opinion, only 32 per cent disagreed. The respondents were also asked if Pétain deserved the death penalty. Only 3 per cent thought so. However interpreted, the results were a political embarrassment to the new order.

It was a further uncomfortable truth for those who hastily donned the prosecutor's gown that the motion abolishing the Third Republic and conferring supreme power upon Pétain had been passed in the National Assembly on 10 July 1940 by 395 votes to 3 and in the Senate by 229 votes to 1. The legislature included 146 Socialists and 72 Communists.

2

Almost 7,000 men and women had been condemned to death in France. Britain had far less scope for bringing heretics to justice. Yet there was one candidate in 1945 who epitomized an idealized version of the British way of life for most people and who was far more famous than Céline or the French journalists. His name was passed to the Director of Public Prosecutions and the Attorney-General.

Though threatened by the gallows, under the Treachery Act 1940, or penal servitude under the Defence Regulations 1939, he was not a Fascist, let alone a Nazi. Most of his readers would have thought that he had little interest in politicians of any kind, except to treat them with ridicule. He had first been denounced for treason in 1941, as a man who had 'broadcast for the Germans'. By 1944 Malcolm Muggeridge, the intelligence officer who had charge of him in Paris, thought 'Wodehouse might well have fared ill if he had come before a British court at the time.'[4]

It was one of the oddest and most instructive stories of the war. In the spring of 1940, P. G. Wodehouse was fifty-nine. He and his wife, Ethel, lived at their home of Low Wood in the coastal resort of Le Touquet Paris-Plage, some fifteen miles south of Boulogne. They had spent six years in France, most of them at Low Wood. Before that, Wodehouse had lived in America since 1909. In May 1940, there was no apparent reason for British citizens to leave Le Touquet. Like other residents, the Wodehouses had given their names to the British Vice-Consul at Boulogne, asking to be warned if it was thought necessary to leave for England. No warnings were issued. The German army was a long way off, hundreds of miles away on the other side of neutral Holland and Belgium. The nearest Franco-German frontier was further still, protected by the Maginot Line; the front appeared as static as the trenches of more than twenty years before.

The expatriates listened to the BBC, which mingled optimism with the easy patriotism of 'We'll hang out the washing on the Siegfried Line'.

Wodehouse had written to a friend the previous year, calling the Germans 'mugs' to take on the British after the defeat of 1918. He thought Churchill's 1939 broadcasts 'fine', and was reading his works with admiration. Then, on 10 May 1940, blitzkrieg overwhelmed neutral Holland and Belgium, after months on a western front where the armies had often been forbidden to fire upon one another. As German tanks broke through, the radio still spoke of attacks repulsed and lines holding. Yet guests from 85 Squadron RAF who had enjoyed the Wodehouses' hospitality now vanished. On 20 May, the radio admitted that the Germans had taken Amiens and Arras.

Wodehouse had not driven a car since 1906. On 21 May, he left in the larger of their two cars driven by Ethel. This had been involved in a collision a few months earlier and had not been used since its repair. It broke down and they had no option but to return. They set out again in the smaller car, accompanied by a friend's car and a Red Cross van. The Red Cross van broke down. The Wodehouses reached the main road to the Somme and found it jammed by refugees heading south at the mercy of the Luftwaffe. They returned to Low Wood again. German planes were circling the house. Le Touquet was cut off and occupied soon after. Wodehouse recalled that he had been listening to a BBC report of the enemy being thrown back when the first German troops appeared.

For two months the couple remained in the house, though food and tobacco was pillaged, their baths commandeered by the German Labour Corps, and their home briefly requisitioned by a German major. Like all British male civilians, Wodehouse had to report every morning to the Kommandantur at Paris-Plage.

On 27 July, he was given half an hour to pack a suitcase and taken with other British males by bus to the prison at Loos in Belgium. He kept a notebook, describing an elderly German sergeant as 'very decent', while a 'pleasant' young soldier gave them his cigarettes. A number of the Germans whom he was to encounter were bullying or brusque, a few were kind. These were not front-line troops nor diehard Nazis but for the most part older soldiers on barrack duties.

His internment lasted almost a year, first at Loos, then at the citadel of Huy and most of the time in an internment camp at Tost, Upper Silesia, a former lunatic asylum. He received no preferential treatment nor did he encounter particular hostility. A German soldier, leaving for other duties, shook his hand and said, 'Thank you for Jeeves.' The days of bread, watery vegetable soup and a portion of sausage were spartan, as were nights sleeping on the floor at Huy with or without straw. Far worse was anxiety at Ethel's fate and the monotony of prison routine.

Living conditions at Tost resembled a prisoner-of-war camp rather than a concentration camp. Wodehouse, a natural anti-authoritarian, compared the experience to being a schoolboy at 'Dr Grimstone's', though the commanding officer at Huy had seemed more like a retired colonel living at Cheltenham or Bexhill. When a Red Cross parcel arrived, it was like a hamper at school. If he enjoyed any privilege at Tost, it was to use the money he had brought to hire a typewriter and buy some paper, on which he began to write *Money in the Bank*.

On his release in June 1941, he was four months short of sixty, when internees were freed anyway. Appeals from American admirers may have brought the date forward: he had received anxious letters and small gifts from America. Such kindness may explain what he came to regard as his greatest act of folly.

Three times he asked permission to leave Germany and was refused. First he suggested that he should go by train through eastern Europe and Turkey, to Palestine and London. Then he proposed that he should return via Lisbon. The third time he asked to be allowed to live in Sweden. At length, the Wodehouses were permitted to go to Paris in September 1943.

On his release from Tost he was escorted to Berlin and lodged at the Adlon Hotel, commandeered for government use. He was given no choice in the matter and was left to make a living for himself or borrow money from such friends as he had in Germany.

He had spent some time working in Hollywood and was now visited by two men he had known there. Werner Planck had been an actor and wine merchant who returned at the outbreak of war to work for the German Foreign Office. Wodehouse also met Major von Barnekow, whom he had known since working in Hollywood in 1929 and who was more likely to be taken for American than German. Wodehouse found it hard to think of either man as 'the enemy'.

For the next six months the United States was neutral and, since he had to support himself, there seemed no reason why Wodehouse should not write for its magazines. For the *Saturday Evening Post* he wrote 'My War with Germany', describing his captivity. Harry Flannery, CBS correspondent in Berlin, asked him for an interview. The request was presented as a chance to reassure American friends that he was safe.

Unfortunately, Wodehouse was not an astute interviewee and had no chance to revise his answers. At one point, for example, he said to Flannery that he thought the world he wrote about might not survive the war, 'whether England wins or not'. In June 1941 England, with no foreign ally but the Russians in full retreat before the Wehrmacht, was not a certainty

to win the war. Yet such views were not to be addressed to a friendly neutral. The words were ill-considered and those who seized on them were
happy to ignore his other comment in the broadcasts that all the internees
at Tost 'fervently believe that Britain will win'. Why or how the Germans
allowed such remarks as that to go out was never to be explained.
Wodehouse was also asked about the move from a prison camp to the
Adlon Hotel and said it was 'very nice too'. The comparison between a
prison camp and a hotel might seem reasonable but it was presented as
meaning that Wodehouse had promoted himself to luxury.

The interview alone was contentious. Worse was the suggestion that
he might broadcast via CBS to the United States. Where was the harm?
It would be a non-political talk of his own composition, certainly not
pro-German, describing his experiences as an internee. It was an acknow-
ledgement to those American readers who had shown him kindness.
Wodehouse was later to describe it as a 'ghastly blunder'.

There were five talks, beamed to America from the Reichsrundfunk
studios at Charlottenberg between 28 June and 6 August 1941. The content of the broadcasts were, as Wodehouse hoped, a demonstration of
English flippancy in the face of adversity and a determination not to whine.
Air Vice-Marshal Boyd, a prisoner of war at the time, read them and said,
'Why the Germans ever let him say all this I cannot think ... There is
some stuff about being packed in cattle trucks and a thing about Loos jail
that you would think would send a Hun crazy. Wodehouse has probably
been shot by now.'[5]

The tone was set by an early remark in the first talk, 'Young men start-
ing out in life have often asked me, "How can I become an internee?"' It
was plainly Bertie Wooster describing internment, comparing the obscene
drawings on the cell wall to living in a bound volume of *La Vie parisienne*
or describing the stench of Loos prison as a self-confident stench, standing
with both feet on the ground and looking the world in the eye.

The broadcasts, unflattering to the Germans, had none the less been
made with their permission. A famous Englishman was demonstrating that
the enemy were not beasts after all, they had treated him more or less
humanely and had now set him free. He was paid 250 marks for talking to
America, after which Goebbels' Propaganda Ministry took over. During
9–14 August, the recordings were beamed to England, which was not part
of the agreement. Wodehouse saw his error far too late. When invited to
broadcast for the Ministry of Propaganda in May 1943, on the Katyn mas-
sacre of Polish officers by the Red Army, he refused and complained to
Werner Planck at the Foreign Office.

Those who disliked the novels of Wodehouse were now quick to allege Fascist tendencies in them. As George Orwell pointed out in his 1945 essay, 'In Defence of P. G. Wodehouse', the reason why there are no Fascist tendencies in Wodehouse's writing is because there are no post-1918 tendencies at all. Moreover, the evidence of the man and his books points the other way. According to a neighbour, Mrs Wodehouse insisted on the day before their abortive escape that he should burn the rough drafts of anti-German articles he had been writing. This was done on the terrace of the house.

Fascism is referred to twice in his pre-war books. In *The Code of the Woosters* (1938) Bertie's antagonist Roderick Spode aims to become dictator of Britain as leader of the blackshirt movement. He is frustrated by Mosley who buys up all black shirts for his own followers. Spode and what Wooster calls his 'handful of half-wits' are obliged instead to become a 'black shorts' movement, unkindly described as swanking about in 'footer bags'. A second reference, this time to Hitler in the story 'Buried Treasure', describes him as a sitter on the fence in great affairs and small. A man has a moustache or he has not. Hitler should either grow it or shave the thing off.

The mask of Wodehouse – or Wooster – is far more that of the youthful anti-authoritarian with a heart in the right place, the protagonist of comic anarchy undermining the pompous and the humourless. Important people who might have been targets of that comedy in the world of his creation were perhaps not sorry to show him up when the chance came.

Almost before the broadcasts reached England, Anthony Eden as deputy premier described Wodehouse in the House of Commons as a servant of 'the Nazi war propaganda machine'. An influential Tory backbencher, Quintin Hogg, put him on a par with 'Lord Haw-Haw'. This cannot have been on the basis of what he said in the broadcasts; indeed only the first one had gone out. Duff Cooper, Churchill's Minister of Information, persuaded William O'Connor, 'Cassandra' of the *Daily Mirror*, to lead the hunt by broadcasting a 'postscript' after the BBC's main evening news. Cooper had presumably forgotten or overlooked the occasion, on 24 September 1939, when as Cassandra in the *Daily Mirror*, his protégé was telling his readers to enjoy the antics of English-language broadcasts from Berlin.

O'Connor accused Wodehouse of spending the first nine months of the war 'gambling' at Le Touquet and of throwing a cocktail party as 'the storm-troopers clumped in'. Truth was the first casualty but there was worse to follow. O'Connor informed the nation that Dr Goebbels had offered Wodehouse release from internment and a 'luxury suite' at the

Adlon Hotel, provided that he made the broadcasts and would 'worship the Führer'. Wodehouse had never set eyes on Goebbels and had no idea he was being released until told to pack his suitcase. His age was the reason and he was given no choice of destination or hotel.

Avoiding the facts, O'Connor clung to self-righteous clichés. He described Dr Goebbels taking Wodehouse into 'a high mountain' and showing him the kingdoms of the world. 'All this will I give thee if thou wilt worship the Führer. Pelham Wodehouse fell on his knees.' The quality of the prose, malevolent and mawkish by turns, had all the pretentiousness of Wodehouse's fictional fools or knaves. 'Fifty thousand of our country-men are enslaved in Germany. How many of them are in the Adlon Hotel tonight? Barbed wire is their pillow.' He scarcely seemed to stop short of Madeline Bassett's insistence to her suitors that the stars are God's daisy-chain.

In justice to the governors of the BBC, they read the script and were appalled by it. They took counsel's opinion and were informed that if the facts were otherwise than asserted by O'Connor, they might face an action for slander. At that point they declined to broadcast it, only to be told by Duff Cooper that he had the power to override their decision and would do so. It went out on 15 July 1941, by which time a number of authors who had not liked Wodehouse or his works anyway had beaten Cassandra to the punch.

On 3 July in the *Daily Telegraph*, A. A. Milne began the attack, noting that Wodehouse had avoided service in the First World War and had then settled in France to avoid paying tax due in America. The truth was that Wodehouse had volunteered for the Royal Navy in 1914 and had been rejected because of defective sight. When America entered the war in 1917, he volunteered for the US Army and was rejected again on medical grounds.

As for American tax liabilities, Sax Rohmer, author of the Fu Manchu crime novels, revealed in an accompanying letter that extortionate sums were demanded by the IRS from 'all English novelists and playwrights, or all of those with whom I am acquainted who derived any considerable rev-enue from the USA'. The only remedy was either a long and expensive legal action, which Rafael Sabatini had undertaken, or to move elsewhere. In Wodehouse's case, the IRS later accepted that he owed not $50,000 but $7,000, which had been paid. Since then, he had paid $40,000 on subse-quent earnings, of which $19,000 was later returned to him as an overpayment.

Professional envy rang clear. On 3 July, E. C. Bentley, of the 'Clerihew'

rhyme and *Trent's Last Case*, deplored Oxford's Doctorate of Letters con-
ferred in 1939 on Wodehouse, 'one who has never written a serious line'.
The honour should be taken from him. Five days later, Sean O'Casey, to
whom Wodehouse's writings and most things British were anathema,
urged the country to waste no more time on 'English Literature's performing flea'.

There was an understandable distaste among those who knew only
that Wodehouse had broadcast from Berlin, as if in the manner of Lord
Haw-Haw. It was eclipsed throughout the controversy by what Gilbert
Frankau called a heresy-hunt inspired by jealousy. As Compton
Mackenzie put it, in a letter which the paper declined to publish, a man
should not be condemned unheard in this manner and, in that context,
he found A. A. Milne's morality more disgusting than Wodehouse's irresponsibility.

Of all the correspondents at this time, the sanest was perhaps Dorothy L.
Sayers. She pointed out that the most important events of the war to date,
including its atrocities, had taken place while Wodehouse was held in a
German prison camp. There was no means by which he could have
'known or appreciated' what was going on except in the version permitted by his captors. It was absurd to judge his 'unhappy broadcasts' as if he
had been free to read and listen during the year of his internment.

It had become a duty of the Ministry of Information to persuade the
nation that it was outraged over things which, in truth, it might know or
care very little about. In this case it was said that bookshops dared no longer
display Wodehouse novels for fear of having their windows broken by
offended patriots, while libraries withdrew his volumes from their shelves.
It was certainly true that in a few public libraries, including Sheffield and
Southport, the council ordered the novels of Wodehouse to be removed
and destroyed. Yet no breaking of a bookshop window was reported and
the novels remained in print. Indeed, all the publicity and argument served
to bring the name of P. G. Wodehouse to the fore. In the remaining four
years of the war, his British sales reached 450,000.

The reckoning came when the Allies took Paris. On 25 August 1944,
as the liberators entered the city, the Wodehouses were at the Hotel
Bristol. Next day, Wodehouse made contact with an American colonel
and was visited by a 'delightful' British major from the Intelligence
Corps, whose name was Malcolm Muggeridge. Muggeridge was an
admirer of the novels and sympathetic to their author, believing unfash-
ionably that so distinguished and original a writer who gave so much
pleasure to so many readers had earned the right to be kept clear of the

'monstrous buffooneries of war'. He discussed the case with Duff Cooper, now British ambassador in Paris and formerly leader of the pack in raising the cry against Wodehouse. But Cooper seemed to have lost interest in the hunt. He had developed a habit of falling asleep in the middle of conversations, including those with Muggeridge. The matter rested there.

Over several days, the Wodehouses were interrogated at the Hotel Bristol by Major E. J. P. Cussen, an MI5 officer and future judge. Wodehouse told his story in detail, producing accounts of money received during his wartime captivity. After his release from internment, he had received royalties in Berlin from countries trading with the Axis powers. While in Paris he also received 320,000 francs, about £320, from his Spanish publishers in Barcelona. The statement to Cussen concluded with an insistence that he had at no time intended to assist the enemy. As to the broadcasts, he admitted that he had suffered a great deal of mental pain as a result of his action.

Though the Wodehouses were arrested briefly by the French, it was decided they had no case to answer in France and they were released. Major Cussen completed his report on 29 September 1944, submitting it to MI5 and the Home Office. He advised that further inquiries could only be made in Germany, when it was invaded. In his view, the broadcasts were not pro-German in character and Wodehouse was not in breach of Section 1 of the Treachery Act 1940, which carried the death penalty.

However, it was possible to broadcast 'with intent to assist the enemy', under Regulation 2A of the Defence (General) Regulations 1939. The maximum sentence was penal servitude for life. Among other post-war cases, Reginald Humphries went to penal servitude for five years, at the Old Bailey in December 1945. He had been released from a German internment camp, having agreed to broadcast for his captors. Gerald Hewitt, a language teacher, had written scripts for German broadcasts. In March 1945 at the Central Criminal Court, Mr Justice Macnaghton told him, 'You sold your country to the enemy.' Hewitt went to penal servitude for twelve years.

Wodehouse protested that he had no intention of assisting the enemy. Cussen thought that the normal and probable consequences of broadcasting from Berlin must have been to assist the enemy. If that were so, Wodehouse might have escaped the hangman but remained within the shadow of the prison walls. Yet Cussen advised that unless Wodehouse's present story could be disproved by investigations in Germany after the war, it might be difficult to persuade a jury to convict him. It was a grudging reprieve.

TOTAL WAR: A SORT OF TRAITORS

Finally, Cussen referred vaguely to 'matters of policy' and advised that Theobald Matthew, Director of Public Prosecutions, should give his decision. Matthew considered the facts and recommended that there should be no prosecution. 'There is not sufficient evidence to justify a prosecution of this man.' What he called 'the nature and content of his broadcasts' would not sustain a charge of assisting the enemy, let alone treason.[6]

There remained a possibility of charges under the 'Trading with the Enemy' regulations. These were intended to prevent firms in England trading with Germany indirectly. Yet it was impossible to live in Germany, buying groceries or paying a hotel bill, without trading with the enemy. Ethel Wodehouse had traded when she sold her bracelet and wristwatch to enable the couple to survive. To make a living, Wodehouse dealt with two German firms at their request, the first time selling rights of *Heavy Weather* to the Berliner Film Company in 1942 for 40,000 marks and receiving 1,000 marks for allowing Tauchnitz to reprint *Money in the Bank*. The two sales totalled 41,000 marks, less than half the money needed to live for two years in Berlin. The rest, 60,000 marks, came from selling possessions or borrowing from friends.

The government argument in the House of Commons, put by Anthony Eden on 6 December 1944, was that it was impossible to have Wodehouse extradited from France to stand trial under English law when there were no legal grounds for a prosecution. On 15 December, an attack on this was led from the Conservative benches by Quintin Hogg. He understood the government's advisers to say that it was not automatically an offence to speak on enemy radio during wartime. If it was not an offence, 'it ought very soon to be made one.' The content of the broadcast was immaterial, 'A person who happens to clown on the enemy wireless . . . is committing just as much an act of treason towards this country as "Lord Haw-Haw" himself.'

In 1946, the Wodehouses were given visas for the United States. The 'war guilt' of the novelist had been equated by the *New York Times* with that of unfortunate dachshunds or 'German sausage dogs' who had been stoned by 'patriots' in 1917. In England, there was a reaction against his detractors who too often seemed to be his rivals. George Orwell had already published his defence of Wodehouse. Evelyn Waugh, who was at first not permitted to broadcast a BBC tribute on Wodehouse's eightieth birthday in 1961, deplored his barbarous treatment during the war. Waugh also settled for all time the nature of the Wodehouse world. It stood alone and apart from modern life, a celestial landscape as unspoilt as Eden before the Fall of Man.

Wodehouse's good nature had seldom been in doubt. In compiling his 'self-portrait in letters' in the 1950s, he was reminded of the insults of 1941, including Sean O'Casey's sneer at the 'performing flea of English Literature'. On the grounds that all the performing fleas he had ever met had been distinguished by sterling artistry and the qualities of a good trouper, Wodehouse repaid O'Casey by calling this account of his life *Performing Flea*. The title revealed much about him and a good deal about O'Casey.

3

Since Wodehouse had escaped prosecution, it might have seemed that Britain alone among Allied combatants would have no great war criminal to try. Minor traitors who could be put to death for their opinions were something of a disappointment. John Amery, scapegrace son of Churchill's cabinet colleague, Leopold Amery, was hanged in December 1945. He was a Fascist and a Franco supporter in the Civil War. In 1940 he moved from Spain to France and found himself in the Vichy zone as the Third Republic collapsed.

Amery's wartime career was erratic. His vision was to create a British division of the SS, to be recruited from inmates of internment and prisoner-of-war camps. The Legion of St George attracted only a few dozen volunteers, quartered in Berlin, their mess decorated with a portrait of the Duke of Windsor in place of George VI. It was a condition of service that the Legion should not engage in 'fratricidal war' between Britain and Germany. It would fight against Bolshevism on the Eastern Front. In truth, it fought no one at all.

There were similarities between Amery and Roger Casement, though Amery's assertions lay somewhere between fantasy and insanity. His book *England Faces Europe* was published in Berlin in June 1943, finding its way into the libraries of camps where British prisoners were held. He was hanged for this publication and for such proclamations as that of 20 April 1943, announcing that 150,000 people in England were in prison for refusing to fight against Germany. In Germany, he added, British prisoners were flocking to join the war on Hitler's behalf. 'Hundreds of soldiers have volunteered to join the Legion and many RAF aeroplanes are coming over to us . . . We are going to write a new name in the story of the British Empire. Englishmen will never, never be slaves of the plutocratic tyranny.' Amery pleaded guilty at his trial and went to the gallows. Once again, John Dryden might have written his epitaph.

> To die for faction is a common evil,
> But to be hanged for nonsense is the devil.

Yet Amery was soon overshadowed by a man who was indeed a famous war criminal. They were hanged within a few weeks of one another.

So far as a street-fighter can have a prose style, William Joyce had one. In his wartime broadcasts from Berlin he saluted 'Mr Bloody Churchill', a man 'remembered by all those who lost their relations and friends in the holocaust of the Dardanelles, so assiduously organized by this imitation strategist . . . Butcher-in-chief to His Majesty the King . . . His personal habits are such that his chief following consists of unpaid tradesmen . . .' He was one of those 'willing to serve under any flag in order to improve their fortune and minister to their self-admiration'.[7]

Joyce took no prisoners. Lloyd George was a 'Liberal animal in a Tory skin', the Liberal party was 'formed out of the scum and dregs of all that was left of the Whig menagerie'. Labour leader, Ramsay MacDonald, 'The Loon from Lossiemouth', became the 'bright hope of socialism, installed as head of a Tory government amidst the ape-like grins of City financiers'. Pathological anti-Semitism was Joyce's stock-in-trade. He saluted Hore-Belisha with the observation that 'Chamberlain was tired of being told that his War Minister was an Oriental pedlar of furniture.' Among gentiles, Prime Minister Baldwin was 'always trying to ape the ways of a country gentleman, with a canting Puritan whine in his voice', his 'swinish physiognomy' appearing on advertisements with such fatuous slogans as 'Trust me!' or 'Safety first!'[8]

Alone among the propagandists of treason, Joyce was known to millions. Apart from Winston Churchill, his was perhaps the best known English voice on radio during the war. He began as a newsreader, at the Reichsrundfunk studios at Charlottenberg. A German radio engineer, trained in England, heard the voice, its timbre the result of a nose badly broken in a youthful brawl. To most Germans, Joyce was simply an English speaker. The engineer noticed that his nasal drawl and abrasive manner gave him the tone of a sneering blue-blooded aristocrat. Joyce was given his own news programme and became known to his listeners, almost at once, as 'Lord Haw-Haw'. William L. Shirer, CBS correspondent in Berlin until December 1941, also thought 'this hard-fisted, scar-faced young Fascist rabble-rouser sounds like a decadent old English blue-blooded aristocrat'. The voice, sometimes pedantic, sometimes sardonic, was famous for its evening announcement, 'Jairmany calling! Jairmany calling! Jairmany calling! Here are the Reichsender Hamburg,

Station Bremen and Station DXB on the 31 metre band. You are about to hear our news in English.'⁹

There was a parallel organization, the Büro Concordia, which pretended to be broadcasting from concealed transmitters in Britain itself, in order to waste the time of the police and the intelligence services. The cockneys of Workers' Challenge urged the people to rise against Chamberlain and Churchill, adding, 'You'll probably hear us again tomorrow night, but it's getting hard. The police are always on our heels nowadays.' Radio Caledonia advised the Scots to make a separate peace with Hitler, meantime broadcasting a weekly 'Sunday evening service in Gaelic', from Hamburg. The Christian Peace Movement begged servicemen to lay down their arms and oppose the immorality of war.

William Joyce's road to Berlin had been as paradoxical as the man himself. He was born in Brooklyn of American parents in 1906. His father, naturalized eight years earlier, and his mother on marriage in 1905, had been born in Ireland but were American citizens under both British and United States law. Though he lived in England most of his life, William Joyce never took British nationality. As an adolescent in Ireland he was educated by the Jesuits, proud to be a British imperialist and to join the Unionist fight against Sinn Fein. In England at sixteen, a fight after an election meeting at Lambeth Baths ended with two men putting a razor in his mouth and cutting his cheek from the corner of his mouth to his ear. He called it an attempt to cut his throat. Whether or not it was so, he remained convinced his assailants were 'Jewish Communists', all the justification his latent anti-Semitism needed in order to assume pathological proportions.

Joyce was briefly a Conservative but in 1923 joined the first short-lived Fascist movement in Britain, Miss Linton Orman's 'British Fascisti Ltd', in tribute to Mussolini. When Sir Oswald Mosley resigned from the cabinet and the Labour party, over unemployment in 1930, taking several Labour MPs and a Conservative into the New Party, Joyce hesitated. When the New Party became the British Union of Fascists, he joined, becoming its Director of Propaganda.

So far, the New Party had not been overtly anti-Semitic. If, as the British Union of Fascists, it chose that position, Joyce was the man to guide it. He reached notoriety by being tried and acquitted of riotous assembly with Mosley and others in 1934. At length, he broke with Mosley in 1937 and set up a numerically insignificant National Socialist League, choosing Hitler rather than Mussolini.

These were his years of street meetings and street-fights. At that level, speakers and audience seemed to have given as good as they got. When freedom of speech was at issue, guidance came in a magistrate's comment to Raven Thomson, charged with using insulting language, on 11 September 1936: 'If fascists come down and make wholesale attacks on a law-abiding community they will be punished fully for using insulting words . . . If, on the other hand, a coterie of Jews . . . challenge the speaker's remarks, Thomson is free to deal with the challenge and comment on Jews in the same way.'[10]

Joyce was largely self-educated. Since his parents were unable to buy him a university education, he enrolled part-time in the University of London, at Birkbeck College, supporting himself as a tutor or crammer. He won a first-class honours degree in English, began a PhD thesis on the English language and published 'A Note on the Mid Back Slack Unrounded Vowel [a] in the English of Today' in the prestigious *Review of English Studies*.

This was no ordinary street ruffian. Cecil Roberts heard him at the Park Lane Hotel, deputizing for Mosley, and was both horrified and electrified by the unknown orator, thin, pale and intense. As a connoisseur of speeches, Roberts had never heard one so terrifying in its dynamic force, 'so vituperative, so vitriolic'. Joyce denounced the democratic system and its leaders, his listeners frozen by the cold, stabbing voice. 'There was a gleam of a Marat in his eyes and his eloquence took on a Satanic ring.' He sat down, 'luminous with hate'.[11]

Joyce was prosecuted twice more in the remaining years of peace. On 17 November 1938 he was charged with assault before the West London magistrate. There had been a street meeting of the National Socialist League which ended when the police ordered it, though Joyce's supporters first sang the National Anthem. There was then a scuffle between Joyce and a bystander. Each accused the other and the case was dismissed. On 22 May 1939 a similar case before the Westminster Police Court followed a street meeting where hecklers sang the Internationale. Again it was hard to say who punched first and the case was dismissed.

Such was the man who slipped away from London to Berlin in the last days of peace to become the mouthpiece of the Third Reich for almost six years. He took with him views of English history and literature which ranged from the odd to the zany. He quoted endlessly, if inaptly, from such favourite poets as Dryden and Pope. He founded a Carlyle Society in Berlin because he believed the great Victorian would have worshipped Adolf Hitler. Among modern authors, he denounced Bernard Shaw as an impious reptile and Noël Coward as 'sickly, putrid, maggot-eaten'.[12]

In Berlin, in 1940, he published his verdict on England's past, 100,000 copies issued in both English and German as *Twilight over England* or *Zwielicht über England*. A second edition was produced in The Hague during 1942. Many of these copies were intended for prisoner-of-war camps, where British servicemen with time on their hands might be re-educated by them. This book would have sealed the fate of William Joyce, even if his broadcasts had not.

His thesis was that after the final defeat of the Stuarts at Culloden in 1745, the country suffered under discredited and successive Whig govern-ments, whatever their party titles. 'Thus did the materialism of finance lay hold on England.' International finance opened the way to capitalism, Jewish or gentile. Capitalism brought the impoverishment of the working class and the corruption of government. Edward Windsor, as Joyce called the Duke of Windsor after his abdication as Edward VIII, had unwisely protested on seeing the destitution of the people in the South Wales coal-fields. '"Something must be done," he said: and it was done – to him.'[13]

If Joyce was likely to be hanged in the end, as he suggested in 1940, at least he would have his money's worth in print. The narrative of his history echoed to shots aimed undeviatingly at the assassination of character. Sometimes there was a degree of justification, often very little. The Lord Chancellor, Lord Reading, formerly Sir Rufus Isaacs, was a 'brilliant lawyer and rascal of the Marconi scandal'. Stanley Baldwin 'owed to his pipe and his piggish countenance a reputation for honesty, which no single act of his career deserved'. Duff Cooper, the enemy of Wodehouse, was known on Joyce's news bulletins as 'The British Minister of Misinformation'. He received a side-swipe in the book by virtue of having married Max Reinhardt's star Diana Manners, thus becoming 'The little cissy whom Diana Manners had adopted'.[14]

A good deal of additional abuse was reserved for Churchill as Chamberlain's 'thing he picked up out of the political gutter to make First Lord of the Admiralty . . . great-grandson of a plantation mulatto . . . in 1911 he showed his friendship for the workers by ordering the military to open fire on the miners of South Wales.' For the future, Churchill is imagined accompanying the Governor of a British prison 'on a cold grey morning just before eight' to the execution shed.[15]

Joyce was even prepared to denounce the father of his fellow Fascist in Berlin, John Amery, for being Jewish. Yet to his British readers he offers hope. Once Britain is defeated, her future will be bright. Under Adolf Hitler, England and Germany will renew their old and traditional friend-ship.[16]

The 1950s was to see a revolution in abuse directed at public figures in the name of satire. Before that, Lord Haw-Haw sent a refreshing cold blast across the airwaves. Of course it was true that most of his charges and innuendoes were unjust, as others were to be twenty years later. Yet protected from the laws of libel and slander, he was able to entertain his listeners every evening with descriptions of figures in English public life which set them chuckling and which went the rounds of conversation in the following days.

It was possible, in areas like South Wales or the East End of London, to be resolute against Hitler yet to detest Churchill. He was regarded as the Home Secretary who had used troops and mounted police to break the 1910 strike in the Welsh coalfields, to send in troops who shot dead unarmed demonstrators at Llanelly. He was the architect of the Gallipolli disaster in 1915; the man who crossed the floor of the Commons to the Conservative benches when it suited him, and espoused the cause of Edward VIII, when it was already lost, in the abdication crisis of 1936. In the peacetime election of 1945, the crowds of the Walworth Road jeered his speeches and scratched his car. Similarly, abuse of Duff Cooper was music in the ears of those who disliked his encouragement of people to eavesdrop and inform on the conversations of suspected defeatists – 'Cooper's Snoopers' as these spies were known.

In his broadcasts, Joyce exploited such antagonisms and played down his anti-Semitism, perhaps sensing that it would repel more listeners than it attracted. He was handicapped, as time went on, by bad news from the battlefronts. At first, during the phoney war, broadcasts to Britain were jovial, offering a knockabout discussion of the news between an Englishman and a German, Smith and Schmidt. Joyce sounded reasonable, well informed, even objective, quoting neutral sources like the *New York Times* or the still neutral Italian and Norwegian press. He differed from the BBC by being the friend who revealed to listeners what others withheld from them.

The BBC had not been popular in the early stages of the war, often associated with bullying commands and propaganda, 'His Master's Voice' and 'Bloody Baptist Cant'. At the beginning of December 1939, a *News Chronicle* poll reported that the corporation attracted more hatred than Adolf Hitler. In March 1940 the BBC circulated its report on *Hamburg Broadcast Propaganda*. It had interviewed 34,000 people, of whom a sixth proved to be regular listeners to Lord Haw-Haw, while a quarter listened to him from time to time. A third who did not listen to him did not often listen to the BBC either.

Of those who listened to him, half did so because they heard other people talking about the broadcasts, 38 per cent found Joyce amusing, 29 per cent wanted to hear the German view and 26 per cent wanted the news that the BBC was holding back. Only 4 per cent disliked Lord Haw-Haw; fewer still felt it unpatriotic to listen. He was now what the report called 'a familiar feature in the social landscape'. In America on 22 April 1940, *Life* magazine rated him as a smash hit and the latest variety show at the Holborn Empire in the New Year of 1940 was called *Haw-Haw*. More ominously, opinion poll results and the Kettering by-election of March 1940 showed about 30 per cent of voters in favour of peace with Germany.

The tone of Joyce's broadcasts changed with blitzkrieg in May 1940. According to his bulletins, British troops at Dunkirk were 'unable to cope with German dive-bombers and other engines of modern warfare . . . The glorious RAF was too busy dropping bombs on fields and graveyards in Germany to have any time available for the battle of France.' Even then, the propaganda contained contradictions. Joyce claimed that the RAF had deliberately bombed German ambulance planes on their runways and the civilian population of Hanover, while insisting that its planes flew too high to hit their targets because they were no match for the Luftwaffe's superior machines and numbers.

At the fall of France, Churchill's order to the Royal Navy to sink the powerful French fleet at Oran, so that it should not pass into German hands, was made to order for Joyce. 'That inspired military genius, Winston Churchill, discovered that it was easier to bomb French ships, especially when they were not under steam, than to save the Weygand line. If it was so hard to kill Germans, why not, he reasoned, demonstrate Britain's might by killing Frenchmen instead? They were beaten and would be less likely to resent it.' Joyce adds that a cowardly surprise attack also has 'certain great initial military advantages, which a genius, such as Churchill, was bound to perceive'.

The manner in which William Joyce's geniality and jokes gave way abruptly to sneers and invective was the most chilling thing about him. The voice which poked fun across the waters of the North Sea before Dunkirk now commanded, 'Lay down your arms, resistance is useless', or predicted ominously, 'The people of England will curse themselves for having pre-ferred ruin from Churchill to peace from Hitler.'

For every listener who scoffed at the absurdity of the broadcasts, another wondered if Joyce might not be right. Like the Büro Concordia broad-casters, he gave the impression that his spies were everywhere in England as invasion threatened. He knew that a particular village clock in a church tower had stopped. How could he know? Simply because the ringing of church bells had been forbidden except as the signal of invasion. Therefore, many clocks were no longer wound. He claimed to know about a pontoon school in the canteen of the Bristol Aeroplane Works. The gamblers must find somewhere else to play after the forthcoming visit of the Luftwaffe's bombers. How could he know about these workers who played cards, unless his spies had told him? The truth was that he knew only that every large factory had a pontoon school somewhere, usually in its canteen. The rest was the bluff of the birthday-party conjuror.

In April 1945, as Allied troops closed in on Berlin, Joyce and a number of expatriate broadcasters were evacuated from Berlin to Hamburg, where they transmitted for a few days longer. His appeal changed again. It was not German victory of which he spoke. 'The horrible war through which we have just been passing is but the prelude to a struggle of a far more decisive kind.' Western Europe, 'without the help of the German legions', would be defenceless before Stalin's millions, now fighting through the streets of Berlin.

British troops were no more than twenty miles away from Hamburg. The expatriate broadcasters gathered all the food and drink on the premises and held what Joyce's interrogator, Commander Leonard Burt of Scotland Yard, called 'a sort of macabre "end of term" party'. Joyce was a heavy drinker. Now he became extremely drunk, went to the studio, switched on the equipment and made his final long and slurred broadcast to England. He repeated all the arguments about the Bolshevik threat. As for his adversaries, 'If they will not hear . . .' At this point his fist hit the table and set the acoustics ringing, 'If they are determined not to hear . . . then the people of England deserve all they get.' It was an astonishing performance and the end was defiant. 'And so I say in these last words – you may not hear from me again for a few months – Es liebe Deutschland! Heil Hitler! . . . And farewell.'

It was not quite farewell. He and his wife escaped to Flensburg near the Danish frontier, Joyce with a passport in the name of Wilhelm Hansen. Admiral Doenitz, as Hitler's successor, had his headquarters in the town, pending the arrival of the Allied occupation force. Joyce's aim was to reach Denmark, which he and his wife did, then cross to neutral Sweden, which proved impossible. They returned to Flensburg. As Joyce was walking through a copse on 28 May 1945, he saw two officers of the Royal Armoured Corps gathering wood. He spoke to them in English and they recognized the famous voice. He put his hand into his breast pocket to get the 'Wilhelm Hansen' passport. Lieutenant Perry, thinking he might have a concealed weapon or a suicide pill, shot him in the leg. When searched he also had a German military passport in the name of William Joyce.

In 1933, hoping to accompany Mosley on a visit to Hitler, Joyce who was an American citizen fraudulently obtained a British passport. Though he subsequently renewed it until 2 July 1940, he used it only to escape to Germany in 1939. No one who met him, including the bank official who signed his first application form, dreamt he could be anything but British. It was now argued that he had enjoyed the protection of the British Crown for nine months in Germany, however fraudulently. Until his British passport renewal expired on 2 June 1940 he never invoked its protection. He took German nationality on 26 September 1940, when the country of his birth was still neutral.

In English law, by the Naturalization Act 1870 and the British Nationality and Status of Aliens Act 1914, Joyce in 1945 was therefore a natural-born American citizen who had been a German citizen since September 1940. Under international law, an alien owed allegiance to a country's laws only while on its territory. Allegiance to Britain apparently ceased for Joyce when he left for Berlin on 26 August 1939.

Much as his enemies wanted him hanged, it was not clear how he could be a traitor to George VI. American by birth, he went to Germany in September 1939, taking German nationality eleven months later. After that he was a German citizen whether or not that country was at war with Britain or the United States. On these facts, he only owed allegiance to the United States until August 1940 and subsequently to Germany. His life depended on whether, by holding a British passport from September until June in wartime Germany, an American citizen could be said to have enjoyed the protection of the British Crown during that time. If so, and if he had performed a traitorous act in those nine months, his life would be forfeit.

Proving treason under the Statute of Treasons of 1351 and its amendments was not easy. The crime and penalties were so extreme that there must be one traitorous act witnessed by two people or two acts witnessed by one person. In Joyce's case, the only witness called against him was Inspector Albert Hunt of the Special Branch. At the Old Bailey on 17 September 1945, Hunt testified that he had been stationed at Folkestone from 3 September to 10 December 1940 and had monitored broadcasts from Germany. He had heard Joyce on one occasion – at least, he recognized the voice from pre-war rallies. He could not say on which day he had heard the broadcast, only that it was 'either in September or early October'. He could not say from which station or from what country the voice came. 'I was just tuning in my receiver round the wavelengths when I heard the voice.'

If that was the prosecution case, no matter that people by the million had heard Joyce's subsequent broadcasts when he was a German citizen, there would have been no case to answer under the statute of 1351. However, the government had foreseen this. After his capture, Joyce was not brought back to England but held in Germany. He was kept there while Parliament amended the law.

This was a procedural amendment only, not affecting the substance of the statute. It altered the level of proof, by abolishing the requirement of two acts witnessed by one person or one act witnessed by two people. Instead the procedure in cases of treason was to be assimilated to that of murder, where one act witnessed by one person might be sufficient. Inspector Hunt was that one person. If the jury believed him, it mattered nothing that he could not say on what date the broadcast was made or where it came from. Once the law had been amended, Joyce was brought back and charged under its new provisions. It might be inaccurate to say that the law had been altered to fit him but it could now put the noose round his neck.

The worst of it was that he acquired the air of a martyr. It was an appalling error. Joyce had quite expected to be hanged if he was caught and in *Twilight over England* he had spoken of it. 'When, however, the writer is a daily perpetrator of High Treason, his introductory remarks may command from the English public that kind of awful veneration with which £5000 confessions are perused in the Sunday newspapers, quite frequently after the narrator has taken his last leap in the dark.' However repulsive his opinions may have been, he faced that reality in 1945 with a wry and unbroken courage.[17]

Joyce had a taste for gallows humour. While awaiting trial he asked his solicitor what would happen if the Old Bailey jury proved to be mainly Jewish. The solicitor assured him that objections could be made. 'When they take the oath they put on a hat or put their hand on their head.' A glint of amusement appeared in the prisoner's eyes. 'Well, if six of them do it, wouldn't it be a good idea if I took the oath the same way?'

He had no need to take the oath. Though he pleaded not guilty, he did not give evidence. The jury convicted him; his appeals to the Appeal Court and the House of Lords were dismissed. He was hanged at Wandsworth on 3 January 1946. A few minutes before his death, he wrote a last letter to his wife, including the salute of 'Sieg Heil!' and describing this moment as 'Beim letzten Appel, Volkssturmmann der Bataillon-Wilhelmplatz', the last roll-call of the Wilhelmplatz Battalion of the People's Militia, recruited to defend Berlin. In a political testament which, for whatever reason, the BBC broadcast on its lunchtime bulletin, he defied 'the Jews who caused this last war' and warned the British people against 'the crushing imperialism of the Soviet Union'. He wished Britain to be great again and the Swastika, in the hour of need, to be raised from the dust and crowned with the words, 'Ihr habt doch gesiegt – You have conquered nevertheless. I am proud to have died for my ideals; and I am sorry for the sons of Britain who have died without knowing why.'

This manner of dealing with Joyce and his ideals was a blunder on three counts. First, it raised a soapbox orator and street-fighter to the level of political anti-hero. A crowd of 300, some of whom had brought their children to share the excitement, had to be held back by police from Wandsworth prison gates as Joyce took his leap in the dark. Movietone News arrived to film the scenes. He was headline news in the press, on radio and on the cinema screens.

Secondly, this punishment of his opinions made him a martyr for his cause and a hero to those who shared his opinions. Others who looked for repentance were to be disappointed. His response to news of the German concentration camps was to say that during the breakdown of supplies and the chaos of invasion, priority had naturally not been given to prison camps. Yet it was difficult not to acknowledge his courage in the face of imminent death. As he walked to the gallows, it was said that one knee trembled. Joyce looked down at it and smiled, knowing that it was not fear but the effect of the bullet wound several months before. Among those who admired him without reservation, a line of men gave a 'Sieg heil!' salute for their fallen hero outside the prison at the hour of his execution. The white supremacist Sons of Liberty in Louisiana produced an edition of *Twilight over England* in 1982, proclaiming his life to be 'sacred and holy', that of a man who represented 'not the last ones of yesterday but the first ones of tomorrow'.

Thirdly and perhaps worst of all, the manner of his trial began to seem like an affront to justice. As the French experience showed, those who pursued the defeated at the end of a war did not always do so with clean hands. Even in England, the *Daily Mail* which rejoiced to see 'Lord Haw-Haw' in the condemned cell, was the same paper which had appeared with a famous banner headline, 'Hurrah for the Blackshirts!' on 8 January 1934, signalling Lord Rothermere's support for Mosley at the time of the BUF Olympia rally.

The definitive verdict on the proceedings for treason was given in the Notable British Trials volume devoted to his case. The press had encouraged a feeling that 'There would have been a public outcry if Joyce had been reprieved.' The trial volume found, 'with a universal reprobation of Joyce's conduct, an almost equally universal feeling, shared by lawyers and laymen, servicemen and civilians that . . . the decision was all wrong and that an unmeritorious case had made bad law'. The feeling was not that Joyce 'having been convicted should have been reprieved, but that he should not have been convicted'.[18]

Despite the headline proclamations of 'fury' and 'outrage', most people had regarded him as a joke – 'Lord Haw-Haw, the Humbug of Hamburg, The Comic of Eau-de-Cologne', as the Western Brothers' music-hall song called him. He was one of a handful of men whom Britain put to death in the twentieth century for expressing their opinions. Yet even by the end of 1946, his conviction and execution had already caused what J. W. Hall, in the trial volume, called 'more disquiet than dissatisfaction in the minds of the public'.

4

William Joyce, despite his first-class honours degree in English Language and Literature or his devotion to Thomas Carlyle, was not a name known to the world of modern writing. By contrast, Ezra Pound was known almost everywhere within the English-speaking world. In Pound's wit, energy and versatility, F. R. Leavis in *New Bearings in English Poetry* (1932) found qualities absent from English poetry since the seventeenth century.

In 1945 Pound was probably the most celebrated of all contemporary American poets. He was almost sixty. From 1908 until 1925, he had combined free verse and Renaissance models. His sources of inspiration were Latin, Italian and Provençal but also, as T. S. Eliot remarked, in Robert Browning, W. B. Yeats and English poets of the 1890s. His influence was evident, as when Eliot dedicated *The Waste Land* to Pound, 'il miglior fabbro'.

By 1920 Pound had reached the height of his achievement with a series of nine autobiographical poems, *Hugh Selwyn Mauberley (Life and Contacts)*, describing a period from the 1890s to the end of the Great War. It included one of the most sardonic denunciations of the waste and futility of that war. From Cambridge, Leavis called it a 'regeneration of poetic idiom'. Those who were tempted by Pound's future conduct to perform a critical backward somersault by saying it was no good after all were sadly in error.[19]

From 1925 Pound's later output was dominated by his *Cantos*. They were sometimes imagistic, including Chinese ideograms for better effect, and they mystified most readers. Where there might have been rhetoric

Pound began to rant. Such openings as 'Hang it all, Robert Browning, there can be but one Sordello', had too much of bar-room argument, or what F. R. Leavis again called 'bullying assertions' or 'platform vehemences'.[20]

Combined with this, Pound became the worst of anti-Semites. Then, brought up short by the news of the German death-camps, he conceded briefly, 'after all, we are all human beings', before going back to his customary hectoring. He had been brought up a Presbyterian in Philadelphia. While denouncing Judaism he added for good measure that Christianity was a 'bastard faith'; Christ was now 'thoroughly' dead. He told H. L. Mencken that he believed religion to be the root of all evil, 'or damn near all'.

In 1924, Pound and his wife Dorothy settled in Rapallo on the Ligurian coast of north-west Italy and lived there for twenty years. He supported Mussolini and after a private interview with the dictator in 1933 was apt to refer to him as 'Muss' or 'The Boss'. By 1938, he was contributing to the *British Union Quarterly* published by the British Union of Fascists. He insisted there was a Jewish conspiracy to take over the world and, incidentally, a conspiracy among Jewish publishers to keep Pound out of print. Usury had brought economic collapse. He wrote to the newly elected President Roosevelt, seeking a place on the President's 'Brains Trust' which was to save the nation.

By the time of the 1939–45 war, anti-Semitism had been ingrained in Pound for a quarter of a century. Anti-Americanism now joined it. Roosevelt was 'our louse of a President', trying to involve the United States in the war at the behest of Jewish interests. Pound offered himself to the Italian Ministry of Popular Culture for radio talks to be beamed from Rome to neutral America. As a neutral, he was entitled to make this offer and gave his first talks on the *American Hour* in January 1941. He attacked London and Washington, Churchill and Roosevelt, and of course Jews and usury. He was summoned to the United States Consulate in Rome, where his passport was renewed for six months only, with a provision that it could be used solely to return to America. He gave the Fascist salute and left.

Pound was not a skilful broadcaster. The mixture of hectoring and a folksy manner gave the impression of a tooth-sucking old wiseacre. The attacks on Roosevelt brought pleasure to some listeners but the constant anti-Semitic jargon and phobias must have wearied all but the most dedicated sympathizers and alienated all who did not share his prejudice to a marked degree. He had nothing like the professionalism of William Joyce, perhaps because Joyce had been a public speaker of sorts, if only from a soapbox. Joyce was well used to heckling and answering back. Pound had the tone of a man who expects his audience to shut up and listen.

On 7 December 1941, he broadcast a talk on the situation in the Far East and the manner in which the British Empire was rotting from within. He did not wish to see his young compatriots 'go git slaughtered to keep up the Sassoon and other British Jew rackets in Singapore and in Shanghai. That is not my idea of American patriotism.' Before that day was over, the Japanese had attacked Pearl Harbor. Whatever had been tasteless or absurd to Pound's listeners so far, an embarrassment to his friends and even his mentors, would be an act of treason if repeated from enemy territory during wartime.

Pound insisted that he was a loyal American who legitimately advocated the defeat of the Roosevelt administration and those who had it in pawn. In any case, America was at war with Japan but not with Italy or Germany. This problem was solved by Adolf Hitler who, in an act of Wagnerian hubris, declared war on the United States in support of Japan and dragged Italy after him. In January 1942, Pound broadcast again and committed treason before the entire world.

Talk after talk flayed Roosevelt as 'below the biological level at which the concept of honour enters the mind' or a man who 'belongs in an insane asylum', or accused America of 'shuttin' out news' while 'Mr Smarmy and Mr Slime are still feeding it you right over the BBC radio.' When American troops landed in North Africa, Pound's voice followed them: 'What are you doing in the war at all? What are you doing in Africa?' At other times, the simple theme was, 'You are going to lose the war.' If the American people trusted their present leaders, 'the American people are mugs.' Sometimes the tone sounded demented as when he offered a Jewish homeland: 'Sell 'em Australia.'

The broadcasts ceased between August 1942 and February 1943, then resumed in their old style. On 13 January 1943, Roosevelt announced that Pound would be indicted for treason. The indictment was handed down by a grand jury in the District of Columbia on 23 July. It made little practical difference to the man, still described as 'a person owing allegiance to the United States'. He had nothing to lose. After the Italian surrender of 1943, the rescue of Mussolini by German paratroops and his installation as a puppet dictator at Salo on Lake Garda, Pound followed to act as propagandist.

By the end of the year he was broadcasting again. His talks were part of *Jerry's Front Calling*. Beamed to the United States, the programme attracted listeners by giving details of American troops who had been taken prisoner and by passing on messages to their families. Those who listened anxiously were subjected to the increasingly disjointed ranting of Ezra Pound. It was an insidious but effective means of propaganda.

Friends and commentators in America were speculating as to the fate of Pound and other traitors once the war was over. Unlike William Joyce, he made no effort to take on the nationality of the country from which he broadcast. It was part of his claim that he was a loyal citizen of the United States. The poet Archibald MacLeish, assistant secretary at the State Department in Washington, tried to prevent the worst. It was a question of time before the Allied advance up the Italian peninsula reached Rapallo. When Pound was captured, he might be tried under martial law and despatched by a firing squad or the noose of the military hangman before anyone in Washington could intervene. He might be executed by Italian partisans. MacLeish asked Harvey H. Bundy, Assistant Secretary of State for War, to ensure that nothing untoward should prevent Pound facing trial in the normal way. Anything else would risk giving the fugitive the status of a martyr.

On 28 April 1945, Mussolini and his mistress, Claretta Petacci, were captured by the partisans. As Mussolini faced the firing squad, Claretta Petacci threw herself across him and both were killed. Their bodies were then hung up by the heels in a Milan petrol station for the crowds to take their vengeance. It was not a good omen for the post-war world.

As American troops reached Rapallo, Pound resigned himself to the worst. He tried to surrender to the first United States soldier he encountered but the man showed not the least interest and tried to sell him a stolen bicycle instead. On 2 May, two Italian partisans came to his house in Rapallo, arrested him and handed him to the Americans. He was taken to Genoa and interrogated. The house in Rapallo was searched and large quantities of paper, as well as his typewriter, were taken away.

There followed some weeks in which he was held at the United States Army's Disciplinary Training Center at Pisa, driven there in a jeep, hand-cuffed to a black soldier arrested for rape and murder. American troops serving sentences imposed by courts martial and waiting to be shipped elsewhere were kept here under canvas. At one end of the camp were ten cages, each six feet square and ten feet tall, containing a single prisoner and a latrine bucket. The cages had cement floors, tar-paper roofs and were on view from all sides. At night the occupants were illuminated by powerful lights. The cages were known as 'death cells' for good reason. Most of the occupants were soldiers convicted by courts martial and waiting to be taken to Naples and hanged.

Among the shaven and uniformed figures of the military prisoners, Pound in his cage looked a bent and bearded old man, wearing what remained of his civilian clothes but with no belt to keep his trousers up for fear of suicide. He was left to endure the heat of the Italian summer, unprotected, and to use the latrine bucket in public view. The danger of making him a martyr by such treatment was evident and, worse still, the defiant captive had begun composing in his head 'Canto 76' of what was to become *The Pisan Cantos*. After twenty-five days in the gorilla cage, as he described it, he was transferred to a tent and given a measure of freedom. He had been examined by two army psychiatrists who found that his memory had failed and he had difficulty in collecting his thoughts. His age and present environment were likely to precipitate a complete mental breakdown.

In the medical compound, he was allowed the use of a typewriter and continued the *Pisan Cantos*. He remained there for four months until, in November 1945, he was abruptly collected by a military escort, driven to an airfield and flown to Washington. What lay ahead of him was a matter of life or death.

Pound favoured fighting the treason charges on the basis of freedom of speech as guaranteed in the First Amendment. Perhaps he imagined something like the three-hour oration in which the Prime Minister of Vichy France, Pierre Laval, had defended himself. The power and cogency of Laval's speech were beyond anything that had been expected of him. Pound compared it to an oration of Demosthenes. It did no practical good. Laval's condemnation was a foregone conclusion and he was shot soon after the trial.

In such a world, Pound's friends were concerned first and foremost to save his life. Death sentences for wartime collaboration with the enemy were being passed and executed in Britain, France and elsewhere. In Norway which, as a matter of humanity, had no death penalty, special legislation was enacted to provide it for one man, the collaborator Quisling. The shadow of the gallows also lay upon the surviving leaders of the Third Reich.

It had yet to be seen what the United States would do in such cases but its indictments for treason were in place. The only safe defence seemed to be a plea of insanity before the trial came on. It was arranged that Pound should be examined by four psychiatrists. Anyone who had heard the wartime broadcasts would hardly have thought them the utterances of a rational man.

Pound agreed. He was examined by four specialists who concluded that he was suffering from a degree of paranoia which made him unfit to stand trial. He was unable to instruct counsel or to participate in the proceedings and needed care in a mental hospital.

The outcome was as welcome to the government as it was to the defenders. A sentence of life imprisonment after a conviction for such treason as his might have been thought inadequate. In practice, he would probably have been free from a life sentence after a few years. To have imposed the customary penalty for treason and hanged one of the most prestigious literary figures of the century would do little for America's reputation in the world.

By the time of the sanity hearing on 13 February 1946, both William Joyce and John Amery had gone to the gallows in London. It seemed that Pound's friends had taken the right course. The jury listened to the evidence and in three minutes came back with a verdict of 'unsound mind'. Pound was to spend twelve years in St Elizabeth's Hospital in Washington before his release in 1958. He had a room and his books, visits from friends, a typewriter and paper. He translated, or at any rate adapted, both the *Elektra* and the *Trachiniae* of Sophocles, as well as poetry from the Chinese. The *Cantos* continued to appear.

On his release, he spent two months in America seeing those whom he might never see again, then sailed for Italy. Life at Rapallo proved to be one of depression, phobias and silence. He lived for a further fourteen years, dying in November 1972 at the age of eighty-seven. At moments he seemed to regret the rantings of the past and at others to reiterate his prejudices. Unlike the wartime years, no one any longer cared.

A few younger writers venerated him for his influence on poetic technique. He was applauded as his translation of the *Trachiniae* took the stage. Yet these portents were misleading in the post-war years and it seemed he was not wanted anywhere. Admirers like F. R. Leavis now distanced themselves from the *Cantos* and by a very wide margin from the person of Ezra Pound the propagandist. Leavis was not a man given to talking about himself in the course of his criticism. However, when he spoke of the general dislike of Pound's Fascism, he thought it prudent to add 'and my own dislike is intense'.[21]

In the event, no traitor to the United States who had done what Pound had done was sentenced to death. In some cases, the indictment was not even upheld. It seemed that he could, after all, have delivered his courtroom philippic in the manner of Pierre Laval and, with remission, still served a shorter sentence than his twelve years' detention in St Elizabeth's Hospital.

The immediate post-war years were the last in which the liberal democracies felt obliged to put to death those who had voiced hostile opinions in wartime under the protection of the nation's enemies. Even by the time of the Korean War in 1950, the world was so far divided by ideology rather than nationality that a paper like the *Daily Worker* was free to report the combat from the Communist north, while its rivals did so from the south. In this, at least, the lessons of the Second World War had secured an important freedom.

8

Tales of Mean Streets

THE CENSORSHIP OF obscene publications had not been a live issue in the first years of the Second World War. Sir Frank Newsam, Permanent Under-Secretary of State at the Home Office, recalled in 1957 that 'prosecutions were few and far between.' The police were heavily engaged in other matters and 'there was no contact with the Continent – because a lot of this stuff is imported.' Worst of all for the pornographers, there was an acute paper shortage. Restrictions under the Paper Order of 1942 made it almost unobtainable, except illegally and in small quantities from jobbing printers and stationers. Paper required Canadian wood pulp, which in turn demanded precious space on the perilous convoy routes, offering further targets for the U-boat wolf-packs.[1]

Governments had also set aside moral qualms in the hope that the evils of obscenity might be useful in the world struggle. The Luftwaffe leafleted the 1944 Anzio beachhead with drawings of a young English-woman stripping off her last undergarments, while an eager US soldier looked on. The picture was intended to remind British troops of the threat to wives and girlfriends from an over-paid, over-sexed and over-here ally. The troops gratefully cut the pictures in half, binning the GI and framing the pin-up. Earlier still, the best brains of British psychological warfare had subjected the enemy to a deluge of 'novelties', as the police described such devices, which would have earned a prison sentence in peacetime.

Among these was a cardboard toy, six inches tall and activated by springs, which caused a painted figure of the Emperor Haile Selassie of Abyssinia to bugger a painted figure of his enemy Mussolini. It was intended that the RAF should drop these on the Italian army in North Africa to undermine morale. The horizon-long surrender columns of Italian troops suggested that undermining was hardly necessary. In any event, the toys landed among German units. They proved popular with the Afrika Korps, many of whom attributed their presence in the desert to the ineptitude and cowardice of their Italian ally.[2]

The monthly glamour magazine *London Life*, whose specialities included underwear, fetishism and discipline, had flirted with prosecution in almost every pre-war issue. No less than the Ministry of Psychological Warfare, it rallied to the nation's cause with such items as its 'blitz' cover of May 1941. This displayed three alleged Windmill Theatre girls, minimally dressed in transparent brassieres and knickers, plus the animal snouts and straps of gas-masks. This combination of rubberwear and restraint proclaimed the importance of ARP drill and reminded readers of the government's appeal 'to wear their gas-masks for fifteen minutes daily'. In small print, the contents of the issue also promised 'Little Man You've Had A Busy Day' by 'Mounted Mannequin'. Pornography in the service of morality survived the war. In 1946, John Willie launched his magazine *Bizarre*. Beneath the more outrageous illustrations of female models trussed up with something like a billiard ball in their mouths was the pious injunction: 'Don't let this happen to you – Learn ju-jitsu'.

Censorship of the sexually explicit in the first two years of the war related principally to female nudity on the London stage. The Lord Chamberlain called a conference of theatre managers in April 1940. The managers obediently passed a resolution deploring nude shows, even though nudes were required to stand motionless. London was by now packed with soldiery. A man who survived the inferno of Narvik or Dunkirk, the Battle of Britain or the Atlantic convoys, ought not to endure the further shock of a woman standing before him with no clothes on.

The BBC, under the Ministry of Information, was reputed like a cushion to bear the impress of the last person who sat on it. Nudity could scarcely be a problem on radio. However, the corporation did its best for propriety in March 1942 by banning the word 'drunk' or any 'suggestions of insobriety'. 'There is considered to be nothing offensive in an occasional "damn" or "hell", particularly in some plays, but producers have been warned that scripts are not to be "spattered with such words".' 'Some plays' usually meant wartime action dramas in which, for example, a ship was torpedoed. The general allocation of swear words in 'torpedo' dramas was one every half hour.

In such circumstances, it was unlikely that the law would turn its attention to obscene books. The ad hoc Obscene Publications Squad of Scotland Yard amounted to only five officers, even in peacetime. As more officers were called up for the army or required to supervise bombed cities, there were few to spare for obscenity. In the blitz, a bookshop or a publishing house might well have been destroyed before a complaint could be followed up. From 1942 onwards some 1,500,000 United States servicemen, consumers and importers of violent books or 'comics', were amenable only to US military law. Recipients of sadism in the comics were brutal Germans and bestial Japanese. Like chewing gum, the issues quickly found their way into the hands of British children, among whom they were extremely popular. It was alleged that the US military authorities kept their front-line troops well supplied with such comics before going into action.

Nevertheless, in the spring of 1942, two obscenity prosecutions came to Bow Street Magistrates Court on 22 April and to the Central Criminal Court on 18 May. The books were of little consequence to literature, yet this case was in its way as significant as any trial of *Lady Chatterley's Lover*. While the Battle of the Coral Sea was fought and the Japanese drove the British back to the border of India, the Old Bailey court argued over material which one counsel insisted 'does not fall within a mile of the meaning of the word indecent'.

The books and authors sounded American, but it was an all-British prosecution. For the first time, the Obscene Publications Act targeted hard-boiled crime fiction. In 1957, the Home Secretary in a memorandum to the House of Commons Select Committee on the Obscene Publications Bill, confirmed that official policy for some years had been the suppression of 'Cheap paperback novels dealing with sordid subjects . . . These works portray crimes of violence, brutal treatment, intimidation and corruption with a strong flavour of sex, and in view of their cheapness may well have a wider and more corrupting effect than works dealing only with sexual matters.'[3]

The first of the 1942 cases involved *Miss Callaghan Comes to Grief*, by Britain's most popular crime novelist, René Raymond, who wrote as James Hadley Chase. It was issued by Jarrolds, a mainstream publisher, 'bombed out' of Paternoster Row in the London blitz and now in relative safety at Prince's Gate, Knightsbridge. The second case concerned two novels by Darcy Glinto who was less famous: *Road Floozie* and *Lady Don't Turn Over*. Glinto was the pen-name of Harold Ernest Kelly, a journeyman of 1940s pulp fiction. As Darcy Glinto he chronicled the world of floozies and their gunmen, while as Lance Carson he rode the range in such unobjectionable westerns as *Dan Furber – Outlaw* or *Cattle Cache at Desert Pan*.

In both cases, there had been a complaint from the public. A plain-clothes policeman paid a visit to the bookshop. He was shocked by what he found, as policemen are apt to be on these occasions. Even if James Hadley

Chase was not recognized, few people were unaware of his notorious best-seller, *No Orchids for Miss Blandish* (1939). It enjoyed a huge wartime audience among servicemen. Its title was a music-hall joke, a byword for sex and violence, a synonym for the racy or improper. Most people assumed it was an import. It certainly read as if author, action, setting and characters were American.

The plot of this earlier novel set a pattern in Chase's stories. A beautiful heiress, Miss Blandish, is kidnapped by a criminal family, led by Ma Grisson. The gang's executioner is her half-wit son, Slim, whom she is said to have made into a gangster. Slim the simpleton has no record for going after women but has 'a bad name for little girls'. As a killer, he skewers one rival to a tree by a knife through his stomach and leaves him to die with the injunction 'Take ya time, pal.' When bones are hit by his life-preserver, they snap 'like the sharp note of breaking wood'. There may be a victim in the book but there is not a single redeeming character. The police are as corrupt as the criminals.

Ma Grisson orders Miss Blandish to introduce Slim to the world of adult sexuality. 'Nothin' you can do will ever make me . . .' is no match for a rubber hose, drugs and rape. Despite such ordeals, the experience of being kidnapped forms an improbable bond between her and the repulsive Slim. When he is killed by the police, she jumps to her death from a high window. On the book's first publication, its jacket promised that publishers, printers and readers were 'convalescing from shock. They thought they could take it until they ran into Slim Grisson.'

Chase had followed this with *The Dead Stay Dumb* and a 'surprise musical', based on his thriller *Get a Load of This*, starring Vic Oliver at the London Hippodrome in November 1941. *Miss Callaghan Comes to Grief* also appeared that year. Set in St Louis, it describes gang rivalry in the white slave trade. The theme of decent girls leaving their homes and being trapped or forced into brothels allowed a little wholesome indignation to creep in. The publisher's blurb prudently described the subject as 'a loathsome corrupt stain on the pages of American history'.

The criminal protagonists are Mendetta and Raven, a former bodyguard to 'Legs' Diamond. In the homicidal passages, Raven's strangling of a prostitute is as detailed and vivid as his own death in the electric chair. The nearest figure to a hero is a reporter on the *St Louis Banner*, whose pastimes include evening visits to the city morgue to admire the day's batch of the young and naked female dead. Sadie Perminger, an innocent witness to the murder of Mendetta by Raven, is abducted and handed over to Carrie O'Shea who runs the only high-class brothel in East St Louis. 'And when she's broken you, you'll be doin' what you said no to in the first place.' The police are dishonest; the District Attorney is corrupt; Judge Hennessey, who supervises law and order, is paid by the gang bosses regularly, on the first of the month.

Despite Sadie's sufferings, the truth of her abduction and Mendetta's murder is discovered by the *St Louis Banner* reporter. There is a riot by the girls which ends in the castration of the two men controlling the brothel and with the execution of Raven for murdering his rival. In terms of obscenity it was a considerable step ahead of *The Well of Loneliness*.

Specific passages were at issue in the trial, which saw the author as well as his publishers standing in the dock. By submitting the manuscript to Jarrolds, René Raymond incurred a charge of 'causing an obscene book to be published'. The same procedure was adopted in the second case, that of Harold Ernest Kelly for *Road Floozie* and *Lady Don't Turn Over*. In his case, Wells, Gardner, Darton & Co. had modestly declined to let their name appear as publishers on the two book-covers but had been traced and brought to justice.

The surprise of the first trial was the appearance of James Hadley Chase. Instead of a shadowy or seedy purveyor of obscenity, he stood in the dock as René Raymond wearing the uniform of an RAF squadron leader, complete with 'wings'. He was at once recognizable as a hero of the hour. Under his own name he was a patriotic propagandist, co-author of *Slipstream: A Royal Air Force Anthology*, published by the king's printers, Eyre & Spottiswoode.

There was some confusion as to what Crown counsel intended. The Common Serjeant, presiding over the trial, remarked: 'I understand that the prosecution are putting forward the book as a whole. If that is so the whole book needs to be read. The best thing would be to give the jury a copy of the book and let them read it.' Twelve copies were handed out. Christmas Humphreys, for the Crown, then announced that he would read out 'twelve particular passages to which the prosecution takes exception'. This was done, though counsel for the publishers objected that 'the passages read in court have been divorced from their context.' Raymond's defender added that the book was not even indecent, let alone obscene.

Unfortunately for the jury, the Common Serjeant was a man in a hurry. He announced that he would begin his summing up that afternoon and finish it next day. The jurors could read the book overnight, if they wished. How many of these fire-watchers, air-raid wardens and Home Guard soldiers would have time to do so was an open question. Next day, the jury convicted both author and publisher. Each was fined £100 with costs,

some £4,000 by modern values, but no prison sentence was imposed. On
seeing this, Darcy Glinto and his publishers withdrew pleas of 'not guilty'
in respect of *Road Floozie* and *Lady Don't Turn Over*. The publishers were
fined £50 for each book and the author £50 for the pair. In such circumstances, a major adaptation of the law relating to obscenity in crime fiction
stumbled into being.[4]

One aspect of the cases was not mentioned in court. All the books on
trial portrayed America at its worst. Yet for two years American dollars had
kept Britain in the war. Three months earlier, the first US servicemen
came ashore to fight a common enemy. 'So we had won after all,' wrote
Winston Churchill. Before American participation, there was little sign of
victory, as opposed to stalemate and a negotiated peace. US troops and
their leaders appeared as saviours, even as guarantors of victory. Was it tol-
erable that best-selling British fiction should portray their country as one
where the police were corrupt on system, district attorneys could be
bought as necessary, and judges received payment from the Mafia on the
first day of the month?

Though this was never asked, it would require some credulity to believe
it was never thought. On 30 November 1942, the *Chicago Sun* attacked the
United States Office of Censorship for banning the shipment to England
of new printings of Erskine Caldwell's novel *God's Little Acre*, previously
published in both countries. 'To win the war, is it necessary to make the
people of England think that there are no depressed economic groups and
no race problems in the United States?' The British authorities also assisted
by having Erskine Caldwell's novel declared obscene in court, nine years
after publication. In December 1942, Alex Faulkner cabled the *Daily
Telegraph* in London on behalf of the *Chicago Sun*. He asked why shipments
of *God's Little Acre* had been banned. He was advised by the US Navy
censor that all reference to the novel in his cable had been deleted. Not
only was the book banned in Britain, it was forbidden to ask – or suggest –
why.

Erskine Caldwell had worked among the 'poor whites' of Georgia; his
novel as well as his play *Tobacco Road* was drawn from this experience. On
first publication of *God's Little Acre* in the United States, a prosecution was
brought by the New York Society for the Suppression of Vice. Objections
to the book were similar to those in the British prosecutions of Zola in
1888–9: the characters were indecent or obscene in language and manners.

In 1933 the New York City Magistrate, Benjamin Greenspan, had ruled
that the book must be considered in its entirety. He found it honest and
sincere in intent, 'not a work of pornography', with no tendency to incite

readers to behave like its characters. Coarse and vulgar language was no reason for banning it. 'The court may not require the author to put refined language in the mouths of primitive people.' A number of other American states and cities banned it – St Paul, Missouri, as late as 1946 and Massachusetts in 1950. Citizens of St Paul were still able to buy it simply by crossing the Mississippi to Minneapolis. In England, individual magistrates were issuing destruction orders for the book as late as 1953, though it might be bought a few miles away.[5]

In the summer of 1942, with two Old Bailey verdicts behind them, the Metropolitan Police sought out individual bookshops. Cecil Charles Reede of High Street, Chatham, supplied books to the crews at Chatham Dockyard, to ease the boredom of Atlantic convoy duty or minesweeping in the North Sea. His shop was raided and he appeared before Chatham magistrates on 5 August.

The magistrates decided that Balzac's *Droll Stories* were not obscene, nor were the novel *Georgette* and *The Second Oldest Profession*. Destruction orders were made for nine books. Those to be burnt were, unsurprisingly, Erskine Caldwell's *God's Little Acre*, and eight volumes of sensationalism: Mae West's *She Done Him Wrong*, *Kiss the Blood Off My Hands*, *Vinegar and Brown Paper*, *Hell's Belles*, *Silken Skin*, *For Men Only*, *Mr Dayton Darling* and *Love Ethics*.

She Done Him Wrong began life on Broadway as Mae West's play *Diamond Lil*. Though she had been arrested and imprisoned for her first play *Sex* in 1926 and the entire cast of *The Pleasure Man* was arrested on stage in 1928, *Diamond Lil* in 1927 avoided such attentions. As *She Done Him Wrong*, it was filmed in 1933 with its authoress as the star. It had appeared as a novel in the previous year. It lay somewhere between the nimble ironies of Anita Loos in *Gentlemen Prefer Blondes* and the comic energy of Damon Runyon in *Guys and Dolls*. However, Chatham magistrates were unimpressed by New York club life at the Bucket of Blood or Suicide Hall, accompanied by forthright language, pimping and white slavery as the small change of Miss West's fiction. Once again, it was an unwelcome portrayal of a new wartime ally.

Apart from the destruction orders, criminal convictions were imposed on Mr Reede for selling three titles: *Miss Callaghan Comes to Grief*, *Road Floozie* and Rex Holt's *Hell's Belles*. He was fined £30 for each book with ten guineas costs. He must pay 'forthwith' or go to prison for three months.

Harold Ernest Kelly kept up his output until 1950. James Hadley Chase had not heard the last of censorship. As late as 17 April 1958, the Minister

of Customs presented the Australian Senate with a list of 178 titles criminalized by the Literature Censorship Board. Chase's novel *Twelve Chinks
and a Woman* rubbed shoulders with D. H. Lawrence, Mae West, John
O'Hara and Grace Metalious's *Peyton Place*. Yet a number of Chase's novels
survived to be filmed by French and American directors. George Raft
starred in *I'll Get You for This* in 1951 and *No Orchids for Miss Blandish*
appeared as the respelt *Grissom Gang* in 1971.

The British film production of *No Orchids* in 1948 attracted ridicule by
using British talent, including the comedian Sid James, to impersonate
American gangsters. Worse still, Miss Blandish fell in love with Slim
Grisson before the kidnap. The violence was of a far lower order than in
the book but any filming of a novel with this reputation provoked outrage.
The *Daily Express* called it 'A disgrace to Britain'. The *Evening Standard*
thought it 'A Disgrace to British Films'. The *Observer* condemned 'A
monstrous exhibition of ill-taste'. The British Board of Film Censors
granted the film an adult certificate but the *Daily Herald*'s critic added, 'I
advise the Plaza management to take it off at once, before the London
County Council steps in to override the censor's lapse.'

The LCC stepped in, while the film was still at the Plaza, Piccadilly
Circus. The council's Public Control Committee ruled on 23 April that it
must be cut or banned. 'The film contains matter of a brutal and sadistic
character, of a sensual nature and of an immoral kind . . . unless certain
modifications which would, in the committee's view, eliminate the most
objectionable features, are made within the next forty-eight hours, the film
must be withdrawn in London.'

The result was chaos. The film was withdrawn and cut in London. In
Surrey it was banned outright. Elsewhere it was shown uncut. In the following year, a far more controversial gangster film appeared, James Cagney
in *White Heat*. As Virginia Graham remarked in the *Evening Standard* on 10
November 1949, 'This film glorifies violence. The terrible thing is its
excellence.'

Censorship of books and films, in the decade of Hitler's war, was active
behind the scenes as well as in public. During the 1942 prosecutions, the
government learned that another well-known firm, Constable, proposed to
issue James T. Farrell's trilogy, *Studs Lonnigan*, a realistic fiction set in the
slums of Chicago. The novel was to be the subject of random destruction
orders until 1953. In 1942, it had already been refused entry to Canada as
indecent and immoral. Because of the paper shortage, Constable agreed to
buy sheets of the American edition and bind them in England. For this,
they required an import licence. The Board of Trade identified the book

and refused the licence. Ironically, 1942 was also the year in which the Nazi regime banned the book for British and American prisoners of war.

2

In 1945 with the advent of a majority Labour government, J. Chuter Ede became Home Secretary. He was responsible for legal censorship of literature and films until the following year when the Home Office lost its power to require the Director of Public Prosecutions to take criminal proceedings. Among other powers, he controlled the reading matter of prisoners. When the double sex-murderer Neville Heath was awaiting execution in the death cell of Pentonville prison his requests included two American crime novels, D. B. Olsen's *Bring the Bride a Shroud* and Paul Whelton's *Call the Lady Indiscreet*. These were refused and he was given instead the more bracing and wholesome adventures of John Buchan, *The Thirty-Nine Steps*.

Ede kept in touch with men like Sir Sidney Harris of the British Board of Film Censors over the depiction of crime on the nation's screens. In 1948, the British Board of Film Censors, which also exercised control over the British zone of occupation in Germany, was persuaded to ban the showing there of the film of Graham Greene's *Brighton Rock* (1947), with Richard Attenborough playing the teenage gangster, Pinkie. When questioned over this, the board explained that it was not prepared to have the British seen by the subject race as 'a nation of razor slashers and racecourse thugs'.

Closer to home, Ede heard with dismay that the major film producer and owner of the Odeon Cinema chain, J. Arthur Rank, was making *Good Time Girl* with a sixteen-year-old starlet, Diana Dors. It was based upon the true wartime story of a US paratrooper deserter in London, Karl Hulten, and Georgina Grayson, alias Betty Jones, his Welsh striptease-dancer girlfriend, the product of an approved school. In reality, the pair pursued a career of armed robbery, ending with the murder of a taxi driver, for which Hulten was hanged and the teenage dancer sent to prison for life.

From Ede's inquiries, *Good Time Girl* glamorized crime. It also depicted approved schools and their authorities as indifferent to the young and incompetent in dealing with them. The Home Secretary took Rank to lunch, threatened to denounce him in the House of Commons and finally obtained cuts in the film. He discovered too late that the material which replaced the cuts was far worse. The censors could not help him. Sir Sidney Harris regarded the film as sordid and undesirable but this could not be given as a reason for refusing it a certificate. However, some films fell victim to censorship of another kind. In September 1952 Rank decided to ban X-certificate features from its numerous Odeons and Gaumonts. Those under eighteen could not be admitted, which excluded family audiences and was bad for business.

Wars and the years which follow traditionally show a growth in crime, a fall in standards of honesty and sexual morality. In Britain, crime had remained stable until 1943, after which it increased dramatically to the end of the war and beyond. Prostitution grew threefold between 1939 and 1945. The post-war years showed a far steeper increase in violent crime among the young. How far were the screen, the comic and the printed word responsible for this?

In July 1943, Dr Temple as Archbishop of Canterbury already saw the heroism of the blitz being overtaken by dishonesty and an 'alarming collapse of sexual morality. There is a danger that we may win the war and be unfit to use the victory.' Nor was this confined to one side of the Atlantic. The Hays Office had felt obliged to censor the strong language used in the British naval epic, *In Which We Serve*. The National Legion of Decency condemned such films as Greta Garbo in *Two-Faced Woman* and Barbara Stanwyck in *Lady of Burlesque*, based on Gypsy Rose Lee's novel *The G-String Murders*, even though the film had been passed by the Hays Office.

The enthusiasm for crime was not new. Depiction of crime in drama and fiction went back at least as far as Aeschylus. Chaucer wrote one of the neatest crime stories ever in *The Pardoner's Tale*. Elizabethan England revelled in 'rogue histories' like Thomas Nashe's *The Unfortunate Traveller* (1594), whose violence might make even James Hadley Chase seem tame. The nineteenth-century broadsheet and the mass circulation newspaper brought tales of murder and execution – the more gruesome, the more tenacious the appeal. In 1879, one Kate Webster boiled the body of her elderly victim, scooped the fat into a bowl and sold it round the neighbourhood as dripping. 'The feelings of those who consumed the dripping are not much to be envied,' wrote one contemporary with healthy relish. How was crime on the page or the screen of the post-war world any different? One answer, directly affecting Britain, lay in a legal decision which occupied US courts from 1940 to 1943.

3

For ten years after the war Britain was caught up in a battle over 'Yank mags', fought three thousand miles away. 'Crime comics' and 'horror comics' were produced there at the rate of 70,000,000 a month by 1950. Every street-corner news-stand might hope to sell more than a hundred a day. A surplus was always allowed for by the publishers. Copies unsold were rerouted, usually as ships' ballast, to Europe and, to a lesser extent, to North Africa. Their contents were of international concern.

Since 1884 the State of New York had had a so-called 'Anti-Sadism Law', copied by other states but never as a Federal statute. Like much legislation passed in haste it proved largely unnecessary and unworkable. Anyone was guilty of a misdemeanour who published a book, pamphlet, newspaper or magazine 'principally made up of criminal news, police reports, or accounts of criminal deeds, or pictures or stories of deeds of bloodshed, lust or crime'. If this meant what it said, the Criminal Law Reports or *The Adventures of Sherlock Holmes* might have been banned. What about stories or articles intended to combat crime? The moral of literary crime was, 'Be sure your sins will find you out.' Yet as children confided to Dr Fredric Wertham, author of *The Seduction of the Innocent* (1955), a study of the 'horror comic' and its evils, to know that crime does not pay, you first have to read about it.[6]

Created after a campaign by the Society for the Suppression of Vice, the statute applied only to the State of New York and its imitators. American domestic history made it an absurdity. How could the press have reported prohibition and the gangs which violated it without breaking the law? Magazines like *Master Detective*, *True Crime* or *Black Mask* sold by the million. Novelists from Conan Doyle to Raymond Chandler and the memoirs of every retired detective passed unchallenged. The law seemed a nonsense until 1940.

That year, a concerned citizen entered the shop of Mr Winters in New York City. He saw copies of a magazine for sale, the June issue of *Headquarters Detective: True Cases from the Police Blotter*. It yielded such illustrated gems as 'Bargains in Bodies', 'Girl Slave to a Love Cult' and 'Girls' Reformatory'. The troubled browser went to the District Attorney. The Attorney read the magazine, ordered a search of the shop, where 2,000 copies of such material were found, and charged Mr Winters under the 1884 statute with possessing 'a certain obscene, lewd, lascivious, filthy, indecent and disgusting magazine'.

Winters was convicted under the Anti-Sadism Law, though his counsel denounced 'the manifest injustice and absurdity' of the charge. The court found the indecency or obscenity of the material proved. It was upheld by six votes to one in the New York Appeal Court. The majority found that 'collections of pictures or stories of criminal deeds of bloodshed or lust unquestionably can be so massed as to become vehicles for inciting violent and depraved crimes against the person and in that case such publications are indecent or obscene in an admissible sense.'

The one dissenting voice, Judge Lehman, maintained that the wording of the statute 'is so vague and indefinite as to permit punishment of the fair use of freedom of speech'. Mr Winters appealed on these grounds to the US Supreme Court, which found in his favour by a vote of 6 to 3. The majority held that the New York Appeal Court had not limited punishment to 'the indecent and obscene as formerly understood'. It had created a new standard of guilt in 'criminal news or stories of deeds of bloodlust, so massed as to become vehicles for inciting violent and depraved crimes against the person'. This was unconstitutional. The New York statute was also repugnant to the Fourteenth Amendment, which prohibited a state from violating an individual's freedom of speech, guaranteed by the First Amendment to the Constitution.[7]

There was, to say the least, a certain majesty about a judgment which allowed life and breath to the Girl Slave and her Love Cult or to Road Floozie, as surely as to Madame Bovary and Sister Carrie. Yet the decision opened a way to liberty, in the name of crime-writing, which critics soon denounced as licentiousness. The effects were felt in Britain as surely as in the United States.

By the war's end, a further threat came from the morality of crime comics and the fiction related to them. America's best-seller of 1947 was by a former comic-strip writer, Mickey Spillane. *I, The Jury* introduced a private-eye hero in Mike Hammer and a new philosophy of righteous violence. In this first novel, Hammer's 'buddy' has been shot in the stomach and left to die. Hammer vows to track the killer, to be judge, jury and executioner, and kill the murderer in the same manner. The culprit proves to be the book's heroine, seen first in a white bathing-suit with legs that 'make you drool to look at'. She performs a striptease on the last page, intending to entice the hero to his death. When she is naked, Hammer shoots her through the navel, the wound described as carefully as her attractions had been. As she falls to her knees, she asks stammeringly how he could do such a thing. His riposte is ready, in the last line of the book. '"It was easy," I said.'

As in comics like *Crime Does Not Pay* or *Gangbusters*, eroticism and sadism are supercharged by the hero's self-righteousness. In Spillane's case, there is often a political or Communist threat to 'Mr and Mrs Average' which enables Hammer to shoot, flog and stab his way through the ranks of evil men and beautiful but treacherous women in a crusade against the underworld or subversives. In *One Lonely Night*, Hammer defends 'Mr and Mrs Average' against 'Russia and the slime that breeds there'. The 'Red sons-of-bitches' will be exterminated soon, 'unless they get smart and take the gas pipe'.

In parallel with Senator Joseph McCarthy's investigations into 205 alleged Communists in the State Department, Hammer claims to be on the side of the angels. In 1948, with a Soviet blockade to force the Western allies from their enclave of West Berlin, all pretence of a continuing wartime alliance was at an end. Even the most vehement campaigner against pulp crime and 'horror comics', Fredric Wertham in *The Seduction of the Innocent*, exonerated Spillane, on the curious grounds that the damage had already been done to his admirers by childhood reading. One of Dr Wertham's targets is a comic-book story of gang murder in which the victims are towed face down over a gravel road at speed until it is impossible to 'identify the meat'. Mike Hammer, in *One Lonely Night*, prevents identification more simply, by wearing his victim's fingertips to the bone on the concrete before throwing him off a bridge.[8]

A number of United States judges in post-war cases where children had injured or killed one another commented on the influence of the comics. When a boy of thirteen mortally wounded a seven-year-old, hid him and left him to die, Judge Daniel A. Roberts took judicial notice of twenty-six comic books in the defendant's possession. They depicted 'homicidal, near-homicidal and brutal attacks'. The boy had followed the illustrations at an age when he was still too young to read the captions. Judge Roberts found the material 'startling in the extreme, and nauseating and degrading to the moral sense . . . That these publications are permitted to be sold to the youth of the country is a travesty upon the country's good name.' Something must be done, 'by law if the publishers will not properly censor their own work'.[9]

Nothing was done. Or, rather, the report of the Senate's 1950 Crime Investigating Committee, chaired by Estes Kefauver, found no link between crime in books or comics and crime in fact. The New York State Legislature thereupon appointed a committee. It accepted Dr Wertham's view that the law should forbid the sale or display of crime comics to children under fifteen. This was opposed by a number of organizations, including the Mystery Writers of America and the American Civil Liberties Union, but the committee was in no two minds. Crime comics 'impair the ethical development of children' and are 'a contributing factor leading to juvenile delinquency'. When the bill to control them was debated, the New York State Assembly voted for it by 141–4 and the State Senate approved it unanimously.

This was outright rejection of the Kefauver Committee. Comic-book publishers had found no friends in New York. They need not have worried. The bill was passed to Governor Thomas Edward Dewey, newly re-elected and in a strong position to use his authority. Dewey exercised his veto. The proposed law was unconstitutional, on the same grounds as the Anti-Sadism Law. The United States, Britain and the post-war world were to be the hunting ground for cartoon villains, as they were for the homicidal talents of Spillane's Mike Hammer.[10]

4

In Britain, it remained an open question whether comics and novels had a corrupting effect on the young. They seldom included explicit sexual content which the Obscene Publications Act of 1857 and the Hicklin judgment of 1868 held necessary to deprave and corrupt. There was no 'foul language', as the phrase had it, no overt descriptions of erotic acts. Spillane's hero did not swear out loud as he broke Communist limbs over a table, used his belt on naked traitresses, or shot and bombed his way through his country's enemies. Instead, he confided coyly, 'I said a dirty word.' Dr Wertham produced a comic-book illustration of a captive heroine with her skirt disarranged and legs apart, bound before a poker-wielding villain. 'Children told me what the man was going to do with the red-hot poker,' he noted underneath the illustration, but suggestion was all.

In its depiction of horrors, the world had moved on since the last days of peace in 1939. Lord Russell of Liverpool in *The Scourge of the Swastika* (1954) and *The Knights of Bushido* (1960) detailed the atrocities committed by Germans and Japanese during the war. There was nothing to prevent an adolescent reading them, in paperback or from a library. The events described would have shown Spillane or the comics for the morally puerile rubbish they were. Yet it was unthinkable that such material as Russell's books should be censored. Those who read them would surely resolve that such things should never happen again. Others sought to exploit wartime horrors. Stories like Alfred Perle's *House of Evil* offered fictional panoramas of helpless women in the hands of a modern inquisition, either with a Nazi or a post-war Communist background. They were the price paid for telling the truth elsewhere.

Since it was impossible to airbrush villains from fact or fiction, there were attempts to eclipse them, notably in the cinema where pre-censorship made control easier. Films like *The Blue Lamp* (1949) showed the youthful London gangster as a bully and a killer but no more than a coward in the end. As a hero, it created a cheerful London policeman, played by Jack Warner, who survived for many years in one of the most successful television series ever, *Dixon of Dock Green*. In many cinemas for fifteen years after the war, the main features were separated by a half-hour episode of *Scotland Yard*, presented in the lugubrious monotone of Edgar Lustgarten, teaching that a squalid cell or an execution shed beckoned at the end of every criminal career. By the time this series transferred to the television screen in the 1950s, it was rivalled by weekly instalments of *Fabian of the Yard*, based on the career of the recently retired Superintendent Robert Fabian, the most famous detective of his day.

There was a world of difference between the new comics or the novels of Mickey Spillane – or those of James Hadley Chase – and the earlier tradition of English crime writing. With a few exceptions, the righteous man had been the example. Sherlock Holmes, Richard Hannay, 'Bulldog' Drummond, Lord Peter Wimsey, and Peter Cheyney's Slim Callaghan dominated the pre-war market. With this in mind, the BBC offered adult listeners such morally and socially impeccable crime-fighters as Paul Temple and his wife Stevie, while for children there was to be a new hero who had nothing whatever in common with the dumb villainy of the comics.

Dick Barton – Special Agent made its debut in 1948. The fifteen-minute episodes were broadcast every evening immediately before the seven o'clock radio news. The signature tune of 'The Devil's Sleigh-Ride' introduced a celibate hero, a total abstainer from alcohol, with his two assistants, Snowy and Jock. Each episode left the drama on a cliff-edge, awaiting a conclusion in which virtue was always triumphant and crime never prospered.

Within weeks the series was on its way to an audience of fifteen million and a lot of trouble. Many children, avid for stories of crime and punishment, failed to notice that the former did not pay. As early as 1 April, when a ten-year-old thief appeared at Horsham Juvenile Court charged with stealing a wristwatch, his father attributed this to listening to *Dick Barton*. 'Children are too fond of playing at Dick Barton. He is the curse of this country.' By 1950, the radio series was the subject of Geoffrey Webb's *The Inside Story of Dick Barton*. '*Dick Barton* has been called everything – an entertainment, a stimulant, a relaxation, a drug, a safety valve, a social menace, a Fascist plot and a pattern for parasites. The important thing is that he has never been called a bore.' The question asked by reviewers in the light of juvenile interest in crime was put succinctly by Virginia Graham in the *Evening Standard* on 21 April, 'Would You Ban *Dick Barton*?' The swiftest reply came from Robin Johnston, aged eleven. He thought it 'very silly' to suggest that *Dick Barton* contributed to juvenile delinquency. The hero of the series was, after all, the crime-fighter who always got his man.

The BBC grew nervous and appointed a 'watchdog' for the series, a former probation officer, to ensure that its content was not subject to criticism. When his name was leaked to the press, contrary to undertakings, he resigned and the series was brought safely to an end in March 1951. By then the authorities were too concerned about the effect on the young of films and comics, and indeed television, to worry much about *Dick Barton*.

Since 1868, it had been accepted that obscenity must deprave or corrupt those whose minds were open to its influence. A similar criterion might surely be applied to works of crime and violence. If figures for violent crime rose at a time when such material was available in such quantities, the causal connection appeared plain. If culprits in court confessed that they had committed crimes under the influence of what they saw or read, that connection seemed proved.

A number of cases had offered such proof. Even during the war, when a thief of seventeen was sent to prison at London Sessions, he boasted that he had been a member of a Soho gang, the 'Dead End Kids', named in honour of a gang in the Humphrey Bogart film *Dead End*, under whose influence he had operated. In 1948 Flying Officer Hobbs, an RAF deserter, chloroformed his guards, then coshed and robbed his aunt and her daughter, crimes for which he went to penal servitude for seven years at Hertfordshire Assizes on 17 June 1948. This was at the height of the controversy over the film version of *No Orchids for Miss Blandish*. The court heard that Hobbs had been incited by seeing it immediately before the assault.[11]

On 26 February 1950, the *Evening Standard* reported that 'Junior Gangs' were copying films and turning what had once been games into actual crimes. On 21 March, in a House of Lords debate, Lord Lloyd demanded that the government should ban outright 'the worst type of gangster films'. However alarmist this might seem, criminals in the courts confessed increasingly that they had been inspired by the screen or the printed page. Four weeks after Lord Lloyd's demand, a youth at Grays, Essex, Juvenile Court on 19 April told the magistrates that he had snatched a woman's handbag 'for fun' because he had 'seen crooks do it at the pictures'. The fact that he needed the money to pay an outstanding fine for shoplifting did not improve his case.

The same excuse was offered in more serious offences, not excluding assault and murder. A seventeen-year-old was accused of murdering a nightwatchman during a robbery in January 1949 by beating him repeatedly over the head with a monkey-wrench. The boy protested that this was the result of having just seen the film *Three Strangers*, written by John Huston, starring Sydney Greenstreet and Peter Lorre. The film's principal characters were lottery winners coming to grief as a result of greed. 'A man hits a woman over the head with an idol and kills her,' the youth pleaded. After that scene, 'Something came over me.'[12]

A fifteen-year-old who inflicted grievous bodily harm on three women in separate incidents told the police, 'After watching a dramatic type of film, I walk out into the cold air and it seems to affect my brain. I feel the urge to attack girls at this time.' A ten-year-old boy who had stabbed to death a nine-year-old girl told Southampton Juvenile Court, 'I have seen stabbing on television . . . I watch all the murders. I like the way they track them down and question them.' An eighteen-year-old bank robber claimed, 'I have seen it all on TV and thought how easy it would be.'[13]

There was one case examined in far greater detail than these. In the view of the journalist Kenneth Allsop it precipitated an emotional crisis in the nation's life equalled only by the sudden death of George VI and the Dunkirk evacuation. On 2 November 1952, Christopher Craig, aged sixteen, and Derek Bentley, nineteen, confronted police while attempting to break into Barlow & Parker's warehouse in Croydon. What followed confirmed the fears of those who saw teenagers corrupted by the examples of cinema, comic books and pulp fiction. Craig was carrying a 1914 service revolver with a sawn-off barrel. He fired and injured a plain-clothes policeman. Bentley was arrested while Craig broke away. The fugitive continued to fire and, some fifteen minutes later, by what was a terrible fluke at such a range, shot dead PC Sidney Miles.

It appeared that a diet of violent fantasy had led to an atrocious crime. Craig confessed that he liked going to the cinema three or four times a week to 'gangster films'. When asked in court what he thought he was doing on a warehouse roof, shooting at the police, he replied, 'In a film or something, sir.' When his ammunition ran out, he dived from the rooftop like a doomed Hollywood gunman, fracturing his spine, breastbone and left wrist. Craig who was too young to hang served a life sentence of eleven years. Bentley, under arrest for fifteen minutes when the fatal shot was fired, went to the gallows as an accomplice to murder.[14]

In this case, there ought to have been evidence of the corruption of two teenagers by films or comics. Books seemed ruled out, since both defendants were illiterate. Yet Craig liked being read to. According to evidence in court, his favourite author was the innocuous and moralistic children's writer, Enid Blyton. However, it was certainly true that both youths had been separately to the cinema on that Sunday afternoon a few hours before the shooting. Bentley had afterwards watched television. Craig and his girlfriend had been to *My Death is a Mockery*, a cautionary tale in which a smuggler shot a customs officer and was hanged for his crime. Bentley had been to the Astoria, Streatham, which was screening Betty Grable in *Lady from the West*. He went home and then watched a television programme of old-time music hall, *Songs from the Shows*. This diet of fantasy offered little comfort to the theorists.

Not everyone believed in a link between criminal fantasy and reality, however strongly they might advocate censorship. As the mood for dealing harshly with young thugs became more apparent, a belief that paperbacks, films and comics fuelled the fantasies of young criminals was not always welcome. It offered an excuse to the defendant who might be presented as a decent and amiable lad. He had acted out of character only because he had been corrupted by the products of a greedy and unscrupulous film-maker or publisher. Was he not a victim rather than a perpetrator? In the Bentley and Craig murder trial Lord Chief Justice Goddard moved quickly to block this defence. 'Now let us put out of our minds any question of films or comics or literature of that sort. These things are always prayed in aid nowadays when young persons are in the dock, but they really have very little to do with the case.' That was not what the moral majority had been saying.[15]

The direct influence of books and films on criminality remained headline news. Six months after Lord Goddard's warning, on 17 June 1953 at the Central Criminal Court, a shipowner was gaoled for attempting to persuade a man to kill his former wife's husband, using a method taken from the fiction of Peter Cheyney. Unfortunately for him, the man he employed was a plain-clothes detective sergeant of the Flying Squad. Pleading on the defendant's behalf, his counsel conceded, 'It is poor stuff compared to Cheyney's work, but there is a resemblance to it.'

The dangers of this approach were shown in a very different trial on 20–21 March 1956. Leonard Atter from Primrose Hill was accused of murdering Robina Bolton at Westbourne Terrace, Paddington. Victim and suspect were known to one another but the case rested largely on the discovery of *True Detective* in the bedroom of the accused. It contained a story,

'The Murderer Walked In', describing an intruder knocking a man uncon-
scious and killing his wife with blows to the head from a hatchet. Mrs
Bolton died in allegedly similar circumstances. Prosecuting counsel read
out the story, pointing out the similarities.

Atter's counsel protested that 'If it is going to be suggested that there are
similarities between the facts and this story, I will have to point out that
there are also a large number of dissimilarities.' The prosecution case was
based on the assumption that Atter would read the story and very probably commit such a murder. Without calling on the defence, Mr Justice
Devlin told the jurors, 'I must satisfy myself there is some piece of evidence
that is more than mere suspicion. You cannot put a multitude of suspicion
together and make proof out of it.' He directed them to acquit the defendant, yet the case illustrated how easily held was the belief that crime in fiction
dictated actions in fact.

It was inevitably argued that there should be a public inquiry into the
cinema and its influence on crime. Yet this had already taken place with
results that pleased no one. In 1948, the Home Secretary, Chuter Ede, set
up a committee under an eminent constitutional lawyer, Professor K. C.
Weare, to consider what harm might be done to children by the cinema.
After two and a half years, the committee reported on 5 May 1950.
Contrary to expectations, 'The "glamour" film, which sets up false ideas of
values, may be more dangerous to the young cinema-goer than the gangster film so widely blamed for juvenile crime. The gangster film may do no
more harm than the reading of detective stories does to its father and [is]
less frightening to a child than an eerie or grotesque cartoon.'

The committee had also concluded that 'The mere fact that a film has
crime for its theme does not seem a necessary reason for refusing to allow
children to see it.' It found little evidence of 'the serious imitation of gangster characters by children in real life and no evidence of imitation that is
anything more than pantomime'. Ironically, it concurred with Sir Harold
Scott, Commissioner of Metropolitan Police from 1945 to 1953, who
thought the influence of crime fiction and the crime film on young adult
males was confined to 'externals', the swaggering walk or the boastful
manner. The far more important moral influence went no deeper than
'imitations of Red Indians or pirates'.[16]

It was not what the hopeful moralists and an anxious public wanted to
hear. 'Screen Glamour More Harmful Than Screen Gangsters, Say 2½
Year Investigators', was the scornful press response. Yet Professor Weare's
committee had at least devised a system of excluding those under eighteen
from a new category of X-rated films. 'Many films contain sequences that

are brutal, anti-social, or licentious. Such films should be banned to children.' It also suggested banning all children from cinemas after 8 p.m. but this was ignored.

Despite reassurances by the Home Office Committee and the Commissioner of Metropolitan Police, imitation might take more than one form. In that respect, the award-winning French thriller *Rififi*, shown in London in 1955, was also nothing less than an instructional film for robbers. It showed professional criminals surveying their target, the chloroforming of the concierge, the duplicate key for the flat above the jewellers, the chipping of a hole in the floor, with an umbrella inserted and opened to catch fragments that might otherwise fall and trigger the alarm sensors, the silencing of the alarm itself by squirting thick foam into its box. Even those too young to see the film assimilated its lessons by word of mouth. 'Foaming' an alarm now became part of every thief's education, until alarm manufacturers defeated this by constructing a box within a box. It was true that the robbers in the film received poetic justice. That would not prevent a wistful member of the audience believing that, having learnt by their mistakes, he could do better.

5

Cinema and broadcasting were responsible to regulatory bodies which were, in turn, directly responsible to the government. The area in which the government had least control was over the reading matter of the nation's youth in crime comics and pulp fiction. Craig and Bentley might have been illiterate but most of their contemporaries were not.

In 1953, the number of books and magazines (including comics) for which destruction orders were granted quadrupled to 167,293, while the number of convictions in England and Wales for publishing obscene material more than doubled from 49 to 111. Sir David Maxwell Fyfe, Home Secretary and avowed crusader against crime comics, had found a further outlet for his energies.

In the weeks following the Craig and Bentley trial, there was one clear and easy target, an author whose books sold by the million. He was a household name in Britain, as even Mickey Spillane was never to be. His was a pen-name, simple and memorable: Hank Janson. The books contained sex and violence, or sex with violence. He was everything that had been deplored since 1945. The covers were seductive in design and suggestively violent in their titles. Sultry heroines, about to meet their fates, challenged the browser in *Bewitched* or *Torrid Temptress*, each boasting on its cover a ten million sale, an eleven million sale or a twelve million sale. There seemed no reason to doubt it.

Hard-boiled contemporary crime with a pseudo-American setting was usually the author's style, though there was room among dozens of covers for a lightly veiled harem captive or a half-dressed victim kneeling before a helmeted guard. These were not books that the great and the good would admit to reading, let alone speak up for in court.

The books were less well written than Chase or Spillane. Their quotient of sex or violence was about the same. The style was represented by several lines on the flyleaf of *Tension*, advertising the forthcoming attractions of *Whiplash*. 'Sharp's fingers stung my cheek. "Come clean!" he snarled. "You killed him. You stripped and bumped off his sister too." "I want to see my solicitor," I croaked through puffed lips.' More than anything the style resembled the film parody *Laughter in Paradise* (1951), where a sensitive and respectable middle-aged author, played by Alastair Sim, dictates penny dreadfuls to his adoring secretary with such lines as, 'I slugged her in the kisser, she sure was a swell tom-ay-to.' The joke in the film had little appeal in reality.

Hank Janson's novels crossed the Rubicon of social class, more surely than James Hadley Chase. The waiting cab-driver read them openly, the travelling bank manager discreetly. Those who read Chase were not, on the whole, the people who committed crime. But *Tension*, *Whiplash*, *Hellcat*, *The Jane with Green Eyes*, *The Lady Takes the Rap*, *Enemy of Men* and their rivals became part of working-class and teenage culture in the early 1950s. They fell easily, at two shillings a time, into the hands of the young, in years when post-war fear of 'young thugs' and violent robbery was at its height. If 'bookshops' were raided to confiscate 'Hank Jansons', they were corner newsagents, tobacconists and other retail outlets far removed from Blackwells or W. H. Smith.

To destroy Hank Janson might behead the monster of pulp fiction. If he or his publishers could be convicted as an example, back-street publishers and opportunist shopkeepers would think twice. For several years, his titles had featured on lists of books for which destruction orders were granted – and still they prospered. The writer or his minions produced a novel every month, as well as several 'specials' a year. Small wonder that he described himself not as an author but as 'a publishing business'.

It was a murder case of 1953 which raised the pursuit of Hank Janson to a full-scale prosecution. In August, John Francis Williamson, a twenty-three-year-old furnaceman of Boundaries Road, Balham, was charged with the murder of his landlady's five-year-old daughter. The child had been put to bed in the kitchen as usual but was found dead next morning. Wilkinson confessed to the police that he hit her on the head with a chair-leg after drinking beer and vermouth. There was no apparent motive but drunkenness. At his trial in November, medical witnesses on both sides agreed that he was a psychopath but also that he was not insane. A psychopath, like a sadist, was not a madman in law but a man with a moral deficiency. Wilkinson's appeal was dismissed and he was hanged.

Wilkinson did not blame the killing on anything that he had read and no evidence to this effect was offered. However, a copy of a Hank Janson novel was found in the room where the murder was committed and it seemed he had been reading it before the crime. The child's murder had been a callous and pointless act, an outrage to millions who read of it. Any jury faced with a trial of the publishers or author of the book in question might find it hard to put aside the thought of its possible responsibility for her death.[17]

Even before Wilkinson was hanged, Scotland Yard raided the London premises of Arc Press, New Fiction Press and Gaywood Press, arresting the two managing directors, Reginald Carter and Julius Reiter. They seized a number of books, including seven Hank Janson titles, *Accused*, *Auction*, *Persian Pride*, *Pursuit*, *Amok*, *Killer* and *Vengeance*, on which the obscenity prosecution was based. On 14 January 1954, the defendants appeared at the Central Criminal Court before the Recorder of London, Sir Gerald Dodson. They did not seem to think they had committed any crime and admitted full responsibility for the books. These were not, after all, works of deliberate sexual obscenity. Reginald Carter told the court that 97,000 copies of *Accused* had been printed and published, 140,000 of *Persian Pride*, 78,500 of *Amok*, 98,250 of *Killer*, and 90,000 of *Vengeance*. No figures were available for the other two books.

Mervyn Griffith-Jones conducted most of the major obscenity prose-cutions of the decade. He assured the jury that the books were freely available from 'various bookstalls throughout the country'. They sold for two shillings, within the reach of every working man or schoolboy. Five dealt with murder, robbery 'and every other kind of crime', while *Persian Pride* and *Auction* showed an unhealthy interest in the Arab world and sexual slavery. 'The main theme running through all the books is sex. The second is sadistic cruelty with the hero being tortured and young girls being tied up.' In his submission, the only possible effect of the books would be to deprave and corrupt. At the request of the prosecution, the jury spent the afternoon reading the books.

On 18 January, the Recorder demanded to know where 'Hank Janson' was. Detective Sergeant Goodall explained that a warrant for his arrest had been issued but he lived in Spain and could not be extradited. The jury convicted both defendants and their companies, despite a plea by their counsel that the public had not protested against the sale of the novels, indeed it had bought them in their hundreds of thousands. The jury should consider 'the general standard tolerated by public opinion today . . . Books which twenty-five years ago raised a storm of protest might today be published without anyone lifting an eyelid.'

Next day, Sir Gerald Dodson passed sentence, having been told by the police that the defendants were of good character. However, there had been 1,400 destruction orders for fifty-two Hank Janson titles in the past three years. There were also criminal convictions against two of the companies. Gaywood Press had been fined £50 at Blackburn in August 1951 for *Temptation* and New Fiction Press fined £200 at Darwen in August 1952 for *The Lady Takes the Rap*.

The Recorder turned to Carter and Reiter. For the benefit of those in the book trade who listened nervously from a distance, he told them, 'It is high time that publishers should realize their responsibilities.' Still less reassuring was the sequel. 'The profit in these books must be prodigious . . . Fines mean nothing to people who can make money on this scale.' The defendants were on their way to prison, as James Hadley Chase, Darcy Glinto and their publishers had not been in 1942. Carter and Reiter went down for six months each and their firms were fined £6,000. The law waited to get its hands on Hank Janson.

'This is literary pollution and it is high time that it came to an end,' said Sir Gerald for the benefit of publishers unhappily aware that their own products differed only in degree from Hank Janson. It was hard to believe that the titles and the covers of his novels, rather than the content, had not been his downfall. Where did this leave such eminent organizations as the Crime Club of Collins with titles like Peter Cheyney's *I'll Say She Does* or *Dames Don't Care* – or the publishers of Chase with *You've Got It Coming* or *Lady Here's Your Wreath*? As for the plea that books were to be judged by modern standards, the Recorder gave it short shrift. 'I profoundly disagree, and to the credit of the jury they showed by their verdict that they disagreed also.'

A purge of the corner shops began and at Maidstone Magistrates Court on 26 January 1954 a further batch of Hank Janson novels were sent to destruction. The chorus of disapproval was unanimous. 'I cannot say I have ever read worse books,' said the shocked Detective Constable McRelf who led the raid. Here, too, a warrant was issued for the arrest of Mr Janson. In another case at Brighton, involving four shops, the court ordered 902 books out of 1,617 to be destroyed. It had taken the magistrates three weeks to examine the material. They did not condemn publications which were merely erotic. Magazines that had been seized for 'including photographic studies' were returned to the retailers. As for the novels, the chairman of the bench remarked, 'It is to be hoped that booksellers will obtain information from the police of those books we have ordered to be destroyed and be careful not to infringe the law.'[18]

Reginald Carter and Julius Reiter appealed against their convictions and sentences. Their cases were heard on 15 March in the Court of Criminal Appeal, where they must have felt they had drawn the short straw by getting Lord Chief Justice Goddard as the senior of the three judges. Gerald Howarth once again argued that, as well as the tendency of the material to deprave and corrupt, 'the standards of today should be taken into consideration, and therefore it is proper for the jury to consider what was going on around them – for example, modern standards of films, and other books printed and published and for sale on bookstalls.' The trial judge should not have excluded that. 'I cannot imagine any age in which these books would not be obscene,' said the Lord Chief Justice shortly.

Gerald Howarth tried to support his argument by submitting a list of books which sold freely and were issued by respectable publishers. He suggested Hank Janson was no worse. It was a waste of breath; Lord Goddard did not even call upon the Crown to reply. 'These men have tried to sail as near the wind as they could and they have gone too far . . . It is high time that publication of this stuff was stopped in such a way as to indicate to other persons the view which this Court takes.' Goddard refused to mention the titles of comparable books submitted 'because I have no desire to give any advertisement to such shocking literature'. However, as their publishers were soon to find out, he had made a careful note of them. Carter and Reiter returned to prison. 'Other persons' had been warned.

The next defendant to appear in court was Hank Janson himself. He was Stephen Daniel Frances and he had returned from Spain to be arrested and charged. He admitted that he had written twenty-five Hank Janson novels between 1947 and 1951. On 22 December he was committed at the Guildhall to the Central Criminal Court, charged with publishing the same seven novels in 1952 that had sent Carter and Reiter to prison.

At the Old Bailey on 1 February 1955, Stephen Frances again admitted writing the twenty-five earlier books but denied writing those which were the subject of the present trial. Reginald Carter, who had printed some of the first books, paid him £4,000 and then took over the business 'including all manuscripts and outstanding debts and the assignment of the copyright in "Hank Janson"'. The author had since written books of a different sort for the English market.

However improbably, Hank Janson now became the subject of an expensive literary seminar. The jurors were locked in their room to read the seven books on trial and two more which the defendant admitted writing earlier, *The Jane with Green Eyes* and *The Lady Takes the Rap*. The jurors must decide whether there was a 'similarity in style and phrasing between these two books and the seven mentioned in the charges'. After nine days they were not sure.

When the adjourned hearing resumed on 11 February, Mervyn Griffith-Jones for the Crown announced that 'evidence has just come to light which appears to establish that four of the books in the case are not by the defendant.' Sir Anthony Hawke, the Common Serjeant, directed an acquittal on these charges and on his advice the jury acquitted on the rest.

The court assumed that the level of obscenity in the seven Carter and Reiter books must differ from the two which Frances admitted. Yet *The Lady Takes the Rap*, which he admitted, was prosecuted successfully at Darwen in August 1952. How much difference was there between the two groups or – indeed – was there any? However, ownership of 'Hank Janson' passed to another publisher who expurgated future novels. British printers refused the risk. The new titles were produced in Paris.

6

Victory over pulp fiction led to a battle against imported American 'horror comics', usually crime comics. In the autumn of 1952, after a series of well-publicized and vicious robberies, a ban on such publications was linked to demands for the return of flogging, abolished in 1948, and for tougher laws to control gun and cosh. On 1 December, from the political right of the national press, the *Daily Telegraph* appealed, 'Ban Comic A Week For Every Child', and on 4 December, 'Only Father Can Stop Bad Comics'. From the political left on 2 December the *Daily Herald* reported the hearings of the Congressional Committee as 'US Attack on Dirty Comics and Magazines'.

Dr Fredric Wertham, though his career lay in the United States, was gathering English friends in high places. He had failed to persuade the Kefauver Committee or to have a new anti-Sadism law enacted in New York. Yet the Conservative cabinet of Winston Churchill in 1952 responded to his ideas. Randolph Churchill, the great man's son, wrote a preface to Dr Wertham's denunciation of such comics in *The Seduction of the Innocent*. He denounced English courts for failing to see that obscenity went beyond sexuality. 'Surely the right course is for the Director of Public Prosecutions to initiate an action against some firms who are seeking to enrich themselves at the expense of the minds of young children?' Yet the comics were not produced in Britain and the target could only be a distributor or the newsagent who sold them. But as Dr Wertham's findings reached politicians, teachers, clergy and welfare workers, the demand for action grew louder.

The time seemed right. In addition to Lord Chief Justice Goddard, David Maxwell Fyfe was now Lord Chancellor and head of the legal system as Lord Kilmuir. In the House of Commons on 21 October 1954, the Home Secretary, Gwilym Lloyd George, promised to receive a deputation led by the Archbishop of Canterbury and to give 'very careful consideration to public unease over comics imported from the United States'. Sir Anthony Eden, the new Prime Minister, was taking a close personal interest. Lloyd George also proposed, as soon as possible, to look into the defects in the law relating to obscenity in literature.

On 12 November, Archbishop Fisher visited the Home Office. A resolution would be put to the Church Assembly: 'That this Assembly views with great concern the great increase in literature of a sordid and horrific nature now offered for sale under the misleading title of "comics", and welcomes every action that can be taken to protect the young people of this country.'

An exhibition of horror comics opened at the headquarters of the National Union of Teachers. Exhibits were gathered by teachers from pupils for viewing by MPs and journalists. Sir Hugh Lucas-Tooth, Parliamentary Under-Secretary to the Home Office, came away convinced. 'This is without any question the most appalling collection of unrelievedly bad taste I have ever seen.' For the press, the *Evening Standard* added, 'Many of the "comics" are packed with violence and morbidity that have to be seen to be believed.' On all sides there was condemnation and dismay at the ease with which the material was coming into the hands of children. The government was adamant that not a moment must be lost in speeding legislation through Parliament to deal with the peddlers of filth and degradation as they deserved.[19]

On 10 February 1955, a bill to ban horror comics, or 'harmful publications' as they were now called, was introduced in the Commons. Penalties were set at a fine of £1,000 and four months in prison, enough to put most corner shops out of business. Difficulties then appeared. Short of an anti-Sadism law preventing the depiction of crime, which had failed in the United States, this was simply a horror comics bill. However, the government also intended the statute to update the 1857 Obscene Publications Act. The Home Secretary was warned that the two things were incompatible. The 1857 Act certainly needed updating but the bill before Parliament dealt with a particular craze or fashion among the young which would probably be forgotten in five years. With the innocence of childhood at stake, however, this was not the time to quibble.

On 4 March, the future Labour leader Michael Foot and his supporters, plus six Conservative MPs, sought to limit the Act's duration. Mr Foot suggested that it should expire after three years, unless renewed. The Conservative members suggested expiry on 31 December 1961. Yet it seemed unthinkable for a measure rooting out such evil to be terminated. If this was murder of the soul, an expiry clause might as well apply to murder itself. Dr Geoffrey Fisher was not only Archbishop of Canterbury but Chairman of the Church of England Council of Education. Close behind him came the Young Men's Christian Association and the Mothers' Union, who had joined the deputation to the Home Secretary. It was an awesomely powerful pressure group.

Other voices favoured caution. Eleven days later a letter appeared in *The Times* from Sir Alan Herbert, novelist and librettist, Chairman of the Society of Authors, former member of Parliament for Oxford University, and architect of the Matrimonial Causes Act 1938. He and the Society of Authors had already drafted a new Obscene Publications Bill and sent it to the Home Office. It would replace the 'deprave and corrupt' test, which had 'worked injustice for a century' and which the Harmful Publications Bill now proposed to entrench. That was a tinkering bill and 'it tinkers badly.' Justice must be done by a new law including the whole issue of literary merit in obscenity publications.

It was not what the government wanted to be told. Next day, however, *The Times* greeted the second reading of the Harmful Publications Bill with a warning to the Home Secretary that he had been 'stampeded into legislation against "horror comics"'. The campaign against 'this latest outbreak of beastliness' had been public-spirited. As it stood, however, the new law might be used against the fairy-tale horrors of *Struwwelpeter* at one extreme and a serious magazine feature on some violent or cruel theme at the other.

The editorial reminded its readers of well-intentioned people 'genuinely convinced that "Three Blind Mice" and similar favourites are so gruesome that they do serious damage to the infant mind'. Neither

Gwilym Lloyd George nor his backers were such people but, said *The Times*, laws live on long after their original intention has become unnecessary or forgotten and 'are sometimes then used as convenient instruments for quite different purposes'. If the law on obscene publications was to be reformed it should be reformed *en bloc*.

It was perhaps injudicious, in the moral heat of the argument, to add that a child's reading was primarily a parental responsibility or that many other influences, good or bad, were as important as horror comics. By next day, the bill was through its second reading and already in committee. It criminalized stories of crime or violence or of a repulsive nature, 'told wholly or mainly in pictures'. *The Times* pointed out that it would only require a thirty-page issue to include sixteen pages of editorial and advertising material to put it beyond the reach of the statute. The bill had been hastily and badly drafted. With government support and moral fervour behind it, however, it passed into law.

The Children and Young Persons (Harmful Publications) Act soon began to gather dust. The craze for comics of all kinds faded as the attractions of television drama grew, its network spreading across most of the country with what the comedian Jimmy Edwards called 'myxomatotic speed'. Circulation figures declined until, by the 1960s, crime comics or *Tales from the Crypt* had become a curiosity. Crime was now beamed into the living room. As early as 30 October 1952, when many parts of the country could still not receive television, a previous Minister of Health, Dr Edith Summerskill, warned the nation's mothers that the current 'ugly wave' of juvenile crime would continue so long as 'boys are taught through the screen, the radio and television that to be tough with the fist or the cosh attracts attention and makes them objects of admiration in their own little world'. She did not mention horror comics.

Throughout the decade, such warnings were echoed. Glorification of crime by radio and television was debated in the Commons on 31 October 1958. G. W. Longdon warned members that large numbers of people glorified the thug when they saw and heard on television and radio, in programme after programme and for ninety per cent of the time, the thug 'being successful and enjoying the fruits of his activities'. This was supported from the Labour benches by J. E. McColl, who denounced the broadcasting companies. Their 'day after day continuous playing on violence seems indicative of profound social malaise and is leading to the growth in the minds of young people of an attitude towards violence which older people find it difficult to understand'.

In the Commons, on 19 February 1959, R. A. Butler, a future

Conservative Home Secretary, revealed that the police were concerned at the way in which crime series revealed their methods and acted as a source of intelligence to criminals. Such programmes were a textbook for criminals. In some respects, *Z-Cars* or *Softly, Softly* did the police a service. Hardly ever when a suspect was arrested did he or she exercise a right to silence, refusing to answer questions without a defending solicitor present. Viewers were left in ignorance of that right. Almost invariably, the script allowed the suspect to blurt out an incriminating or compromising reply, as no true professional would ever do.

The demand for crime, which had existed for centuries in the form of gallows speeches or true confessions by notorious criminals, made it unrealistic to suppose that it could be kept off the screens of cinemas or television sets. The traditional solution was to show virtue as being triumphant most of the time. In due course, the entertainment value of a series like the BBC's *Crimewatch* would coax viewers on to the side of the hunters rather than the hunted.

Ten years after the war, Lord Campbell's 1857 law on obscenity was ill-suited to modern literature and the modern world. As Lord Goddard had described it in 1954, no adjustment was necessary. The criteria set out in 1857 and the 'deprave and corrupt' judgment of 1868 remained valid. The battle over artistic freedom in the 1950s was an encounter between traditionalists like Goddard or Maxwell Fyfe and others who insisted that the world had moved on. A major issue was whether works of literary merit should still remain at risk from the law. Whatever the outcome, by 1955 both sides were ready to fight.

9

New Laws for Old

I

FOR FOURTEEN YEARS after the war, the dividing line between literature and obscenity was, more than ever, a matter of chance for the publisher facing trial. A housebreaker or a bank robber could hardly be unaware that he was committing a crime. A publisher, or indeed an author, could have no certainty until the jurors brought in their verdict.

It was common sense that anyone who published *Fanny Hill* or *Lady Chatterley's Lover* could expect to go to prison. Yet *The Well of Loneliness* was now published without difficulty, as were James Hanley's *Boy*, Jack Lindsay's translation of Petronius' *Satyricon*, and a number of other books condemned in the pre-war years. The more important question was how far public opinion had moved since those years and to what extent that movement might protect literature. In this context, neither Hank Janson nor *Tales from the Crypt* stood in danger of being mistaken for literature.

Faced with a new politics and increasing criminality in the new world of peace there were those who still pined for the stability of the old order, the 'normalcy' of 1920s nostalgia. Others had seen six years of total war and, set against its atrocities, were not dismayed if a novel contained an expletive which might be heard at any hour on the shop floor or a building site, nor were they disturbed by an appealing description of a sexual act.

In the immediate post-war years one historical romance and one masterpiece of war fiction set new standards of tolerance. *Forever Amber*, by the American novelist Kathleen Winsor, was placed in the reign of Charles II, embracing the royal court, Newgate prison, the Great Plague of 1665 and the Great Fire of the following year. The heroine marries four times and bears three sons by men she does not marry. It was less racy than novels written close to the time, notably Daniel Defoe's *Moll Flanders*, which was still apt to be the subject of magistrates' destruction orders in Britain. It acquired a reputation for being 'hot stuff', its fame sung from the music-hall stage by Cardew Robinson and others. 'When we played at True Confessions, Mrs Price, they made *Forever Amber* look quite tame.' On 18 June 1948, the British Board of Film Censors was obliged to explain why it had allowed the film an 'Adult' certificate, rather than banning it outright. The Board argued that it had already been released in this 'modified' version in America.

The novel had been published in the United States in October 1944. By January 1947, it had sold 1,300,000 copies as well as 100,000 of a British reprint and thirteen translation rights. It seemed a little late to bring a criminal prosecution on either side of the Atlantic. The State of Massachusetts passed a law in 1945 allowing civil litigation against books considered obscene. An action was brought against *Forever Amber* and a temporary injunction granted against further sales. At the full hearing, the book was acquitted. The plaintiffs appealed to the Massachusetts Supreme Court.

Judge Frank J. Donahue found that the book was not 'obscene, indecent, or impure'. In a famous judgment, he remarked unkindly of the plot's sexual episodes that he had found them 'a soporific rather than an aphrodisiac . . . while the novel is conducive to sleep, it is not conducive to a desire to sleep with a member of the opposite sex.' It was hardly a precedent that encouraged action in England against a book which promised much by its reputation but delivered very little on its pages.[1]

A far more serious threat attended the publication in London of Norman Mailer's epic of war in the Pacific, *The Naked and the Dead*. Its story was the invasion and conquest of the Japanese-held island of Anopopei. For six hundred pages it detailed the horrors of battle as graphically as Erich Maria Remarque had described the trenches of 1914–18 in *All Quiet on the Western Front*. By the time it was brought before the House of Commons at Westminster, it had already been banned in Canada and Australia, though not in the United States.

The omens were not particularly favourable for its London publisher, the small but prestigious firm of Allan Wingate. The vocabulary of the novel's characters, though containing far fewer obscenities than in everyday military life as millions of men had just experienced it, came close to prosecution by British standards. Mailer had veiled such crudities lightly. Among the group of infantry in the first wave of the Anopopei beach landing is the Boston Irishman, Gallagher. He is allowed to use the word 'fug', as in telling someone to 'shuffle the fuggers' in a card game or looking at his hand and asking, 'What the fug do you think I got?' It was said that

Tallulah Bankhead, on first meeting Mailer, had inquired, 'Are you the young man who can't spell "fuck"?'

Subject matter was as difficult a problem as expletives. Among topics of conversation in the infantry was the effort to recall, after years of deprivation, 'what a pussy feels like'. Yet this was a major novel of the Second World War, all the more important in the Old World because it described an area of the conflict less familiar to Europeans. Even so, a pre-war English publisher would certainly not have got away with it.

With far more reason than Kathleen Winsor, Mailer had deflected his critics by saying that this was the way the past had been. There were, after all, horrific but necessary accounts of atrocities in wartime Germany or in the fight against Japan. It was unthinkable that Lord Russell of Liverpool should be banned. Mailer's novel had nothing to match Russell's photographs of naked women being herded to their deaths at a run in one of the Nazi camps. As for tender sensibilities, British children as young as ten had been taken by their parents to sit through the newsreel scenes of Belsen's horrors, as the camp was liberated, in order that they might see and never forget.

Yet Mailer had written a novel. Fiction was seldom thought to carry the moral weight of reality and Allan Wingate was soon in trouble. On 1 May 1949, a *Sunday Times* editorial demanded that the book should be withdrawn at once. It acknowledged Norman Mailer's exceptional gifts but large parts of the book were so grossly obscene that it was unfit for circulation. It was predictable that the editorial should find the language 'incredibly foul and beastly' by comparison with any other novel being issued. No decent man could leave the book lying about or 'know without shame that his womenfolk were reading it'. It was almost exactly what the *Spectator* had said of *Ann Veronica* forty years before.

Allan Wingate replied next day in the Liberal morning daily, the *News Chronicle*, insisting that the book was 'a true picture of the way soldiers talked and behaved during the war'. American reviewers had compared it to Stendhal and Tolstoy. On the following day, the *Evening Standard* came to Mailer's defence. The book was not pornographic – and this was certainly true if pornography required any presence of the erotic. Its depiction of war, in the paper's view, was as dreadful, lurid, real and terrifying as an etching by Goya. On 8 May, the *Sunday Times* demanded a prosecution of the publisher. The paper offered the standard reassurance of most censors – that it was opposed to censorship. However, there was a limit to freedom of the press and *The Naked and the Dead* had crossed it.

It seemed that shades of the prison house were beginning to gather round Allan Wingate. As the law stood in 1948, it was impossible to plead the book's literary merit as a justification, even to show that the book's characters talked as soldiers talk. The Director of Public Prosecutions, Sir Theobald Matthew, had his attention drawn to the novel. Fortunately for Allan Wingate, questions had now been asked about it in Parliament and the director could not pre-empt the proceedings of the legislature. The constitutionally correct procedure was to refer the matter to the Attorney-General. In the new Labour government, that post was held by Sir Hartley Shawcross.[2]

The young Sir Hartley Shawcross was an incisive, debonair figure of the English bar, whose allegiance to red-blooded socialism was so fragile that his House of Commons nickname was 'Sir Shortly Floorcross'. He was now the only man who stood between Mailer's publishers and an Old Bailey trial. In the House of Commons on 23 May 1948 he explained that he must serve two public interests. 'No publisher should be permitted to deprave or corrupt morals, to exalt vice or to encourage its commission.' On the other hand there should be 'the least possible interference with the freedom of publication'.

> The Attorney-General should not seek to make the criminal law a vehicle for imposing a censorship on the frank discussion or portrayal of sordid and unedifying aspects of life simply on the grounds of offence against taste or manners. While there is much in this most tedious and lengthy book which is foul, lewd and revolting, looking at it as a whole I do not think that its intent is to corrupt or deprave or that it is likely to lead to any other result other than disgust at its contents.

It was hardly the ringing praise of those who saw in Mailer a new Stendhal or Tolstoy. Yet it was the most libertarian judgment upon alleged obscenity for many years. Indirectly, the freedom of literature in Britain owed a good deal to Norman Mailer and Allan Wingate, as well as to Shawcross himself. In 1957, the Commissioner of Metropolitan Police gave evidence that he had several times had to consider prosecutions in respect of modern fiction, which members of the public had demanded. He cited the case of James Jones' *From Here to Eternity*. Though it had been necessary to have the book read, he had always refused to prosecute. Such decisions had been far easier for him in the light of *The Naked and the Dead*.[3]

2

Despite such misgivings over fiction, it was radio, cinema and the stage which seemed the more immediate threat to the nation's post-war morals and morale. In 1947, the BBC was denounced, by the Vicar of All Saints, Nottingham, for broadcasting Eugene O'Neill's play *Ah, Wilderness*, 'the kind of play the devil would use in his propaganda to break up homes'. Having kept judiciously to the strait and narrow path in wartime, the corporation now strove to head an avant-garde of drama. In 1954, it commissioned Sasha Morrison to adapt *The Decameron* as a radio play, though censoring it as necessary. In the following year it offered Marilyn Monroe the radio lead in a new and lightly expurgated translation of the *Lysistrata* of Aristophanes. The play had never been translated so frankly before, let alone performed in England.

The stage continued to suffer the incubus of the Lord Chamberlain's duty to pre-censor all plays appearing on the English stage. When an attempt was made in the autumn of 1949 to abolish this power of an unelected court official, the reaction was so strong that the reformers could not even get a quorum of fifteen members of the House of Commons for their Censorship of Plays (Repeal) Bill. Next day, the house heard that morals in contemporary plays were 'like a farmyard'. Chuter Ede, as Home Secretary, rejected any reform of stage censorship. That Christmas, after the O'Gorman Brothers appeared in the annual pantomime at the Empire Theatre, Sheffield – *Little Bo-Peep* – they were convicted by Sheffield magistrates of 'acting parts not approved of by the Lord Chamberlain . . . certain indecencies and certain political references'.[4]

Though a ban was lifted on the Arthur Schnitzler play *Fraulein*, this served only as a reminder that its performance had been prohibited for eighteen years. In November, another ban was reiterated, this time upon Lillian Hellman's earnest and anodyne discussion of lesbianism in *The Children's Hour*. Whatever the public might want to see on the London stage, the Lord Chamberlain was still deemed to know best.

Film censorship, however controversial, was at least more than the whim of a court official. The British Board of Film Censors remained answerable to the Home Office and through Parliament to the electorate. Nor did it any longer have the last word in every case. There was a growing appetite for continental cinema. When two French films, *Manon* and *Traffic in Souls*, were refused certificates in October 1950, the London County Council intervened and licensed them, so that they might at least be seen by London audiences.

3

The victory of *The Naked and the Dead* soon proved to be misleading. Despite the Attorney-General's assurance that censorship was a last resort and that even the 'foul, lewd and revolting' was not necessarily a publisher's passport to the criminal dock, the next six years saw an astonishing increase in the prosecutions of those who published material deemed obscene. At the least punitive level were the destruction orders granted by local magistrates, which ended the matter by destroying the culprit's stock without a criminal prosecution. In 1950, in respect of books and magazines in England and Wales, the number ordered to be destroyed was 40,404, according to Home Office figures. By 1954, that had more than quadrupled to 167,293. In another field of endeavour, the number of obscene photographs destroyed had almost tripled by 1953.

The biggest increase in destruction was not in books but in what were termed 'postcards', comic but vulgar cards beloved of George Orwell and the English on their seaside holidays. These suffered only 297 casualties in 1950 but 16,646 four years later. The caricatures of sozzled latchkey husbands returning home to amply endowed wives, or embarrassed honeymoon couples and the like, were a national institution. The most respectable people posted them to friends and neighbours during their week of sun and sea. As one of six defendants remarked at Bournemouth Magistrates Court on 20 October 1953, 'There are two ways of looking at the cards, and the wording on them depends on the way they are read.' It was the meaning, rather than the wording, which was ambiguous and 751 of his cards went up in smoke.

There was a large number of such prosecutions in 1953–4, culminating in the trial of a man whom Orwell had hailed as England's greatest folk-artist. It was at Lincolnshire Quarter Sessions in July 1954, following raids in resort towns on the North Sea coast. Donald McGill was then almost eighty, a man who looked more than anything like a neatly suited academic. He had done hundreds of cards, each design sold for a fee rather than a royalty. He died eight years later and was buried in an unmarked grave at Streatham.

At his court appearance, a number of cards were produced. One showed a fat swim-suited woman on an overburdened seaside donkey, with a message to her friends, 'I'm sitting on my ass on the sands.' A red-faced husband, holding a telegraph-sized stick of rock in a phallic manner, inquired, 'A stick of rock, cock?' A pretty girl at the races informed a bookie, 'I want to back the favourite, please. My sweetheart gave me a pound to do it both ways.' The justices decided that the sight of such cards would deprave and corrupt anyone who beheld them. McGill was fined £50, or some £1,500 by modern values.

On similar grounds, Sir Frederick Wells had condemned 'sunbathing magazines' in the Lord Mayor's Court, at the London Guildhall, on 3 October 1952. The defendants were the British Sunbathers Association of Finsbury Park. He ordered the destruction of the magazines on the grounds that they 'offended against modesty and decency'.

It might seem, despite the decision over *The Naked and the Dead*, that not a great deal had changed since 1939. Yet still it was a matter of luck as to which magistrate the defendant came before and in which area. On 7 September 1954, Halifax magistrates were presented by the local police with demands for the destruction of several obscene books and magazines: *Windows in Paris: Eight Beautiful Nudes*, *The Dreadful Disclosures of Maria Monk*, *Eves Without Leaves* and *Diana Dors in 3D*. It escaped constabulary notice that *Maria Monk* was still the anti-Catholic sermon published by the Presbyterian Tract Society in 1833.

There was further difficulty as the magistrates struggled with the red and green spectacles required to see Miss Dors as anything but a two-toned blur. Though John Bastian for the prosecution assured them that she was 'practically nude', this was not at all evident. Mr Bastian insisted, however, that 'Coming into the hands of any person, it can have nothing but a corrupt and depraving influence.' Fortunately, Detective Inspector C. C. Payne was at hand with experience of red and green spectacles. The magistrates learnt how to manipulate them.

The unfortunate shopkeeper who had sold the pin-up magazines, John Gray of Hunger Hill, Halifax, could only plead that he thought them 'works of art – the female form divine'. The chairman of the bench adjourned the hearing so that the material might be studied. A month later, the court reconvened. No destruction orders were made. *Eves Without Leaves* had already been acquitted at Norwich in October 1953 and had been in print for three years, its contents exhibited at the London Salon of Photography. Diana Dors' reputation was restored and there was a certain local hilarity at the prospect of the magistrates taking a month with two-toned glasses to make their decision.

Mr Gray might count himself fortunate. In the following week, a few miles away, Leeds stipendiary magistrate, Mr R. Clewerth QC, took a very different view of the October issue of *A Basinful of Fun*, published by F. Youngman, and ordered the destruction of 108,000 copies of the magazine.

They had been seized by the police on 24 September, 'after an anonymous complaint'. K. H. Potts for the prosecution pointed out 'a revolting picture' of a girl who had won a bikini competition. There were also two 'completely unnecessary pictures, one of which was called "wolf defence"'. He complained that the drawings of characters were 'exaggerated' and that 'one is particularly reprehensible and goes beyond vulgarity, which is commonplace in the publication.' The police assured the court that many of those who bought the magazine were schoolchildren and adolescents.

The magistrate hesitated to condemn the magazine on the strength of two pictures, 'which could be taken in more ways than one . . . but there are too many "lavatory jokes"'. In vain did the defence argue that American horror comics circulating in the country were far worse or that the pictures were 'no worse than those of film actresses which one sees on the hoardings'. The magistrate told him that he had condemned the publication for two reasons, 'and I could give another 101 reasons if I had to do so'.

Mr Clewerth, a Queen's Counsel, than added a significant remark. 'A work of art like *The Decameron* or Chaucer is not considered obscene, but if it is sold at sixpence halfpenny on a bookstall to attract customers, it could well be so.' The magistrates in the drab Wiltshire railway town of Swindon had needed no persuasion of this.

In July 1954, police officers in Swindon descended on the premises of Mrs Elsie Foulds, at 274a Commercial Road. It was rather less than a bookshop in the usual sense. The officers confiscated a number of titles, including *Corpse in the Boudoir*, *Dames Fry Too* and *Desire*, the last of these by Hank Janson. Among other books seized was a handsome two-volume edition of *The Decameron* by Giovanni Boccaccio, Italian scholar and diplomat of the fourteenth century. As its title suggested, it contained a hundred stories told to one another by a group of courtiers and ladies, who were refugees from the Florentine plague of 1348. The book was written ten years after that event.

The present edition had been translated by J. M. Rigg and published by the Navarre Society with sixteen illustrations. One thing distinguished it from the other books. They were marked at two shillings and sixpence, *The Decameron* at three guineas, about twenty-five times the price. It was the best part of a week's wages for the young and innocent of Swindon. The police seized 261 books from Mrs Foulds and the magistrates ordered 61 of them to be destroyed, including the handsomely bound *Decameron*. Mrs Foulds' solicitor warned them that 'The police will be held up to the ridicule of the whole country if it is considered obscene.' Unimpressed, the

Swindon bench ordered its destruction, together with *Dames Fry Too* and its companions.[5]

Mrs Foulds took her case to the Appeal Committee of Wiltshire Quarter Sessions at Trowbridge. Some embarrassment had already been caused to the police when it was discovered that the identical edition of *The Decameron* was to be found just down the road from the shop, in the town library – and indeed just down the road in Trowbridge at the County Library.

The appeal involved counsel for the Director of Publication Prosecutions. J. T. Malone QC took on the case at short notice and had to read the book while on his summer holiday. He complained to the appeal committee that it was not 'holiday reading'. Though the appeal succeeded, he tried to dig Swindon out of the hole it had got itself into by arguing that while there might be copies in public libraries, any book which kept company with *Foolish Virgin* and *Corpse in the Boudoir* at 274a Commercial Road deserved all that it got.[6]

When questioned by the House of Commons Select Committee on the Obscene Publications Bill in 1957, Sir Theobald Matthew recalled that it was not the selling-place of the book but its sixteen illustrations which were at issue. That, however, was not what his counsel said to the appeal committee. The book displayed 'an inordinate interest in the sexual topic' and 'the book was displayed among a variety of books, the titles of which were calculated to attract those looking for undesirable literature, and particularly young people'. He had no objection to it being read by 'students of social history'.

All this was soon beside the point. The appeal committee overruled the magistrates and *The Decameron* was saved from burning. Swindon, a town whose name was not often on the lips of literary critics, was briefly and unwillingly famous for the conduct of its police force and its magistrates.

In the light of such cases as this the Home Office became more closely involved, principally to stop magistrates from making fools of themselves and undermining public confidence in the system. Destruction orders became widespread thereafter, but now under the guidance of the Home Secretary, whose officials issued a list of 4,000 titles to assist the courts.

4

Despite all this, cases before magistrates courts and the destruction of stock in some instances seemed unlikely to have a decisive impact on the circulation of 'undesirable literature'. It had become evident to the Home

Office, presided over by Sir David Maxwell Fyfe, as well as to Lord Chief Justice Goddard, that corruption must be attacked at its source. Publishers should be held to account. In some cases, these were opportunist two-man firms issuing a sheaf of lurid paperbacks and then moving on. If it were also possible to put several otherwise respectable London publishers in the dock and convict them, the entire trade would pay attention.

Two incidents precipitated a campaign of censorship in 1953–4. One occurred in the Isle of Man, which had its own laws and was not answerable to the Westminster Parliament. Boots Library, an offshoot of the famous high street chemist, was fined by the High Bailiff on 18 September 1953 for circulating two obscene novels. *Julia* by Margot Bland was published by a reputable London firm, Werner Laurie, well known for fiction, biography and translations of Maupassant. The second book was an American novel, *The Philanderer* by Stanley Kauffmann, published in New York and then in London in April 1953 by Cassell & Co.

Cassells were another respected firm whose dictionaries and textbooks were on most students' shelves. Reviews of the book had been favourable, notably in the *Spectator* by Marghanita Laski on 10 April and in the *New Statesman* by Walter Allen on 25 April. Allen saw in the book 'the rendering of the moral struggle', a man torn between the pleasures of the philanderer and the knowledge that he is destroying himself. However, this was also judged obscene by the Manx court, who made 'very strong observations' on it, inviting the Home Office in London to consider a mainland prosecution. The island court was 'rather surprised' that the book should circulate in England. *The Philanderer* and *Julia* were laid before Sir Theobald Matthew.

The two references from the Isle of Man offered a beginning but hardly made up a campaign. However, by 19 January 1954, Julius Reiter and Reginald Herbert Carter had both gone to prison for six months as publishers of Hank Janson and his competitors. In sentencing them, the Recorder of London, Sir Gerald Dodson, remarked, 'If it is to be said that an obscene publication is to be judged in the light of modern standards, I profoundly disagree.'

It had been argued by the defence that what constituted obscenity must be decided by the standards of the present age. The same argument was used when Reiter and Carter appealed against conviction in March 1954. In order to sustain the point, it became necessary to cite examples of novels 'getting away with it'. Three were chosen: Vivian Connell's *September in Quinze*, an American novel published in London by Heinemann; Walter Baxter's *The Image and the Search*, published by Secker

& Warburg, and Charles McGraw's *The Man in Control*, published by Arthur Barker, an imprint of Weidenfeld & Nicolson.

From the bench, Lord Chief Justice Goddard familiarized himself with the titles. Sir David Maxwell Fyfe now had five novels in his sights and apparent cause to prosecute five London publishers. If the charges were proved, no British publisher would be likely to risk prosecution for a very long time. Authors might also think twice about what they wrote, if they were reminded that they would sit with their publishers in the dock of the Central Criminal Court. The alter egos of James Hadley Chase and Darcy Glinto had sat there in 1942 but that had seemed something of an aberration. In the present prosecutions only two of the five authors were available. Stanley Kauffmann and Vivian Connell were American and stayed put in America, Charles McGraw was dead. However, Kathryn Dyson-Taylor, who wrote as 'Margot Bland', and Walter Baxter could and did share the dock with their publishers.

The first trial was of Kathryn Dyson-Taylor and T. Werner Laurie Ltd, as well as their printers, for publishing *Julia*. The case was not typical, since this was a small firm of good reputation, which went out of business a few years later. The problem was its size, or lack of it. It had neither the staff nor the resources to fight a case to the House of Lords. Nor could it face the disruption of business that this would involve. The defendants pleaded guilty, so that the case could be settled inexpensively at Clerkenwell Magistrates Court.

There was a plea in mitigation, which Frederick Lawton, a future Lord Justice of Appeal, performed eloquently. Mrs Dyson-Taylor was thirty-five, American-born, and had spent much of her life in Canada and France. She had no deep roots in any one country and 'has difficulty in appreciating those nuances of standards which are so important in literary work'. Mr Lawton agreed that the novel would be perfectly readable 'without those purple passages', which were only a fraction over the borderline of legality. 'The incidents only add a little more colour than was required.' In the circumstances, the magistrates could afford to be lenient. They fined Mrs Dyson-Taylor £25 with five guineas costs, Werner Laurie were fined £30 with £10 costs and the managing director of the printers was fined £5. It would not be so easy, in future, to find a printer for such books.[7]

Before the next trial, that of *The Philanderer* at the end of June, a public row broke out. It was started by Graham Greene in *The Times* on 5 June. He denounced the 'Manichaean nonsense' of the current prosecutions, which would be impossible in continental Europe. He reminded his readers of the absurd police seizures of William Blake's drawings between the wars, the banning of *Ulysses* and *The Well of Loneliness*, both of which were now freely available. Was it necessary to 'go through all this again'? When Greene was attacked as a Catholic who must support the Index, he replied that he had little regard for it when it touched imaginative literature. In a further letter Herbert Van Thal gleefully recalled the French police commissioner who tried to prosecute *Le Paris* for a line of asterisks, on the grounds of what they might suggest. Another publisher, Paul Elek, was having difficulty with his new edition of Zola's *La Terre*, unpublished in English since Henry Vizetelly was sent to prison in 1889. Printers were now afraid to touch it because of 'a single paragraph of animal mating in a novel of some 200,000 words'.

In the trial of *The Philanderer* at the Central Criminal Court, the atmosphere was distinctly different to the case of *Julia*, let alone Hank Janson. Mervyn Griffith-Jones, for the Crown, instructed the jury in their duty to accept the deprave-and-corrupt doctrine of obscenity laid down in 1868. Mr Justice Stable did not contradict him but added that the problem was whether 'the impact of certain passages on a Victorian mind [in 1868] would be the same as on an Elizabethan mind [in 1954]'. The 'modern standards' argument, which both Sir Gerald Dodson and Lord Goddard had denounced, was back in play.

To make the point, the judge recalled his parents discussing the propriety of going to see Bernard Shaw's *Pygmalion*, knowing that it contained Eliza Doolittle's line, 'Not bloody likely.' When this was used, 'It was the biggest social shock I can remember. If I had used that word when I was twenty-one, I would have been ordered out of any respectable house in England.' To compound the embarrassment of the prosecution, he instructed the jury to go away and read the novel, before the Crown presented the passages to which it objected. In the *Julia* case, only what Frederick Lawton called the 'purple passages' were in issue. Where such passages occurred in *The Philanderer*, they rang true to the sexual experience of the 1950s young, the furtive meetings, mutual nudity, disappointment on occasion. The jury retired to read the book.

The true legacy of the case was the judge's summing up. He did the work of the defence as surely as its own representatives. He began by criticizing the prosecution, which had told the jury that its decision would determine what books would or would not be published for the future. 'We are not sitting here as judges of taste. We are not here to say whether we like a book of that kind. We are not here to say whether we think it would be a good thing if books like that were never written.'

There was the gleam of an acquittal ahead. It brightened as the judge added, 'The charge is not that the tendency of the book is either to shock or disgust. That is not a criminal offence. The charge is that the tendency of the book is to corrupt and deprave. Then you say: "Well, to corrupt or deprave whom?"' He answered his own question with another. 'Are we to take our literary standards as being the level of something that is suitable for the decently brought up female aged fourteen? Or do we go even further back than that, and are we to be reduced to the kind of books that one reads as a child in the nursery?'

Once again Sir Wintringham Stable answered his own question. 'A mass of literature, great literature from many angles, is wholly unsuitable for reading by the adolescent but that does not mean that a publisher is guilty of a criminal offence for making those works available to the public.' There followed his definition of the function of a novel, which was 'not merely to entertain contemporaries; it stands as a record or picture of the society in which it was written.' This time, it seemed that 'modern standards' had won the day.

Finally, the judge knocked away the main support of the prosecution case. The Crown had read this candid account of a philanderer's decline and fall and had concluded, 'Well, that is sheer filth.' He paused and added, 'Members of the jury, is it? Is the act of sexual passion sheer filth? It may be an error of taste to write about it. It may be a matter in which perhaps old-fashioned people would mourn the reticence that was observed in these matters yesterday. But is it sheer filth? That is a matter, members of the jury, you have to consider and ultimately to decide.'

It was one of the great judgments of its day, clear, fair and humane. Mr Justice Stable spoke for the whole morning and part of the afternoon. The jury retired, returned and found the publishers not guilty. The decision had tripped up Maxwell Fyfe and his cohorts when they least expected it, given the conviction of *The Philanderer* in the Manx court. For the defence, the trial provided nationwide publicity. The novel was first published in London in March 1953 and had sold a handsome 6,000 copies in six months before Cassell had to withdraw it. Now it sold many times more, the judge's summing-up reprinted in it and adding an important coda to the law on obscenity.[8]

Through the summer and into the autumn of 1954, the remaining cases provided a Wimbledon tournament of litigation, as the ball went to and fro between prosecution and defence. In September, it was the turn of Hutchinson & Co. (Publishers) Ltd, as well as their printers, to answer charges at the Central Criminal Court of publishing an obscene libel in *September in Quinze*. This was the American novel by Vivian Connell, not the first of the author's books to appear in England. It had been published in June 1952 and no objection had been heard for a year. Since Vivian Connell was not available as a defendant, Katherine Webb, a director of Hutchinson, was additionally charged in her own right and occupied the Old Bailey dock.

The novel was described by Mervyn Griffith-Jones for the prosecution as portraying 'the life of persons at a Riviera resort, the name Quinze quite clearly intended to be the town of Cannes'. The book was available at libraries and bookshops throughout the country, which might either be taken as showing how innocuous it was or how far the contagion had spread. However, the atmosphere in this courtroom, where Sir Gerald Dodson once again presided as Recorder of London, was less cordial than it had been at the trial of *The Philanderer*. The jurors were sent away on Wednesday to read the novel by Friday morning. Unlike the case of *The Philanderer*, they were first shown which pages in the book the prosecution had taken exception to.

On Friday 17 September, the jury returned a verdict of guilty on all counts. Hutchinson, their printers and Miss Webb were each fined £500, the publishers also being ordered to pay £100 towards the costs of the prosecution. All those convicted were left to pay their own costs. The Recorder congratulated the jury on helping to protect the country from 'this sort of thing' and on realizing how important it was for the youth of that country to be protected and 'the fountain of our national blood not to be polluted at its source'. As for the publishers' plea of innocence, 'I should have thought any reader, however inexperienced, would have been repelled by a book of this sort, which is repugnant to every decent emotion which ever concerned man or woman.'

Yet for a year no one had been repelled and, taken in conjunction with *The Philanderer*, the impression grew that the outcome of such cases depended upon whether the defendants came up before the likes of Sir Wintringham Stable or the likes of Sir Gerald Dodson. The publishers, printers and Miss Webb might count themselves lucky not to have been the defendants in another case which came before the same judge in the same court during the following week.

In that case, Bernard Kaye and Alfred Kaye, publishers, were sent to prison for six months each. Two of their printers and one of their authors were fined £100, some £3,500 by modern values, with the alternative of three months in prison if they failed to pay. A third printer and a second author were fined £250, some £9,000 each in modern terms, with the alternative of six months in prison. The novels whose authors were not named were *Shameless, Soho Street Girl, Academy of Love* and *The Big Sin*. It might have been thought that these were more flagrantly illegal than the output of Hutchinson, had it not been for the Recorder's assertion that there could be nothing much worse than *September in Quinze*.⁹

The Crown had succeeded in dealing with the Kaye brothers, as also with Werner Laurie and Hutchinson. Yet it had been badly beaten in the case of Cassells and *The Philanderer*. The campaign was decided in two more trials during the autumn of 1954, the first involving Charles McGraw's *The Man in Control*, published by Arthur Barker, once again a reputable firm. Charles McGraw was dead and once more a director of the firm occupied the dock. This was Herbert Van Thal, who had tried to score off the censors in June by writing to *The Times* about the Parisian chief of police who prosecuted a row of asterisks.

Mervyn Griffith-Jones appeared for the Crown. The objection to the book was that it concerned lesbians and a girl who was corrupted at seventeen. It was not his contention that the whole of the book or even the greater part of it was obscene but he suggested 'the smell of the book was directly obscene'. How this could sustain a charge under the Obscene Publications Act was not clear and the jurors acquitted the publishers after a retirement of thirteen minutes. There had been a hint of desperation in the suggestion that the jurors could tell the character of a book by what was vaguely described as its 'smell'.¹⁰

Worst of all for Sir David Maxwell Fyfe and his supporters, indeed for everyone concerned, was the trial of Heinemann for publishing Walter Baxter's novel, *The Image and the Search*. This was a second novel, following *Look Down in Mercy*, by a gifted young novelist, published by a firm well known for issuing the fiction of such writers as Graham Greene and Somerset Maugham. The plot of *The Image and the Search* concerned a young wife whose husband was killed during the war and who, in the wake of this, involved herself in a number of affairs, all of them temporary and none of them satisfying. Perhaps in some views she was intended to be a nymphomaniac but the sense of sexual urgency is no stronger than, for example, in Graham Greene's *The End of the Affair*.

The book was a skilful evocation of a decade recently past and of a London which had already changed. It contained no obscenities and most of the bedroom scenes went little further than a description of a couple cuddling together naked. The conclusion of the wedding night is merely the groom's realization that 'he was not impotent after all.' At the end there is one page, in more than three hundred, to which objection was easily taken. Yet it describes only the young Englishwoman's desperate attempt to force herself upon an Indian who draws back with a cry of disgust and terror.

Reviewers had not liked the book, though E. M. Forster thought it 'serious and beautiful'. A *Sunday Express* editorial on 7 March 1954, the year following publication, denounced it as written 'in language abhorrent to a civilized palate' and demanded that the publishers should withdraw it. At Bow Street on 8 October, A. S. Frere, company chairman, said forthrightly, 'I regard Walter Baxter as one of the most gifted writers of this generation.' Baxter, charged with causing an obscene libel to be published, described his aim as 'a serious portrayal of the vulnerability to evil of any egocentric personality, and the disintegrating effect of sin on such a personality'.

At the trial before Mr Justice Devlin in October, after the jury had read the book, Mervyn Griffith-Jones, for the Crown, dismissed it as 'pornography dressed up as a twelve-and-sixpenny novel'. The jurors tried twice and could not agree upon a verdict. They were discharged and a retrial was ordered. The second hearing began before Mr Justice Lynskey at the Central Criminal Court on 24 November with a new defence counsel, Gerald Gardiner QC, who was to defend Penguin Books in the 1960 *Lady Chatterley* trial.

By contrast with Sir Wintringham Stable, Mr Justice Lynskey reached only the third sentence of his summing-up before breaking into language so violent that it opened the way to an appeal by Heinemann, if convicted. 'You have only got to look at my list at this Assize to see the kind of immorality of a criminal character that exists in this country – case after case of buggery, case after case of incest and case after case of abortion. So you will realize this is not an evil lightly to be brushed aside. It is an evil, if it exists, that has got to be cleaned up.'

There was no buggery, incest or abortion in *The Image and the Search* and the reason for the outburst was never explained. Lynskey was an eminent and respected member of the judiciary, a devout Catholic, famous for chairing the so-called Lynskey Tribunal of 1948, investigating allegations of corruption among ministers of the post-war Labour government. First thing next morning, he endeavoured to put matters right but the damage was done. 'I did not want to suggest to you, did not even want to hint to you that the book had had anything whatever to do with those cases . . . There is not a single scintilla of evidence that any one of those people with whom I have had to deal has ever read the book or seen it or heard of it.'

The jurors retired, came back two hours later and could not agree. They were irreconcilably divided in their view of the novel. 'If we were to stay here for a few hours or a few days,' said the foreman sadly, 'I do not think we should get any further.' The jury was discharged and Mervyn Griffith-Jones, for the Crown, informed the judge that the Director of Prosecutions would proceed no further with the case. A formal verdict of 'not guilty' was returned.[11]

In the legal battles of 1954, even if one includes the Kaye brothers and their *Soho Street Girl*, there were six cases of importance and the Crown had won three. *The Philanderer*, *The Man in Control* and *The Image and the Search* had been acquitted. Perhaps to Sir Maxwell Fyfe and the Director of Public Prosecutions, a fifty per cent success rate was disappointing but acceptable. Leaving out *Julia*, where Werner Laurie had opted to have the charges set-tled by the Clerkenwell magistrate, and the Kaye brothers, who were by no stretch of the imagination mainstream, the future looked less promising. Of four cases where books issued by major publishers had been before higher courts, the Crown had won only a single case and had lost three.

In borderline cases, such as *The Image and the Search*, juries seemed likely to disagree. Since verdicts depended entirely upon opinions of books and not at all upon the evidence of facts, this was not surprising. Yet like the 1920s it reflected a point in the nation's history where those who pined for the values of a pre-war world were balanced by those who wanted change, not least in the freedom to read what they chose to read. At the same time, the country was now under threat from publishers over whom it exercised no control whatever.

5

The new threat from France began with a single book, which had been that country's notorious best-seller in 1948. It was a crime novel, but crime as even Mickey Spillane had never known it. The author was a young surrealist, Boris Vian, a contributor to the literary monthly, *Les Temps Modernes*, who became a protégé of its editor, Jean-Paul Sartre, and of Raymond Queneau. Vian's world evoked the Englishman's dream of post-war Paris, from Gauloise cigarettes, Left Bank café tables and jazz clubs to earnest existentialism and brooding obsession. In 1947, at twenty-six, he had been on the shortlist of the Prix Goncourt for his first novel *L'Écume des jours*, translated as *Froth on the Daydream*, whose heroine established her own surreal credentials by having a water-lily growing in her lung. The author's foreword, dated New Orleans 10 March 1946, remarks that the only two things worth living for are pretty girls and the music of Duke Ellington.

In the following year Boris Vian assumed the pseudonym of 'Vernon Sullivan' for hard-boiled crime novels written in French but set in America, presenting them as if they had been translated from an English-language original. He was a distinguished translator of Gallimard's versions of Raymond Chandler, Peter Cheyney, James M. Cain and Nelson Algren. The first of four Vernon Sullivan novels was published in November 1946 and became the French best-seller next year. Its title was *J'irai cracher sur vos tombes*, literally translated for the Vendome Press edition of 1948 as *I Shall Spit on Your Graves*. It was to cause a good deal of trouble and was said by British customs officers to be the banned novel they found most revolting and the most dangerous.

It was first published in French by Editions du Scorpion, owned by Vian's friend Jean d'Haullin, who had asked him if he knew of American writers of pulp crime whose works might be profitable in France. Vian gave him his own manuscript, describing it in a preface as one which had reached him from an intermediary. He placed it in the tradition of James M. Cain but with the language of Henry Miller and a sadistic violence in advance of James Hadley Chase. Though it was hard to see much that could be thought erotic in the book, it combined sexual violence with mutual racial hatred. It also showed a moral nihilism of the kind associated with the existential avant-garde of post-war France. It was favourably reviewed by those who thought Vian was a new William Faulkner or a neglected Ernest Hemingway.

The setting of the book is Buckton, in the American Deep South. The narrator, Lee Anderson, is the manager of a bookstore, the son of a black family who like his father can pass as being white. His race is suspected only once when he is said to have shoulders with the slope of 'a negro boxer'. His mission is to avenge the lynching of a younger brother, 'le gosse', after an affair with a white girl. For some time he is content to join the promiscuous couplings of white teenagers who frequent the nearby drugstore, 'un club de bobby-soxers', where white girls who wear ankle socks, tight sweaters and write to Frank Sinatra, are 'like goats' by fourteen, while the boys are so instinctively bisexual that they serve his purpose almost as well.

His planned vengeance against the white race is the seduction and murder of two adolescent sisters from a wealthy family, fifteen and seventeen years old, Lou and Jean Asquith. He accomplishes the seduction of the elder, while she is drunk and sick at a party, with the assistance of his favourite girl, Jicky, from the drugstore. In the end, both sisters are murdered during the kind of sexual attack that Jack the Ripper might have perpetrated. Hanged by the outraged townsfolk, the physiological effect of this on the victim is to produce an erection which confronts them as 'une bosse dérisoire'.

It was not a novel likely to linger on bookshop shelves, however appalled moralists and prophets of racial harmony might be. It was far more subversive than titillatory pornography of the kind that the English language press in France was known for. The British customs could do nothing but attempt to stop the English translation entering the country. In France, its sales continued and it was dramatized in 1948. Plans were made for a film version. In the same year two more Vernon Sullivan novels appeared, *Les Morts ont tous la même peau*, or *Dead Men Look Alike*, and *Et on tuera tous les affreux* or *All Hoods Will Die*. The last of the four Sullivan novels, *Elles se rendent pas compte* or *Dames Don't Get It*, appeared in 1950.

In France, moral unease over *J'irai cracher sur vos tombes* was heightened when a copy of the book was found in a hotel bedroom next to the body of a murder victim. Vian was prosecuted in 1949 on a charge of *outrage au bonnes moeurs par la voie du livre*, corrupting public morals by means of the book, and was fined 100,000 francs. Though the novel was banned in France, the English edition was still on the customs 'stop list' in 1954. The lesson of history appeared to be that while censorship may delay the appearance of a book, play or film, it seldom prevents that appearance sooner or later. In 1973 Christian Bourgeois published the novel in France without difficulty. In 1988, it was issued as a cover-to-cover audio book by La Voix de Son Livre, alongside George Sand, Stendhal and Balzac.

The story had been adapted for the screen by Vian and Jacques Dopagne, in a version directed by Michael Gast in 1959. This was not the same film as the 1978 feature by Meir Zarchi, *I Spit on Your Grave*, the most frequently cited title in the 1984 row over 'video nasties'. Vian was appalled at the 1959 version and died of a heart attack during its first screening.

By the time of the 1954 trials in England the production of English books in Paris was dominated by the Olympia Press of Maurice Girodias, the son of Jack Kahane, who had prudently taken his mother's name during the German occupation to conceal his Jewish ancestry. The new press followed the example of Kahane's Obelisk Press, publishing Henry Miller's *Plexus*, Samuel Beckett's *Watt*, Jean Genet's *The Thief's Journal*, Alfred de Musset's *Gamiani*, under the title of *Passions' Evil*, Pauline Reage's *The Story of O*, and three volumes of Sade, *The 120 Days of Sodom, Justine: or Good-Conduct Well Chastised* and *The Bedroom Philosophers*.

Sade's status in France, in whatever language, was still contested. In Britain no publisher in his right mind would have thought of issuing an edition of such works as Girodias had circulated. Yet Sade was now increasingly regarded as one of the most remarkable minds of the revolutionary period. Scholars in France held conferences to discuss his work and the veteran man of letters Gilbert Lely had published a selection of prudently chosen *Morceaux choisis* in 1948 without trouble. Jean-Jacques Pauvert began a complete edition for subscribers in 1947. Unfortunately for him, it soon spread beyond the subscribers and proceedings were taken against him in 1953. He was brought to trial three years later. He presented a confused defence, first claiming that he was publishing great literature, then changing tack and suggesting that he was a small publisher, hardly worth bothering about, and that only a select group of intellectuals and scholars would read the books. Unsurprisingly, he lost the case. *Les 120 Journées de Sodome, Philosophie dans le boudoir, La Nouvelle Justine* and *Juliette* were banned.

As well as Sade, Miller, Genet and Beckett, the Olympia Press by 1954 had issued John Cleland's *Fanny Hill*, as *Memoirs of a Woman of Pleasure*, translations of Guillaume Apollinaire as *Amorous Exploits of a Young Rakehell* and *The Debauched Hospodar* and a number of newly written entertainments. By the 1960s, the lifting of censorship in Britain and the United States destroyed its market.

Among its other titles were *The Black Diaries of Roger Casement*, whose publication had been prevented by the British Home Office in 1925 and which was now issued unexpurgated beyond the reach of the Official Secrets Acts. In 1964, Olympia also published *Murder vs. Murder* by Jean Justice. This, too, was a book which would have encountered legal problems in Britain. It was a polemic on the A6 murder for which James Hanratty had been hanged in 1962, though another man had initially confessed to the crime. DNA evidence was later to suggest that Hanratty had been rightly convicted of murdering a young woman's lover, as well as having raped and maimed for life the young woman herself. Even so, the possibility that the DNA evidence from the exhibits had been contaminated during thirty years of inexpert storage remained a possibility. At the time of the murder no one knew in what form DNA existed or how it should be stored.

In Britain there was little provision for objection to customs seizures and destruction. Few of those caught with literary contraband wanted anything other than a quick exit into obscurity. One exception to this was a case involving a French-language edition of the works of Jean Genet in 1956. Birmingham Central Library had ordered the three volumes for their reference library through the Oxford booksellers B. H. Blackwell.

Two of the volumes were confiscated by the customs authorities on arrival in England.

What followed was not a prosecution but a public row as to whether customs authorities should have such powers over the works of an author, published in French and freely available in France, when they were to be held in the reference section of a major public library. It was certainly the case that Cambridge University Library held copies of *Lady Chatterley's Lover*, while the Bodleian Library at Oxford listed Henry Miller's novels *The Tropic of Cancer* and *The Tropic of Capricorn* in its catalogue. Among its rare books was the original edition of Sade's *La Nouvelle Justine* and *Juliette*, published together in 1796. Were such institutions to enjoy privileges denied to the main library of England's second largest city?

The argument continued in the press and in Parliament. Denis Howell, Labour member for Birmingham, All Saints, tackled the Treasury minister responsible for customs and excise, Enoch Powell. The government insisted that customs were doing their job and that, if it seemed they were not, then it was open to the importers of the volumes to appeal against the decision. Unfortunately for Mr Howell and Birmingham City Library, the importers were not the library but B. H. Blackwell, who wanted nothing more to do with the matter.

Not only was Genet a professional thief, he was a homosexual whose encounters were graphically described in his work. The Treasury gathered together its literary talents and instructed them to produce a translation of the most lurid episodes so that those in authority at Birmingham might be invited to London to read it for themselves. There was stalemate and the confiscated volumes went to their fate, not necessarily to destruction but to the library of obscene literature which the Treasury collected for its own purposes. It mattered nothing that the books in this case were in French. The Treasury kept linguists on call to read suspect books in foreign languages, 'including *argot*'. There were, after all, such rare and exotic items as the *Kama Sutra* in Danish.

The world of the Olympia Press and its rivals, like the invigorating world of Boris Vian's post-war Paris, was to pass as the 1960s saw a false dawn of liberty and enlightenment. Even so, the stop list issued to British customs officers searching luggage in 1960 still contained a final instruction that any book published by the Olympia Press or its sister the Ophelia Press should be detained and examined. By then the olive green paperback covers of the 'Traveller's Library' series, which was what this press existed to produce, were in any case vanishing from the stalls by the Seine and from the bookshops of the rue de Rivoli or Brentano's in the Avenue de l'Opéra.

The end came on the day when Her Majesty's Customs seized imported copies of J. P. Donleavy's novel *The Ginger Man*, which the Olympia Press had published in 1955. By then the book was freely available in Britain and the time had long passed for an obscenity prosecution. These copies were a reprint produced overseas as a matter of economy for the existing London publisher. Customs and Excise did not operate under the Obscene Publications Act 1959 but under the Customs Consolidation Act 1876. The 1959 law required that copies of the book should be found obscene. The Act of 1876 still required only that they should be shown to be indecent, a far lower degree of proof. It was within the country, not outside it, that *The Ginger Man* was now safe. This distinction put an end to English publishing in Paris.

6

Reactions to the failure of the 1954 prosecutions at home and the growth of English publishing on the Continent remained irreconcilable. Maxwell Fyfe as Lord Kilmuir, Lord Goddard, Sir Gerald Dodson, and judges who felt as Mr Justice Lynskey had done stood on one side. If the law against obscenity had not worked, that was because it needed strengthening. On the other side were those who saw the reluctance of juries to convict or heard the plea of Sir Wintringham Stable that literature should reflect the modern world and concluded that the law required liberalizing. It was the liberalizers who won the day, largely because they proved better organized and got their bid in first.

Authors and publishers were dismayed to see how easily a book which seemed unexceptionable might land them in the dock. In November 1954 the Society of Authors set up its committee under Sir Alan Herbert to consider how the law might be improved. The committee included a sitting MP, Roy Jenkins, later to become Home Secretary and Chancellor of the Exchequer. The removal of Maxwell Fyfe from the Home Office to the Lord Chancellor's office was fortuitous after all. His replacement, Major Gwilym Lloyd George, was sympathetic to reform of the law, if only because it could hardly be left as it was.

In Parliament, the proposal for reform drew support from all sides. Roy Jenkins not only represented the Labour party's interest but was so closely associated with the proposed legislation that it was sometimes known as 'The Jenkins Bill'. Nigel Nicolson, son of Sir Harold Nicolson and partner in the publishing firm of Weidenfeld & Nicolson, was a Conservative supporter. Following a spectacular by-election victory at Torrington in 1958, a publisher, Mark Bonham-Carter, represented the interest of the Liberal party. There might be opponents of the bill but they lacked cohesion in the House of Commons.

The law which was proposed as a result of the Society of Authors' deliberations left a good deal of the Obscene Publications Act 1857 intact. The principal change was a provision by which the 'public good' might be considered. Publication might be in the interest of art, science or learning. Judges and magistrates had consistently refused to hear evidence on this point, though A. S. Frere in his statement at the trial of *The Image and the Search* had managed to slip in the comment that he considered Walter Baxter to be one of the best novelists of the new generation.

Roy Jenkins persuaded the House of Commons that a private member's bill should be referred to a select committee on the subject. According to parliamentary convention, the membership of the committee would reflect the numerical strength of the political parties in the house. There were fourteen members, including Jenkins himself and Nigel Nicolson, as well as Chuter Ede who had been Home Secretary in the post-war Labour government. The committee sat and took evidence from 20 May 1957 until 30 January 1958.

Those who appeared before this committee included the Permanent Under-Secretary of State at the Home Office; the Director of Public Prosecutions; senior officials of Customs and Excise; the Commissioner of the Metropolitan Police; representatives of the Society of Authors and of the Publishers Association, and of the Association of Chief Police Officers of England and Wales. After the summer recess, the committee also took evidence from the Public Morality Council, the British Federation of Master Printers and two distinguished authors, T. S. Eliot and E. M. Forster.

The witnesses confirmed a good many views and facts. The Home Office still regarded literature as a twin threat. First there were cheap paperback novels produced in Britain and dealing with 'sordid subjects'. Second, since 1953 there were printed books from abroad 'of a gross obscenity previously only met with in typescripts or manuscript books or letters'. These imported books were passing to the underground trade in London and being hired out to customers at £1 a time. In the case of Sade's *Justine*, the hiring fee was £8, the equivalent of the net average wage for a working week. The Home Office was more concerned with stamping out this trade than with liberalizing the law.[12]

Perhaps the most important point in the mass of evidence was made by T. S. Eliot. In discussing the literature of the past, he pointed out that what may deprave and corrupt a reader in one age will have no effect in another. The literature of the Ancient World or the Renaissance, which may seem to threaten corruption now, did not do so then. By implication, what may have seemed corrupting to a past age may now appear as quaint or tedious.

When the committee reported, it advised the House of Commons to retain the definition of obscenity as that which tends to deprave and corrupt, simply because a better definition had proved impossible. The existing reference to depraving and corrupting those into whose hands a book was likely to fall still required further definition in the light of Mr Justice Stable's comment that this did not require all literature to be suitable for a girl of fourteen.

In any prosecution, the committee recommended that the book must be judged as a whole and not by selected passages. There should be a defence of literary or artistic merit and witnesses should be called on either side. A prosecution should be brought against a publisher rather than an author, though the author should have the right to be heard. Booksellers should have an automatic defence of 'innocent dissemination', since they could not be supposed to know the contents of every book on their shelves. To ensure uniformity, all proceedings must be brought with the consent of the Attorney-General. Authors and publishers should have the right of opposing applications for destruction orders at individual magistrates courts. The government sought to turn the bill into a more draconian measure. There was to be a clause making it an offence to possess obscene material for purposes of gain, for example, and this was used in future prosecutions.

Fortunately the bill found general sympathy. The new incumbent Conservative premier, Harold Macmillan, was the son of a famous London publishing house. In the House of Lords, the legislation was guided through its stages by a formidable champion and by the end of the following parliamentary session, in June 1959, the bill had received the royal assent as the Obscene Publications Act 1959. But whatever euphoria the libertarians might have felt, they were soon reminded that the Obscene Publications Act was only one of several laws which might be used to take a publisher to court.

7

The occasion of this reminder was the new Street Offences Act 1959. This measure was designed to sweep prostitution from the city streets and oblige the girls to find a room, a maid, a telephone number and a space for their trade card in the showcase of the local newsagent – a revolution in the vice trade that introduced the 'call girl'. Frederick Charles Shaw saw an opportunity to do a little good by publishing a *Ladies Directory*, listing the girls and their phone numbers. He also included photographs and what the House of Lords, upholding his conviction, described disapprovingly as details of the more unusual 'services' which some were prepared to perform.

Shaw began like a responsible businessman by going to Scotland Yard to ask if what he was proposing to do would be legal. 'Look, officer,' he said to a detective constable, 'I am going to publish this book. I am trying to make money out of this because since the new Act has been brought in the girls need a bit of publicity.' It was Mr Shaw who got the publicity. Scotland Yard was non-committal, saying that it was 'not in a position' to advise him whether to publish the directory or not, but it prosecuted him when he did.

It was not clear what he should be charged with. *Harris's List of Covent Garden Ladies*, as far back as 1794, was regarded as an obscene book and treated as such by the courts. It was sold at the time as a 2-for-1 offer with *The Racing Calendar* and drew a fine of £200, more than £100,000 in modern terms, with a year in prison for James Roach. Unfortunately, any charge under the new Obscene Publications Act might bring a tribe of 'expert' witnesses for the defence to talk endless nonsense about the social value of the publication. In the event, most witnesses were called for the prosecution of Mr Shaw and were call girls listed in his directory. 'I do strip tease, massage and correction,' said one of them brightly.[13]

The Director of Public Prosecutions sidestepped the new law and charged Mr Shaw with common law conspiracy to effect a public mischief and to corrupt public morals. The second count was something of a novelty, not covered by Act of Parliament. It would be an addition to common law if he were to be found guilty, as he was. However, any common law conspiracy carried a maximum sentence of life imprisonment rather than three years under the Obscene Publications Act. Frederick Shaw was badly shaken but lucky. He went down for two years. He then appealed to the House of Lords on the grounds that there had been no such offence as conspiring to corrupt public morals until he was charged with it; it certainly did not exist when he published his book. The law lords ruled there had not been one then but there was now, and sent him back to prison.[14]

The case did little to clarify the law on obscenity. In 1973, the *International Times*, or *IT*, published advertisements for homosexuals to meet for homosexual purposes. A 'public good' defence was avoided, the defendants being convicted of conspiring to corrupt public morals and a further new common law offence of conspiring to outrage public decency. On appeal, the conviction for conspiring to outrage public decency was quashed because the objective was 'too vague'. On the precedent of Mr Shaw, the conviction for conspiring to corrupt public morals was upheld.[15]

The Shaw case was a landmark in constitutional law but it sent a shiver through Bloomsbury and Soho alike. What if a reactionary Home Secretary chose to ignore the new obscenity law and charge publishers and authors under the even newer judge-made law with a conspiracy to corrupt public morals? A maximum sentence of life imprisonment was unlikely but the thought of such a provision in the hands of Lord Goddard or even Sir Gerald Dodson was less than encouraging.

IO

The Policing of Literature

EVEN AS THE new law on obscene publications came into force, there was discussion at Penguin Books over publishing D. H. Lawrence's novel *Lady Chatterley's Lover*. Its narrative was sexually explicit as no other novel commercially published in England had been. Its language was everything that had traditionally marked the vocabulary of an obscene publication.

Penguin Books were unrivalled as publishers of modern literature in paperback, including Lawrence's other novels, essays and poems. The motives which inspired Sir Allen Lane when he founded the firm, in 1936, had been part literary or educational, aiming to bring great literature and modern writing to those with sixpence in their pockets, the price of ten cigarettes. In part, he saw commercial potential in doing this on a grand scale. The parallel with Henry Vizetelly in the 1880s was both flattering and cautionary.

More than twenty years after the firm's inception it was also natural that Penguin as the publishers of Lawrence in paperback should want to include the most controversial of his titles in their series. If it was necessary to resort to the defence that the novel might be obscene but that its publication was for the public good, it would have to be justified as a 'classic'.

Translations of older classics could scarcely be a reliable guide, though the firm had issued its Penguin Classics series without much trouble. Among the earliest was Robert Graves' translation of Apuleius' *The Golden Ass* in 1950. While it was true that the narrator's love-making with the slave girl Fotis had been available in English since William Aldington's translation of 1566, the Graves version was far more spirited and appealing to the modern reader. For that reason it was banned in Australia. Graves' translation of Suetonius' *The Twelve Caesars*, issued in 1957, also contained a comprehensive list of the sexual perversions of Tiberius and Nero. Again, there was no trouble.

On the other hand, Penguin had published a distinguished and popular study of the Ancient World in 1951, *The Greeks* by H. D. F. Kitto. In the course of this, Professor Kitto had referred to Athenian comedy of the fifth century BC, that of Aristophanes and his rivals, as having 'roaring obscenities that could not be printed today'. It was less than ten years since that had been written.[1]

Among other publishers, Paul Elek had issued his unexpurgated translation of Emile Zola's *La Terre*, though he had difficulty in finding a printer. In the matter of Greek obscenity, Faber & Faber had published Aristophanes' phallic comedy, *The Lysistrata*, in 'an English version' by Dudley Fitts which made its way to the stage of the Oxford Playhouse two years later.

The reappearance of *The Lysistrata* was long overdue. Aristophanes wrote his play in 412 BC, a comedy of Athenian women banning their menfolk from sexual intercourse until peace should be agreed in the war with Sparta. In 1878 Benjamin Bickley Rogers had avoided reproach by producing what he called a 'free translation', also changing the title to *The Revolt of the Women*. Laurence Housman had offered 'A Modern Paraphrase' in 1911. Even in 1955, Dudley Fitts explained that it was necessary to use 'a comparable indelicacy' rather than a translation when, for example, Kalonike asks Lysistrata what the women should do if their men desert them. The answer, as critics through the ages had noted in Latin, referred to a phallic joke of the comedian Pherekrates. Not until the Penguin Classics translation of 1973 was this made more specific.[2]

If the fate of *Lady Chatterley* and Penguin Books depended on the novel being a modern classic, the omens were not entirely unfavourable. Even before the new legislation, on 5 January 1956, the London Sessions Appeals Committee had quashed a sentence of two months' imprisonment and a fine of £5 5s. imposed by the Bow Street magistrate on George Vinn, a bookseller of Old Compton Street in Soho who had sold the unexpurgated Paris-printed edition. On appeal, a fine of £50 with £10 10s. costs was substituted for imprisonment. John Phipps, on behalf of the Director of Public Prosecutions, conceded that 'There is great literary quality in the book.'

In the House of Commons on 3 December 1959, Dr Alan Thompson had questioned Anthony Barber, Economic Secretary to the Treasury, over a customs seizure of both *Lady Chatterley's Lover* and Henry Miller's *Tropic of Cancer*. 'It is absurd that in 1959 Customs officers should be rampaging through the luggage of British or foreign citizens living in Britain looking for copies of *Lady Chatterley's Lover*.' Both titles had been confiscated in a search of personal effects in transit to a Swedish citizen. Mr Barber replied that the confiscation was being investigated. In another incident a young girl was reduced to tears by an unidentified customs officer who found Lawrence's novel in her luggage and demanded to know her father's phone number, so that he could be phoned and his daughter's misdemeanour reported.

Arguing the case of the Swedish citizen, Dr Thompson added, 'Will you bear in mind that this controversy over D. H. Lawrence has been dead for over twenty-five years? He is now recognized as a major English novelist.' Barber replied half-heartedly, 'I am afraid I have to abide by the law. As recently as 1956 this particular book was ruled to be obscene by a magistrate at Bow Street.' A magistrate's ruling was binding on no other court, however, and applied only within a limited area of jurisdiction.

Interest in Lawrence's novel had never been greater. A film version, far more bland than the novel but cashing in on the title, was already circulating. It had been passed by the Board of Film Censors, though Croydon Town Council decided on 14 September 1959 that it would be banned from exhibition on Sundays. Indeed, some members of the Sunday Film Selection Committee wanted a total ban on the film in Croydon but the committee lacked the power to impose this.

2

By 1960, with the new law in place, the next step was bound to be a test case. The publication of *Lady Chatterley* and the subsequent prosecution resembled a gentlemanly duel rather than a legal brawl. Penguin had published several series of titles by individual authors, including Bernard Shaw, Somerset Maugham, Aldous Huxley and Evelyn Waugh. They had issued ten novels by D. H. Lawrence in 1950 to commemorate the twentieth anniversary of his death. All his novels were now in Penguin with the exception of *Lady Chatterley's Lover*. It seemed inevitable that the firm should now publish the book and equally inevitable that the Director of Public Prosecutions should test the new law.

How many jurors, faced with the text, would decide that it was a sincere and sympathetic account of an unmarried man and woman in love? How many – and there would certainly be a significant number – would echo the views of *John Bull* on the novel's first clandestine appearance in 1928? 'The sewers of French pornography would be dragged in vain to find a parallel in beastliness. The creations of muddy-minded perverts, peddled in the back-street bookstalls of Paris are prudish by comparison.'

The book's moral authenticity was said to lie in such aspects as a 'phallic tenderness' with which Lawrence endowed the affair between Sir Clifford Chatterley's wife and his gamekeeper. Constance Chatterley had been driven into the arms of Mellors only by Sir Clifford's inability to satisfy her sexually, following his injuries during the war. The language of courtship and passion is realistically that of Mellors and his class. The conduct of the couple is neither more nor less moral than nature. Even so, 'phallic tenderness' was not a quality to commend itself to Treasury Counsel at the Central Criminal Court.

Language was a problem. There remained a presumption that the use of certain words in print was criminal. The forbidden words of English literature, used with brutalizing regularity in many areas of English life, were inescapable in Lawrence's novel. Prosecuting counsel was to point out, as meticulously as an abacus, 'The word "fuck" or "fucking" occurs no less than thirty times . . . "Cunt" fourteen times, "balls" thirteen times, "shit" and "arse" six times apiece, "cock" four times, "piss" three times and so on.' It was a curious analysis of the quality of Lawrence's prose and counterproductive. It meant, for example, that these words amounted to no more than one in a thousand in the entire book. The complaint that a word like 'cunt' occurred six times also meant that it occurred rarely.[3]

Yet 'foul language', however rare, was a serious matter. When Penguin had published the autobiography of the distinguished American defence lawyer Morris Ernst, *The Best is Yet*, in 1947, it faced the problem of the word 'fuck'. Ernst used the word only in quoting material at issue during his successful defence of the Random House edition of *Ulysses,* in 1933. His autobiography containing it was freely available in America. *Ulysses* itself, with the offending word, was marketed openly on both sides of the Atlantic. The legal advice given to Penguin in 1947 was that they would face prosecution unless they shortened it to 'f . . k'. They did so. Morris Ernst, a veteran campaigner against censorship, was dismayed.

Yet there was some comfort in precedent. *Ulysses* had been acquitted in the United States and the British government had realized that banning it was no longer realistic. In 1959 there had been an action in New York between Grove Press and the Postmaster-General after the firm's edition of *Lady Chatterley's Lover* was banned from the mails on the grounds of obscenity. The publisher had won; the book passed freely through the mails. This verdict might, at the least, discourage a conviction in England.

Even on the most pessimistic analysis, if the matter were handled properly, Sir Allen Lane need not go to prison. The prosecution conceded at the trial that the reputation of Lane and his firm was above reproach.

Indeed, his reputation was said to be of a kind that stands like credit at the bank to a defendant in criminal proceedings.

The novel was printed by Western Printing Services, after Hazell, Watson & Viney of Aylesbury had withdrawn from the contract over protests by the typesetters. They also feared prosecution. The print run was 200,000 copies at 3s. 6d. and publication was scheduled for 25 August 1960. Earlier that month news of the printing reached Sir Theobald Matthew, Director of Public Prosecutions. It was decided to bring proceedings. A summons was served on 19 August and the defendants made a point of cooperating fully. Scotland Yard were invited to collect twelve copies from Penguin's offices, rather than raid a bookseller or wholesaler. The books were called for by Detective Inspector Monahan and his sergeant. Michael Rubinstein, the firm's solicitor, made the point to Scotland Yard that publication in this way had been 'symbolic'. It was likely that any sentence would be nominal. Accordingly, charges were brought against Penguin Books, not against individual directors.

Yet in the cold world of the courtroom there were perils that had appeared insignificant or went unnoticed in the safe confines of parliamentary debate. The new law still defined obscenity as material likely to deprave and corrupt those who read it. Of course, if it were found obscene but its publication appeared to the jury to be for the public good, as being in the interests of literature, art or science, the publisher and his book were to go free. This meant that the jurors would have to consider whether they themselves, or at least their families or their children, were likely to be depraved or corrupted by it. Yet somewhere, probably in university departments, there would be those in whose interest the book ought to be available. Which interest would they put first? It seemed unlikely the book would clear the hurdle of 'public good'.

In the event, the jury were said to be 9 to 3 for acquittal before the hearing began. This may have had less to do with new legislation than with a feeling in the post-war world and the reformist decade of the 1950s that what people chose to read was up to them. Deference had been at a discount since 1945 and nowhere was this more evident than in matters of taste.

So far as a trial is a public performance, counsel for the prosecution and the defence, as well as the judge, were to be eclipsed by the witnesses. Sir Laurence Byrne, now Mr Justice Byrne, had featured in a well-known obscenity case twenty-eight years earlier when he prosecuted at the trial of Count Geoffrey Potocki de Montalk, who in 1932 went to prison for six months after trying to persuade a typesetter to print his poems, *Here Lies*

John Penis. Gerald Gardiner, briefed for the defence of Penguin Books, was one of few advocates to deserve the epithet silver-tongued. His manner betrayed a youthful ambition to be an actor. He was one of the reformers of the decade, founder of the Campaign for the Abolition of Capital Punishment, destined to became Lord Chancellor in the Labour government of 1964, and the first Chancellor of the Open University, in which he also became a student.

Mervyn Griffith-Jones, for the prosecution, had a long and distinguished record as Treasury Counsel, some of it in the business of prosecuting obscenity. He was ridiculed after the *Lady Chatterley* case for having told the jury: 'Ask yourselves the question, would you approve of your young sons, young daughters – because girls can read as well as boys – reading this book? Is it a book you would have lying around in your own house? Is it even a book that you would wish your wife or your servants to read?' This last question drew smiles from the jurors at its antique quality. The truth was that Mervyn Griffith-Jones was capable of solemn facetiousness. In the present trial there was also a point when he explained to the jurors that 'phallus' meant penis, 'for those of you who have forgotten your Greek'. Such moments were his only approach to humour in an arena where he now had few friends. Unfortunately, as the trial seemed to turn against him, he became more outlandish and fared badly against the cultivated and reasonable arguments of Gerald Gardiner.[4]

For the first time in such a case it was open to defence and prosecution to offer expert witnesses who would testify to the book's literary qualities – or lack of them. They were not allowed to give evidence as to whether they thought the book would deprave or corrupt those who read it. This was a question for the jury alone and the jury must not be swayed in advance, except by the arguments of counsel. When Gerald Gardiner QC for the defence asked Graham Hough his opinion of a passage from Jacques Barzun, including the words, 'I do not consider Lawrence's novel pornographic', Mervyn Griffith-Jones for the Crown was on his feet at once. As a result, Mr Justice Byrne ruled that Mr Gardiner might question the witness about Barzun but not on the point of whether the novel was pornographic, which was for the jury.[5]

The prosecution offered no witnesses. It was left to Mervyn Griffith-Jones to act the part of a puzzled and disgusted reader. It might not have been difficult to find witnesses prepared to say that, compared with other novels by Lawrence, *Lady Chatterley* was not a particularly impressive achievement. However, in weight of numbers and reputation they would have been hard pressed to outgun the heavy artillery of the defence.

Among distinguished academics and experts on Lawrence who gave evidence were Graham Hough of Christ's College, Cambridge, Helen Gardner from Oxford and Joan Bennett from Cambridge. Vivian da Sola Pinto was a friend of Lawrence's surviving sister and had created a special collection at the University of Nottingham, where Lawrence was a student. Professor Richard Hoggart was not only a distinguished scholar but author of *The Uses of Literacy*, a fine and definitive analysis of contemporary literature and society. Among authors were the novelist Dame Rebecca West and Dame Veronica Wedgwood, who as C. V. Wedgwood was a biographer, as well as one of the greatest authorities on seventeenth-century English and European history and literature.

Among clergy were Dr John Robinson, Bishop of Woolwich, and Canon Milford, Master of the Temple. Just before Dr Robinson left the witness box, he was asked by Gerald Gardiner whether this was a book Christians should read, meaning presumably that they should feel it permissible to read it. 'Yes,' said the bishop, 'I think it is.' When this reached the press, a single word was added to the headlines, giving Penguin Books its best advertising slogan ever, '"A Book All Christians Should Read" – Bishop'. Among other witnesses, Norman St John Stevas spoke for the new law which he had largely created and Sir Allen Lane for Penguin Books.[6]

The evidence of these witnesses was impressive but less dramatic than a single incident on the third day of the trial. An elderly man walked slowly across the courtroom, bowed to the judge, and entered the witness box. When asked by Jeremy Hutcheson for the defence, 'Is your name Edward Morgan Forster?' he said, 'Yes.' Five members of the jury turned towards him with renewed interest. A list of his novels was read out. When Mr Hutcheson reached *A Passage to India* the heads of the other seven jurors also turned. A dramatization of the novel was currently running in the West End. He was the only witness who had known Lawrence personally. 'I saw a great deal of him in 1915. That was the time when I saw him most but we kept in touch.' Had Mr Forster described Lawrence at the time of his death as 'the greatest imaginative novelist of his generation'? 'Yes, I would still hold to it.' On that basis, he conceded, *Lady Chatterley's Lover* was 'not the novel of Lawrence I most admire. That would be *Sons and Lovers*, I think', but it showed 'very high literary merit'. Mervyn Griffith-Jones did not cross-examine.[7]

The battle between Mr Griffith-Jones and witnesses in cross-examination assumed an almost predictable form. The prosecutor would read out a description of sexual intercourse in which the words 'fuck' and 'cunt' or even 'womb' and 'belly' were repeated. Was this supposed to be great writing? The witnesses were skilful enough to avoid the trap of trying to justify everything offered them. They either said that this particular passage was not remarkably good or that it was not representative of the quality of the book as a whole, which was the test required by law. They all said that while they thought this a very fine novel, they were not arguing that it was Lawrence at his best. One or two went on to the attack and challenged Mr Griffith-Jones as to whether a particular 'purple passage', as he called it, was bad writing. Whichever course they took, the impression was of an integrity and honesty of view not universal among defence witnesses in a criminal court.

Mr Griffith-Jones helped this impression by making tactical errors in cross-examination. When questioning Professor Richard Hoggart, perhaps the most cogent and best-informed of all the defence witnesses, he queried the description of Lawrence's writing as puritanical. 'I thought I had lived my life under a misapprehension as to the meaning of the word "Puritanical". Will you help me?' Professor Hoggart explained that, in English historical tradition, Puritanism was not synonymous with prudery but meant 'an intense sense of responsibility for one's conscience'. 'I am obliged for that lecture upon it,' said Griffith-Jones sarcastically. He then asked a question which occupied twenty lines of the trial report. When Professor Hoggart answered him in two lines, he was told that the question was 'a simple one to answer without another lecture'. It was a bad mistake. A few minutes later Griffith-Jones was called to order by the judge and was apologizing to the witness. All this damaged him before the jury. Presumably his ill-temper came from knowing by this point that he had lost his case.[8]

In the end, during his final address to the jury, he fell back on a line of attack which had not matured much since *John Bull* in 1928. He seized on page 217 of the novel, where Mellors stroked Lady Chatterley's breasts and pulled off her nightdress over her head. 'Why introduce a little striptease into it all? What is the point of taking off the night-dress? What a passage! Is that the kind of thing that qualifies a book as great literature? You would have to go, would you not, some way in the Charing Cross Road, in the back streets of Paris, even Port Said to find a description of sexual intercourse which is perhaps as lurid as that one.'[9]

Gerald Gardiner's reply was fluent and finely crafted, arguing a point forbidden to the expert witnesses – *Lady Chatterley's Lover* would corrupt no one. 'My submission is that this book would not corrupt anyone in real life, young people included. With deference to my friend I should add, not even your wives or your servants.' The jury smiled again at this. It was a smile that all the talk of Port Said and Paris, even the unjustly maligned Charing Cross Road, would not undo. 'Members of the Jury,' said Mr Gardiner, 'I leave Lawrence's reputation and the reputation of Penguin Books with confidence in your hands.'[10]

Mervyn Griffith-Jones had ended with a glancing blow at the 'so-called experts' who had spoken for the defence. Mr Justice Byrne, in his summing-up, commended the prosecutor's advice to the jurors to 'Keep your feet on the ground.' They did so – and acquitted Penguin Books. Gerald Gardiner applied for costs on behalf of his clients. 'I will make no order as to costs,' said the judge, which left the publishers with a bill estimated at £14,000 – almost half a million pounds in modern terms. The trial was dubbed the most expensive seminar on D. H. Lawrence ever held. It also made *Lady Chatterley* one of the best-sellers of all time and Penguin Books a wealthy publisher. Fifteen years later its sales had reached four million. The public flotation of the firm in 1961 was oversubscribed fifteen times. The result weighed heavily in the Director of Public Prosecutions' refusal to bring proceedings in several controversial cases over the next thirty years.[11]

The great and the good had their day of triumph. Others were not called because there were already so many. T. S Eliot was among those in waiting. Graham Greene favoured publication but found parts of the book absurd and feared that he might damage Penguin's case. Among those who would have been happy to see the book fail were Edith Sitwell, because she believed the character of Sir Clifford Chatterley was based upon her brother Osbert, and Sir John Sparrow, barrister of the Middle Temple and Warden of All Souls College, Oxford. He was to publish an elaborate critique in *Encounter* for February 1962 of the 'night of passion' on page 258. He concluded that the passion on this occasion was 'that known by the English law as buggery'. What would the verdict have been had this been made plain to the jury? Yet the jury read the book and, presumably, came to a conclusion other than Sir John's.

Another absentee was F. R. Leavis, perhaps the most influential and certainly the most combative academic critic of his day. He had written a major book on Lawrence and was a Penguin author. He was not called because he told the firm bluntly what many others may have felt privately, that the publication of the novel in this manner had done Lawrence's reputation a disservice.

3

Few of these witnesses entered the witness box in such a trial again. The book that next faced the law had more in common with *The Ladies Directory* than with Lawrence. Its heroine's adventures were more extensive and exotic than anything Constance Chatterley encountered. John Cleland's *Fanny Hill* was more than two hundred years old and a stalwart of the criminal courts. It had first appeared in two volumes, in November 1748 and February 1749, as *Memoirs of a Woman of Pleasure*. Subsequently it was far better known under the name of its heroine. Even in 1749 the authorities were in no two minds about it. The office of the Secretary of State, the Duke of Newcastle, tracked down the publisher 'G. Fenton', who proved to be Fenton Griffiths. The publisher then betrayed the identity of the author. John Cleland protested that he had written it without any intention of publication until he found himself in the Fleet prison for debt. Encouraged by others, he polished up the narrative and offered it to a publisher. When it was printed, 'more clergymen bought it than any other distinction of men.'

Though the first edition was doomed, the novel was reprinted in an expurgated version in 1750 as *Memoirs of Fanny Hill* with a disclaimer on the title page that the author had described vice 'solely to make the worthier, the solemn sacrifice of it to virtue'. Among these opportunists, John Cleland had enjoyed a gentleman's education at Westminster School without the income to support it afterwards. Now forty, he had been British Consul at Smyrna, served in the East India Company and then, as he complained to the Secretary of State, was driven to become 'a writer for Bread'. He tried novels and journalism. As a last resort, he turned to Celtic philology. He survived the *Fanny Hill* scandal by forty years, dying at the age of eighty in the year of the French Revolution.[12]

Fanny Hill's memoirs are a section cut through the sexual underworld of George II's London. There are such eccentricities as the alleged delights of flagellation, mention of which would have seemed impossible in any novel of Lawrence. It is rather as if Daniel Defoe's *Moll Flanders* had been rewritten for the age of *Playboy* and *Penthouse* magazine. However, it was far more ornately composed than either *Lady Chatterley's Lover* or the contents of the 1960s magazines – nor did it resort to so-called four-letter words. John Cleland had, after all, received the education of an eighteenth-century gentleman.

The 1963 edition was a paperback from Mayflower Books, a main-

stream firm. An expensive hardback was published by a rival and no action
was taken. Unlike Penguin, Mayflower did not invite Scotland Yard to collect copies. The case began when a plain-clothes detective inspector went
to the Magic Shop in the Tottenham Court Road, owned by G. Gold &
Son, subsequently known as publishers of a range of sex magazines. He
bought a copy of the novel. Two days later, the Metropolitan Magistrate,
Sir Robert Blundell, granted a search warrant and 171 copies were
impounded from the shop.

At the magistrate's hearing, Mayflower Books were legally entitled to
intervene but not to demand a jury trial as of right. The book's fate would
be decided by Sir Robert Blundell, who had already granted the search
warrant. Mayflower also asked the Director of Public Prosecutions to proceed against them rather than the bookseller, but this was refused.

When the case opened at Bow Street on 20 January 1964, it was difficult to imagine Rebecca West or E. M. Forster – let alone the Bishop of
Woolwich – standing up for *Fanny Hill*. This was not to be a book all
Christians should read. The historian Peter Quennell, the novelist and
critic Marghanita Laski, H. Montgomery Hyde, author of *A History of
Pornography* and former member of Parliament, led a small team of defence
witnesses. Mervyn Griffith-Jones headed the prosecution and he called no
witnesses.

Peter Quennell conceded that this was not a literary masterpiece but the
equivalent of William Hogarth's etchings in *The Harlot's Progress*. He quoted
from the preface to the American edition, now circulating freely there,
'Fanny Hill would have shuddered at Lady Chatterley.' Other witnesses
pointed out that the novel had a good deal in common with the work of
Smollett or Henry Fielding, whose *Tom Jones* was its exact contemporary.

At the end of the closing speech for the defence, Sir Robert Blundell
announced that he would not call upon the prosecution to reply. 'Doing
the best I can in the circumstances, I have no hesitation in saying that the
order should be made.' The forfeited copies were removed by the police
and the law was in confusion once more.[13]

Sir Robert Blundell's decision affected only the area of his jurisdiction
as a magistrate, which was roughly central London. It did not apply to the
expensive hardback edition which continued to be sold. The Mayflower
paperback was prosecuted again in April 1964, when it was condemned by
magistrates in Manchester. The book might be sold in other parts of the
country but the outlook was not promising. Mayflower cut their losses and
reissued it in an expurgated version. Even the expurgated edition was
banned by magistrates in Edinburgh but survived elsewhere. In 1970, it was

not a reform of the law but a change in the climate of opinion which persuaded Mayflower to risk an unexpurgated edition. This time there was no prosecution.

As a result of the case, an Obscene Publications Act 1964 amended its predecessor. A publisher might now claim the right to a jury trial, rather than a magistrate's decision. Yet a publisher might be convicted of possessing obscene material even if it was merely a manuscript under consideration, providing that some intention to publish could be shown.

Titles routinely prosecuted in the past were now sidling into print. Whether they were slipping through the net, as the phrase had it, or ignored because the authorities preferred to avoid another confrontation of the Chatterley kind was yet to be determined. Among the most notorious, Henry Miller's *Tropic of Cancer* was published by John Calder in 1963 without difficulty and *Tropic of Capricorn* in 1964, even as *Fanny Hill* was being banned. Pauline Reage's novel *The Story of O* was published by the Olympia Press in a London hardback without a prosecution. In 1969 Lytton Strachey's *Ermyntrude and Esmeralda*, a bisexual romp written half a century earlier, first appeared and in 1971 E. M. Forster's *Maurice*, a novel of homosexuality from the same time, was first published. A number of other titles, including Lawrence Durrell's *The Black Book*, came home from exile in Paris.

4

Future prosecutions were divided between texts of literary or historical interest and those which, in the name of rebellious youth, sounded to most people over thirty not unlike a tantrum in a middle-class nursery. The last major prosecution of what was recognizably a traditional work of literature was of Hubert Selby Jr's novel *Last Exit to Brooklyn*, toiling through various stages from November 1966 until July 1968. Anyone seeking to demonstrate the pointlessness of obscenity trials for such fiction need have looked no further.

Sections of this American novel had appeared in prestigious 'little magazines', including *Black Mountain Review* and *New Directions*, for ten years past. As a novel published in New York it gathered tributes to its power and sincerity. *Newsweek*, hardly a forum of the literary avant-garde, thought it a 'serious work of literature' and was grateful to Selby and to Grove Press for believing in his fatal vision and strong, original talent. The *Nation* invoked Dostoevsky.

Yet unlike *Fanny Hill* or *Lady Chatterley*, Selby offered a troubled and repellent view of the contemporary world. The *Saturday Review* warned of 'an account of the life of people at the bottom of the heap'. Selby had seen the world, as a merchant sailor, a TB patient, a copy-holder and wire-boy. What he saw, he wrote. To the *Chicago Sun-Times* his style was a battering ram, and to the *Los Angeles Times* a flick-knife. His themes, said the *Sun-Times*, were sex and violence. Anyone finding that distasteful should read something more reassuring.

In the shadow of the Brooklyn army base or naval yard, an assortment of thieves, pimps, prostitutes of both sexes and casual killers infested the streets, bars and cafés. Their street violence was routine and extreme, aimless yet often fatal. The style of the novel with its elimination of the narrator had echoes of James Joyce; the bleak atrocities and forlorn landscape suggested Dickens and Zola in a century far more evil than their own. As a portrait of a post-war criminal society, it recalled *The Thief's Journal* of Jean Genet. The most abhorrent episode, to judge by the level of complaints, was the street murder of the female prostitute Tralala, abused and violated before death and desecrated afterwards. Yet the narrative also had the freshness of experimental writing in the literary magazines where it had first appeared.

Calder & Boyars acquired British and Commonwealth rights. Before publication, their solicitors sent a copy of the novel to the Director of Public Prosecutions, acknowledging that this was a controversial book, which portrayed drug-taking and homosexuality – both illegal in England at the time – and sexual perversion. In reply, the DPP's deputy wrote what he described as 'a most unhelpful letter . . . Not because I wish to be unhelpful but because I can get no help from the Acts.' Professor Barbara Hardy, author of a distinguished study of George Eliot and one of the foremost authorities on Victorian literature, advised publication. The book appeared in January 1966.[14]

It seemed that Professor Hardy's advice and the instinct of the publishers had been right. Reviews were respectful, including those from Kenneth Allsop in the *Spectator* and Anthony Burgess in the *Listener*, who wrote that no book could be 'less obscene'. If obscenity must titillate, the novel was a failure. It sold in hardback for some months without interference. There was no murmur from the DPP. Then, on 2 March in the House of Commons, a Conservative MP, Sir Charles Taylor, directed the attention of the Attorney-General to what he called a filthy and disgusting book. It had been sent to him by the well-known Oxford bookseller and magistrate, Sir Basil Blackwell.

Sir Elwyn Jones, as Attorney-General, declined to take action. The book had been available for five months. It had sold 11,247 copies and its publishers had made a modest profit of £1,184, one year's income for a single person on an average wage. Critics were 'almost unanimous' in praising its literary merit and the DPP was 'far from certain' that a prosecution would succeed.[15]

A private prosecution of Calder & Boyars was undertaken by a well-known right-wing Conservative MP and Baptist lay-preacher, Sir Cyril Black, supported by a far better known Labour MP, Robert Maxwell, who described the book as 'muck'. Proceedings before the Marlborough Street magistrate ended with a conviction, despite evidence from Anthony Burgess and others for the defence. The magistrate described the book as worse than any typewritten pornography which had come his way from Soho.

Once again, the verdict was binding only in the Marlborough Street jurisdiction and the publishers announced that they would continue to sell the book. At this point the DPP intervened and they were charged under the Obscene Publications Act. It was not until November 1967, a year and ten months after the book's appearance, that the jury trial began at the Central Criminal Court. The jurors read the book and then heard evidence from defence witnesses including both Barbara Hardy and Frank Kermode, who compared Selby's exploration of the lower depths with Dickens and Galsworthy.

The prosecution produced the Reverend David Shepherd, once an opening batsman for England and now a worker with deprived youth in the East End of London. Sir Basil Blackwell turned the tables on his cross-examiner when asked if the book had depraved and corrupted him. He said it had. This was a trick, as it soon proved. Sir Basil explained that he was an old man and the short remainder of his life would be sullied by the memory of Selby's fiction. As a magistrate he might reasonably be required to know that this was not what the law had meant by 'deprave and corrupt' in *Regina v. Hicklin* (1868).

That 1868 judgment went on to define 'deprave and corrupt' as being likely to suggest to readers of all ages 'thoughts of a most impure and libidinous character'. Had Blackwell not known this definition to begin with, then his professional journal, the *Justice of the Peace and Local Government Review*, had set the whole problem out fully in a series of articles in 1954, reprinted as a pamphlet, *Obscene Publications*, in 1955 with the details of the *Hicklin* judgment. It was not likely that Blackwell, bookseller, magistrate and anti-pornographer, was unaware of the contents.[16]

Such devices worked well enough for present purposes and the jury returned a verdict of guilty. Yet Calder & Boyars had behaved responsibly. They escaped with a fine of £100 and £500 costs. Far more serious, the case was to cost them £15,000. In a further gamble, they appealed against conviction and were represented by John Mortimer. A further eight months passed before the appeal hearing, two and a half years after the novel's first appearance in Britain.

As Lord Justice Salmon made plain, the Appeal Court did not propose to express a view as to whether the book was obscene or publication was in the public interest. Those had been matters for the jury alone. The basis of the appeal was that the trial judge had failed to sum up adequately to the jury a vital part of the defence case. The defence had maintained that publication was in the public interest because the book was so shocking that readers would want to eradicate the evils it portrayed. This might or might not be true but Judge Rogers should have included it in his summing-up.

The appeal succeeded. Lord Salmon said that Judge Rogers had thrown the jury in 'at the deep end' and left them to sink or swim. They should have been told to consider, on the one hand, the number of readers who might be depraved and corrupted by reading the book, as well as the strength of that tendency and the nature of the corruption or depravity. On the other hand, they should have been told to allow for whatever literary, sociological or ethical value the book might possess and then weigh the two sets of factors against one another. This direction had not been given. 'It is impossible for the court to be satisfied that the flaws in the summing-up caused no miscarriage of justice.'[17]

The publishers and the novel had been cleared and the sentence of £100 with £500 costs was quashed. The Director of Public Prosecutions declined to bring charges again. Sir Cyril Black MP might have done so, had he not been overtaken by the Criminal Law Act 1967, passed during the long progress of this case through the courts. It had never been intended that concerned citizens should be allowed to take the law into their own hands, causing chaos by persuading magistrates to ban a book in some parts of the country while it was freely available in others. The Criminal Law Act now provided that no private citizen might seek a destruction order from a magistrate without leave of the Director of Public Prosecutions.

It seemed that Sir Cyril Black and Sir Basil Blackwell had wasted their time, the courts had been put to a good deal of fruitless trouble and the publishers were £15,000 out of pocket. The novel was reprinted as a 'Post-Trial Edition Complete and Unexpurgated' with an introduction by Anthony Burgess. The temporary loss sustained by Calder & Boyars was turned into a handsome profit. Those who had most to lose were the pornographic booksellers of Soho and elsewhere. After the prosecution before the Bow Street magistrate in July 1966, copies from under the counter doubled in price from 30s. to £3. When the Old Bailey trial began, the book was selling illegally at £5 or £6 a copy. Such entrepreneurs had reason to be grateful to Sir Cyril and his supporters. The censors' dilemma had not changed much since James Bramston wrote *The Man of Taste* in 1733.

> Can Statutes keep the British Press in Awe,
> When that sells best that's most against the Law?

5

In parallel with the battle to save the literature of the present from the laws of obscenity there was a fight on behalf of books whose appeal was historical. The fact that a publication had historical interest might seem to make it more respectable than if it had been modern and revolutionary. Yet historical interest did not help Mayflower Books with *Fanny Hill*. When Peter Quennell told Mervyn Griffith-Jones, under cross-examination, that the novel had been recommended by a Cambridge tutor before the war as a text to be studied for eighteenth-century social history, he received short shrift. A greater obstacle faced the first two volumes of the anonymous Victorian confession, *My Secret Life*, at Leeds Assizes in 1969, though the book in question was not a novel.

This diary was the work of 'Walter', who if his account is to be believed was born about 1820 and was still alive in the late 1880s. In 1888, for his own amusement, the eleven volumes of this memoir were said to have been printed in an edition of six copies. Three of these survive. One is in private hands, one was left to the British Library by C. R. Dawes and one is in the Kinsey Institute at Bloomington, Indiana. In appearance, it is a book printed at the turn of the century or a little earlier in France, Belgium or Holland.

From infancy to old age, it describes its author's life from the perspective of prolific sexual experience. He claims sexual relations with some 1,200 women, many of them prostitutes or 'casuals'. Some, like Camille or Yellow-Haired Kitty, became the objects of a long affair. The figures of his narrative, his mother, his godfather the surgeon-major, cousin Fred who died with his regiment in India, the lewd old major at his club with whom Walter 'chummed', are as vivid as any in a novel. They are, as Steven

Marcus described them at the trial, 'novelistically drawn'. Yet they are no more the conveniently crafted characters of fiction than are those of Henry Mayhew's *London Labour and the London Poor*. Beyond them, the streets of London, the women of the Strand in black dresses on a blazing summer afternoon, have the suggestive realism of early photographs.

The voices are a match for those of Mayhew. Fifteen-year-old Kitty, a prostitute in the late 1850s, is asked what made her turn to this way of life. Better food than her mother can afford to give her, is the answer. 'Pies and sausage-rolls! O, my eye, ain't they prime!' The ring of reality rather than the artifice of pornography echoes in these outbursts. The reactions of the people have a novelty and authenticity. Driving in a London cab with Camille in the 1840s, Walter exposes himself to her, unaware that they are about to be overlooked by passing traffic. '"The omnibus! The omnibus!" she cried out suddenly. Forgetting myself and all but my wants, I had exposed my randy doodle just as an omnibus passed, and as I looked up, there was the conductor laughing at me.' It is a more probable and a more human response than a stare of shocked propriety.

Walter is a predator and a knave. In general, however, his account gives the lie to the legend of Victorian prostitution by girls under the age of consent, if only because that age was twelve until 1876, when it was raised to thirteen, and then sixteen from 1885. There is one harrowing and repellent encounter with a girl of ten and a pander who claims to be her mother. It is the more harrowing because, had the girl been two years older, it would not have been illegal.

Walter's comment on the diary, in his second preface, rings true for much of Victorian England. 'Whatever society may say, it is but a narrative of human life, perhaps the every day life of thousands, if the confession could be had.' In 1857, the Metropolitan Police put the number of London prostitutes at 8,600, when the total population of the capital was 2,800,000. Henry Mayhew and Dr Phillpotts, Bishop of Exeter, thought the number was 80,000, perhaps more. These figures, if nothing else, would support Walter's account.

If the Obscene Publications Act of 1959 meant what it said, this was surely a work whose publication was 'for the public good', in the interest of literature or learning. It was, on the evidence, a unique historical document, however repellent the character of its author.

In 1967 the book had been published by Grove Press in the United States, and a Bradford printer, Arthur Dobson, was now producing a reprint of this edition for the English market, on his own account. Before the printing of the first two volumes was complete, someone found a discarded sheet of the galley proof in a wastepaper basket. That evening it was being handed round among the customers of a local pub for their amusement. Not everyone was amused and someone went to the police. Mr Dobson found himself at Leeds Winter Assizes in January 1969 before Mr Justice Veale and a jury, charged with possessing obscene material for purposes of gain, contrary to Section 2 of the Obscene Publications Act.

Mr Dobson had been in trouble before, though his prison sentence had been quashed on appeal. The courtroom was now stacked with two of his other products which were to be the subject of a separate trial but remained in full view of the jury at this one: *Bawdy Set-Up* by Tim Selmand and *Sex Name* by Virgil Canning. It was someone's equivalent of a nod and a wink to the jurors. The police evidence given was that when arrested he had said, 'You can't pin *this* on me', as if other things had been successfully pinned in the past. What he claimed to have said was, 'You can't pin this on *me*', which suggested an innocent past. He had the air of a culprit who was 'well overdue'. All the same, it was natural to wonder whether, if Mr Dobson had been the Oxford University Press and had published the book he would have been standing in the dock.

To the extent that lawyers have to assume a distinctive role for each case, John Cobb, Recorder of Bradford, prosecuted with an air of one who finds even the thought of sex distasteful. His attack began with an extraordinary assertion that the book must be recently written. The evidence was that it contained the word 'fuck', which everyone knew was a twentieth-century lawyers' mnemonic for 'felonious and unlawful carnal knowledge'. When this had been disproved he still claimed that Walter's diary was a modern book, presumably originating in the United States. It required evidence from David Foxon, Reader in Textual Criticism at Oxford, to establish from contemporary advertisements and editions that the first volume had not only been printed but reprinted by 1901.

For almost a fortnight Mr Cobb, tall, thin and bespectacled, maintained a pained expression and tone. Opening his case on 14 January, he had described the book as 'utterly and totally obscene'. It was the work of a man who 'from a very early stage in his life gave himself over to a life of unremitting fornication and diverse and perverted sexual malpractices'. The prosecution was particularly keen on perversions. At the committal proceedings counsel for the Director of Public Prosecutions had assured the court that the book 'describes in complete detail every form of sexual perversion on virtually every page'. How it was possible, on a single page, to describe 'every' form of sexual perversion 'in complete detail' was something neither he nor the DPP cared to demonstrate. As a matter of record, the references in the book to homosexual conduct or sado-masochism, neither of which was more than a curiosity to Walter, amounted to no more than a few pages out of some 2,500.

In all the circumstances, it seemed unlikely that there would be an out-right acquittal. John Mortimer, for the defence, assembled his experts who spent most of their time going in to bat against John Cobb. The prosecu-tion's tactic was to discredit them from the outset. The incident in which Walter encounters the girl of ten and her mother was the subject of a well-rehearsed trick. 'Is this not the vilest thing you have ever read?' It was distressing, harrowing, and made the narrator a repulsive brute, but that was not the question. 'Vilest' was chosen to reflect discredit on the writer and reader alike. The witness who says it is the vilest gives away much of the case. The witness who says 'no' makes the jurors wonder how vile the rest of his or her reading matter may be.

Several of John Mortimer's team stumbled, though recovering their bal-ance in due course, until the arrival of Steven Marcus from America. A courteous, mild-mannered professor from Columbia University, he was an expert on Charles Dickens and author of *The Other Victorians*, including a study of *My Secret Life*. He too was asked if this extract was not the vilest thing he had ever read. Unabashed by the dignities of a British court, Professor Marcus asked quietly, 'You don't mean that question literally, do you, Mr Cobb?' John Cobb appeared shaken by this. In part he had lost the initiative and, in the classic nightmare of the cross-examiner, had got an answer he was not expecting. Far worse, it seemed that this benign aca-demic had seen a major flaw in the carefully prepared case. He could only say that of course he meant it.

'Mr Cobb,' said Marcus gently, 'have you never heard of the concentra-tion camps of the Third Reich . . .' What was coming was plain. Whatever the Victorian child had suffered, perhaps on only one occasion, perhaps more, it was not what some children had endured in Buchenwald or Auschwitz. John Cobb, having to respond in seconds, made an appalling choice. 'Come, Professor Marcus, it would have been better for this child had she been dead.' Dead as a result of being brutalized and murdered in a concentration camp? One observer in court murmured that he had been 'interfered with' as a child and was so glad his parents had not had him put down. The judge, who had shown a certain weary detachment during the evidence of so many academics, stared at the prosecutor. There were audible gasps.[18]

As the case went on, it seemed the defence witnesses were winning the argument. The prosecution produced two witnesses whose thesis was not that the book should be banned but that it was of insufficient interest to be published in the 'public good', if the jurors should find it obscene. They seemed heavily outweighed.

The jurors retired to consider their verdict, came back and convicted Arthur Dobson. The defence case had made little impression on them. When taken to the jury room to read the first two volumes of *My Secret Life*, all that the defendant had printed, it was reported that most read only a few pages before closing the book. Only two of the twelve appear to have been in the habit of reading books and most, on seeing the language in which this one was written, were said to have gone no further.

Arthur Dobson was sent to prison for two years, reduced to one year on appeal. He was fined £1,000, ordered to pay £2,000 towards prosecution costs and left to pay his own costs of £17,000, a total of some £600,000 in modern terms. He seemed unlucky in his judge. Historical value, even the defence of publication for the public good, counted for very little in the end. Most juries seemed bored rather than impressed by expert evidence – and perhaps resentful at having to sit through it. In any case, a publisher might be well advised to avoid such provincial venues as Leeds Assizes.[19]

6

Taken together, it was hard to say where the cases of *Last Exit to Brooklyn* and *My Secret Life* had left literature. *Last Exit*, condemned as obscene by a jury, was freely available to young and old alike. Walter's diary was banned and Arthur Dobson was in prison. No one from Calder & Boyars had been sent to prison and the £600 penalties imposed were small by comparison with £3,000. No one could argue that one book was more or less obscene than the other, for that was the very thing the law of evidence prohibited. Yet there was nothing as barbaric or sadistic in *My Secret Life* as the slaughter of Tralala in *Last Exit*.

There were other factors in the equation. The Labour government of Harold Wilson, re-elected with a three-figure majority in March 1966, seemed almost immune from criticism. The liberal Attorney-General, Sir Elwyn Jones, had not wanted a prosecution of *Last Exit* in the first place. Books of all kinds were finding their way into the country and magazines whose format was copied from *Penthouse* or *Playboy* were generally accepted. As for the young, the greater concern was not that they read pornography but that they did not read at all – or at least to little purpose. The television screen was far more familiar to them than the printed page.

The evil example of literature was less often cited but there was one striking exception. It concerned the horrors of the Moors Murders trial in 1966 and the Marquis de Sade. On 19 April at Chester Assizes, Ian Brady and Myra Hindley faced charges of murdering a youth of seventeen, a boy of twelve and a girl of ten. The bodies were found in makeshift graves on the windswept moors of the Pennines between Manchester and Huddersfield, hence the name of the case. Two more victims, a boy and girl of sixteen, were not found at the time.

The behaviour of the accused gave the case its notoriety, particularly their tape-recording and photographs relating to the death of Lesley Ann Downey. So too did the books from which the murderers were said to have drawn inspiration, rather as the Chicago child-killers Leopold and Loeb claimed it from the supremacist philosophy of Nietzsche forty-two years before. The books in the Moors Murders case testified to an admiration for the Nazi regime and the philosophy of Sade. Among them was Russell's *Scourge of the Swastika*, written to denounce the Third Reich. Brady also had a copy of *Mein Kampf* but since it was in German he could not read it. On the other side, there were such paperback 'sucker traps' as *High Heels and Stockings* or *The Kiss of the Whip*, which Mr Justice Fenton Atkinson described: 'I suppose the titles are more sinister than the contents. One was enough for me.' Finally, there was Sade.

Two books were found in Brady's possession. One was a 1964 paperback reprint of Geoffrey Gorer's *Life and Ideas of the Marquis de Sade* (1934), in itself no more pornographic than Bertrand Russell's *History of Western Philosophy*. Gorer was best known as a distinguished anthropologist. His book was an account of Sade's indebtedness to the mechanistic theories of the French philosopher La Mettrie, debunking human spirituality, in *L'Homme machine* (1748). His account of Sade's life was brief and bland, some forty pages in all. Ian Brady, in evidence, claimed that he had enjoyed it. So, for that matter, had reviewers in the *New Statesman* and the *Times Literary Supplement*.

The second book was more contentious. What Brady read, though newly published as a translation of Sade's *Justine*, was an earlier and shorter version, *The Misfortunes of Virtue*, unlikely to have trouble with the law. Sade wrote three versions of his novel. This first was written in a fortnight in 1787 during his imprisonment in the Bastille. It is an eighteenth-century philosophical tale, showing the world as a place in which the wicked prosper while the good are punished – and deserve to be according to nature's laws. It is the best of the three versions. *Justine: or, The Misfortunes of Virtue* was the second, 'warmed up' at the request of Sade's publisher Girouard and issued in 1791. *La Nouvelle Justine* (1796) was an inflated four-volume preamble to *Juliette*, the story of her evil sister.[20]

The murderers' reading matter was a curiosity of the case. Yet the inspiration of Sade came less from his books than from the fact of his existence and his reputation. The Moors Murderers were no doubt people of vicious and violent tastes, who might otherwise have been cautious or reticent in respect of them. Yet they discovered that they were not alone – 'Thank goodness I'm not the only one!' as correspondents confided to agony columns. A famous French nobleman had thought and felt as they did, commemorating this in books that had scandalized the world. Indeed, a scandalized summary was far more accessible and welcome to the killers than a detailed account. It might have been inconvenient, for example, to learn that their idol was a man opposed to capital punishment, sentenced to death himself for the crime of 'moderation' – saving defendants from torture and death – as a judge under the Revolution.

They hardly needed books to confirm what they already felt with such strength. Indeed, all the stimulus required for fantasy and homicide could be obtained as easily and conveniently from an entry in an encyclopaedia. A further irony of Brady's admiration for Nazism was that the Third Reich, despite its own record of murder, did not abolish the criminal law in respect of it and would have executed these two admirers in short order.

Life, rather than literature, seemed to have played the dominant role. Brady was a child of the Glasgow streets, never to know his father, whose mother left him to the care of foster parents. He lived with four children in one of the worst Gorbals tenements. As a primary school child he was known for his skill with a flick-knife and its use to torture and kill cats or other animals. He tied a classmate to a post, heaped paper round him and set fire to it. By eleven, he was practising Nazi salutes and shouts of 'Sieg Heil.' After school, he worked as a butcher's assistant, the slaughter of animals a grim anticipation of his murder of Edward Evans by blows from an axe. The difference between reading a book and killing a victim was a good deal greater than between using an axe on an animal or on a human. Yet Sade as the invisible presence died hard.

Even without the Moors Murders, Sade symbolized literature which no parliamentary legislation could legitimize. Otherwise, it seemed, there could be no limits at all. In Britain, the last battle in the campaign between those prepared to publish him and those prepared to stop them was not fought until the 1990s. Like many final battles it was something of an anticlimax. In 1991, Arrow Books, a major paperback firm, published an unexpurgated English edition of *Juliette*. On 13 August in *The*

THE POLICING OF LITERATURE

Times, Moyra Bremner, a television presenter, urged a prosecution. Like many people who advocated a particular prosecution, she was opposed to censorship but felt there must be an exception. Sade's association with the Moors Murders was cited and such incidents in the novel as villains forcing parents to eat their children, which deranged criminals might imitate. The Director of Public Prosecutions refused to take action. Miss Bremner asked the Lord Advocate of Scotland to prosecute and ban further works by Sade as inciting child abuse and rape. The Lord Advocate declined.

It was the end of a chapter: if such books as this could not be prosecuted, it was hard to see what publications could be. Yet there were also procedural problems. In an age of growing 'reading difficulty', a trial of *Juliette* would require the jurors to read with care an eighteenth-century historical novel of well over a thousand pages. It seemed a fair bet that there would be one or more on any jury who could not do it. Without that, a trial could not be fairly conducted under the current legislation and the case would go to appeal with a good chance of success. The whole process might well end in acquittal and hugely increased sales. Sade's heroine would be freely available with a storm of publicity behind her for another 'Book They Would Not Let You Read'.

7

There was an even more decisive impediment to obscenity prosecutions long before 1991. History had moved on and jurors showed themselves less likely to listen to the prosecution and the police. This had little to do with the book or publication on trial. For several years after 1972 such prosecutions at the Central Criminal Court brought a high number of acquittals. There was little question of publication for the public good in titles like *US Bondage* or in the sexual entertainment of such specialist or fetishistic magazines as *Slant*, *Relate*, *Search* or *Mentor*. At any other time, there would surely have been convictions. No one complained longer or louder to the public than Mrs Mary Whitehouse.

Seven of the twelve cases, including *Inside Linda Lovelace* and *US Bondage*, ended with verdicts of not guilty. Three more were abandoned and there was no retrial, after the jury failed to agree. In the remaining two cases, the jury convicted on only four counts out of thirteen in the first, and one count out of six in the second. Since the material seemed unselfconsciously pornographic, how could the prosecutions have miscarried? Mary Whitehouse insisted it was the result of defence counsel challenging jurors who looked as if they might be hostile. In eight of the twelve cases which she had cited, however, there was no challenge by either side. Mrs Whitehouse also suggested that 'clever' defence lawyers bamboozled the jurors. Yet it seemed unlikely that so many defence counsel could be clever while so many prosecutors were stupid.

Inside Linda Lovelace was a test of public opinion – or lack of it – for the jury of nine men and three women. 'If this book is not obscene within the definitions of the Act, it might well be difficult to imagine anything that would fall into the category,' said Judge Rigg in his summing-up. It was acquitted by male and female jurors alike. Defence witnesses in such cases no longer talked of Dickens, Galsworthy or Zola. At this 1976 Old Bailey trial, they described the essentially benign effects of reading about abnormal sexual experiences. 'Yes, this has therapeutic value . . . I have known patients who could benefit by masturbating on this . . .' Such material could be 'helpful to couples'.[21]

'Oh, this is all too technical for me,' said Judge Rigg helplessly. The closing defence address to the jury denied that the book would deprave or corrupt. Judges had read it and it did not corrupt them, otherwise we should expect 'orgies in the Garrick Club, the Central Criminal Court chugging at the hum from vibrators and daisy-chains in the lunch hour while eating cheese-and-pickle sandwiches'. It was reported that the jurors laughed. The book was 'a bit rude and a bit silly', but 'should we make up our own minds about it or do we need Big Brother to decide?'[22]

No one at the time seems to have pointed out that the name 'Lovelace' had been traditionally pronounced 'Loveless'. In the 1950s, Lord David Cecil lecturing to Oxford undergraduates on the eighteenth-century novel, made the point that the seducing man of fashion in Samuel Richardson's *Clarissa* had been given the name of Lovelace or 'Loveless' in order that no reader should mistake his character from the outset – nor be greatly distressed by the manner of his disgrace and death on the duelling ground.

In 1972, there was an unwelcome explanation of some recent acquittals. During that year the 'Longford Committee', including authors, journalists, clergy, social workers, lawyers, publishers, academics and students under the Earl of Longford, made its report. It was an independent initiative whose fifty-three members, like their chairman, were concerned at the unopposed progress of pornography. Among them were the Archbishop of York and Dr Donald Soper of the West London Methodist Mission, Cliff Richard representing pop culture, Lord Shawcross as Chairman of Thames Television, authors including Kingsley Amis and Malcolm Muggeridge.

Almost buried towards the end of their report was a passage which was to prove far more significant than its authors could have imagined. It acknowledged 'the widespread allegation which it would be dangerous to shirk' that members of the Metropolitan Police were taking bribes for showing favours to pornographers. The report acknowledged that the *Sunday People* had first suggested this on 28 June 1964.[23]

Even as the Longford Report appeared, another Conservative MP, Raymond Blackburn, applied for an order in the High Court, compelling Robert Mark, Commissioner of the Metropolitan Police, to enforce the laws against obscenity. The High Court rejected the application and Mr Blackburn went to the Court of Appeal on 16 November 1972. Lord Denning, Master of the Rolls, asked him about one particular police raid. 'You are suggesting that, before the police came, the hard pornography was withdrawn and after they had gone it was put on sale again. Are you suggesting that the proprietor knew in advance the police were coming?' 'It has happened not only in one case but in thirty cases,' said Mr Blackburn firmly. 'Everybody in Soho knows it. I have been told it by villains and policemen.' None the less, he lost his appeal.

The Longford Report estimated that Soho bookshops had 'at least doubled in the last three years'. This was not surprising if figures given by the *Observer*'s Business Review on 15 August 1971 were at all accurate. Pornography, cheaply produced from master copies, was sold at very high prices, bringing £1,500 a week to the smallest bookshops, and £10,000 to the most successful. This was cash-in-hand and its practitioners felt no need to trouble the Inland Revenue. Soho takings, £10,000,000 annually according to the *Observer*'s accounting, were almost entirely profit.[24]

Police tolerance of the trade had been evident to the public for decades, even if outright bribery had not. How had dealers thrived so openly otherwise? If the Obscene Publications Squad had been in doubt, thousands of London residents could have enlightened them. Anyone living in such areas of prostitution and pornography as Soho or Paddington could hardly be unaware of what was going on. Why did the Obscene Publications Squad not raid the shops day after day until the entrepreneurs turned to other professions? Fly-spotted second-hand paperbacks filled their windows with titles like *The Road to Buenos Ayres* or *White Slaves in a Piccadilly Flat*, containing earnest tracts which piously denounced the evils enticingly portrayed on their covers. These were quite safe in any court of law. The main premises contained innocent glamour magazines. Under the counter or in a back room lay the money-spinners.

The stock of these shops was conveniently summarized in a memorandum submitted by the Commissioner of Metropolitan Police to the Select Committee on the Obscene Publications Bill in July 1957. It contained few surprises. Photographs came in four categories. The first was 'Homosexual: pictures of two male persons engaged in sodomy or other perversion; nude pictures of small boys; nude pictures of particularly well-developed male persons'. In the light of later preoccupations with paedophile pornography, it is interesting that there was little apparent demand for photographs showing the sexual abuse of children as opposed to 'naturist' pictures.[25]

The second category of photographs was 'Heterosexual: pictures of a man and woman copulating; pictures of "eccentric" sexual engagement; nude women in suggestive attitudes; nude women exposing their private parts'. The third category was 'Lesbian: two women engaged with the aid of an imitation penis in sexual intercourse'. The fourth category, 'usually from America', was 'Sadism in various forms'. It included women beating women, women beating men, men beating women, women being tied up, 'women tied to trees or furniture, etc.', and 'torture – women'. If the price – from ten shillings to twenty-five shillings a set – was any guide to popularity, then heterosexual, homosexual or lesbian copulation were favoured. Sadism and paedophilia were at a definite discount.

The second commodity was magazines, all imported. Denmark and Germany provided 'pictures of nude females'. France offered 'Stories and pictures . . . Usually of nude females in suggestive positions'. Magazines from America were 'in effect, an advertisement for obscene films', though some contained pictures and stories.

'Books' were either pamphlet-sized typescripts from America or printed books from Paris. Some typescripts were 'locally produced'. Books from France were smuggled by easing off the paperback cover, dividing the book into its twelve or sixteen sections and posting each as a rather bulky letter. The parts were glued together again on arrival at an apparently innocent address in England. Such books were the most expensive commodity, now hired out at £5 and taken back for £2.[26]

None of this was new. In 1845, Alfred Carlile traded in the same way and fell victim to the same perils as Soho merchants in the 1960s. Nemesis came in the shape of a plain-clothes agent from the Society for the Suppression of Vice.

> I went to the shop two or three times before the day when the sale took place, and bought several innocent publications. On the day in question, the prisoner showed me a French print in the window, which I asked to see. I

asked him if he had anything more curious, and he at length invited me to go into the back shop. He then shewed me several indecent prints. I asked him the price, and selected two which I produce. These form the subject of the present indictment.[27]

In the early 1970s, rumours of police corruption spread, though raids on shops and warehouses continued at a rate of about 170 a year in the London area and sixty in Soho. In the year of the Longford Report, 1972, there were forty-five Soho raids in the first five months. Of seventy-five men arrested, sixty-four had been cautioned and signed disclaimers allowing their stock to be confiscated. What the Longford Committee did not know was that the culprits had then been taken to Holborn police station where the merchandise was held and were allowed to buy it back. To prevent the Soho pornographer Ronald Mason being noticed by other officers, Commander Wally Virgo lent him a CID tie when they went to collect his stock, redelivered to Mason's home by police transport.

As these stories were retailed and investigations began, they inevitably reached jurors chosen for the Central Criminal Court who lived in the central London area. As early as 15 August 1971, the *Observer* described the trade as running on 'sweeteners to the police'. Small wonder if juries were increasingly unlikely to convict on evidence given by officers whom rumour and the media told them were probably corrupt. The Obscene Publications Squad consisted at its maximum of eighteen officers, though the personnel varied from time to time. Had three new arrivals not proved incorruptible, the scandal might have gone on far longer. Being summoned to the squad office on their first Friday night to collect a weekly share of the take, each was dismayed. One put the banknotes in the drawer of his desk and waited his chance to report what was going on.

Commander Wally Virgo and fourteen members of the conspiracy continued to take £2,000 a week from Soho bookshops with Christmas bonuses and other favours, at a time when a parliamentary answer on 28 January 1971 put the average weekly wage in the country at £28. The Obscene Publications Squad became what the judge at the first trial in the autumn of 1976 called 'a vast protection racket'. At the end of the trials of Chief Superintendent George Fenwick and others in December that year, Mr Justice Mars-Jones calculated the takings as in excess of £100,000 a year.

When pressure from senior officers made a raid necessary, an officer would telephone first and say, 'W. H. Smith.' This was the instruction to clear the shop of all stock that might cause trouble, replacing it with innocuous books and magazines. The squad could be seen to do its job while causing little inconvenience to its clients. Even if it was necessary to take away the more expensive products, these could always be sold back.

The dishonesty was on such a scale as to be farcical, the stuff of a *Carry On* screen comedy. James Humphreys, dubbed 'The Emperor of Porn', was asked how he knew a particular policeman could be trusted to be corrupt. He replied simply to a reporter, 'I never knew one who wasn't.' A trader would pay something for a 'licence' to open a shop, perhaps about £16,000 by instalments. If he refused, he would be raided repeatedly until he became reasonable. Thereafter, there would be a weekly payment. In addition, as James Humphreys described it, the protecting officer would expect to be taken out to lunch or dinner regularly. On each occasion, at Stone's Chop House or the SPQR in Dean Street, the helpful officer would expect a casual 'bung' of £100 to be going on with.

Once the investigations began and the trial publicity of senior officers like George Fenwick, Bill Moody and Wally Virgo became national news, the prospect of getting a conviction for obscene publications became ever more remote. Commander Virgo's story was more remarkable than most. When the Drug Squad was accused of paying off informants with narcotics confiscated from others, he had been the senior officer who investigated and gave his colleagues in that squad a clean bill of health. He himself was involved in bribery and corruption on a daunting scale. He was luckier than other defendants, however. Sent to prison for twelve years, his sentence was quashed on appeal.

The worst of this publicity, as Sir Robert Mark the new Commissioner of Metropolitan Police described it, was that dishonest policemen were now matched by dishonest defence lawyers. A cross-examiner would ask a police witness if he was a member of a particular squad. The witness would agree. 'And is that a squad which is currently under investigation on allegations of corruption?' A good advocate could deliver most, if not all, of this question before the judge intervened to tell him it was improper. Counsel would apologize and withdraw the question but not, of course, before the jury had heard it and connected it with what they had read in the press.[28]

A small number of prosecutions were successful, usually involving imported magazines or films. Elsewhere money was being paid to have charges dropped. What lay ahead was an armed truce, legislation to control pornography rather than to stamp it out. The Indecent Display Act 1981 banished what was called 'hard-core' from public view and the Local Government Miscellaneous Provisions Act 1982 rehoused it in licensed 'sex shops'. Mrs Whitehouse spoke on behalf of an indignant moral majority: 'I can't believe it!'

She was not alone in wishing that liberal legislation and the literature it sheltered might be wiped from the face of the earth. In December 1981, a *Guardian* correspondent deplored the far-off occasion in 1960 that gave freedom to *Lady Chatterley's Lover*, which was nothing more than a 'sexually repressive fascist novelette' and a specimen of 'cheating obscenity'. Where censorship by evangelical Christianity failed, militant feminism might succeed. Yet this was also the dawn of the Internet. It was to make the computer keyboard a universal provider of pornography on a scale to dwarf Soho and Lawrence's novelette alike.

I I

Beyond the Pale

I

ONE NOVEL, CERTAINLY a candidate for prosecution under the 1959 Obscene Publications Act, escaped altogether. The English edition of Vladimir Nabokov's *Lolita* was published by Weidenfeld & Nicolson in October 1959. Its author had a distinguished literary output in Russian and English. Educated at St Petersburg and Trinity College, Cambridge, he was now Professor of Russian Literature at Cornell University. He was best known for two post-war novels, *Bend Sinister* (1947) and *Pnin* (1957), as well as a collection of short stories.

For reasons no one could foresee, the name and subject matter of *Lolita* were to linger in public consciousness for over half a century. Despite a liberalization of moral censorship, it was easier to publish the book in 1959 than it might have been twenty years later, when figures plucked from the air asserted that ten per cent of all schoolchildren, more than a million, were victims of sexual abuse.

Lolita had been in difficulties before its appearance in England. It was the confession of Humbert Humbert, a middle-aged European man of letters awaiting trial in America for seducing the twelve-year-old Dolores Haze, 'Lolita'. His quest for the ideal 'nymphet' is the subject of the book. The issue for critics and legal advisers was whether Humbert's apologia was likely to deprave and corrupt the reader by enticing him – or indeed her – into the practice of what was soon to be widely known as 'paedophilia'.

Humbert, an unrepentant predator, is the lodger of Mrs Charlotte Haze in the American town at whose college he teaches. Besotted by the winsome daughter, he allows himself to marry her mother, a coy yet vulgar widow. His dream is to dispose of her, becoming guardian and possessor of Lolita. Mrs Haze discovers this truth in his secret diary and confronts him. She is immediately killed by a black Cadillac as she runs out to post letters denouncing him. The gods of irony deliver Lolita to her admirer, that she may destroy him.

There is little sexual behaviour in the book but its narrator thinks of almost nothing else. Its pages are populated by grotesques, not least Humbert Humbert, whose name is frequently taken to be Humbird or Homburg. Lolita is a garish vision of the Awful American Child, sly, vulgar and avaricious. She is as knowing and lewd-minded as her mentor, sexually experienced with boys and girls of her own age. On their first night, it is she who seduces him, revealing that her virginity was lost to a loutish fellow pupil and that other techniques were learnt in lesbian experiments with schoolfriends. There is no room for childhood innocence. Even so, in any prosecution, this authorial slander on the child victim might have gone badly. Mrs Haze is little more than a stage mother-in-law, whose slaughter by a passing car is a matter for applause.

Five words encapsulate the narrator's furtive self-admiration: 'Oh, what a crafty Humbert!' The characters have a quality of circus slapstick. Humbert had previously married a wife of childish appearance. She put on adult fat and left him for a Russian émigré colonel, now a Paris taxi-driver. As she stoops over her luggage, packing to leave, he has a vision of putting on his mountain boots and taking 'a running kick at her rump'. Such moments share the anarchic zest of P. G. Wodehouse or Kingsley Amis.[1]

The way in which Humbert mocks American municipal and family decencies – in Lolita's summer camp each cabin is dedicated to a Disney character – compounds his crime. Old and amoral Europe debauches young America, while young and vulgar materialism corrupts old-fashioned dignity. The narrative recalls Aldous Huxley's *After Many a Summer* or Evelyn Waugh's *The Loved One*, rather than pornography. In milder terms, it might have been a subject for Henry James.

The prospect of being bound to such an appalling creature as Humbert's nymphet would deter all but the most resolute paedophile. Yet as Philip Toynbee remarked, if it could be shown that one little girl was seduced as a result of the book's existence it should be suppressed. More to the point, jurors would have before them such passages as Humbert's orgasm, achieved by a girl of twelve sitting on his lap – and his assurance that it was a harmless pastime.

The story is set in 1947 and the book was completed in 1953. Four New York publishers rejected it. It was then read by Maurice Girodias of the Olympia Press. Paris seemed a natural home for such moral anarchism and Olympia published the book in two volumes in September 1955. Individual copies began to reach London and New York. Yet the Permanent Secretary of State at the Home Office confirmed that it was not on the customs stop list, forwarded to the French government for their cooperation in suppressing certain English titles published in Paris.[2]

Very few people in England or the United States had heard of *Lolita* until 1956. On 29 January, in the *Sunday Express*, John Gordon demanded to know whether Graham Greene had been 'pulling the leg' of the *Sunday Times*. The paper had invited eminent authors to name the three best books of 1955. *Lolita* had been one of Greene's choices. Gordon acquired the Olympia Press edition, 'the filthiest book I have ever read . . . Anyone who published it here would certainly go to prison.' In anticipation of trouble over the book, twenty-one writers and scholars had addressed a letter to *The Times* on 23 February 1956. The signatories included Compton Mackenzie, Iris Murdoch, Stephen Spender, Angus Wilson, Sir Herbert Read, Sir Maurice Bowra and Sir Isaiah Berlin. They deplored the threat to *Lolita*, cited the suppression of *Madame Bovary* and *Ulysses* and added, 'it is Flaubert and Joyce whom we admire not the Public Prosecutors of the time.'

The Home Office denied putting pressure on the French Ministry of the Interior to suppress the Paris edition. Yet it certainly was suppressed, on 20 December 1956, under the 'Loi de 29 juillet 1881 sur la Liberté de la Presse'. US Customs detained copies, examined them and let them go. G. P. Putnam bought US rights and published in New York on 18 August 1958. It outsold all other titles in the United States except Boris Pasternak's *Dr Zhivago*.

At the same time, Olympia Press won an appeal against the French ban, only to have the book banned in July 1958 under the 'Loi sur la Presse Enfantine', implemented by Charles de Gaulle's government of national safety. A French translation from Gallimard in April 1959 became freely available but the same text in English was still banned. The French government therefore lifted the ban and a new English-language edition was issued by Olympia in September.

In London there had been prosecutions in 1956 of travellers caught with copies of the Olympia Press edition. A man was conditionally discharged at Bow Street on 9 April for having in his possession a copy of volume one. At the same court on 12 September a defendant who was found with a copy of volume two was fined £20 and ordered to pay £5 costs. The penalty was light but he acquired an entry in the Criminal Record Office of Scotland Yard.

In these circumstances Weidenfeld & Nicolson acquired British and Commonwealth rights. Even before this, copies of the New York edition were reaching Britain. The open border between the United States and

Canada made it hard to stop the book crossing it and there was little censorship of the post between Canada and the United Kingdom.

Weidenfeld & Nicolson sought legal advice. In the autumn of 1958, the book was read for obscenity by an experienced literary solicitor, Peter Carter-Ruck. The new Obscene Publications Bill was still on its way through Parliament and would become law in the following July. It would then be possible to claim publication 'for the public good'. As to whether the book had a tendency to deprave or corrupt, Carter-Ruck found it exceedingly difficult to advise. He concluded that it was a fair business risk, if four sentences in more than four hundred pages were altered. Nabokov refused to alter them.

Despite the age which the author gave his heroine, the publishers saw her as that 1950s icon the 'sex kitten', of whom Brigitte Bardot was the most celebrated example. Evidence from *Lolita*'s well-wishers would also be admissible. The defence might call upon Graham Greene, V. S. Pritchett, Bernard Levin, Terence Rattigan, Lionel Trilling, James M. Cain and Dorothy Parker, not to mention the twenty-three signatories of the 23 February 1956 letter to *The Times*.

Nigel Nicolson, a partner in Weidenfeld & Nicolson, was also Conservative MP for Bournemouth West. He had not read the novel before the contract to publish was signed. On reading it he was dismayed. Hints from political colleagues were not encouraging. The Home Secretary, R. A. Butler, suggested that it would be best to wait and publish under the new Obscene Publications Act. Next day, Nicolson was confronted by the Attorney-General, Sir Reginald Manningham-Buller.

Manningham-Buller warned Nicolson that if he published *Lolita*, 'you will be in the dock.' As Attorney-General, he was the man to put him there. In any case, the Director of Public Prosecutions would take action. That, said Manningham-Buller, was ninety-nine per cent certain. Nicolson was also summoned by the government's Chief Whip, a future Prime Minister, Edward Heath. Heath argued that publication must be stopped, though he had read the novel and merely found it boring.[3]

In the face of threats and admonitions, Gerald Gardiner QC, defender of Penguin Books in the *Lady Chatterley* case, advised that prosecution was unlikely and that if brought it would fail. Two other QCs, Sir John Foster and Brian Neill, concurred. It was decided to print 20,000 copies, though as yet no firm could be found in England willing to undertake the typesetting. To show good faith, six copies would be printed. The Home Secretary would be informed that they were on public sale. If action were to be taken, these copies offered sufficient grounds. At the same time, it was evident that the publisher had merely sought to establish whether the book was thought to be obscene and not to cash in on its notoriety by printing 20,000 copies straight away.

Harold Macmillan called a general election in September 1959. R. A. Butler was informed of the copies on sale. Like his colleagues, he was occupied in fighting for his parliamentary seat. He was also campaigning as a government leader and conducting the business of his office. *Lolita* was not his first concern. It was not certain that his party would win the election. If it did, there was no guarantee that he would still be Home Secretary. It was not surprising that Weidenfeld & Nicolson's letter went unanswered. By the time the new Parliament met, Nabokov's nymphet was on her way to the best-seller lists.

2

For a decade after the publication of *Lolita* 'child pornography' or 'paedophile pornography' was scarcely a headline issue. A film series based on St Trinian's, the anarchic girls' school of the Ronald Searle cartoons, met with success and no moral objections. Its pupils, despite black stockings and abbreviated school uniforms, were unlikely to see twenty-five or thirty-five again. *The Passion Flower Hotel* (1962) and its sequels by Rosalind Erskine, in which the sixth form of a girls' public school provided what it imagined to be a brothel for a boys' school, brought neither a bark nor even a yelp from a moral watchdog.

A paragon of comic-novel writing by a well-respected author, Leslie Thomas, appeared in 1970. His gifts were summarized by the *Evening News*, which saluted him as 'anatomically naughty but hilarious'. *His Lordship*, published by Michael Joseph, followed by Pan paperback in 1972, was of the type to make the reader laugh out loud. Its narrator, in Wandsworth prison awaiting trial for activities with girls under the age of consent, had been tennis coach at Southwelling School. He was arrested after sitting down drunk and incapable in a pensioner's dinner-plate at the Victoria station buffet. When his suitcase was searched, it contained the Clifton Tennis Cup and five pairs of knickers.

As the only male at the school, William Herbert's virtue was under siege by determined adolescents. In his cell he is interrogated by a police officer, Rufus, eager for salacious details of the accused's adventures. Rufus is not averse to purloining prisoners' property nor to extracting evidence by squeezing the nose violently between two knuckles until the eyes water. The novel ends with the cry of the helpless prisoner, 'Rufuth! Oh, for

Godth thake . . . thath my nothe!' Ten or twenty years later, it would not have been as easy to publish such a novel, however splendid its comedy. Far from attracting paedophiles, its ridicule of their obsession might unite them with police and social workers in an increasingly familiar response: 'That's not funny.'

Yet even as *His Lordship* went its way, the defence of children against certain forms of publishing and the arts became a topic of debate. The rebellious young had to be protected from themselves and their radical sympathizers. In 1971, after complaints from Mrs Mary Whitehouse, charges were brought against Richard Handyside and his firm Stage One, publishers of *The Little Red Schoolbook*. This originated in Denmark and owed its title to the currently fashionable *Little Red Book* of Mao Tse-tung. Stage One had also issued the works of Chairman Mao and Che Guevara. Among other radical ideas, the 'schoolbook' encouraged children to experiment freely in sexual matters. In its defence, Dr James Hemmings insisted that adults holding 'taboos and negative attitudes towards sex' had no business to impose them on the young.

Well-known firms, including Penguin and Faber, considered reissuing the book with their own imprints, in defiance of Mrs Whitehouse and what they saw as her misuse of the Obscene Publications Act. Nothing came of this. Mr Handyside was convicted at Clerkenwell Magistrates Court in June 1971 and fined £50. His appeal to the Inner Sessions Appeal Committee was dismissed on 30 October.

In the following summer the three editors of *Oz*, an underground magazine, were prosecuted for the contents of their 'schoolkids' edition, whose cartoons and commentary had been produced by the children themselves. As well as obscenity charges, the editors were charged with 'conspiracy to produce a magazine containing obscene material with intent to corrupt children'. Even so, this issue with its cartoon antics of Rupert Bear and Gypsy Granny, its mockery of teachers as frustrated flagellants, was not so much obscene as youthfully irreverent. For the defendants and their witnesses, the trial seemed like a chance for 'ragging sir', in the person of Judge Argyll and prosecuting counsel.

It was unfortunate for the defendants that the proceedings lasted from 21 June until 4 August, giving ample time for what *The Times* called the carnival atmosphere of the opening to grow stale before the end. The defence presented the accused as modern dissenters who 'wear long hair, colourful clothes and have their dreams of a better world in small bed-sitters in Notting Hill Gate'. Some saw themselves not as dissenters but as the revolutionaries of an alternative society whose dreams might be

fuelled by what the law unsympathetically classed as 'controlled sub-
stances'.

Judge Argyll took his revenge when the three editors were sentenced to
prison terms of fifteen, twelve and nine months respectively; the magazine
was bankrupted by a fine of £1,500 and £1,250 costs. The terms were so
harsh that there was little surprise when they were quashed on appeal, not
before the judge had been burnt in effigy outside the Old Bailey.

3

The protection of children against literature which was unsuitable for
them, because they were children, was joined in the 1960s by protection of
children against books and stories which had been popular among them
for generations. In July 1968, the Advisory Centre for Education issued a
caution against some of these dangers in *Books for Children*. It was thought
not impossible that *Cinderella* might encourage boot fetishism, *Alice in
Wonderland* and Tom up the chimney in *The Water Babies* could recall the
birth process, *Three Blind Mice* was a castration parable and Andrew Lang's
Brown Fairy Book in which a beautiful girl is whipped might open the way
to sado-masochism. These were cautionary comments rather than censorship. In February 1970, however, Ipswich's Chief Librarian withdrew the
Billy Bunter volumes from public view. Bessie Bunter, the stout sister of
'The Owl of the Remove', was also withdrawn, since such classics were
'unfair to fat children'.

Where there was the political will, an entire class of books might be
banned from children's libraries. As early as 1953 the seven public libraries
in St Pancras, on the decision of the Borough Librarian, dispensed with
Enid Blyton, the flying adventures of Captain W. E. Johns' 'Biggles' and
the escapades of Richmal Crompton's 'Just William'. 'We don't have them
here,' the Borough Librarian explained ten years later. 'There are about five
authors whose books we don't want. They have not been put on a banned
list. We just don't buy their books, that's all.' The books were all 'badly
written' and did nothing to expand a child's imagination or 'horizon'.
Biggles reflected 'an outmoded Kipling approach', which was bad for the
young. Of course, children still asked wistfully for their favourites, 'but we
recommend other books we consider better. The children go away quite
happy.' The explanation had an eerie similarity to those currently given for
the non-publication of dissident authors in the Soviet Union.[4]

The protection of children in the areas of paedophile pornography and
child abuse seemed to spring fully armed to the centre of debate in the

1980s. This was denied by those who insisted that both had always been a major threat to childhood but, in the cliché of the day, had been 'hushed up'. Recent cases, in another overused phrase, were 'only the tip of the iceberg'. So far as child pornography was concerned, the sceptics might cite evidence against this.

For example, when the 1957 Parliamentary Committee on the Obscene Publications Bill heard evidence from the Metropolitan Police, it received details of all obscene material seized in recent years. This was meticulously categorized. What was later termed child or 'paedophile' pornography was absent with one exception. One category of homosexual pornography consisted of photographs of naked boys, posing but not engaging in sexual activity. The grosser sexual abuse of children, let alone the 'snuff' movies, talked of twenty years later were happily absent.[5]

It was less easy to pass judgment on a distant past. If child pornography requires that the subject shall be under the current age of consent, a major collection of earlier material like the British Museum Private Case scarcely confirms its popularity. Fanny Hill was fifteen at the beginning of her career of vice in the 1740s. Yet this was in a society whose age of consent remained twelve until 1876, thirteen until 1885 and was only after that raised to sixteen. The diary of *My Secret Life* (1886) recording encounters with 1,200 women has only one description of a girl under the prevailing age of consent.

If the Metropolitan Police evidence or the Private Case questioned the existence of a vast hidden market for child pornography this did not automatically invalidate such claims in the paedophile-conscious 1970s. At all events, new crimes were created or defined by the Protection of Children Act 1978. The standard of proof was lowered so that child pornography need not be obscene but merely indecent, a definition already used in customs legislation. In the case of photographs, the Metropolitan Police at length defined indecency relating to children as a posed portrait of any naked person under the age of sixteen. Applied literally, this would criminalize even Lewis Carroll's photographs, taken in conditions of extreme propriety with mothers present and with a result that was not so much pornography as kitsch.

A campaign against child pornography was interwoven with a belief in paedophilia as a widespread aberration. The Obscene Publications Branch spoke of 'habitual filming' of such crimes against children either for gratification or for sale in an underworld market. Thanks to the advent of the video camera, such material could be circulated among paedophile rings. Its subject matter was said to beggar belief but included ritual or satanic abuse and 'snuff' films which depicted murder. The crimes depicted as well as the films or photographs of them now came under the reformed Obscene Publications Branch, renamed the Child Pornography Branch.

Growing fear of paedophile pornography caused a number of false alarms. In May 1978 a primary school headmaster was visited by the police because a seven-year-old girl, whose name was on the school roll, was being offered as a pornographic model in California. The girl had by then left the school and 'moved on'. Happily, it later proved that the girl on the American list merely shared the same name and was not a child.

The extent of child pornography was apt to be correlated to the incidence of sexual offences against children. Anyone who followed the more lurid weekend newspapers was aware of prosecutions for such offences against children since newspapers began. Those who doubted the continuing physical ill-treatment of children need only read the stories of Jasmine Beckford in 1984 or Kimberly Carlisle in 1986, doomed by violence and neglect. Yet most adults might feel they had come through childhood without encountering victim or abuser, if they equated such abuse with sexual molestation.

In 1990, the NSPCC dealt with 18,799 cases of abuse. Of these 15,119 or 80 per cent were cases of physical abuse, neglect, children left at home alone or emotional abuse. Sexual abuse accounted for 3,680 or almost 20 per cent. A National Children's Home report published on 23 April 1992 added that a third of sexual abuse of children was carried out by other children. 'Sexually inappropriate behaviour' had been found in children as young as three. Some £50 million was needed urgently to provide 'facilities' for dealing with the problem. In *The Times* on 9 February 1991, the findings of the Director of Aycliffe Centre for Children, for those in their care, put the average age of child abusers at fifteen and that of their victims at nine.

The problem of defining such abuse and calculating its extent had been illustrated by a MORI poll in September 1984. This purported to show that ten per cent of those questioned had been abused in childhood. The figure was widely used by the media as if proved beyond question. It also gave social workers a figure to aim at. The figure was later qualified by Bob Worcester, founder of MORI. The actual finding was not a hundred in every thousand but seven in every thousand. It seemed that sexual abuse had been overstated fourteen times. Moreover, the poll's definition of abuse included such items as adults 'talking about things in an erotic way'. At the Headmasters Conference on 18 October 1987, even a pay strike by teachers had been denounced as 'a form of child abuse'. The Orwellian semantics shifted beneath the debaters' feet. However reprehensible erotic talk or pay strikes might be, they were not what most people thought of as abuse.[6]

It remained to be seen what practical consequences would follow the censorship introduced by the Protection of Children Act. Shortly before it became law, representatives of the DPP went to a showing of the new Louis Malle film, *Pretty Baby*. This had won prizes at the Cannes Festival, was admired for its photography, which suggested a recreation of Impressionist painting, and was playing to packed houses in the United States and France. Its subject was the life of a twelve-year-old child prostitute in a New Orleans brothel just before the First World War.

This case was contentious since the new law, unlike the Obscene Publications Acts, made no provision for artistic merit or a 'public good' defence. Louis Malle's reputation stood high. Though Britain was one of the most censored countries in what was still called the Free World, it would look ridiculous by banning a film available almost everywhere else. Yet there were certainly episodes of nudity and sex which appeared to breach the new law. The film was duly released and there was no prosecution.

Other decisions seemed to show what was not criminal rather than what was. The heroine of Sade's *Juliette*, published in translation in 1994, is a paragon of vice by fifteen and many of her victims over the next thousand pages are children. The DPP and the Lord Advocate turned deaf ears to appeals for a prosecution. Similar refusals followed in 1997 in the case of an American novel, *The End of Alice* by A. M. Homes. The narrator is a paedophile, twenty-three years through a prison sentence for murder. The National Society for the Prevention of Cruelty to Children in London demanded a prosecution.

It was hard to imagine that anyone in the NSPCC had read the novel, harder still to believe that anyone could find it appetizing. Well reviewed and well written, it was in a style that a jury might find opaque. The paedophile narrator has a female correspondent who is nineteen years old, unlike the little girl whom he stabbed to death. Her letters describe a boy of twelve whose repulsive habit it is to keep his scabs until they are ripe enough to eat and who, at her suggestion, allows her to eat one fresh from his knee. In the prison cell, buggery and other sexual distractions between two ageing homosexuals sustain the plot. It was hardly a prospectus for paedophilia and, again, a prosecution was refused.

By 1990, the Obscene Publications Squad was the Child Pornography Squad. Its target was not the mainstream sex magazines nor the bookshops of Soho. The shops remained under the control of a licensing system. The magazines were sworn enemies of child pornography, whose ill-fame might indirectly tarnish them. Their nude models were well over the age of consent. Their policy on fiction required all characters to be over eighteen, even if the story had no sexual content and all a character did was to cross the road fully dressed. Child pornography implied instead a network of individuals trading pictures or videos among themselves. Some viewers were also creators of material. The Internet gave access to websites in countries such as Holland or Denmark where such material was tolerated, enabling them to exploit traditional freedoms. The rest of Western Europe and the United States was also less censored than Britain. As laws became more hostile, sites reappeared in Eastern Europe or the Far East.

Criminal proceedings had usually been brought against the provider or retailer of obscene material. This was plainly impossible with an Internet whose websites were beyond national jurisdiction. Yet it was easier to monitor the Internet than it was to tap a phone line. Purchasers who accessed a site to download paedophile material were punished by a fine or imprisonment. A good many sites incorporated the name 'Lolita' as a code, showing how far Nabokov's heroine had fallen in her middle age.

From 1986 onwards the trade in paedophile obscenity was a periodic television feature. The extent of the market and the size of individual seizures were described as vast. Viewers were shown the reconstituted Obscene Publications Squad at work and even some of the material at issue. Pages of photo albums were opened to show snapshots unobjectionable in themselves but sinister by association. With the camera hovering close, the remaining pages of far worse pictures were turned, too fast to show anything but a blur of colour and patches of black and white. The same video of a child was shown more than once, the camera pulling slowly back during the less repellent opening so that the more repellent sequel was beyond the viewers' vision. It was uncomfortably close to a voyeuristic entertainment in the name of righteousness.

The murky frontier of censorship seemed plainer in one respect. No one could reasonably argue that the murder of a victim in a crime novel constituted a crime in reality. The sexual ordeals of Sade's *Justine*, whatever reservations might be held about the book, were not crimes in reality. Even if the reader of Agatha Christie or Sade or Nabokov condoned the acts described, there was no specific crime in reality to which that reader could be a party. A reader might admire a book whose influence others deplored but that was not the same thing.

Acts against children under the age of consent, filmed or photographed, were themselves crimes. Those who filmed or photographed them became accessories. The law now argued that those who became purchasers of the material were accomplices in the crimes portrayed. They might look in vain to John Stuart Mill who placed restrictions on actions, as opposed to opinions. In a man's actions, 'he must not make himself a nuisance to other people', let alone take part in crimes against them. On the other hand, 'in things which concern himself' alone, he should be free to put his opinions into practice. He must presumably be free to argue that the age of consent should be lowered or raised or even abolished.[7]

However just the cause, the new form of censorship penetrated a little further into those few cubic centimetres inside the skull, which even Orwell's Winston Smith in *Nineteen Eighty-four* erroneously believed to be his own. An individual might enter a room alone and remain alone, tap a keyboard, look at a screen and come out again, facing a prison sentence. In the case of such a trade, few tears may be shed. Reservations were directed towards detection or surveillance applied to political opinions deemed by a government to be terroristic or to an image which it is in the interest of a particular government that the public should not see.

Police action spread beyond the world of the paedophile networks. At dawn on 28 January 1993, the Metropolitan Police raided the West London home of a photographer for *Vogue* and *Harper's & Queen's*. Over 20,000 negatives, transparencies and prints were seized. Almost all had been taken in the course of his work for the magazines and were entirely uncontroversial.

Most of his other work consisted of portraits, commissioned at £4,000 a set, from the wealthy and the titled, including solicitors, magistrates and members of the House of Lords. These were family groups and individual members including children, clothed, and in a few cases where it was requested, unclothed. He had never taken a child's photograph without being asked or commissioned by a parent and never, in either case, when a child seemed reluctant because the result would be a poor photograph. Some of his prints, highly praised, were in the Victoria and Albert Museum, others in the Prints and Photography section of the Bibliothèque Nationale. The problem was not whether he or the police might be in the right but, as Lord Houghton of Sowerby warned the House of Lords when the Protection of Children Bill was debated, 'Some people's minds are like cesspools and they cannot see anything beautiful about some aspects of behaviour and human form.'

After questioning during twenty-four hours at Notting Hill police station, the photographer was released pending a decision. His files, invoices and computer had been seized. It was impossible for him to continue working in England. Seven months later Scotland Yard could only say that three of his prints, out of more than 20,000, might contravene the Protection of Children Act. The Crown Prosecution Service had not yet made up its mind. The *Independent* came to his support. On 4 September, its weekend magazine contained an account of his work with photographs including six children, four clothed, one showing chest and face, one nude turning away from the camera. His supporters, including seventy parents who had commissioned him and their children, made their views known. The police thereupon demanded the names and addresses of all his clients. In his favour, there had been an acquittal at Preston Crown Court in June 1989. A photographer who photographed his three children playing naked in his garden was arrested when Fylde Colour Laboratory alerted the police. The jury unanimously acquitted him.

By no means all those who were investigated proved to be innocent. A procession of otherwise unknown and nondescript defendants went through the courts, charged and convicted for having downloaded images of naked children under the age of sixteen. From time to time there was a more detailed celebrity trial as in the case of Paul Gadd, 'Gary Glitter' the pop star, in 1999. There were two trials on this occasion. He was first acquitted of sexual assaults on a former girlfriend and fan when she was still under sixteen. They had subsequently lived together for several years but she was now married with children of her own. Though she had informed on him, the case collapsed because she had sold her story to the *News of the World* with provision for a bonus of £25,000 if the singer was convicted.

The case of the downloaded images began when a laptop computer was taken for repair and they were discovered. A good many had been simply downloaded, others appeared to be the work of patient hours during which images of children's heads were pasted on to the bodies of naked adult women. The singer was said to have spent twelve hours at a time absorbed in this occupation, which in itself seemed an aberration that was more mental than criminal. In the course of sentencing, Mr Justice Butterfield remarked, 'This is not a victimless crime. The victims are the little children whose images you wish to view.' The definition and distinction were important. It appeared that the victims of *Juliette* or *The End of Alice* were figments of their authors' imaginations, the downloaded images were not.[8]

A similar consideration might apply to the art of the past. In November 1995, a television presenter and her partner were arrested after photographs of her young daughter in the bath were sent to the police by Boots the Chemist. Despite media excitement, the couple were exonerated. David Hockney responded on 7 November at a Royal Academy opening of a retrospective exhibition of his work. He attacked certain members of Parliament as 'Philistines who are not concerned with beauty', adding that 'There is something a bit odd and deeply wrong when somebody is trying to make warm pictures and are questioned by police.' If existing laws were implemented in this way, 'we will have a lot of fun. They will have to start taking a lot of pictures down.'

In a gesture for the press, worthy of Henry Vizetelly or George Moore, Mr Hockney held up a postcard reproduction of Jean-Honoré Fragonard's often-reproduced painting of the 1790s, *La Gimblette* or 'Girl with Dog'. A girl whose age Mr Hockney put at 'twelve or fourteen maybe' is lying on her back, knees drawn up and naked below the waist. She holds up a fluffy white lapdog whose tail lies between her splayed thighs. It was hard to believe that a posed photograph of such a subject downloaded from a website might not be criminal. Would the police now prosecute galleries who showed the painting or the many publishers who reproduced it? A note on an early engraving by Bertony read: 'This subject ought not to be put on display – Ce sujet ne doit pas être mis à l'étalage.' Next morning's newspapers displayed it by the million.[9]

4

Growing concern for children's moral welfare in the 1970s prepared the way for another form of censorship. The voluntary restrictions imposed by the film industry on itself in 1912 were being increasingly disregarded, given the absence of compulsion. Had control remained in the hands of cinema managers or local councils this might not have mattered. Instead, the decade brought video libraries to the high street and the neighbour-hood shopping parade. Many were opened by the newly unemployed from the closure of mines and smoke-stack industries. Redundancy payments financed them.

The absence of censorship and the easy availability of videos with vio-lent or sexual content made them playground 'swops'. Children forbidden to see them at home might watch them at the houses of friends. The most lurid footage could be played repeatedly. Most 'video nasties' were not sexu-ally obscene but sex and horror were often mingled. This was the world of *The Last House on the Left* (1972); *I Spit on Your Grave* (1978), which had no connection with Boris Vian's novel; *Zombie Flesh Eaters* (1979); *The Driller Killer* (1979); *The Bogey Man* (1980); *Nightmares in a Damaged Brain* (1981);

The Evil Dead (1982). The most frequently cited, *I Spit on Your Grave*, depicts its heroine as the victim of multiple rape, then as an avenger dismembering, hanging, drowning or castrating her former assailants.

At one level, the videos were stronger versions of the Hammer horror movie, a staple of the British cinema for twenty years. At another, they were animated and lurid versions of the 1950s horror comics. At yet another, they were not so much video nasties as video sillies, whose victims exuded joke blood or a curious green effluvium. It was sometimes doubtful how seriously their makers took them. In one drama of world-destroying villainy, the advertisement displayed for an Armageddon device adds, 'all major credit cards accepted'. Defenders of the genre insisted that 'it's only a film' and asked why, if Margaret Thatcher was so appalled by killing and maiming in taped fantasy, she had sent a task force to the Falkland Islands in 1982 to do it in reality.

The battle opened on 30 June 1983 with a front-page headline in the *Daily Mail*, 'Ban the Sadist Videos', and a full-page feature, 'Rape of Our Children's Minds'. By this time, the censorship campaign was led by Mrs Mary Whitehouse and her Viewers' and Listeners' Association, which claimed a membership of 30,000. Though Mrs Whitehouse said that she had never seen a video nasty and did not propose to, they had been described to her by correspondents who begged her to take action. In one interview she spoke of a battle for the 'soul of the nation' but retracted this.

The issue was whether children were watching such videos and being depraved and corrupted or scarred for life by the experience. One problem with this, as the campaign turned video nasties into front-page news, was that no self-respecting child could any longer go to school without claiming to have seen at least one of the kind. Those pressing for a ban carried out research in schools. Children were given a six-page questionnaire including 113 titles and asked which, if any, they had seen. The result made further headlines. Forty per cent of all six-year-olds had seen at least one video nasty. Almost half of those between seven and sixteen had done so.

The anti-censorship campaign then moved in. Once again children were asked to say which videos they had seen. This time, however, the questionnaire listed titles which did not exist, such as *Cannibal Feast*, as well as those which did. The children not only claimed to have seen the non-existent videos but went on to describe their contents.

In the absence of censorship, the police and the Director of Public Prosecutions moved in to seize videos under the Obscene Publications Acts

1959 and 1964. The DPP's office issued to the police a stop list of seventy-nine titles, later reduced to thirty-nine as some juries failed to convict. Many police raids on individual video libraries resulted in the removal of the entire stock for examination. On the basis of their titles alone, unexceptionable films were charged as video nasties, including the war features *Apocalypse Now* and *The Big Red One*, as well as the musical *The Best Little Whorehouse in Texas*. The raids also included major public companies who had the bad luck to be in the video industry, among them Thorn EMI.

From time to time in the years that followed, raids and seizures of obscene and violent videos became television news features. One pile of seizures appeared on the BBC, the camera moving too rapidly for a viewer to read the titles. Those who had been recording the news for later viewing could pause the tape. The titles on display included two films familiar on cinema circuits before 1984 and a series on 'Sex and the Elderly'.

The fate of videos in court was uncertain. On 13 April 1983, John Sawyer of Hackney was acquitted for selling *I Spit on Your Grave*, *Nightmares in a Damaged Brain* and *SS Experiment Camp*. The jury had laughed while viewing them. A less fortunate defendant was convicted for *Nightmares in a Damaged Brain* and went to prison for eighteen months. At Leeds, a case of *The Evil Dead* ended with an acquittal. To many jurors, it may have seemed the videos had a good deal in common with the children's favourite *Fungus the Bogeyman* (1977), a loveable anti-hero of filth, slime and ghoulishness created by Raymond Briggs.

The outcome of the controversy was decided by the election of Graham Bright as a Conservative MP in 1983. Mrs Whitehouse met him on her campaign tour and asked him if he would bring in a bill to censor all videos. He promised to do so. The odds were heavily against winning the parliamentary lottery which would give him the chance to bring in a private bill, but he won it. The odds disappeared altogether when Mrs Thatcher and the government gave him their support. The Video Recordings Act 1984 came into operation on 1 September 1986. As the time approached for the destruction of uncertifiable horror and obscenity, and such videos were destroyed, it seemed to the press that the country was a cleaner and a nobler place.

All films and videos past and present, however innocuous, were to carry a certificate from the government's new British Board of Film Censorship. Those refused a certificate, including Pasolini's *Salo: The 120 Days*, were banned outright. Films that might be seen anywhere else in Europe would face a criminal prosecution if shown in Britain. Among those now banned because they had not received a certificate in time were the *Woman's Own* 'weepie', *Who Will Love My Children?* and a 'child-friendly' adventure, *The Riddle of the Sands*. Foreign language films of minority interest were effect-ively banned from Britain because their sales would not warrant the high cost of certification.

There was some unease that Britain should be the most strictly censored democracy in this respect. Accordingly, the government with Orwellian sleight of hand changed the name of the censorship body in 1988 to the more appealing 'British Board of Film Classification'. It did not censor films but merely prosecuted those who showed or sold them without a certificate. Otherwise, it certified films as licensed for sale or showing to those under twelve, over fifteen or over eighteen. Licensed videos now carried a soft-voiced reassurance by the board, as the viewer's friend, that it was merely 'helping you to choose'. It did not add that in the matter of cuts or a total ban, the viewer would get no choice, except perhaps to disobey the law.

The appetite for censorship grew by what it fed on. By March 1988, there had been only two prosecutions. However, Mr John Patten, Under-Secretary at the Home Office, insisted, 'We believe that enforcement of the Act must be stepped up . . . We must not allow this position to falter.' To this end, trading standards officers were given police powers in the new Criminal Justice Act, removing from the police the 'unfair burden' of enforcing the law.[10]

Television was exempt from the 1984 law and when Channel 4 decided in 1986 to show films which would not have passed cinema or video cen-sorship, it was agreed that they should carry a small warning triangle in a corner of the screen. The result was to boost viewing figures considerably. For the benefit of members of Parliament, the Viewers' and Listeners' Association put on a showing of the worst material, promising 'horrific, barbaric scenes totally unacceptable for public viewing'. During a long extract from a French sample, one MP announced, 'This is boring. I would have switched off by now. I would have switched over to the snooker.' He left the showing later, remarking that the makers of such rubbish would go bankrupt before the nation was corrupted. A second MP left saying that he could not see what the fuss was about and that Mrs Whitehouse had set her cause back by such a performance.[11]

Elsewhere, a succession of dealers in illegal videos across the country was tracked down in May 1992. Culprits were found in possession of such long-banned titles as *Cannibal Holocaust*. Yet the tide turned against video censorship. 'Are British VCR-owners really happy to be subjected to this Mrs Grundyish nonsense?' asked the *Financial Times* on 24 September 1994.

Two dealers in pornographic videos were told by a judge at Nottingham Crown Court on 9 June 1999 that he had seen worse on television. 'I have to ask myself, having looked at that video, if this is the best you can do'. They were discharged. The Viewers' and Listeners' Association was quick off the mark. 'If the judge says this material is no worse than what is seen on television, then clearly we need to clean up television.'[12]

In 2005, the British Board of Film Classification confessed that it had given up trying to ban films, in an age when they were increasingly down-loaded from the Internet anyway. It was concerned only to issue certificates for guidance. Those which would once have been banned would get the most restrictive rating. Titles that had caused such trouble twenty years before were now freely available. *I Spit on Your Grave*, *Nightmares in a Damaged Brain* and their companions went on sale in the nation's high streets as DVDs.

In 1984, opponents of the Video Recordings Act described it as the result of a moral panic. As a form of censorship, it failed. The pied pipers of the computer with its video games and chat rooms lured away the children who might once have sat attentively before cannibal holocausts or nightmares in damaged brains. It seemed in 1984 that the history of thirty years earlier, specifically of the Children and Young Persons (Harmful Publications) Act 1955, had been repeated. At the time, it was feared that the innocence of post-war childhood had been corrupted and the fight against rising crime hampered by the morbid viciousness of 'horror comics'. Hardly was the new legislation enacted than the comic had been overtaken by the television screen with its appeal to a universal taste for crime in fact or fiction. Now the world of the video nasty in its high street library had yielded to universal access through the Internet.

5

In the 1980s and 1990s, the Obscene Publications Squad had become responsible for more than the mere confiscation of pornography or the prosecution of its providers. Two notorious areas of child pornography involved the filming of criminal acts by those who perpetrated them. The acts themselves therefore became the squad's concern. One was the satanic or ritual abuse of children. The other was the elusive 'snuff' movie which recorded murder.

In March 1990, press headlines reported, 'NSPCC says ritual child abuse rife'. Child protection authorities of high repute spoke of satanic abuse.

They cited rituals requiring under-age girls to be impregnated as 'brood mares', aborted, their foetuses sacrificed and eaten. One source of this story was the National Society for the Prevention of Cruelty to Children, presenting its annual report on 12 March 1990. Fourteen of its child protection teams had heard from children of satanic abuse: seven were investigating it. Children as young as five were said to be involved. A spokeswoman added that the society was 'absolutely sure that we are dealing with a problem that's happening and that the children we are dealing with are telling us the truth'. A first-hand account by a former 'brood mare' came from Childline. Kidscape showed a child's drawing of a witch and a burning candle. Suspected locations were in Nottinghamshire, Cheshire, Leeds, Manchester and the West Midlands.[13]

The Obscene Publications Branch waited for evidence. Five months later, Detective Chief Inspector Stuart Baker told a conference on incest and related matters that witnesses to ritual abuse had a moral duty to come forward. In his many years in the police force he had never come across any evidence of such activities nor knew of anyone who had. There were no videos. Charities had said 'there may well not be any evidence in terms of the police being able to make prosecutions.' The police said there was no evidence of any kind at all.

Chief Inspector Baker was seconded by Detective Inspector Sylvia Ashton from the West Midlands, an alleged hotbed of satanic abuse. 'There is a group of people going round the country, and indeed the world, making these claims . . . doubtful claims by fringe elements detract from the real problem of child abuse.' One psychotherapist had claimed that 10,000 human sacrifices a year took place in the United States alone.[14]

In 1990, the Obscene Publications Department also launched Operation Orchid to establish the truth or myth of the 'snuff' video. Months later there was no evidence to support anecdotes of murder being filmed to supply a small but lucrative market. Rumours of such films had existed for thirty years or more in the United States but all had so far proved hoaxes. In London, a teenage boy had been suffocated during an orgy in Hackney in 1985. Those responsible were gaoled for manslaughter. A video of the crime was said to be circulating in Holland. No copy was ever found.

In May 1990 the police were told that the victim of such a film had been buried in a Hackney car park. The car park was dug up and bones were found, which were those of an animal. In the most literal sense, however, millions of people had seen a snuff movie on television news during the Vietnamese war. A Viet Cong prisoner appeared on the screen. A South

Vietnamese officer put a pistol to his head, pulled the trigger, and the man's body crumpled while the cameras rolled.

Belief in ritual abuse was not easily exorcized. At the Old Bailey on 15 November 1991 two sisters of ten and fourteen described being taken by their parents to nocturnal devil-worshipping orgies in Epping Forest nine years earlier. Their godfather ritually slaughtered babies on a memorial stone. 'Sometimes he would cut the arm or the leg off, and sometimes he would make us take a bite off it.' Members of the orgy danced naked round a fire and the sisters claimed they were raped and buggered by various men. Prosecuting counsel warned the jury that the police had found no evidence to support the stories; no babies' bodies were discovered where they were supposed to have been buried. It was questionable whether the younger girl could have remembered from when she was little more than a year old that certain things happened on Tuesdays and Thursdays or that she had a drink and felt 'sort of sexy'.

Four days later the prosecution collapsed because the children were unable to continue giving evidence. It was the worst of all outcomes. Child support agencies claimed that giving evidence was an ordeal for the two children, which no doubt it was, and that child witnesses should be believed without such barbarities. The sceptics were able to point to the lack of any corroborative evidence at all and, indeed, to the police investigation which indicated that the children could not be telling the truth. To maintain untruth in court would be a far greater ordeal. The unanswered question was why the children had told such stories, if they were not true. Where had they got them from?

Also in 1991, social workers removed nine children from the Orkneys after accusations of ritual abuse. All the children were returned after it was discovered that the 'rituals' included a ploughing match and races at a Halloween party organized by the entire community. In 1994, what seemed a major miscarriage of justice occurred at Swansea Crown Court. Twelve defendants from Pembrokeshire, seven of whom were ultimately acquitted, were prosecuted on the evidence of a child in care who described satanic rituals. The rites were allegedly performed in a barn, directly on the bend of the main road. Its doors were missing so that whatever happened inside must have been in full view of passing traffic. Orgies were also alleged to have been held on a beach during August, at a time when it would have been frequented by holidaymakers and campers. As one neighbour who was not involved in the accusations put it: 'Something stinks about this case, mate, and people know it.'

Though it might seem there could not be a word of truth in these stories, it was argued that the children 'could not have made the whole thing up'. Yet just a year earlier, a senior officer of the Obscene Publications Squad had never come across such things and knew of no one who had. G. K. Chesterton once prophesied that if people gave up believing in the established forms of religion, they would not believe in nothing – they would believe in anything, even perhaps in the supernatural demons of Epping Forest.

Where did the children's stories come from? Possibly it was only coincidence that what the children described and the dates from which they recalled it were a match not so much for what might have happened in reality but for the wilder fantasies of the black-market video nasty still so freely available at the time. Despite the government's assurances, in 1988, that its new powers would prove effective, illegal copies of videos continued to circulate across the country, in defiance of trading standards officials. This nationwide distribution of favourite titles was usually in the form of easily imported foreign copies with English subtitles. Some of those convicted had set up a postal business at home, copying titles to order. Others copied them in order to swap. It was perhaps coincidence that the trade itself was particularly evident in areas like South Wales, where satanic orgies had been 'disclosed' by children to social workers.[15]

12

The Enemy Within

AFTER A BRIEF period of peace in 1945, it appeared that the Second World War had ended only to make way for its successor. The point at which peacetime darkened into forty years of a cold war with the Soviet Union and its allies depended on the perception of the observer. William Joyce, in his last drunken harangue of May 1945, already warned his listeners that Britain and the West, 'without the German legions', would never contain the tide of Bolshevism which the advancing Red Army represented. Within a year, Winston Churchill issued his warning of an 'iron curtain' descending across Europe, 'from Stettin in the Baltic to Trieste in the Adriatic'.

The the more casual issues of public life, the state retained such weapons of wartime censorship as the Official Secrets Acts and the D-Notice system. The judiciary and Parliament still controlled the press through attachments for contempt of court and breaches of parliamentary privilege. The British Board of Film Censors obligingly banned such films as *Sword in the Desert* in 1950 as being pro-Zionist, and *Titanic* because it was made for Dr Goebbels in 1942 during his 'God Punish the English' campaign.

The antique stage censorship of the Lord Chamberlain was adjusted to post-war politics. So, for example, 'Bevin, Bevan, let's call the whole thing off' – a song in a 1946 West End review, *Between Ourselves* at the Playhouse Theatre – was removed as being offensive to ministers in the new Labour government. The song reminded the audience that 'You put us in and now, no doubt, you wish that you could put us out.' The government discouraged any attempt to abolish this useful theatrical censorship. The parliamentary motion proposing abolition on 29 November 1949 was to fail in the absence of sufficient members to form a standing committee in the House of Commons.

Political impersonations were equally unacceptable. On 16 April 1958, five members of the prestigious Theatre Workshop Company at the Theatre Royal, Stratford East, were convicted and fined for an imitation of the voice of Winston Churchill in *You Won't Always Be at the Top*. On 12 November 1957, the BBC had cut an imitation of his voice from a recording: 'It is against our policy to broadcast impersonations of Churchill's voice.'

Where the government could not censor television directly, pressure of political opinion was brought to bear. Labour supporters used the *Daily Herald* to attack the BBC for a television broadcast of a light comedy, *Party Manners*, on Sunday evening 1 October 1950. The *Daily Herald* denounced 'one of the most astonishing political blunders in the history of the BBC' and the play as being 'steeped in class snobbishness and anti-Labour prejudice'. At the request of 'a Socialist spokesman', the BBC cancelled the Thursday repeat showing.

Responses to pressure varied. The National Coal Board's lawyers visited the Adelphi Theatre in 1949 to see Jack Buchanan in *Castle in the Air*, which included jokes at the board's expense. The management called their bluff. In May 1949, however, when the Royal Navy frigate *Amethyst* was trapped by Chinese Communists on the Yangtse, the BBC agreed to ban Larry Adler from playing the hit of the day, 'Slow Boat to China', on *Saturday Night Music Hall*.

Yet it was international rather than domestic politics which determined the nature of political censorship for the next forty years. At first, nostalgia for the wartime Russian alliance was not easily discredited. Less than two years before the war's end, factory slogans and graffiti urged 'Second Front Now', or 'Tanks for Joe'. British working-class sentiment and productive effort rallied to secure Soviet victory on the Eastern front. Communism in 1945 was acceptable enough for the party to win parliamentary seats at Stepney and West Fife, coming within a few hundred votes of winning others like Rhondda East, which normally had large Labour majorities. Later revelations by former Communists suggested that a significant number of new Labour MPs were secretly fellow-travellers.[1]

Few people doubted the existence of a cold war by the time of the Berlin blockade in 1948, when the Soviet Union attempted to force the Western allies out of their sectors by closing land routes to the city, over a hundred miles inside East Germany. The survival of West Berlin and the airlift which supplied it appeared as the first Western victory of that war. If confirmation of hostilities were needed, it came in 1950 with the invasion of South Korea by its northern neighbour. United Nations troops, mostly

American and British, did battle with the 'Reds', while American and Russian pilots fought one another overhead on behalf of their client states.

Western journalists and visitors sympathetic to the Communist cause, notably the London *Daily Worker*, were free to report the war from the North Korean side and some paid propaganda visits to countrymen who were prisoners of war. It was as if a London paper had reported the Second World War from Berlin or the British Union of Fascists had paid sympathetic visits to Allied prisoners. William Joyce and John Amery had been hanged five years earlier for doing no more than some post-war Communists were now doing. Yet neither the United States nor Britain was technically at war with North Korea. They were part of a United Nations action to restore peace. There was no treason in supporting the de facto enemy.

Long before this, in September 1945, the first post-war traitors who defied the Official Secrets Acts were being identified. Igor Gouzenko, a cipher clerk in the office of the Soviet Military Attaché in Ottawa, defected to the Canadians. The intelligence which he brought implicated a number of scientists in the betrayal of nuclear information to the Soviet Union. These men had worked at Los Alamos on the Manhattan project, producing one atom bomb to be tested and two to be dropped on Hiroshima and Nagasaki, only a month before Gouzenko's defection.

It had been assumed that the Soviet Union was many years behind in nuclear research and posed no threat. In the event, its first atom bomb was tested in the Urals in 1949, only four years after the Americans and three years before the British. A Soviet hydrogen bomb was tested in August 1953, nine months after the Americans. The nuclear shield of Western defence seemed no defence at all.

One scientist whose betrayals first altered the nuclear balance was British, Alan Nunn May, named by Gouzenko. As an undergraduate, Nunn May was a Cambridge contemporary of Guy Burgess and Donald Maclean. Like them, he remained secretly an active Communist. He also took the view of a former US Ambassador to Moscow that 'in self-defence, Russia has an absolute moral right to obtain atomic secrets by military espionage.' If so, her informants had a moral right to ignore censorship imposed upon them by official secrets acts or by national allegiance. What the West saw as a nuclear shield appeared to Moscow as a sword unsheathed.[2]

Nunn May pleaded guilty at the Central Criminal Court in May 1946. His information, given to Colonel Nicolai Zabotin, included documents detailing atomic tests and constituents of the Los Alamos bombs. He also passed on a piece of platinum foil with 160 microgrammes of Uranium 233. As a further bonus, there were specifications of electronic fuses, shells, radar and a powerful new explosive known as RDX. He was not tried for treason but under the Official Secrets Acts and sent to prison for ten years. Russia had been an indispensable wartime ally and the reality of the cold war was not yet universally admitted.

That admission was plain by the time Klaus Fuchs, head of theoretical physics at Harwell, was arrested in January 1950. A German-born naturalized Briton, Fuchs confessed he had been passing information on atomic research to the Soviet Union for eight years. Like Nunn May, he had worked at Los Alamos. As a result of the 'Venona' partial decryption by MI5 of KGB messages between Moscow and the West, Fuchs was identified as the Harwell spy who had 'given' the Russians atomic weapons. He went to prison for fourteen years under the Official Secrets Act. Had he been caught in the United States, he might have followed Julius and Ethel Rosenberg to the electric chair.

In 1971 Peter Deeley's book *Beyond Breaking Point* revealed that Fuchs would have been caught long before but for the fact that an MI5 official who interviewed him on the previous occasion, in 1946, was the same man who had been a double agent between Fuchs and the Russians. When this was about to be revealed twenty-five years later, the D-Notice system was implemented. Mr Deeley was informed that his book could not be published without deletions to safeguard another agent whose identity must still be protected.

The post-war intelligence services were already penetrated by Soviet espionage long before these betrayals. Guy Burgess of MI5 and Donald Maclean, who had been First Secretary at the British Embassy in Washington, caught the Southampton ferry to St Malo on 27 May 1951 and disappeared. They surfaced in Moscow, revealed as Communist agents since they were Cambridge undergraduates in the early 1930s. In 1963 a more important member of the secret service now under suspicion, Kim Philby, followed them shortly before he was to be interrogated by MI5. There were a 'Fourth Man' and a 'Fifth Man', in the persons of Sir Anthony Blunt, Keeper of the Queen's Pictures, and John Cairncross of the Treasury. They were of less importance, long since inactive, and no charges were brought against them.

It was not surprising that Soviet spies operated with some success under such protection as Burgess and Maclean offered. A number were subsequently caught, notably the Krogers and 'Gordon Lonsdale' in 1960, as well as their informants at the Portland Underwater Warfare Research

Establishment. George Blake of MI5 turned traitor out of political conviction. He was caught and sentenced to forty-two years' imprisonment in 1961.

The powers of censorship had done nothing to prevent these nuclear and diplomatic secrets from reaching the Soviet Union. The most bizarre aspect of the major cases was that Burgess and Maclean had openly told colleagues or friends that they were agents of the Soviet Union – and had not been believed. Burgess, who was both a homosexual and a drunkard, was said to have become rowdy at parties, uttering shouts of 'I am Stalin's bum-boy.'

By the beginning of the 1950s the existence of an enemy within was an established and demonstrable reality. The only doubt was over the extent and dedication of this Fifth Column. If ever a nation had needed a workable system of official secrecy, capable of keeping secrets and information from the press, the public and the enemy it was surely Great Britain at mid-century.

2

The most formidable weapon of governments remained the Official Secrets Acts. Against espionage and treachery, however, their function was too often a bolting of stable doors to the echo of receding hooves. They might punish those who were caught or intimidate those who were tempted but they were no match for ideological commitment or simple greed. They were principally used to punish, and more frequently to threaten, editors, publishers and authors.

Questions from two world wars remained unresolved. Were such laws to censor only information or opinion as well? Were they confined to material whose disclosure would prejudice the interests and safety of the state or also those of the government of the day? In time of war the expression of opinion had certainly been criminalized. Yet the laws were originally intended to protect national defences and not to shield ministers who had strong personal interests in concealing the truth, as Winston Churchill described it.

In the first post-war decade of the 1950s it was the institution of National Service, with two million young men in uniform, which offered the most instructive case. It marked a division between generations as well as loyalties. On 26 February 1958, two undergraduates published an article in the Oxford weekly *Isis*, hardly a magazine regarded as a security risk. This, however, was a special edition devoted to the cause of nuclear disarmament. The contribution was based upon the experiences of Paul Thompson and William Miller as National Servicemen in the Royal Navy.

The title of the article was 'Frontier Incidents Exposure', attacking the misreporting of news from Western Europe. Such news highlighted 'Western sincerity and the good fight against Russian wickedness'. The article then described a chain of listening posts, manned largely by National Servicemen trained in Morse code or Russian. From these posts the linguists of the Intelligence Corps monitored Soviet military broadcasts, listening for 'the least squeak' from Russian transmitters. From such transmissions it was possible to estimate the numbers, locations and movements of the opposing forces. A second revelation was that Western aircraft and ships, including West German torpedo boats with British captains, deliberately provoked radio traffic by violating air space or disrupting naval exercises.

Most of the magazine's readers were undergraduates who had also completed National Service. The revelations were unlikely to startle them. Even the wider public could not be surprised that NATO, and indeed its adversaries, kept surveillance on one another's movements. If Russian-speaking units of the Intelligence Corps were not monitoring the Soviet transmissions, what on earth were they doing in Germany? Yet the authors of the article, like two million reluctant conscripts, had signed the Official Secrets Acts. The first paragraph of the article, making plain that it was not a betrayal of secrets but a protest against an aspect of military policy, was no defence. Scotland Yard sent to Oxford its most redoubtable spy-catcher, Superintendent George Smith. Two years later he was to track down the Portland Ring, including the Krogers and the Soviet master spy 'Gordon Lonsdale', in reality a KGB colonel, Konan Molodi.

The Old Bailey *Isis* trial was worthy of a wartime espionage hearing. Much of the prosecution evidence was heard in camera. Wooden screens covered the glass panels of the courtroom doors. Lord Chief Justice Goddard presided, Sir Harry Hylton-Foster, Solicitor-General, appeared for the Crown and a future Attorney-General, Peter Rawlinson, for the defence. In law there was no defence. The defendants had put conscience before the Official Secrets Acts and on this basis pleaded guilty to one charge in exchange for the Crown dropping the rest.

When passing sentence, Goddard warned them that he did not regard their action as trivial. 'If I did, I should not be doing my duty as a judge and I should be making a farce of the Official Secrets Act.' However, he was prepared to see it as 'an act of more or less youthful folly', the result of being 'led away owing to the enthusiasm you were showing to other causes'. The two undergraduates were to go to prison for three months, 'in the most favourable conditions away from other criminals'. Having been detained for a month before the trial and with remission for good conduct, they would be released a month later.[3]

The farce, if it was one, was evident to hundreds of conscripts who served in the listening posts. Whatever information was given away in the *Isis* article might have been news to the British public but certainly not to the Soviet Union. Every 25 December, Soviet broadcasts were said to break briefly into English with a salutation copied from the BBC: 'A Happy Christmas to all our listeners.'

In 1962, a second secrets trial resulted from opposition to nuclear arms. The Committee of 100, leaders of the Campaign for Nuclear Disarmament, considered a sit-down at the War Office, or at the Atomic Weapons Research Establishment at Woolwich, finally deciding to enter and disrupt RAF Wethersfield in Essex. The base was what the Attorney-General called 'an airfield which is required for the safety of this country to be at constant alert'. A search of the campaign's headquarters by Special Branch revealed a document which acknowledged that 'our stated aim is to occupy a rocket base but we expect to be arrested as soon as we put a foot across the entrance.' There was a letter of encouragement from Bertrand Russell, advising the organizers not to involve the entire leadership, in case they were all in prison at the same time.

What the members of the campaign intended was plainly illegal. They knew it was so, though they did not expect the disruption to be more than symbolic. Chief Detective Inspector David Stratton of the Special Branch admitted there was no evidence that they intended to spy or obtain secret information. Yet they were charged under the Official Secrets Acts with 'conspiring to enter' and 'conspiring to incite others to enter' the air base. Though they might not intend to communicate information, their conduct was 'prejudicial to the interests or safety of the State'.

It might seem they had been charged under the wrong legislation. A political demonstration was far removed from a spy communicating secrets. It was apparently one more case of governments using laws in circumstances that had never been envisaged. In this instance, the jury did not find it easy to agree. However, after deliberating for some hours they returned verdicts of guilty against all the defendants. They may have wondered why the law officers had not charged the culprits with incitement to trespass or something that more accurately reflected the purpose of their alleged conspiracy.[4]

Increasingly it appeared that the true post-war purpose of the Official Secrets Act was not so much to protect the realm as to put into authors, publishers and editors alike the fear of a long stretch in Wakefield's maximum security wing – provided that a jury could be persuaded to put them there. The *Isis* journalists had got off lightly but elsewhere official secrets sentences had lengthened dramatically since the atom spy cases of the 1940s. Forty-two years, allegedly under pressure from Harold Macmillan as Prime Minister, was the total in 1961 for George Blake, who betrayed to the Russians a tunnel dug under East Berlin by MI6 and the CIA. The sentence was so vindictive that two pacifist sympathizers, gaoled in the CND case, facilitated his escape from Wormwood Scrubs, his safe passage to Berlin and a career as a KGB colonel in Moscow.

Faced by such penalties, it was not surprising if authors, publishers and editors succumbed to blatant or subtle intimidation. Of the blatant variety was that employed against Lieutenant-Colonel Alexander Scotland in 1954–5. Scotland was seventy-three and had served in military intelligence during both world wars. In 1954 he submitted *The London Cage*, an account of his service, for clearance by the War Office. The War Office did not merely censor the book, it informed his agent that it could not be published at all. The reasons seemed to be that it would offend Britain's new NATO ally in West Germany and that it revealed the War Office's own incompetence.

When Colonel Scotland protested, his home was raided by Special Branch and his personal papers were taken away. The matter was raised in the Commons on 3 March 1955. The Home Secretary, Major Gwilym Lloyd George, was cornered by members who demanded to know on what authority a search warrant had been issued. Was it because 'the book might give offence to the Germans'? Was the Home Secretary aware that those who knew anything of wartime security could find no breach of it in this book? Was the true offence that 'Colonel Scotland has questioned the efficiency of the War Office'?

There was a more general objection, voiced by Anthony Greenwood from the Labour benches. 'Don't you think it is a little unfortunate that this 73-year-old soldier should be hounded in this way while more influential people like Field Marshal Montgomery and the Prime Minister [Sir Anthony Eden] have published their memoirs based largely on official information?' That was an objection heard many times again. The Home Secretary withdrew from the debate after a particularly lame performance, pleading that he 'could not make any further statement'. In the face of mounting publicity, the War Office capitulated. Yet it insisted on a bizarre disclaimer in the book. This explained that the account of War Office ineptitude did not represent the office's view of itself. *The London Cage* appeared belatedly in 1957.

Such cases reinforced a particular objection to official secrecy, the manner in which some writers of history were favoured and others barred from access to material. It was a question, in any case, whether history could prejudice the present interests or security of the state. The 'Black Diaries' of Sir Roger Casement were now generally known to be type-scripts produced by Scotland Yard to persuade influential neutrals not to support moves for the reprieve of a homosexual. On 19 April 1956, half a century after Casement's execution, the government confirmed that they must remain secret indefinitely. In defiance of this, in 1959 the copy of the typescript which had been in the hands of Peter Singleton-Gates for thirty years, was to be used to publish editions beyond the reach of the English law, in Paris and New York.

It was still argued that the high and the mighty, of whom Winston Churchill was the most frequently but unjustly cited example, published their memoirs without interference, using official documents which came into their hands during their tenure of office. Churchill had, in fact, taken advice from the cabinet secretary. It was usually the awkward squad of politics who felt the force of threat of prosecution under the laws relating to official secrecy.

A member of this squad was the maverick Labour politician Richard Crossman, a member of the Wilson cabinet from 1964 to 1970. After Crossman's death in 1974, his diary for 1964–6 was edited for publication. A copy was sent to the cabinet secretary who rejected it as against the public interest and 'harmful to the doctrine of collective responsibility'. It was debatable whether this threatened the safety or interests of the state.

When it was decided to publish diary extracts in the *Sunday Times*, the Attorney-General sought an injunction restraining the newspaper from doing so. Lord Widgery in the High Court refused this on the grounds that 'we are dealing in this case with a disclosure of information nearly ten years later.' This was a far more liberal interpretation of the law than might have been expected, given the half century or more for which some documents in the Public Record Office remained closed.[5]

3

When intimidation of the press by the government took a direct form, it was frequently through the D-Notice system, instituted during the

'German spy' scare of 1912 but still in regular use half a century later. A number of notices, warning the press that it might be liable to prosecution, were issued after the defection of spies to the Soviet Union, sometimes long after. In 1967 an attempt was made to prevent the *Sunday Times* and the *Observer* from belatedly reporting on the careers of Burgess, Maclean and Philby in Moscow since their defection.

It was sixteen years since Burgess and Maclean had fled to Moscow, though only four since Philby had followed them. Yet neither newspaper had thought it necessary to ask for official clearance. Surely the KGB must know what these agents had been doing in Moscow since they got there and began working for it. Once again, those whom the Defence Committee in London proposed to keep in the dark could only be the British public. Both newspapers ignored the threat and published their features without repercussions.

The antagonism over the issue of Defence Notices came to a head in 1967 when the *Daily Express*, in the person of Chapman Pincher, discovered that copies of all overseas cables in Britain were taken every day to the Ministry of Defence for vetting. He inquired of Colonel Leslie Lohan, Secretary of the D-Notice Committee, whether a D-Notice would apply to his scoop. He was told that there was one D-Notice which did not apply and another which was too vague to have any effect. Colonel Lohan asked him as a favour not to print the story. The *Express* published Pincher's 'Cable Vetting Sensation' on 21 February. That afternoon in the House of Commons, the Prime Minister, Harold Wilson, accused the newspaper of 'a clear breach of two D-Notices'.

The press representative on the Defence Committee, Lee Howard of the *Daily Mirror*, thereupon resigned in protest, ending the pact between government and editors. That the people of Britain should be subject in peacetime to this wholesale censorship of their correspondence by cable was bad enough. That they should not even be allowed to know that they were being censored was insupportable. It was characteristic of a system which, as the distinguished historian Hugh Thomas remarked, was itself set up without publicity and, indeed, in complete secrecy.[6]

To calm the objectors, Harold Wilson hastily set up a committee of inquiry, chaired by Lord Radcliffe, deputy director of the wartime Press and Censorship Bureau, now a Lord of Appeal in Ordinary. It included two former Secretaries of State for Defence, Emanuel Shinwell from the Labour benches and Selwyn Lloyd from the Conservatives. Its report coincided on 13 June with a government white paper which appeared to pre-empt the conclusions of the Radcliffe committee. In wholehearted support of Wilson's allegations, the white paper denounced the *Express* article as 'inaccurate in matters of fact and misleading in its treatment of the story'. By informing readers that cables were being censored, the paper tried to persuade them that the Wilson government was responsible for 'new invasions of privacy or for distorting existing procedures to this end'. The newspaper had also breached two D-Notices.

Unfortunately for Wilson and his colleagues, the Radcliffe inquiry had concluded that there had been no breach of the D-Notice system. On the facts, Chapman Pincher's story 'was not inaccurate in any sense that could expose it to hostile criticism on that score'. The government, it seemed, had been caught bending the truth.

4

Far from being resolved, by 1970 the conflict over secrecy between press and government soon embroiled a major national newspaper, the *Sunday Telegraph*, whose editor together with a journalist and an informant shared the dock at the Central Criminal Court throughout most of January 1971. The occasion of the alleged offences was the so-called 'Nigerian Civil War' of 1967–70, during which the breakaway state of Biafra fought bravely but unsuccessfully for the right of independence from the federation of Nigeria.

In Britain, the Wilson government had decided to arm the military government of Nigeria. As the slaughter and starvation of Biafrans continued, it was a decision that became increasingly unpopular. Towards the end of the civil war, in 1969, Colonel R. E. Scott, Defence Adviser to the British High Commission in Lagos, produced a report for the British government. He described the Nigerian army, though heavily armed by Britain and the Soviet Union, as incompetent. That it took three years to defeat the outnumbered Biafrans was some confirmation of that.

Jonathan Aitken, a journalist and prospective Conservative candidate for the 1970 election, went to Lagos and interviewed both Colonel Scott and Colonel Douglas Cairns, a member of the neutral team of international military observers. Mr Aitken returned home and joined others in supporting the Biafran cause. In December 1969, he dined with a friend, General Henry Alexander, whose service had included a spell in West Africa and who received from Colonel Cairns reports on the civil war from time to time. One of these, subsequently known as the Scott Report, was that of Colonel Scott in Lagos: 'An Appreciation of the Nigerian Conflict'. Its principal interest was the revelation that the Wilson government had provided a far greater proportion of arms to the Nigerians than ministers had admitted to the House of Commons.

General Alexander offered to lend his friend this copy of the report, with no suggestion that it was an official secret. Jonathan Aitken, who was working on a proposed television feature on the civil war, took the report with him to the studio and showed it to his producer. The producer photo-copied it. The report itself was returned to General Alexander but, on the basis of the photocopy, Jonathan Aitken offered to write an article for the *Sunday Telegraph*. The article appeared on 11 January as 'Secret Biafra War Plan Revealed'. It had been read before publication by the paper's legal advisers and cleared with the Secretary of the D-Notice Committee, Vice-Admiral Sir Norman Denning. Since it dealt with a foreign army it did not, according to Denning, imperil British national security.

In quick succession, there was outrage in Lagos among those criticized in the report, Colonel Scott was expelled from Nigeria, and an official inquiry began in London. Detective Chief Superintendent Kenneth Pendred of Scotland Yard arrived with his sergeant at the *Sunday Telegraph* offices to question the editor, Brian Roberts, in the presence of the paper's solicitor. The investigation then gathered pace. In March charges were brought against Brian Roberts and Jonathan Aitken under the Official Secrets Acts. For good measure, charges were brought against Colonel Cairns, of the international military observers, because he had sent a copy of the report to General Alexander.

Even at the committal proceedings in the Guildhall, it seemed that someone in the hierarchy of government feared the prosecution might go wrong. The Attorney-General privately offered a deal, whereby the accused would plead guilty at the magistrates court, would be let off with a maximum fine of £50, and a major Old Bailey trial would be avoided. The offer was rejected.[7]

At the Central Criminal Court in January 1971, there was a fourth defendant, the *Sunday Telegraph* itself. So far as the responsibility for pub-lication went, it appeared that Mr Aitken had assured General Alexander that he had not photocopied the report, though his producer had. At the same time Mr Aitken was not told that his subsequent conversation with the general was bugged for the purposes of the prosecution.

James Comyn, for the defence, pointed out that the Scott Report betrayed no secrets whatsoever. The purpose of the article was to reveal that 'inaccurate and misleading statements had been made in Parliament by Mr Wilson, then Prime Minister, and Mr Michael Stewart, the Foreign Secretary: that was the duty of any citizen.' Jonathan Aitken, in evidence, insisted that what he had done was not an offence against the official secrets legislation but an attempt to unmask the butchery of Biafrans resulting from the policy of the Wilson government. Parliament had been misled and 'this was not just a little issue: a thousand Biafran children were dying daily as a result of British bullets.'

The plain implication was that certain leaders of the now-defeated Labour government had been liars and scoundrels. Indeed, Jonathan Aitken's counsel, Basil Wigoder, bluntly described the prosecution to the jury as politically motivated, an attempt to soothe the feelings of Nigerian leaders in their war against Biafra and to soothe the feelings of those members of the government who had been angered by the publication of the *Sunday Telegraph* article.

Whatever hope there might have been of a conviction faded when Mr Justice Caulfield began his summing-up. He suggested that the official secrets legislation under which the case had been brought, having reached its sixtieth birthday, should be 'pensioned off'. What he called the 'warning bark' of the press was necessary to a free society. 'If the press is the watchdog of freedom and its fangs are drawn, all that will ensue is a whimper.'

Verdicts of not guilty on all charges were unanimous. At the general election of 1970, the Conservative manifesto had promised that 'we will review the operation of the Official Secrets Act so that Government is more open and more accountable to the public.' The party was to be in power for twenty-three of the remaining thirty years of the century. On the evidence, it seems not to have learnt much about official secrecy from the downfall of its opponents.[8]

5

Two major cases in the 1980s suggested that the official secrets legislation had better be interred than pensioned off. In the first of these, the Falklands War of 1982 was everything that the Nigerian conflict was not. The invasion of the islands by Argentina on 2 April was met by a military response that was brief, precise and apparently successful in its execution. By recapturing the islands, eight thousand miles away, with a relatively small task force exposed to considerable apparent risk, the combined services had fought a model campaign. Though there were British losses, they were far lighter than anyone might have expected. For the Argentines, though they had occupied the islands, the losses were far greater.

The immediate response to invasion was the despatch of a task force including the carriers *Invincible* and *Hermes* as well as the liners *Queen Elizabeth II* and *Canberra* in the role of troopships. On 7 April, Britain announced the setting up of an exclusion zone, a circle of 200 miles round the islands. Any Argentine ship entering it did so at its peril though, as yet, there were apparently no Royal Navy ships there to present the peril. On 30 April this circle became a total exclusion zone for all shipping, as if in preparation for an invasion. The task force had arrived safely in the South Atlantic by the end of April. Ahead of it and unannounced were nuclear-powered submarines, including HMS *Conqueror* and HMS *Splendid*.

On 30 April, the first air strikes on Port Stanley airfield were carried out by a Vulcan bomber flying from Ascension Island and Harrier fighters from *Invincible*, preparing the way for an invasion. By now the opposing fleet had put to sea. HMS *Splendid* was ordered to track the only Argentine aircraft-carrier *25 de Mayo* and sink her. The hunt for the carrier failed.

On 2 May the Argentine cruiser *General Belgrano*, bought from the United States and dating from the 1930s, was steaming south-east with two destroyer escorts in international waters beyond the southern limit of the exclusion zone. Despite her age, she carried fifteen 6-inch guns with a range of thirteen miles, as well as Sea-Cat anti-aircraft missiles. The British government claimed that her escorting destroyers were armed with Exocet anti-ship missiles having a range of twenty miles. On 13 May, the Secretary of Defence added that *Belgrano* had been 'closing' on the British task force. She was sunk without warning by three torpedoes from *Conqueror* and 368 Argentine sailors died.

A government statement in the Commons on 4 May explained that *Conqueror* detected the cruiser and her escorts at 8 p.m. on 2 May, when she was 'closing on elements of our task force'. The decision to fire the torpedoes which sank her was said on 5 May to be 'one clearly taken by the submarine commander'. These explanations were challenged as inconsistent with the facts. The Argentine cruiser had apparently been detected on *Conqueror*'s sonar two days earlier. She had not entered the exclusion zone but was patrolling well to the south, 200 miles from the task force on which she and her escorts were later said to be closing. The order to sink her had been issued in London and was not a decision of the submarine commander. When *General Belgrano* was sunk, she had been steaming away from the task force for eleven hours towards the naval base of Ushuaia, one hundred miles distant.

The Labour opposition, notably Tam Dalyell, were persistent in challenging the official account. At the worst it seemed that senior figures in the government had misled or lied to the House of Commons. Crucial in any investigation was a top secret government report on the sinking, a document which became known as 'The Crown Jewels', drawn up by an Assistant Secretary in the Head of Defence Secretariat 5, Clive Ponting. It was now 1984 and the task was to square the facts as they were known with what had been said by ministers in the House of Commons two years earlier.

Clive Ponting's account of the response from the Minister of Defence to Tam Dalyell described it as an attempt to conceal information which would reveal that ministers had gravely misled Parliament for the previous two years. He added that Mr Dalyell was simply referred to previous letters with the assurance from the minister that 'There is nothing I can usefully add.' In consequence, Mr Ponting forwarded to Tam Dalyell information contained in a draft for a letter he was never sent. It confirmed that *General Belgrano* had been steaming away from the task force for eleven hours when she was sunk.[9]

Clive Ponting also sent Mr Dalyell a Defence Ministry minute which he alleged advised the withholding of information on the sinking from the House of Commons Foreign Affairs Committee inquiry. It would be best not to reveal that the engagement of the Argentine aircraft-carrier *25 de Mayo* outside the total exclusion zone was permitted from 30 April and that the change on 2 May was not restricted to *Belgrano* but included all Argentine warships over a large area. It was also thought unwise to reveal that there was a delay until 7 May before the appropriate warning was issued for the 2 May change.

The 'leak' was soon hot news. By January 1985 Clive Ponting found himself at the Central Criminal Court facing charges under the Official Secrets Acts and a lengthy prison sentence if convicted. He had acted as a matter of conscience, putting duty to the nation before obligations to the incumbent government. He had done so in circumstances where he believed the House of Commons had been lied to or misled by that government. Yet he had surely broken the law by telling what he believed to be the truth. That he should then be prosecuted had led to what many people, including the leader of the Liberal party David Steel, regarded as 'an East European-style secret trial'.

The most influential witness for the defence was a former Home Secretary and senior Labour politician, Merlyn Rees, who described the moral priorities of a civil servant: 'Loyalty to a minister and a Government must be there, but loyalty to the nation is greater . . . I would put truthfulness to Parliament above all.' Mr Rees recalled that an MI5 officer in the 1930s had briefed Winston Churchill, out of office at the time, because he thought it his duty.[10]

Such arguments were wasted on the trial judge, Mr Justice McCowan. His comments and interpretations of the law, even his summing-up, appeared to leave no room for an acquittal. He defined 'the interests of the state' as the policies of the present government. He was prepared to consider prosecution submissions, which if accepted meant that 'I shall have to direct the jury to convict.'[11]

The jurors went out and came back with a unanimous acquittal. They preferred their view of the law to the direction given them by the judge or the wording of the statutes. The interests of the state were not, for them, those of the party in power but of the whole nation. Ministers were accused of misleading or deceiving Parliament and yet it seemed they were to be protected by the law at the expense of a man who had told the truth. The verdict suggested that it was not the first duty of a civil servant to save members of the government from embarrassment. Mr Justice McCowan's hostile interpretation of the law had unwittingly secured Clive Ponting's acquittal.

After this humiliation, it might seem that the Thatcher government had not much further to fall in such confrontations. Yet what lay ahead was ridicule and rebuff on a global scale, as if the Ponting case were a parochial quarrel. The occasion was the proposed publication of *Spycatcher* by Peter Wright, an MI5 officer who retired in 1976, having joined in 1955 after a wartime career in the Admiralty Research Laboratory and as a Principal Scientific Officer with Marconi. Indeed, he was recruited as the principal scientist of MI5.

Wright's book did not betray significant new information. His own experiences added colour and detail to what was already generally known. His book described how he and his colleagues had 'bugged and burgled our way across London at the State's behest, while pompous bowler-hatted civil servants in Whitehall pretended to look the other way'. These details were scarcely a novelty to readers of Len Deighton or John Le Carré. An early example of Wright's activities was the discovery that the files of the Communist party were kept in the home of a wealthy member in Mayfair. The phone was bugged by the security services and the man's wife was heard promising to leave the key under the mat for a visitor. Wright was there first and a wax impression was made. When the occupants left for a holiday in the Lake District, MI5 officers picked the locks of filing cabinets in the house and microfilmed all the party documents.[12]

Similarly, the story that Harold Wilson had been suspect as a fellow-traveller for his involvement with those who traded with the Soviet Union was not new. It was now linked with the sudden and mysterious death of the previous Labour party leader Hugh Gaitskell in 1963 from 'influenza' of a type almost unknown in Britain, which cleared the way for Wilson's premiership in 1964. Gaitskell's death was now portrayed as a KGB plot to provide a more compliant British leader. It was also linked to a conspiracy by elements in MI5 to destabilize the Wilson government of 1974. Throughout the book, Wright was obsessed by a belief that the Soviet mole in MI5 was none other than Sir Roger Hollis, the head of the service.

Wright was no liberal, let alone a socialist or communist. The author of *Spycatcher* hated Communism and the Soviet Union quite as much as he did those in the Civil Service who retired him on what he regarded as a miserly pension. As if in revenge, he wrote his memoirs and offered them to a London publisher. The publisher was tempted but was then warned off by MI5. The objection was not to the recycling of 'revelations' but to any breach of the lifetime silence owed by Peter Wright under the Official Secrets Acts.

Wright then offered the book to Heinemann in Australia, controlled by a major chain, the Octopus group, and outside British jurisdiction. Its head, Paul Hamlyn, was prepared to publish as a matter of principle and had the money to fight whatever legal battles might be necessary. A first skirmish occurred in London. On 11 July 1986, the Treasury Solicitor obtained High Court injunctions restraining the *Guardian* and the *Observer* from publishing material from *Spycatcher* or from Peter Wright, or in connection with the case which the British government was mounting in the Australian courts. A similar injunction was later granted against the *Sunday Times*.

If the British government believed that it would be shown special favours by another Commonwealth country, it was disappointed. In the New South Wales Court of Appeal on 24 September 1987, Mr Justice Michael Kirby held that 'the case has been brought by a foreign power, and the court has to ask what its attitude would be if the appellant were the South African or Libyan government seeking to prevent a former security agent from revealing embarrassing secrets.'

Margaret Thatcher's advisers were said to have assured her that the government had 'a watertight case' in asking the Australian Supreme Court for an injunction to prevent Heinemann publishing *Spycatcher* in that country. The proceedings, from September 1986 to September 1987, hardly suggested this. One of the worst moments was when the British Cabinet Secretary told the court that he was obliged to be 'economical with the truth', and no less embarrassing was the attempt to hold back certain documents on the grounds of 'public interest immunity'. Mr Justice Powell, in the New South Wales Supreme Court on 26 November 1986, described this as 'offensive', 'odd' and 'hard to accept'.

The attempt to prevent publication collapsed, when the court ruled that Australians had 'a right to know' the contents of the book. In the New South Wales Court of Appeal the British government lost again. By this time, the book had sold more than 500,000 copies in the United States, where an attempt at censorship would have run foul of the First Amendment. It was also said to be selling well in Moscow and Peking. It had even proved impossible to prevent copies entering Britain. Indeed, Heinemann had arranged for a printing to be run off in Dublin.

The Prime Minister and her government appeared determined to walk the plank to the last inch. On 30 July 1987, during the final stages of the action in Australia, the government injunctions in London were upheld in the House of Lords, by three votes to two, banning the British press from reporting anything in the Australian proceedings − or indeed reporting anything in their own parliamentary debates − which would reveal Peter Wright's allegations. The Attorney-General charged the editor and publisher of the *News on Sunday* with criminal contempt for revealing such matters.

Lord Bridge, a former chairman of the Security Commission, dissented from the majority decision in the Lords. He described the government's attempt to insulate the British public from information freely available elsewhere as a significant step down 'the very dangerous road to censorship, the indispensable tool of the totalitarian regime'. He warned the government that it faced condemnation and humiliation in the European Court of Human Rights. 'Long before that they will have been condemned at the bar of public opinion in the free world.' Unfortunately, Mrs Thatcher as Prime Minister had vowed publicly to take the case to the highest court. On 26 November 1991, her successors lost the final round in the European Court by twenty-four votes to nil.[13]

In 1988, however, the Attorney-General had sought a permanent ban from the British courts to prevent the media publicizing or commenting on Peter Wright's revelations. Both the High Court and the Court of Appeal refused the application and, in June 1988, the case reached the House of Lords. On 13 October the law lords ruled that the press was free to report and serialize the book. However despicable Wright's conduct, it would now be absurd to impose a censorship on the British press, when the book and comment on it were freely available everywhere else in the world. To be effective, it would require that the British people should be prevented from reading the foreign press or listening to overseas news coverage. The damage had been done and publication could no longer prejudice the security or interests of the state, which was what the Official Secrets Acts required.

The Shadow Home Secretary, Roy Hattersley, thereupon accused Mrs Thatcher and her government of making Britain a 'laughing-stock' throughout the world. More important was the way in which the issue had involved the world rather than the nation whom it most concerned. The Internet was a revolution struggling to be born but it was already apparent that the power to exercise censorship by one government in matters of this kind had not long to run. Even as the litigation continued, imported copies of *Spycatcher* were sold by independent booksellers and, at the height of its notoriety, from suitcases outside the Houses of Parliament.

The most memorable aspect of the case was the denunciation by senior judges of the government's attempts at political censorship and warnings of the threat of dictatorship. Politically independent judges now emerged as defenders of the people against the government. It was small wonder that the remaining decade of Conservative rule echoed to demands for judges to be more 'accountable' – a demand adapted by the incoming Labour government of 1997 to a policy of 'modernizing' the judiciary.

In tandem with the later part of the *Spycatcher* case, the government was engaged in a battle with BBC Television over the *Secret Society* series by Duncan Campbell. Six programmes, made in Glasgow for BBC2, accompanied articles in the *New Statesman*. Particular exception was taken by the government to two features, 'Cabinet' and 'The Zircon Project'. The first revealed the existence of secret cabinet committees and the use of money from the Ministry of Defence information budget to discredit or harass members of the Campaign for Nuclear Disarmament. The Zircon programme described plans for developing a British spy satellite. The existence of such a project was scarcely likely to surprise the Soviet Union.

The programmes in the series also covered computer data banks, government war powers, radar defences, and the powers of police chiefs. No attempt was made to suppress these. 'Cabinet' was banned by the governors of the BBC, whose Director-General, Alasdair Milne, was peremptorily dismissed. Instead of seeing 'The Zircon Project', however, viewers were treated to newsreel coverage of BBC studios being raided by Special Branch.

Ironically, the BBC had withdrawn the film on 21 January 1987, as the government obtained an injunction forbidding Duncan Campbell from revealing its contents. Next day an injunction forbidding the showing of the film to MPs in the House of Commons was refused. However, the

Speaker of the House banned the showing. On 24 January, Special Branch raided Duncan Campbell's home, taking away all documents concerning the programme in an attempt to find the 'mole' who had provided secret information. A raid and a five-day search of the *New Statesman* offices was also carried out. On 31 January, with newsreel cameras watching, Special Branch raided the BBC studios in Glasgow, removing all material connected with the programme. The police were armed with warrants under the Official Secrets Acts.

Scenes of the BBC being raided by Special Branch were, according to the former Home Secretary and leader of the Social Democrats, Roy Jenkins, like watching events in 'a second-rate police state'. Some of the material was returned soon afterwards and the rest ten months later. No action was taken against the BBC or the programme makers. Two years after it had been made, the programme was shown. The most embarrassing secret was an allegation that the Ministry of Defence, having earmarked £500 million for the Zircon project, was required to keep the Public Accounts Committee of the House of Commons 'reliably informed'. It had hidden the sum in another part of its accounts and told the committee nothing.

No sooner had the material for 'The Zircon Project' been returned by Special Branch than the BBC was in trouble again. This time it was a radio series, *My Country Right or Wrong*, which was about to be broadcast and contained contributions from those who had worked for British intelligence. On 18 December, the Attorney-General obtained an injunction preventing the broadcast on the grounds that former security officers might have breached confidence in the course of their interviews. The High Court also granted discovery, which required the BBC to hand over copies of the tapes to the government. Once again, it was a damp squib. There was no breach of confidence and the programmes were broadcast six months later.

In response to the series of reverses in the courts, the government added the Official Secrets Act 1989 to its armoury. This tightened the net by making the disclosure of information by a Crown servant criminal if the effect was 'damaging' to the security services, the armed forces or international relations. A damaging disclosure by a second party, probably a journalist, into whose hands the information had come was also criminal. The concept that disclosure might be for the public good was not enshrined in law.

While the new law was going through Parliament, the Home Secretary also used the powers of the Broadcasting Act 1981 to prohibit the BBC and the Independent Broadcasting Authority from broadcasting 'any words spoken' by representatives of Sinn Fein, Provisional Sinn Fein, the Ulster Defence Association or any proscribed terrorist organization. This was challenged by the broadcasters but upheld by the House of Lords. The broadcasters thereupon used actors to read the words so that they were no longer 'spoken' by terrorists.[14]

For all the good it had done to governments of either party, official secrets legislation became to many people what Richard Crossman called it in the *New Statesman* of 11 February 1971, 'the toothless old watchdog', fighting the wars of the future with the weapons of the past. It had certainly reached the headlines more often after the Second World War than before it, at a time when secrets of strategic importance were betrayed without the nation's rulers noticing until it was too late. At the same time, information that could no longer damage the interests of the state or whose exposure was in the public interest became the object of ministerial retribution, frequently with no effect but to publicize an offending book or article.

Labour and Conservative governments alike proved capable of astonishing ineptitude in such cases as those of *Spycatcher*, *Secret Society*, Jonathan Aitken and the *Sunday Telegraph*. Their handling of such crises might have evoked H. L. Mencken's title for his description of American political leaders in action in 1924: 'The Clowns March In'. Yet Crossman had prefaced another comment to his description of the toothless old watchdog of official secrecy. If the beast were not preserved, might it not be replaced by a disagreeable young mastiff in Whitehall?[15]

6

By no means all forms of controlling the post-war press were twentieth-century innovations. To many people, the offence of breaching parliamentary privilege had an air of seventeenth-century quaintness. However, the Bill of Rights 1689 provided for freedom of speech within Parliament, not for those outside. It resolved: 'That the freedom of speech and debate or proceedings in Parliament ought not to be impeached or questioned in any Court or place out of Parliament.'

On 1 May 1947, for example, when the Labour government's Transport Bill was carried through the House of Commons, Labour members sang 'The Red Flag' at midnight and the stout figure of Bessie Braddock was reported dancing a jig across the floor to sit in a seat normally occupied by Winston Churchill. The *Bolton Evening News* describing her 'jig' as 'a sorry degradation of democratic government'. She sued for libel and lost.

She learnt better than to sue again. When Lord Mancroft described to the Primrose League 'MPs larking about at night in the Division lobbies with Bessie Braddock and the rest of the girls', this was called by Barbara Castle a 'grave reflection on the House', was ruled a breach of privilege by the Speaker, and the errant peer was made to apologize. On 26 April 1953, the *Sunday Express* described a room with 'a couple of beds in it', where the 'old stagers' slept during all-night sittings. 'One night I found Mrs Bessie Braddock and Dr Edith Summerskill stretched out on them and both snoring.' Mrs Braddock recalled that 'this House has even more powers than the courts to deal with things that happen inside its own area.' She and Dr Summerskill had never snored or slept in the twin-bedded room. The author of the article and the editor of the *Sunday Express* grovelled before the Committee of Privileges. On 9 January 1957, during the fuel crisis which followed the Suez invasion, the paper was in trouble again, for noticing a privileged petrol allowance enjoyed by members of Parliament at the expense of the rest of the nation.

An ancient legal curiosity which played a far more important part as a form of press control was 'contempt of court'. The presumption of innocence in criminal proceedings was sacrosanct. A judge might issue a 'writ of attachment' against anyone, usually newspapers and their editors, when that presumption was compromised. Protection also extended to the character and dignity of the judge. In 1918, for example, Marie Stopes published *Married Love*, a controversial work on contraception but not entirely reliable if the popular limerick was to be believed.

> Jeanie, Jeanie full of hopes
> Read a book by Marie Stopes,
> But to judge from her condition
> She must have read the wrong edition.

In 1928 the editor of the *Morning Post* brought a libel action against Dr Stopes, who lost her case after a hostile summing-up. The trial judge, Mr Justice Avory, was known as a short-tempered reactionary. To the *New Statesman,* the verdict was both an outrage and 'a substantial miscarriage of justice' after a prejudiced summing-up. 'An individual owning to such views as those of Dr Stopes cannot apparently hope for a fair hearing in a court presided over by Mr Justice Avory – and there are so many Avorys.' Avory summoned the editor of the *New Statesman* to his court, demanded a public apology and made him pay costs.[16]

Far more common was a contempt which prejudiced a fair trial. At mid-century the definition of this was much stricter than it was to become in an age of tabloid journalism. In 1949 the murderer John George Haigh was brought to justice. Known as the 'Acid Bath Murderer' and the 'Vampire', he claimed to have murdered nine people, drunk their blood and dissolved the bodies in a vat of acid. His plea of insanity failed and he was hanged. He could only be tried for one murder at a time and that of Mrs Durand-Deacon was chosen by the Crown.

On Haigh's first appearance before Horsham magistrates, the *Daily Mirror* published a front-page picture of him leaving court, next to a photograph of alleged victims for whose murders he was not to be tried and of which crimes he remained technically innocent. The jury at his trial was not entitled to consider these cases. For the *Mirror* to inform potential jurors that 'So far five murders are attributed to him' was a blatant contempt of court. Under another picture of a woman was the caption 'Haigh and I weren't engaged', which identified him beyond question.

The *Daily Mirror* and its editor, Sylvester Bolam, were defendants before Lord Chief Justice Goddard on 25 March 1949. Goddard described this as a 'gross contempt', committed 'not as an error of judgment, but as a matter of policy, pandering to sensationalism for the purpose of increasing the circulation of this paper'. If the directors ever again published such material, they might find that 'the arm of this Court is long enough to reach them individually.' The *Daily Mirror* was fined £10,000, and ordered to pay the costs of the case. Its editor, Sylvester Bolam, went to prison for three months.[17]

A 'gross contempt' was rare. If there was one to rival the *Daily Mirror's* report on Haigh, it was the conduct of the American magazine *Newsweek* during the trial of Dr John Bodkin Adams in March and April 1957 for the murder of Mrs Edith Alice Morrell. Dr Adams practised in Eastbourne, a resort with more than its share of elderly ladies of means. His patients found him a kind and humane physician. He was known for his skill in easing their last days or hours with the aid of drugs. The question was whether he eased them on their way earlier than was justified. This question might not have been asked but for the money and valuables, including a Rolls-Royce car, bequeathed to him. Did Dr Adams know of these bequests when he sped the elderly ladies to eternity?

He was acquitted at the end of a long trial for the murder of Mrs Morrell, not least through skilful cross-examinations in which his counsel, Geoffrey Lawrence QC, reduced expert evidence to questionable opinions. On 1 April, the American magazine *Newsweek* published an account of the proceedings to date as 'The Doctor on Trial'. This was written in America but a European edition was printed in Amsterdam. In America the law of contempt was far more liberal, though more time was spent in the pre-trial selection of a jury to exclude those already swayed by prejudicial material.

From its first lines, the *Newsweek* article violated the English law of contempt. 'Not since the trials of John George Haigh "The Vampire" (nine victims), and John R. H. Christie "The Strangler of Notting Hill" (seven women victims) had a criminal trial roused such avid interest in Britain.' There followed a touristic setting of the courtroom scene 'with a ritual going back to Norman times'.

To compare Adams as he faced trial with Haigh and Christie, convicted of monstrous crimes, was asking for trouble. In a paragraph headed 'Bequests' the magazine added that 'Over a period of 20 years, 17 of Dr Adams' grateful patients bequeathed to him the sum total of 90,000 dollars and this is what started the teacups rattling in Eastbourne . . . Eastbourne's frenzied gossip pushed Dr Adams's alleged victims as high as 400.' The Attorney-General also cited 'highly prejudicial statements relating to a number of wills under which Dr Adams was alleged to have benefited and the amounts alleged to have come to him. That could not have failed, if it had come into the hands of the jury, to have had a prejudicial effect.'

Newsweek's author in the United States was beyond the jurisdiction of the Queen's Bench Division. However, the magazine was distributed in Britain. When the judge in the murder trial warned jurors not to read it, remaining copies were withdrawn from their shelves by W. H. Smith and other outlets. Contempt proceedings began against Eldon Wylie Griffiths, chief European correspondent of *Newsweek* in London; the circulation director of Rolls House Publishing Co., which distributed 7,500 copies to the trade; and W. H. Smith, which had distributed some 1,800. Eldon Wylie Griffiths was discharged while Rolls House and W. H. Smith were each fined a nominal £50, leaving the Lord Chief Justice to regret that 'the court could not deal with those who were far more responsible, but who were out of the jurisdiction of the courts.' *Newsweek* was registered in Dayton, Ohio.[18]

For the next half-century, the powers of the courts confronted an increasing determination by mass circulation newspapers to get a story. The arrival of the Internet and the world-wide web made it all the more difficult to prevent such stories circulating anyway. In 2003, when premier division footballers were suspected of rape in London's Grosvenor Hotel, the Attorney-General warned the press that the famous names must not be divulged, under threat of prosecution for contempt of court. The names rattled round the Internet web, as though the Attorney-General had never existed. Responsible providers closed down the sites under their control.

They confessed that there was no means by which thousands of 'chat rooms' could be policed or silenced.

A number of cases had compromised important prosecutions. In 1997 the trial of five IRA men and an armed robber who escaped together from Whitemoor high-security prison was abandoned for a second time because the *Evening Standard* had published an article in which the men's previous convictions were revealed. Mr Justice Kay ruled that they should not be tried a third time. 'I am satisfied it is no longer possible for justice to be done and be seen to be done in this case in relation to all the defendants.'[19]

In a far more important case five years later, the trial of Ian Huntley and Maxine Carr followed the murder of the two Soham schoolgirls, Holly Wells and Jessica Chapman. 'Grief tourists', as they became known, infested the village as they had besieged London following the death of Diana Princess of Wales in 1997, but the two obvious suspects were not charged for some days. During that time they and their histories were available to tabloid press and television journalists. This included the revelation that Huntley had previously been sectioned and held at Rampton Mental Hospital.

Before the suspects were charged, the press had gone far towards building up a picture of Ian Huntley with his psychiatric record as an active paedophile and Maxine Carr as his accomplice. Only after the arrests did contempt of court restrictions apply, and then it was too late. Few people in the country were not drawn to the story, if only by television pictures of a crowd shouting abuse at a police van carrying the two prisoners or individual bystanders demanding the return of hanging for such crimes.

A few British newspapers wondered if the accused had any hope of an impartial trial by jury. Newspapers from abroad, including *Le Monde* on 31 August 2002, thought not. Some politicians and lawyers remained unconvinced that jurors were swayed by prejudicial publicity. They pointed out that in any case the government was legislating to allow juries to be told of a defendant's previous convictions before a trial. If contempt of court could no longer control the media, perhaps the law rather than the media should give way. Yet the television images had brought about an easy change of popular mood in the present case from the emotionalism of grief tourists to the rage of a lynch mob.

In December 2006, after the arrests of two men for questioning over the murders of five prostitutes in the Ipswich area, Lord Goldsmith as Attorney-General issued a warning to the press. A good deal of press coverage was hardly distinguishable from the identification of the suspects with murders not connected with their arrests. Some comments were little different from those which led to the imprisonment of the editor of the *Daily Mirror* in 1949. Almost sixty years later, in an age when more aggressive reporting claimed to give the people what they wanted, Lord Goldsmith issued 'guidance' on the Ipswich case, urging the media to 'show restraint' and to bear in mind the dangers of 'prejudicing any future trial'. The interviewing of witnesses by the press might also impede the police investigation. Editors were warned to take legal advice because 'they could be prosecuted if they cross the line.'

7

Prejudicial publicity was not the only form of contempt of court. Political or journalistic defiance came within its ambit. In 1963, one journalist from the *Daily Mail* and one from the *Daily Sketch* went to gaol for refusing to disclose sources of information to the committee investigating John Vassall, an Admiralty clerk who had spied for Moscow. In 1983, the House of Lords forced the *Guardian* newspaper to hand over a leaked memorandum on Cruise missiles, which led to the imprisonment of the newspaper's informant. Revealing a name rather than concealing it might be contempt. In 1979, the pacifist *Peace News* and the left-wing *Leveller* identified a witness who had been allowed to give his name as 'Colonel B' in an official secrets case. The papers were fined £500 each. On appeal to the House of Lords, it was ruled on 1 February 1979 that identifying the witness involved 'no interference with the due administration of justice and was not a contempt'.

Journalists who refused to name their sources might also be gaoled. Yet journalists who named them might find that their sources of information ran dry. The Contempt of Court Act 1981 therefore provided that disclosure could not be demanded unless the court was satisfied that it was necessary in the interests of justice or national security or the prevention of disorder or crime.

The most controversial attack of this kind on the media came in 1992. The Director of Public Prosecutions sought to sequestrate the assets of Channel 4 and close the company down. Channel 4 and Box Productions had made a documentary about Northern Ireland, 'The Committee', in the *Despatches* series. It alleged collusion between Royal Ulster Constabulary officers, the security services, loyalist paramilitaries and business or professional men in Northern Ireland to murder people suspected of being IRA members. The conspiracy included about sixty people and was accused by the programme of twenty sectarian killings over a two-year period. One informant was a self-confessed loyalist terrorist who was interviewed. He admitted his role in planning the murders and was named only as 'Source A'.

Channel 4 refused to name 'Source A' on the grounds that he and those who had made the programme would face a serious risk of assassination. Lord Woolf ruled that the company must reveal the man's identity or be responsible for 'collaborating in the continuing of the killings'. After a further refusal, the Crown Prosecution Service asked that the company's assets should be forfeit. To suppress one of Britain's four television networks was an unprecedented act of public censorship. The court might set a 'rolling fine' of £75,000 a day until Channel 4 named its source or went bankrupt. In the end, a single exemplary fine of £75,000 was imposed. 'Source A' remained protected.[20]

8

The last decade of the old millennium saw a change which was perhaps an omen of what was to come in the first decade of the next. A traditional taste for libel as a public blood sport, where no holds were barred and muck was raked in large heaps, gave way to gentler pleas for privacy. In the entertainments of the past, heavyweight libel actions involving Oscar Wilde, Lord Queensberry, Winston Churchill, Horatio Bottomley, the Duke of Windsor, Randolph Churchill, Harold Laski, Lord Alfred Douglas, Robert Maxwell, Metro-Goldwyn-Mayer, Twentieth Century-Fox, even the wife of the Yorkshire Ripper, had rivalled headline murder cases or Test match scores in selling newspapers. Murderers in the condemned cell had sought a libeller to sue as a means of delaying their appointment with the hangman. Now, in the assault on privacy as much as reputation, the tabloids ferreted among the sexual failings of the famous and the royal in a manner more vicious and intrusive than the ancient scandalmongers of the Sunday press.

Threatened with retribution by Act of Parliament, the industry set up its own Press Complaints Commission in 1990. This would still leave the industry in control of areas of controversy. Its fears seemed confirmed when the government ordered a committee of inquiry under Sir David Calcutt QC into the behaviour of the press. That committee, predictably, dismissed the PCC as a creature of the newspaper business. The commission retorted that in its first eighteen months only 1.6 per cent of 2,069 complaints involved the often alleged invasions of privacy or harassment.

Indeed, 61.7 per cent raised issues of fact and 96.9 per cent were resolved without need of adjudication.

To the sceptics this was further proof that the PCC was a lapdog. The Calcutt committee cited the deplorable tabloid treatment of the Prince and Princess of Wales' marriage; the telephoto pictures of the Duchess of York at a bathing pool; the treatment of cabinet ministers, guilty or innocent of adultery. It recommended a tribunal, headed by a judge, to control the press. Its general powers were potentially greater than any since the Second World War. In the view of a veteran libel lawyer, Peter Carter-Ruck, it would 'provide a half-way house to the introduction of the press laws which expired at the end of the seventeenth century. Then there was no real freedom of the press.'

Yet the tribunal sounded formidable only until its powers were revealed. They did not include imprisonment and the maximum fine would be £5,000, next to nothing in the budget of a tabloid editor. The PCC seemed, after all, the best that could be done. The Lord Chancellor of the new Labour government in 1997 promised that even the incorporation of the European Convention on Human Rights into English law would not favour the individual against the press where 'there is a public interest in publishing.'[21]

The gentler values of privacy, rather than the abrasive encounters of a libel action, appealed to conciliatory instincts. A new government was to initiate forms of censorship to maintain peace in a society of the over-crowded, the short-tempered and the litigious. It was not a measure to preserve a traditional way of life but a means to reconcile people to social changes beyond anything most had expected and which many deeply resented. Indeed, they were changes which were too often beyond the government's control. Those who denounced the new restrictions on personal freedom of expression often described them as enshrining in law an attempt at ideological control, known previously, but not always accurately, as political correctness.

13

'Enoch Says What Everyone Thinks'

I

O N 5 APRIL 1963, the BBC broadcast its weekly radio discussion programme *Any Questions*, with a panel of politicians or journalists
answering questions from a live audience on the issues of the day. It was a
popular Friday night feature which drew an audience of five million. A
question was asked about the future of British commonwealth states
grouped together in the so-called Central African Federation. In discussing
race relations in these territories, Sir Gerald Nabarro MP inquired, 'Would
you be happy if your blonde blue-eyed daughter came home with a big
buck nigger and said she wanted to marry him?'

It was the BBC's worst nightmare. Since the war years it had prided itself
on moral and cultural sensitivity. The rules of broadcasting forbad anything
that might appear derogatory to the royal family, religion, disability, race or
nationality. Hence the schoolboy riposte fondly remembered by Denis
Norden, '"Christ!" said the King to the one-legged wop.'

Any Questions was broadcast live, recorded and repeated a few days later.
There was nothing to be done about the live broadcast. However, the corporation informed the press that it would delete the remark from its
recording. By opening its heart in this way, it ensured that the offending
words were printed in newspapers up and down the land. Sir Gerald
remained robust, arguing that 'nigger' was the same as 'negro' and 'buck'
was a flattering description of masculinity. Yet by 1963, what might once
have been a trivial blunder was no longer anything of the kind. The country was split between a ruling class, appalled at such remarks, and a
significant proportion of ordinary people who found them acceptable.

Censorship in public life was to change a good deal in the second half
of the century. Nowhere was this more evident than in legislation which
criminalized or strongly discouraged popularly used language in racial matters. The stirring up of hatred or the incitement of violence in general had
long been criminalized by the Offences Against the Person Act 1861. At

common law, the anti-Semite Arnold Leese had been convicted in 1936 of a seditious libel calculated 'to promote feelings of ill-will and hostility between different classes of [His Majesty's] subjects'. The need for further legislation was still uncertain.

The boundaries of free speech in the immediate post-war world had been indicated in the 1947 case of James Caunt, editor of the *Morecambe and Heysham Visitor*. Like Arnold Leese in 1936 he was charged with seditious libel on the nation's Jewish population, as 'a class of His Majesty's subjects'.

The circumstances were more complex than those of 1936. Until the creation of the state of Israel in May 1948, Britain held a United Nations mandate to keep the peace between the Jewish and Arab populations in Palestine, home of the Arabs and future homeland of Jewish migrants. As the Prime Minister Clement Attlee recalled, both parties had for many years been given 'incompatible promises'. The British army tried to hold a 'fair balance' between the claimants and 'as usual, got small thanks from either side'. It was also left to the army to turn back shiploads of Jewish refugees, as illegal immigrants. British troops came under armed attack from the Stern Gang and Irgun Zvai Leumi. Irgun's emblem was a fist clutching a rifle and bearing the motto, 'Only thus.'[1]

By contrast, the Jewish self-defence group Hagana appeared politically responsible and was acknowledged as such. It was recruited mainly from the Ashkenazi of the European middle class, while Irgun and Stern were, as *The Times* described them on 5 May 1947, 'for the most part poor and fanatical Yemenites and Sephardic Jews, that is to say orientals'. Their 'directing heads' were often Europeans, including Menachem Begin, right-wing prime minister of Israel in 1977. In May 1947 Hagana was to take up arms against Irgun on behalf of a peaceful and negotiated settlement.

Animosities had already come to a head in June 1946, when thirty-one members of Irgun were caught with a large quantity of firearms, bombs, grenades and ammunition. They were sentenced to long terms of imprisonment by a British military court. A month later, Irgun bombed the King David Hotel in Jerusalem, which was also the site of British military headquarters. There were more than a hundred deaths and numerous injuries among British, Arabs and Jews. In November, Irgun claimed responsibility for bombing the British Embassy in Rome, where it was 'strangling repatriation of Jews' to Palestine.

The situation was ripe for exploitation by anti-Jewish agitators in Britain. In London, there were attacks on synagogues and bombs or warnings of bombs. At the same time a female agent of Irgun left a bomb at the Colonial Office which, according to Commander Leonard Burt of Special

Branch, would have blown 'the sort of hole' caused at the King David Hotel. Fortunately, a pocket-watch was used as the timer and one of its hands jammed against the face before the time for the detonation. The surviving mechanism included the thumbprint of a known Irgun agent. This evidence led to Monty Harris who was making incendiary devices on his premises at Gravel Street near Petticoat Lane. He was sent to prison for seven years.[2]

In Palestine, on 4 May 1947, Irgun terrorists in British army uniforms blew a hole in the wall of Acre prison, allowing Jewish and Arab prisoners to escape. There were several deaths. Three of those responsible for the attack were caught, tried and sentenced to death. Irgun thereupon kidnapped two British sergeants and warned the authorities that if the executions went ahead both captives would be killed. The British refused to bargain and the two soldiers were found hanged in an orchard, the ground surrounding their bodies mined.

One of the two murdered men had connections with Lancashire. James Caunt, editor of the *Morecambe and Heysham Visitor*, included a leading article in the issue for 6 August under the heading 'Mustard'. He claimed that the Jewish community in Britain only pretended to condemn the outrages against British soldiers in Palestine and were gross hypocrites. He might have said this and kept out of court. Two further sentences ensured his appearance at Liverpool Assizes. 'If British Jewry is today suffering from the righteous wrath of British citizens, then they have only themselves to blame for their passive inactivity. Violence may be the only way of bringing them to a sense of their responsibility to the country in which they live.'

This rebuke ignored the truth that most of those whom he attacked were British citizens. Some had sons and, indeed, ATS daughters among the troops under attack by Irgun and its allies. Jewish MPs, including Sidney Silverman and Konni Zilliacus, had been critical of the government's handling of the Palestine problem but were quick to denounce the 'criminal insanity' of Irgun. Mr Caunt's second and third sentences had appeared to advocate violence against British Jews. Though he was charged with the same offence as Arnold Leese in 1936, the cases were not alike. Leese's assertions over the use of Christian blood in Jewish rituals belonged to the realms of lunacy. James Caunt's allegations might sound plausible to some people in 1947.

In his defence, Caunt admitted that he intended the article to be 'offensive to the Jews', indeed, 'as offensive as possible', but he denied inciting violence. Being offensive was not criminal. The rest of his editorial was merely a warning of 'what would eventually happen to them if they did not change their ways'.

Throughout the trial the danger of inciting violence contended with liberty of opinion. 'This is not a matter of Jews and non-Jews,' said G. O. Slade for the defence. 'It is a question of whether an editor has a right to say what he thinks and believes to be true without being hauled through the criminal courts.' To suggest that the words complained of incited violence was to echo Cardinal Richelieu: 'Show me six lines written by the most honest man in the world and I will find enough in them to hang him.'

The defendant was lucky in his judge. Lord Birkett was a son of Wesleyan Methodism, a political Liberal, and the best-known advocate of his generation. During the inter-war years, he put aside his lucrative practice and undertook poor persons defences, often murders, and in only three of these did he fail to save his client's life. As a judge at Nuremberg, he had seen the Third Reich at first hand, in the persons of Goering, Hess and Streicher. Their example was not lost on him. Yet in summing up, he asked the jury to put aside preconceived ideas, favourable or hostile to Judaism, and consider only the evidence. 'It is in the highest degree essential – and I cannot over-emphasize its importance – that nothing should be done to destroy or weaken the liberty of the press.'[3]

Half a century later such importance might seem easier to downgrade. As it was, the jury acquitted James Caunt. He left court, presenting himself as a champion of press freedom. Next day, 17 November, the *Manchester Guardian* reminded him that, despite his acquittal, what he intended to be offensive to Jews was 'offensive to many others as well'. Birkett cut the article from the paper and pasted it in his scrapbook.

2

In the case of James Caunt only the jurors knew whether they acquitted him because they judged he had not incited violence or because they put freedom of speech before all other issues or even perhaps because they resented the murder of their compatriots in Palestine. There was not to be such another case to test freedom of opinion until the prosecution of the Racial Preservation Society's newspapers in 1968. Yet Fascism, more specifically anti-Semitism, was not dead in post-war Britain.

In the 1960s a ghost from the past returned from France in the shape of Sir Oswald Mosley. He was still leader of the Union Movement, as it was now more palatably called. Two anti-Jewish meetings, held by rival organizations in 1960 and 1961, were not much noticed. On 1 July 1962, another was held in Trafalgar Square, this time by the National Socialist Movement. The Minister of Works raised no objection because Trafalgar Square had 'long been a traditional place for the free expression of views'.

It was easy to see why the earlier meetings drew little attention. Despite its sinister title, the National Socialist Movement had fewer than a hundred members in the entire country. What it lacked in size it made up for in spite. It was heir to the National Socialist League founded by William Joyce in 1938. The folly of the post-war Labour government in hanging Joyce for treason had given the league a martyr. Yet in Trafalgar Square, the faithful were heavily outnumbered by a phalanx of several hundred opponents stationed immediately in front of the platform, some wearing badges of the Campaign for Nuclear Disarmament, others giving the Communist clenched-fist salute.

The meeting was addressed by Colin Jordan and his lieutenant John Tyndall. Jordan began by saying, 'On 3 September 1939, the blackest day in British history, the long and intensive Jewish campaign was crowned with success and the Jews of the world rejoiced.' That was as far as he got. Several thousand sightseers now watched a fight between Jordan's supporters and opponents. Superintendent George Burgoyne, commanding a large body of police, interrupted the meeting three times to preserve order. He stopped it altogether after Jordan shouted, 'Hitler was right. Our real enemy was the Jew.'

Not only was the meeting stopped, Jordan and Tyndall were arrested and charged with using insulting words. They were also served with summonses under Section 2 of the Public Order Act, which prohibited quasi-military political organizations, such as their own Spearhead. On 20 August, at Bow Street Magistrates Court, Jordan went to prison for two months and Tyndall for six weeks. The magistrate ruled that 'the words used by the two men are very offensive to the large majority of people in this country, whether they be Jews, gentiles or Christians, and by using them they were asking for trouble.'

Both men were also committed for trial at the Central Criminal Court for running a paramilitary organization. As Jordan left the magistrates court he gave a Hitler salute to the crowd. At the Old Bailey he was sent to prison for nine months, Tyndall for six months and two other men for three months each. On 31 July there was further trouble at an open-air meeting in Ridley Road, Dalston, when Mosley had to be rescued by the police. Thirty defendants were convicted at Old Street Magistrates Court as a result of the fighting and twelve more at North London Court.

None of these were landmark cases nor did they involve publications.

Indeed, it was arguable that the expression of such views where everyone might hear and oppose them was preferable to the rancour which festered behind closed doors in the upper room of a Shoreditch public house. As Justice Oliver Wendell Holmes had remarked, 'With effervescing opinions, as with not yet forgotten champagnes, the quickest way to let them get flat is to let them get exposed to the air.' The private gathering in Shoreditch was visited by Mosley himself. His admirers assured him that 'The Jews of today have lived off the story of Belsen and Buchenwald for the past twenty years.' The majority in the crowded room were not pre-war veterans but the post-war young, one of whom seized Mosley's hand and kissed it.[4]

R. A. Butler, as Home Secretary, condemned 'the abuse of free speech' in Trafalgar Square which the Fascists represented. Reluctantly he banned the use of the area. Even the President of the Liberal party told the press on 7 July: 'It is scandalous that such a pernicious doctrine, which caused a six years war and perpetrated such brutality, should be provided with public facilities to spread its poison again.'

The government began a review of laws curbing freedom of speech. It was proposed from the Conservative benches by Tom Iremonger who moved an amendment to the Public Order Act, criminalizing the creation of prejudice against a racial or religious group. Meantime, the Minister of Works banned three more Trafalgar Square meetings: Colin Jordan's National Socialist Movement on 19 July; John Bean's British National Party on 2 September and Sir Oswald Mosley's Union Movement on 23 September.

3

Before the Conservative government could legislate against Fascism, it was voted out of office in 1964. A new Labour government introduced a Race Relations Bill and a Race Relations Board of paid officials to deal with incidents of 'Racialism' or 'Racism' as the offence was now called. By this time, the principal object was not to protect Jewry against the slanders of Fascism but to offer redress to tens of thousands of West Indian immigrants in the disputes of daily life. To many people the Trafalgar Square rallies by small Fascist splinter groups were a psychopathic aberration. Mass immigration from a non-white commonwealth was to involve difficulties of a different order.

The Conservative government had invited immigration from the West Indies in the 1950s to boost the British workforce. All young men in the indigenous workforce were liable to conscription for two years' military service at eighteen. The resulting shortage of labour was severe enough, for example, to lead to cancellation of train services for lack of crews. Yet despite the government's welcome to commonwealth workers and their families and despite a liberal middle-class belief in the virtues of a rich cultural mix of all creeds and colours, the immigration experiment was a doubtful success. The introduction of the Race Relations Act 1965 and the powers of compulsion delegated to the Race Relations Board suggested as much. So did the need for CARD, the Campaign Against Racial Discrimination.

On 17 February 1961, Cyril Osborne warned the House of Commons that there would be two million 'coloured people' in Britain within twenty years. A far more formidable dissident was Enoch Powell, a rising Conservative star and a daunting adversary in parliamentary or television debate. While his party's vote fell almost everywhere in 1964, Powell's majority in Wolverhampton was secure. Immigration had affected the West Midlands more than most areas. In Walsall, a previously safe Labour seat, a Conservative alderman with an anti-immigration message defeated Labour's Foreign Secretary designate, Patrick Gordon Walker. Gordon Walker was selected for another safe seat at the Leyton by-election and lost that as well. The new Prime Minister, Harold Wilson, told the Walsall victor that he would be regarded as 'a parliamentary leper'. It was a foolish remark which served only to anger those who had elected their member.

The Labour government's Race Relations Bill 1965 become law with the support of most of the Conservative party in Parliament. It would protect the rights of immigrant communities in housing or employment and prevent racist attacks upon them in books, periodicals or newspapers. Three years later, the government was ready to test its powers against racism in print. The target was the Racial Preservation Society's *RPS Southern News*. The society professed to believe that 'all those people of other races who have entered this overcrowded island should be given the opportunity to return to their own countries and be assisted to build up their own countries and economies.'

This seemed far removed from the Trafalgar Square ranting of Colin Jordan or John Tyndall. In its newspapers, however, the RPS was more forthright. Included in its denunciations were ministers and officials responsible for continuing and approving the policy of mass immigration. It ran an illustrated series showing the expensive homes in which the comfortable advocates of coloured immigration lived, well away from the crowded city streets which bore the brunt of the influx. It found titles for its subjects, branding the former Conservative Home Secretary, Reginald Maudling, as 'a great pink cream-puff'. It was hard to see how such personal insults could result in a conviction under the Race Relations Act. The board and its legal advisers searched the columns in hope and found four items. The choice reflected little credit on their common sense.

The first extract on which the prosecution was based was a single sentence: 'We are far advanced along the road to 1984. That road starts in the class room!' To many jurors this would seem non-racist and very probably true. Second, came an absurd report on a new medical condition, 'ethnomasochism', contributed by 'our medical correspondent', who appeared to be a porter at Brighton station. This disorder was 'a self-destructive impulse with an erotic basis . . . in government, politics and administration'. Being 'closely akin to all other sexual perversions', it explained 'the fellow-feeling that "liberals" have for other deviants such as homo-sexuals'. The symptoms included a desire for the destruction of one's own race, an eagerness for race-mixing and pleasure in seeing 'co-racialists' humiliated, particularly abroad.

Only in the third extract did the *RPS Southern News* turn to the topic of immigration. It compared the breeding rates of the indigenous white population with those of 'the feckless coloured masses who have been allowed to flood into Britain in the last few years'. A final extract attacked the 'myth' that inferior races might be raised to equality by improved standards of living and education. 'Most of the leaders of corrupt African states were educated in Britain or European seats of higher learning . . . Not much of that influence seems to have rubbed off on them.'

Whatever offence was contained in these samples seemed to fall short of the viciousness shown by James Caunt or, indeed, by Fascist speakers at the Trafalgar Square rallies. Yet governments of both parties had underwritten immigration and multiracialism. The Labour leadership dared not back away. On such material, the Race Relations Board was obliged to bring its case against five defendants at Lewes Assizes. In reply, a Free Speech Defence Committee was set up to collect money for the defence of the 'five British patriots' who had been charged.

The result of the trial on 27 March 1968 was scarcely in doubt. The passages in question may have incited amusement but hardly racial hatred. Some of the jurors may, indeed, have supported the views expressed and would not be likely to convict whatever the law or a judge might say. Moreover, however tasteless the references to breeding rates might be, one issue of the day was certainly the extent to which immigrant mothers were filling the beds of maternity wards in the main areas of settlement. Indeed, the matter was raised in Parliament, let alone in the *RPS Southern News*. Like James Caunt, the acquitted defendants were enabled, by the zealous miscalculation of their prosecutors, to emerge from court as champions of the nation's ancient liberties.[5]

There were no more trials of this kind in the immediate future. To say that the policy of immigration was thoroughly unpopular was not to say that it need necessarily have been. The handling of it appeared in retrospect as the greatest ineptitude of governments in the post-war period. In censorship of opinion on such matters, the embarrassment deepened. It had not been supposed that race relations laws would target the black community, whom they were intended to protect. However, in the wake of the 1965 assassination of Malcolm X, the American Black Power leader, Britain offered a curious replacement, Michael X. Born in Trinidad of a European father and a West Indian mother, Michael de Freitas had gone to sea, landed in Cardiff in 1957 and done well as a pimp and drug dealer in Tiger Bay. He thought its race relations were good.

In London three years later, he became a rent collector and 'eviction agent' for the notorious Peter Rachman, before launching himself as Michael X. A veil was briefly drawn over his past activities. By the 1960s the Black Power movement on both sides of the Atlantic had become fashionable and exciting to celebrities – white as well as black – and de Freitas had an undeviating eye for the possibilities of white middle-class guilt. He was taken up by the well-heeled and the well-known, including John Lennon and Sammy Davis Jr.

In pursuit of funds, the new black leader traded on guilt. For example, he persuaded Lennon that the Beatles owed their success to the rhythms of Liverpool's blacks, which they had stolen. He collected money from the affluent and gullible for his Racial Adjustment Action Society. Too late, they discovered that RAAS, as it was known, was Jamaican slang for 'arse'. His patronage of a public meeting on racial tolerance lasted only until an earnest radical suggested that the Queen should be petitioned to adopt a black baby. 'Don't encourage her to adopt one,' shouted de Freitas. 'Let her have one.'

On 24 July 1967, he took the place of yet another American Black Power figurehead, Stokely Carmichael, who had cut short his visit to England. Addressing a meeting at Reading on Carmichael's behalf, Michael de Freitas recalled the Notting Hill race riots of 1958. 'I saw white savages kicking black women in the streets and black brothers running away. If ever you see a white laying hands on a black woman, kill him immediately . . . Whitey is a vicious, nasty person. Fear of this white monkey is nothing. We will deal with him, if necessary. The white man has no soul. You are dealing with a heartless sort of person, if you are talking to a white man.' Then, to the astonishment of his audience, he boasted that he was not only prepared to kill whites, he had already done so. 'A book I read said I would not be able to sleep at night. But that is not true. You can sleep at night. And I sleep very well. I am no longer afraid.'

He now changed his name to Michael Abdul Malik, self-announced leader of Britain's Black Muslims. As Malik, he stood trial at Berkshire Quarter Sessions, for inciting racial hatred in his Reading speech. He took his oath on the Koran. Indeed, he was not the first Muslim to face such charges. Despite the tradition of absolute freedom of speech at Speakers' Corner in Hyde Park, another defendant had been convicted of racial incitement after saying, 'If I call a white man a monkey, I am paying him a compliment. Killing whites does not count as murder. English people should be shot and you should shed blood for your freedom.'

Representing himself at Reading, Malik opened his defence with a Muslim greeting. When asked by the judge if he wanted to question witnesses, he replied, 'I will but you have to understand this – I am not an Anglo-Saxon. I do not think like you, I do not react like you. If you will sit down as you are paid to do, cool it for a few seconds, I will get around to asking questions. Don't push me, brother.'

He was convicted and sent to prison for a year. This needed no Race Relations Act. All incitement to murder had been criminal by statute since the Offences Against the Person Act 1861. Whether it was useful or wise to 'racialize' such crimes seemed doubtful. Soon after his release he was convicted again of possessing cannabis and later charged with robbery. While on bail, he escaped to Trinidad and founded a commune. Among those who followed him was the daughter of a British MP, Gale Benson, who changed her name to Hasle Kimga and became his uncomplaining and sometimes beaten slave. In February 1972, the bodies of his deputy and Gale Benson were found buried in the commune grounds. In 1975 Michael de Freitas was hanged at the Royal Gaol, Trinidad. During his years in the squalid death cell, it may have consoled him to know that John Lennon considered him to be a political prisoner.[6]

4

In the division of opinion over coloured immigration, a white liberal middle class faced a resentful white working class whose lives were changed fundamentally as streets and neighbourhoods, in the unappealing phrase of the day, 'went black'. The middle class continued to preach toleration, even the exciting promise of a multicultural mix. Despite a general loyalty to the Labour party, the working class remained instinctively conservative, loyal to an England it believed it had always known. The speed of change, over which it was seldom if ever consulted by the government it had elected, was frightening to many. When they protested, they were dismissed as bigots or racists and told to keep their mouths shut. For the first time, in conversation on such topics, people would confide to one another, 'Of course, you've got to be careful what you say.' It was small wonder that they saw a saviour in John Enoch Powell, the one figure of influence who seemed prepared to listen to them.

Enoch Powell attracted greater unquestioning support and a good deal more loathing than any politician of his time. He was supremely clever, perhaps too clever for the menial and compromising world of party politics. A lower middle-class scholarship boy at King Edward's School, Birmingham, he became Scholar and then Fellow of Trinity College, Cambridge, winner of the university's Porson and Craven prizes for classics, and Professor of Greek at the University of Sydney by the age of twenty-five. Students of Thucydides in the 1942 Oxford Classical Texts edition found that it had been edited by a Latinized and youthful 'Johannes Enoch Powell'. He published four collections of his own poetry and two studies of Christianity. In wartime he rose from the ranks to brigadier. In 1950 he became a Conservative member for Wolverhampton South-West. He was Financial Secretary to the Treasury and Minister of Health, resigning both offices over matters of principle. As a man of the Conservative right he campaigned with Tony Benn on the Labour left against Britain's entry into Europe, the two men united in opposing the subordination of the Westminster Parliament and the loss of national sovereignty to civil servants in Brussels.

On the front bench during hours of tedious parliamentary business, Powell and Quintin Hogg 'capped' one another's quotations from Greek literature on slips of paper. Powell's principles were High Tory and free market. When George Brown, on behalf of the Labour government, demanded of heads of industry why they had raised their prices, Powell advised them that the only possible reply was, 'Mind your own business.'

Following the 1964 election, out of office and with his party out of power, Powell came to the fore in the immigration debate. He held that it was not racial prejudice to argue that significant additions to the immigrant population must be prevented so that immigrants already in the country could be properly assimilated. In the nation as a whole, despite widespread opposition to further immigration, opinion polls found a 55–35 majority in favour of race relations legislation as a means of ensuring equal and decent treatment of immigrants already settled. Powell argued that the immigration figure of 50,000 a year, which had by then risen to 75,000, was unsustainable without a breakdown in race relations. More controversially, he advocated paying the passages of those immigrants who wished to return to their countries of origin.

Before long Powell's rhetoric, driven by a fierce rationality, became more colourful. In the *Daily Telegraph* on 16 February 1967 he compared the assault of immigration on the towns of the West Midlands to the German blitz. The white inhabitants were to be 'driven from their homes and their properties deprived of value' with the approval of the government and the indifference of the rest of the country. Six months later he warned his readers that to speak the 'undeniable truth' that there is a difference between those who belong to the country and those who do not was to be 'hounded and pilloried as a racialist'.

In retrospect all this seemed a preliminary to a single afternoon on Saturday 20 April 1968, when Powell addressed the West Midlands Area of the Conservative Political Centre at the Midland Hotel, Birmingham. The press received advance copies of his speech and had little doubt what the Sunday morning headlines would be. The subject of the speech was 'preventable evils' and within a minute or so immigration was highlighted as the first. Powell recalled a recent encounter with a working man who said, 'If I had the money to go, I wouldn't stay in this country.' The man would not be satisfied until he had seen his three children safely settled overseas. 'In this country in fifteen or twenty years time,' he told Powell, 'the black man will have the whip hand over the white man.'

Nothing in the earlier speeches had matched this. 'I can already hear the chorus of execration,' Powell told his audience. 'How dare I say such a horrible thing? How dare I stir up trouble and inflame feelings by repeating such a conversation? The answer is that I do not have the right not to do so.' To add evidence to his argument, he quoted the Registrar-General's figure of 3,500,000 commonwealth immigrants and their descendants who would be settled in Britain 'in fifteen or twenty years'. His own guess was five to seven million by 2000, an overestimate (the 2001 census would put the figure at just under four million). His demand was that the 'total inflow' must be stopped at once. Of the present level of immigration and the official attitude he could only say, 'We must be mad, literally mad.' It was 'like watching a nation busily engaged in heaping up its own funeral pyre'.

The speech became more passionate as it progressed, including the emotive story of a widow who was the last white inhabitant of her street and feared that her refusal to let rooms in her house to black tenants would lead her to prison under further race relations legislation. What followed gained notoriety as Powell's 'rivers of blood' image. Ironically, he did not use the phrase by which his most famous utterance was to be known. He made the point that in looking across the Atlantic he saw the ferocity of interracial violence in urban riots. The worst had been in the Watts district of Los Angeles in 1965 and 1966, though Newark, Detroit, Chicago and Washington had their share as the summer 'season' came round. In Britain, the same chaos would threaten if immigrant communities sought to 'over-awe and dominate the rest with the weapons which the ignorant and the ill-informed have provided'. There had already been race riots in Notting Hill in 1958 and others were to follow until Brixton in April 1981. The Scarman inquiry into this last outbreak blamed both the police on one side and community leaders on the other.

What Powell said next was, 'As I look ahead, I am filled with foreboding. Like the Roman, I seem to see "the River Tiber foaming with much blood".' His prophecy derived from 'That tragic and intractable phenomenon which we watch with horror on the other side of the Atlantic' in Watts and elsewhere. His reference was to Book VI, line 87 of Virgil's *Aeneid*. The Sibyl had prophesied that Aeneas and his companions, seeking to found a new kingdom at Rome, must face grim warfare first 'et Thybrim multo spumantem sanguine – and the Tiber foaming with much blood'. Powell later wished that he had left the words in Latin but had feared it would sound pedantic.

Next morning his speech was the main headline in every Sunday paper. In the evening Edward Heath sacked him, by telephone, from the Shadow Cabinet. In Parliament and among the ruling class it seemed he had scarcely an ally left. The quality press denounced him while most of the populist papers came out on his side. In the country, if opinion polls were to be believed, he was supported by more than three quarters of the population. When pollsters asked if Edward Heath had been right to sack him, a good many respondents added to their replies, 'Sack Heath, not Powell.'

On Monday morning, up and down the country, workers downed tools and staged impromptu marches in his support. From the London docks, 1,300 men set off for Parliament, representatives of far more. Among their banners were 'Back Britain, Not Black Britain' and 'Enoch Says What Everyone Thinks'. One of them read, '45,000 Dockers Support Enoch

Powell.' There seemed no reason to doubt it. Alongside the London dockers, the porters of Smithfield marched in his support. On the other side, students – and undergraduates – marched in protest. Those who represented the University of Oxford arrived in Parliament Square at the same time as the dockers' demonstration and a running fight ensued.

Enoch Powell's career in parliamentary politics seemed over, though he was elected as an Ulster Unionist, having resigned from the Conservative party in opposition to its policy of joining the European Community. Yet his influence survived, as did his popularity in the country. One thing was certain. Despite denunciations of his 'racism' and calls for his prosecution, no case against him under race relations legislation was likely to succeed. He would, in any case, have been a formidable courtroom antagonist. More to the point, there was not a jury in the land likely to convict him. The Wolverhampton *Express and Star*, for example, received some 5,000 letters in his favour and only 300 against. The publicity of a trial would have given him an unrivalled platform for his views. It would also have given him the status of a popular hero even more surely than the status he already enjoyed, a situation far more dangerous to his political rivals than to their *bête noire*.

5

Enoch Powell might have been too formidable an antagonist for the modest talents of the Crown Prosecution Service. The same could not be said for other defendants who appeared in court from time to time over the next thirty years. It was not the more bourgeois protests of the Racial Preservation Society which characterized these cases but publications of a proletarian and Hitlerian Fascism. In 1979, for example, Rupert Relf was charged with possessing material designed to stir up racial hatred. Unfortunately, left-wing activists who tried to get such offenders into court were apt to be a severe liability. In this case, the prosecution depended on an agent provocateur who worked in the local education department but had also gone under cover as a Nazi to entrap Relf. He spied on Relf and his group, wearing a swastika badge, and even went so far as to visit a black man in the area and threaten that his house would be burnt down. Embarrassingly, the witness had to admit in court that in reality he had previous convictions for gross indecency, receiving, larceny, criminal damage, and obtaining property by deception.[7]

It was argued, by Bernard Levin among others, that legislation criminalizing publications and opinions as racist had achieved little or nothing.

330

Indeed, it might make matters worse. This was true in the sense that it often did not require such legislation to criminalize them as inciting violence or murder or a breach of the peace. Where there was a dispute between two parties, perhaps the unwisest thing was to penalize one side only, as the law on race relations too often seemed to do.

So, for example, in June 2002 a falling-out occurred between two neighbours in Exeter. One was a white electronics engineer, the other an Arab postgraduate student. In the wake of the 11 September 2001 bombings of New York and Washington, the engineer was insulting to three Arab neighbours and, having had a friend killed in the Twin Towers attack, began arguing abusively with the Arab over Islamic belief. The engineer was arrested. He had no previous criminal record but pleaded guilty and was fined £100 as well as being told that he was lucky not to go to prison. All this might seem perfectly reasonable but there was some indignation in the neighbourhood that no action was taken against the Arab neighbour who had announced, '11 September was a great day. Osama bin Laden is a great man and all Americans deserve to die.' By such casual inequalities did resentments breed.[8]

In the case of Nazi movements, it was arguably better to let them exist in the open rather than to drive them into an underworld of hatred and conspiracy. The 1990s produced titles like *Combat 18* and *Stormer*, which would have horrified Enoch Powell and probably the Racial Preservation Society. They were not merely racist but specifically Hitlerian.

Combat 18 was so called in tribute to its idol because Adolf Hitler's initials were the first and eighth letters of the alphabet. The manner in which the third issue demanded a 'white revolution' would, once again, have been criminal under the Offences Against the Person Act without assistance from race relations legislation. When three men who produced that issue of the magazine were prosecuted at the Central Criminal Court in March 1997, its rhetoric was a good deal more murderous than the output of 1960s racism. It advocated 'shipping all non-whites back to Africa, Asia, Arabia, alive or in bodybags – the choice is theirs'. It also included instructions on making bombs and detonators for the revolution to come. The three authors were sent to prison.[9]

Stormer's vitriol was more widely spread, citing the names and details of individuals whom it judged worthy of retribution, regardless of religion, race or creed. Its targets also included 'thousands of mosques, synagogues, communist headquarters, nigger estates, TV companies and newspapers all waiting to be blown to bits'. Once again, incitement to murder was not confined to any race or group.

It was easy to dismiss such publications as evil. At another level they seemed ludicrous. For example, the leading light of *Stormer* was a local dustman rather than a figure of any political influence. Since the 1960s, there had been a widespread resentment of political leaders and their appointees who had abandoned ordinary people to the problems of multiculturalism. This grievance was harnessed by *Combat 18* and *Stormer* who identified the traitors and provided details to enable them to be tracked down. Collective denunciations in *Combat 18* also covered homo-sexuals and the IRA – not surprising in a publication of its sort – and the police and government for good measure.[10]

One of the oddest incidents in the battle of race and religion occurred in the Bristol suburb of Frenchay on Sunday 11 December 2005. Stickers with a swastika, a slogan and the website address of a small Fascist splinter group, N9S, appeared on a number of lamp-posts. As with *Combat 18*, N9S appealed to a curious sense of the arcane and the recondite. The group, founded in 1977 and registered with the Electoral Commission as a polit-ical party, took its name from an abbreviation of the November 9th Society. November 9, 1923 was the date on which sixteen members of the Nazi party were murdered during a Munich march.

N9S believed that only Aryans should be British citizens and that non-Aryans who entered Britain after 1 May 1997 should be made to leave. It wanted to make the promotion of homosexuality illegal and to require that all incomes must be earned by work. None of this appeared on the Frenchay leaflets. Their slogan read simply: 'We are not P.C. we are Nazi.'

Despite the address of the N9S website underneath, it might be doubted if the stickers had any immediate connection with the party except as a background for someone else's slogan. They lacked the more obvious attacks on racial or religious groups. A Nazi organization would surely pro-duce something more acerbic. N9S claimed no responsibility for them. The Bristol Muslim Society wisely refused to be alarmed. 'We in the Muslim community don't regard these groups as a threat . . . the people who run them have such low IQs they don't know how to keep them going.'[11]

Yet the slogan did not suggest racial or religious spite so much as resent-ment against the approved forms of education or training in gender studies or racial awareness. Was it possible that a handful of the young – perhaps the adolescent and only one or two of them – had thought it amusing to scare those 'do-gooders' who had imposed such studies upon them? How better than by promising that the target of Nazi revenge for hours of sanctimonious tedium should be 'political correctness' and those who preached it? The young were certainly capable of responding with vindictiveness. A month later, only thirty miles away in Swindon, a boy of seventeen was sent to prison for daubing swastikas and graffiti on mosques and a Sikh temple, as well as making an ineffectual attempt at arson.[12]

6

Combat 18 and *Stormer*, however vicious, were doomed as political weapons. The association with Adolf Hitler and Germany was electoral poison so far as the overwhelming majority of disaffected voters in Britain were concerned. Far more significant, especially on a relatively low turnout, was the total of over 800,000 votes cast for the British National Party in the European parliamentary elections of June 2004. This total was not enough to win a seat but it was a sizeable showing.

The BNP was not by any means new. Its leader in the 1960s had been John Bean and it had inherited the leadership of the far right from the National Front of John Tyndall in 1982. It had succeeded in winning a very small number of local council seats, totalling twenty-one throughout the country by 2005. It made further gains the next year in the most deprived areas of East London, among voters who concluded that the major parties had done nothing for them and never would. It even campaigned as 'the Labour party your grandfathers knew'. The BNP also did relatively well among white voters in the Asian-settled areas of industrial Yorkshire and Lancashire. Its leader was not the local dustman of *Stormer* but a Cambridge graduate in law and history, Nick Griffin, elected in 1998. He won 16 per cent of the vote in the parliamentary seat of Oldham at the 2001 election. This did not put him in danger of winning but it was one of the best results by a far-right candidate in recent years.

The racist credentials of the BNP were seldom in doubt. Yet its opposition to immigration and immigrant communities was blended with other populist causes. The restoration of capital punishment for terrorist murderers or child sex-murderers, abhorrent to the main parties, would in themselves have attracted votes. Even in mainstream politics, appeals for the castration of sex offenders had been heard in the 1990s from the Conservative benches of the House of Commons and from the Chief Constable of Manchester. The proposal to withdraw Britain from the European Community in order to regain national sovereignty, rejected by all three major parties, might command a majority of national opinion and had already gained seats for the United Kingdom Independence Party in the European parliament.

333

Not for the first time in modern politics, there was a large section of the working-class Labour vote which felt that its party in government had betrayed it. In the early 1930s, this had promoted the Fascist party of Sir Oswald Mosley, a former Labour cabinet minister, and those Labour MPs who defected with him. In 1945, it had delivered parliamentary seats like West Fife and Stepney to the Communist party and had very nearly done the same in a Labour heartland seat like Rhondda East. As another century began, the deprived who felt they had been disinherited by New Labour found a sympathetic reception among the BNP, especially in areas of mass immigration. The BNP alone seemed prepared to think the unthinkable about multiculturalism, which its leader described as a 'hell-hole' created by government. Yet the party was quick to put its hand on its heart and deny, however unconvincingly, that it was racist.

In its efforts to silence the BNP, the political establishment, assisted in this case by the BBC, seemed to make almost every mistake open to it. Even before its criminal trials of 2006 were over the BNP, in the words of its leader, had received 'the largest wave of donations in the history of the party, the best publicity in the history of the party'. Its gains in the following local elections suggested that the prosecution had done it a favour. A great many people now knew what the BNP was, some discovered that they agreed with it, and contributed to its funds. In that respect, it had much for which to thank all those who brought it to court.

In 2003 the BBC had infiltrated an undercover reporter with a concealed camera into the BNP organization, posing as a rabid right-wing supporter. A left-wing group had also planted one of its members. The object of the BBC was presumably to gather sufficient evidence for an investigative programme and perhaps charges of incitement to racial hatred against Nick Griffin and his associates, the maximum prison sentence for which would have been seven years.

Three less important members of his party were caught on film, mouthing racial abuse and threats of violence against Muslims. It was alleged by the BNP that the BBC's agent provocateur had 'poured lager' down the throat of one man to get him to perform as he did. He had previously been what the party called 'ethnically cleansed' by young Pakistani men who drove him from his home. This was suggested as the reason for his drunken daydream of shooting them all dead. The left-wing plant, again according to the BNP, had engineered the choice of the two others as candidates for council elections before they were disgraced. The organizations referred to denied this.

Whatever the truth, the trap was sprung in the summer of 2004. Films secretly made for the BBC recorded speeches given to BNP members in a public house. They were shown by the BBC and Nick Griffin was interviewed on television. The evidence of racial abuse and threats by the three people filmed in disputed circumstances was double-edged. In his television interview Mr Griffin turned the tables by claiming that the three men concerned had already been expelled from the party for racist conduct which he described as 'disgusting'. The BNP was not a racist party and did not tolerate racism; these were three 'bad apples' out of a membership of 10,000.

The secretly filmed speeches which Nick Griffin and his lieutenant, Mark Collett, had made were addressed to private meetings in the Reservoir tavern at Keighley, West Yorkshire. The fact that the meetings were private raised a doubt about prosecutions for racist incitement. If all those present held the same racist beliefs, perhaps there was no opportunity for inciting them to become racist. Furthermore, the speeches contained attacks on both race and religion. At the time, incitement to racial hatred was automatically a crime but incitement to religious hatred was not.

In attacking Islam, Nick Griffin described it as a 'wicked, vicious faith', if judged according to the precepts of the Koran. Those precepts advocated the spread of Islam by violence. In the BNP's interpretation, they also permitted the faithful 'to take any woman by the strength of their right arms', so long as she was not a Muslim, and do as they pleased with her. It was true, at least, that few people had managed to reconcile the literal text of the Koran with the rights of women as understood in modern Western democracies. The danger of Islam, as Mr Griffin described it, was of a religion that had expanded from 'a handful of cranky lunatics' thirteen centuries earlier to a movement that now swept country after country.

His speech had also attacked the government and the governing class. 'They turn a white homogeneous Britain, where everybody was English, Scottish, Irish or Welsh and we all basically got on, and we were the same, and we understood each other, and we had the same language, they turned that into a multiracial hell-hole.' As for the religion of aggression and violence which he portrayed, 'First our police force and our elected government haven't done a damn thing properly about it, and the second is that their good book [the Koran] tells them that that's acceptable. Now that sentence could get me seven years.'

The decision as to whether he should be held to account, let alone whether he would get seven years, rested with the Crown Prosecution Service. Nick Griffin had already done his BBC interview following the showing of the secretly filmed speeches. A consideration which the CPS must surely have weighed and presumably rejected was that he would either be convicted at a trial and appear as a martyr for the cause of free speech – or he would be acquitted and able to claim that the people of Britain, represented by the jury, were on his side. In either event, given an unparalleled opportunity of addressing his views to the world, the principal casualty might be racial harmony. None the less, the CPS chose the high-risk strategy of prosecution. Mr Griffin professed to be delighted. 'See you in court,' was his confident response.

The first trial of Nick Griffin and Mark Collett took place at Leeds Crown Court in January 2006. As the judge reminded those present, it was not a political trial. Yet it could hardly avoid being one. The leaders of a political party, however minor and despised, were in the dock because of what they had said. There were noisy demonstrations outside by supporters and opponents, including such placards as 'BLAIR THE LIAR SHOULD BE ON TRIAL, NOT NICK GRIFFIN'. In his opening address, Rodney Jameson QC for the Crown was painstakingly impartial. 'Some of [Griffin's] analysis of a situation is, you may think, perfectly legitimate political comment . . . He deals with serious issues. He accurately predicts events that happened in London in July 2005.'

This last concession was important. The prosecution was not helped by a series of suicide bombings carried out by British-born Muslims in London on 7 July 2005 and an attempt to carry out further attacks two weeks later. The attacks came a year after the BBC exposure of the BNP and six months before the trial. On 7 July the terrorists had blown up three tube trains and a bus, killing fifty-two people and injuring scores of others. Opinion had inevitably turned against Islamic fundamentalism and, to some extent, against Islam in all its forms. Nick Griffin had forecast an attack and had even suggested that the bombers might come from Bradford. In the wake of the explosions there was a new British National Party leaflet headed, 'If only they had listened to the BNP.'

To the jury at Leeds, Mr Jameson made the point that freedom of expression could not be 'unfettered' and Mr Timothy Kay QC for the defence responded with the equally familiar argument that freedom of expression was vital in a democratic society, including the freedom to offend. Then it proved that Mr Griffin, perhaps like many believers in their own infallibility, made a persuasive witness. He dealt confidently with Islam: 'It's a dragon. It's something which unchecked will bring misery and disaster to this country.' Very few people in court could fail to remember the London bombings at that point. When accused of racial incitement by attacking Islam, he had a ready answer. 'There's a huge difference between criticizing a religion and saying this is an attack on the people who follow it.'

He was not an easy witness to score points from in cross-examination and he used his table-turning to advantage. For example, he had said in his speech at the private meeting that the murdered black teenager Stephen Lawrence, whose death was claimed to have been inadequately investigated by Scotland Yard and who was regarded as a martyr to police institutional racism, was in truth a dealer in drugs and one who 'taxed' the dinner money of younger children. Mr Griffin was asked, 'Do you think it made his parents' ordeal better or worse by you saying he was a taxer or a drug dealer?' It was an open goal and the defendant's aim was sure. 'It's utterly irrelevant. There was no chance of them finding out. It's your fault and your bosses', not mine.' Following this exchange, his version of the Stephen Lawrence story also reached the tabloid press.

At another point in his speech he had used the term 'Paki thug'. Now he was asked, 'This is pure, overt out and out racism?' 'It's not racism. Paki is not a racist phrase in that community.' 'They ['Paki thugs'] stab on sight, don't they?' asked the cross-examiner ironically. Once again, Mr Griffin seized the opportunity. 'Yes, they do. How many of them come through this court for doing that? Hundreds of them.' In the freedom of a Miltonic debate, there might have been leisure to argue that in nearby Preston there were four gang attacks by whites on Muslims for every one attack by Muslim gangs on whites. Unfortunately this criminal trial was not designed for such a debate. Instead, Mr Griffin went on to explain that his main worry was being murdered by Muslims. He coupled this with the case of Salman Rushdie, whose ordeal by Iranian-sponsored Islamic terrorism was thereby filed away in the jurors' minds next to the London suicide bombings.

As in his original speech, Nick Griffin remembered who his immediate enemies were. Through the press reporters and television journalists he told the world as well as the jury, 'The politically correct establishment want to outlaw any criticism of Islam in this country by saying it is a Muslim people. It is not.' The argument that Islam constituted a religion and not a race was a shield against charges of inciting racial hatred.

The question for the ten white jurors and one Asian was not whether he was right or justified in everything he had said, nor even whether he was privately a racist or a hypocrite, but whether he had incited racial hatred on a particular occasion. His speech had been made privately to those who shared his views. Did that leave scope for incitement? He attacked a form of religious belief when an attack on religion was not in itself criminal. Finally, he was entitled to freedom of expression within the law.

In closing their cases, both prosecution and defence counsel cited the latest definitive judgment on freedom of speech from Mr Justice Sedley in the High Court in June 1999. 'Free speech includes not only the inoffensive but the irritating, the contentious, the eccentric, the heretical, the unwelcome and the provocative, provided it does not tend to provoke violence. Freedom to speak only inoffensively is not worth having.'

The jurors acquitted Nick Griffin on two counts of incitement to racial hatred but, after nine hours, could not agree on the other two. Mark Collett was acquitted on four counts and there was disagreement on four others. That might have been the end of the matter, had the Crown Prosecution Service dropped the charges which produced disagreement. Yet it had now manoeuvred itself into a position where it could hardly abandon the case without seeming to concede that the two defendants were entitled to speak as they had done. The first trial had accomplished nothing except to transmit the defendants' words and opinions to millions of people, perhaps in excess of the five million who had first watched the speeches on television, instead of the 10,000 members of the BNP.[13]

If a probable conviction was the criterion for a retrial, the omens were not good. As Mr Griffin remarked to a journalist, a third of any Yorkshire jury were likely to sympathize with the BNP anyway. What if jury after jury simply disagreed? He was undismayed when a spokeswoman for the CPS assured the press that there would be a retrial on the remaining charges. 'If the Crown Prosecution Service feel they must continue to persecute us for telling the truth, we will see them in court.'

In the worst of all possible outcomes for the CPS, at the retrial of October 2006, the jury unanimously acquitted both defendants on all remaining charges. No one would know why the juries at the two trials behaved as they did. Perhaps they disliked the BBC's secret surveillance of a private meeting. Perhaps legal arguments about words spoken at a private meeting or attacks confined to a religious system carried weight. Perhaps the jurors even sympathized with too many of the defendants' views – or just with their sincerity – to convict them. It would have been encouraging to think that they believed, with Voltaire, that much as they might dislike what Mr Griffin and Mr Collett had said, they would defend to the death their right to say it.

Even while the trial progressed through January and February 2006, the government was struggling to get its new Racial and Religious Hatred Bill through Parliament. The law seemed to be unwanted by members of almost every religious denomination, as well as by writers and artists who saw its threat to freedom of expression. In the Commons, the government faced a rebellion on its back benches. The House of Lords thought the proposed legislation unworkable and altered it. It went through the Commons at length, after concessions, with few hopes of its success in practice.

As though this were not enough for a month or two, Abu Hamza, formerly imam of Finsbury Park mosque, occupied the dock of the Old Bailey. A figure of some menace with one eye and hooks where his hands had been, his career had also included a spell as a Soho nightclub bouncer and as a construction project engineer at the Royal Military Academy, Sandhurst. His hatred for all that the West, including Christianity and Judaism, represented was unconcealed. He now faced charges of inciting religious hatred and also of inciting murder. An arsenal of weapons at Finsbury Park bore witness to his intentions. He had urged his followers to bleed the common enemy to death; if not with a nuclear weapon, then with a kitchen knife; if not with chemical weapons, then with pesticide. If the BNP was right to believe, as it claimed to do, that immigration or multiculturalism would produce conflict and disintegration in Britain to rival Bosnia, no one would have been more jubilant than Abu Hamza.

As the two trials ran their course, more than two hundred miles apart, there was little in either case that seemed humorous. Yet political irony was not entirely missing. On 8 February, *The Times* published a photograph. It was not a particularly good one but the profile nearest the camera was identifiable as Abu Hamza. He was on the platform of a public meeting, held to defend freedom of speech, including his own homicidal ravings. Just beyond him and more sharply in focus, sat Nick Griffin. The ghost of John Stuart Mill chose to remain invisible.

14

God Is Not Mocked

FOR MUCH OF the twentieth century it had been assumed that religion in Britain, let alone blasphemy, would play a decreasingly important part in national life. As church attendances, baptisms and marriages fell, while those for 'priest-free' funerals rose, the trend seemed irreversible. Belief and sentiment would linger for a generation or two, ebbing uncomplainingly away. Crowds with bared heads might sing 'Abide With Me' at the Wembley Cup Final or 'Cwm Rhondda' at the Cardiff Arms Park but not for much longer. Community hymn singing would probably be the last thing to go. Aldous Huxley in *Brave New World* (1932) envisaged a post-believing world with 'Community Singeries' of secular songs and even an 'Arch-Songster of Canterbury'. As it happened, people stopped singing and fought over religion.

With the conclusion of the Cold War, which in some ways was a belated conclusion of the Second World War, it was possible for Francis Fukuyama to write a book on *The End of History and the Last Man* (1992) whose thesis was its title. More generally, there was a hope that universal economic prosperity would sap the urge and remove the need for war, systematically undermining what remained of the world's tyrannies. A future of uneventful affluence, if that was what the end of history meant, might follow. The assurance was uncomfortably reminiscent of the promise that the conflict of 1914–18 had been a war to end all wars.

On 11 September 2001, as two passenger jets hijacked by Islamic terrorists demolished the Twin Towers of New York's World Trade Center, history assumed its command of human affairs once more. Yet those who gave their lives to crash four aircraft into their targets on the same day did so in the certain faith of a martyr's reward. As if in response to these acts, religions everywhere began to take themselves more seriously.

In the matter of Islam, it was as if a fault-line of unresolved historical antagonism cracked open. This ran through the Siege of Vienna in 1529, the fall of Constantinople in 1453, even to Charles Martel driving back the Arab armies at Poitiers in 732. The victory of self-styled 'Cool Britannia' at the British general election of 1997 was, in truth, only a prelude to very hot wars in Iraq and Afghanistan, often fought in apparent ignorance of the past and its lessons.

In consequence, members of the Muslim faith who wished no ill whatever to Christianity or non-believers were transformed in popular imagination. They were pictured either as bloodthirsty fundamentalists, vigilant for whatever might offend them, or a beleaguered minority who must be protected from offence or harassment by stricter official censorship imposed on the entire population. It was in vain to protest that they were not offended. Legislation was in place to give the government and those who acted on its behalf a firmer control over opinion and the forms in which it might be expressed.

2

For more than half a century, after the downfall of William Gott in 1922, the suppression of blasphemy was little more than an historical curiosity. Several times during these years there were demands for the prosecution of those who denounced or ridiculed Christian belief but they came principally from the fringes of orthodoxy. It would have puzzled most people to imagine what social, political or doctrinal developments could make blasphemy a matter of national security before the century's end.

A Blasphemy Laws (Amendment) Bill was introduced in the House of Commons in 1930. It would have removed common law blasphemy and the Blasphemy Act 1698 from the calendar of crime. There was much sympathy and practical support for the measure; it had passed its second reading before the Home Secretary intervened. While he approved of the bill in general, he must prevent 'breaches of the peace by unbridled attacks upon religious feeling' and the public disorder which might follow.

The bill's supporters were divided between those who rejected compromise in the matter of free speech and others prepared to accept the limitations which the Home Secretary outlined. The proposed bill was withdrawn and the Blasphemy Act of 1698 remained on the statute book. It made very little difference. From time to time, thinly supported allegations of blasphemy or profanity were heard. One of the most pertinent involved the BBC's broadcasts of Dorothy L. Sayers' *The Man Born to be King*, in 1941–2. This was a cycle of radio plays depicting the life of Christ. Their author, famous for her 'Lord Peter Wimsey' detective novels, was a devout Anglican who had produced a distinguished translation of Dante's *Divine Comedy* into English verse. The purpose of the plays was to make Christ an approachable and sympathetic figure to modern listeners.

Though the BBC was not subject to theatrical censorship, any stage portrayal of God the Father or Christ the Son was still forbidden. Marc Connelly's *Green Pastures*, a Pulitzer prizewinner, and George Moore's *The Passing of the Essenes* remained under a theatrical ban on these grounds. Cecil B. de Mille's *King of Kings* (1927) had portrayed Christ on the screen but films were still silent at the time and this film could be allowed as part of Christian iconography, albeit with pictures that 'moved'. The voice of Christ was more contentious.

The BBC decided to broadcast *The Man Born to be King* in parts, between December 1941 and October 1942. The first episode was followed by a number of individual protests and a particularly vociferous one from the Lord's Day Observance Society. The objections were principally to the imitation of Christ's voice and to the use of colloquial expressions. So, for example, in the scene depicting Christ's preaching at the temple, one of the opponents among the Sadducees present is told forcefully to 'sit down and shut up'.[1]

In reply to these criticisms, the corporation reported on 8 January 1942 that its Central Religious Advisory Committee, chaired by the Bishop of Worcester, had carefully considered the series and the views of the objectors. 'The committee has unanimously recommended that the proposal should be proceeded with and the Board of Governors has accepted the recommendation. The second broadcast will accordingly be given on 25 January.'

Dorothy Sayers assured the press that her scripts had not been censored in any way by the BBC and she defended her work. 'The suggestion that any person who may speak in an uneducated voice and use slang cannot be a saint of God and is not fit to be associated with Christ should be repudiated by every Christian.' Yet the success of the series did nothing to persuade Parliament to relax stage censorship.

As in the Victorian period, those who professed a religious belief were not exempt from accusations of heresy or blasphemy. Yet they remained far removed from threats of prosecution in the ecclesiastical courts, let alone at the Old Bailey. When Dr Barnes, Bishop of Birmingham, questioned received orthodoxy in his *Rise of Christianity* in 1947, the Archbishop of Canterbury, Dr Fisher, remarked, 'If I held his views, I would feel compelled to resign.' Dr Barnes felt no such compulsion and no steps were taken to remove him.[2]

Dissent might be political rather than doctrinal. Dr Hewlett Johnson, the 'Red' Dean of Canterbury, was a friend and apologist of the Soviet leadership. Canon Stanley Evans, in 1953, urged Christians to join mourners the world over following the death of a great liberator and 'outstanding leader in the struggle for world peace' – Joseph Stalin. Their detractors grumbled but that was as far as the matter went.[3]

Doctrinal disputes in the ecclesiastical courts were far more likely to involve an incumbent who had annoyed his parishioners by using incense and celebrating 'Mass' rather than 'Holy Communion'. The criminal courts dealt solely with scurrility or extreme profanity, in effect an outrage so violent as to threaten a breach of the peace. Gentle fun or mockery of religious institutions pervaded such series as the BBC's *That Was The Week That Was* by the start of the 1960s. Its 'best washing-machine' comparisons of the benefits offered by rival denominations revealed the Church of England as the churchgoers' best buy, 'a handy little faith with optional extras. If you want Transubstantiation you can have it. If you don't, you don't have to.' Neither this nor the fatuous sermon preached in *Beyond the Fringe* on the text from Genesis, 'Behold Esau my brother is a hairy man and I am a smooth man', stood in any danger. Even in 1882, it had taken a private prosecution, two trials and a further retrial to get convictions in the case of material as offensive as the *Freethinker*'s 'Comic Bible Sketches'.

What might have been a test of church discipline occurred in the spring of 1963 when the Bishop of Woolwich, Dr John Robinson, published a short book, *Honest to God*, issued by the Student Christian Movement Press. Its title sounded uncontroversial but in a few weeks the bishop and his book had brought religious debate to the centre of national life. Dr Robinson had already made headlines in 1960, agreeing at the *Lady Chatterley* trial that this was 'a book Christians should read'. A good many of them now took far greater exception to *Honest to God* than they had done to Lawrence's novel.

On 4 April, an anonymous reviewer in *The Times* quoted Oscar Wilde's description of the English Church as one in which 'a man succeeds not through his capacity for belief but his capacity for disbelief'. Dr Robinson had set out to demythologize and demystify the faith, though at the same time he claimed he was merely 'thinking aloud'. He dismissed much of the New Testament as mythology. The Incarnation was 'God dressed up – like Father Christmas' or a fable in which 'God took a space-trip and arrived on the planet in the form of a man'. A personal God with whom the individual might communicate was dismissed in favour of God as 'ultimate reality'. Nor was there room in this new theology for the Resurrection or the New Testament miracles.[4]

The publishers got their word in first. 'Free speech is what the Church of England needs, not a heresy trial,' said the managing director of the SCM Press anxiously, preaching in Westminster Abbey. From the diocese of Bristol, Bishop Oliver Tomkins assured readers of his diocesan gazette that the author's offence was not heresy but mere irresponsibility. Archbishop Michael Ramsey of Canterbury reminded Dr Robinson publicly that the right to 'liberty of thought' carried with it obligations of consideration and restraint. If the author of *Honest to God* claimed he was only thinking aloud, this plea was a means of having his theological cake and eating it. The book had done hurt to divinity students and to 'struggling faithful members of the Church'. Dr Robinson thereupon complained that Archbishop Ramsey misrepresented him.

The Bishop of Peterborough thought the book 'derisive' and its tone deplorable. *The Times* on 8 August announced that 'Anglicanism is closer to Hinduism than to the particular form of religion adumbrated by the Bishop of Woolwich.' Six days later, the Examining Chaplain to the Bishop of Southwark confessed that he could not remain in the Christian Ministry, 'if I held the views (or doubts) expressed in *Honest to God*'. The hint, if it was one, left the Bishop of Woolwich unmoved. More forthright reviewers, including T. E. Utley in the *Sunday Telegraph* of 24 March, advocated that church discipline should be used to remove the bishop from his see.

The argument became so warm in the course of the summer that the publishers of Dr Robinson's book, which had now sold almost a quarter of a million copies, announced a sequel. It was to be *The Honest to God Debate*.

Many whose faith was undermined or whose souls were scorched by the new light could only look on. It seemed that a bishop might deny the fundamentals of the faith with a light heart while incurring no risk whatever of proceedings for heresy or charges of blasphemy. As the row continued, those who grieved for their belief were able to draw comfort from a reader's letter to *The Times* on 6 April. It simply quoted the farewell of the dying Benjamin Jowett, a veteran of Victorian religious controversy, to his young friend Margot Asquith. 'My dear child,' said the old man gently, 'you must believe in God, no matter what the clergy tell you.'

3

If it was possible, as the *Church Times* put it, for a bishop to remain in place while 'denying almost every Christian doctrine of the church in which he holds office', there was an end of censorship in matters of religious opinion. Elsewhere, the risks were greater.

With the end of the Lord Chamberlain's powers in 1968, producers and theatre owners became liable to the laws of the land controlling blasphemy and obscenity. In 1970 a mainstream London theatre, the Criterion, staged *The Council of Love*, translated from Oscar Panizza's *Le Concile d'amour* (1894). Mingling satire and comedy, it depicts a heaven in which God the Father, Jesus Christ and the Virgin Mary have patched up their quarrel with the Devil. Their purpose is to introduce syphilis into the court of the Borgia pope, Alexander VI, in 1495 as a punishment for promiscuity. Following its first publication, the author had been sent to prison for a year by a Munich court in 1895.

At the Criterion in 1970, the play ran for ten weeks. On 21 August, Milton Shulman reviewed it in the *Evening Standard* under the heading 'And Now Full Frontal Blasphemy'. He concluded that 'So majestic a subject is hardly likely to suffer from such weak and dubious ridicule.' None the less, on 25 August a theatrical producer, Mr Geoffrey Russell, made a complaint to Scotland Yard and the matter was investigated. In December, Lady Birdwood unsuccessfully attempted a private prosecution of the directors. Earlier in the year she had in vain sought leave to bring a prosecution against Kenneth Tynan's 'nude revue', *Oh! Calcutta!* On 31 July, Sir Peter Rawlinson as Attorney-General turned down that application.

Before long, a force more powerful than Mr Russell or Lady Birdwood had found a more promising target. Following the 1967 legalization of homosexual conduct between consenting adults in private, a weekly magazine had appeared, *Gay News*. It reached issue 96, in June 1976, when it became the defendant in a successful private prosecution for blasphemous libel. The occasion was a poem, 'The Love That Dares Not Speak Its Name', by James Kirkup. Kirkup's work already had a considerable reputation. His poem describes a Roman soldier attracted by the crucified Christ and it depicts an act of homosexual necrophilia.

More than half a century after William Gott's last appearance, Denis Lemon as editor and *Gay News* itself faced charges under the ancient law of blasphemy. The prosecution was brought by Mrs Mary Whitehouse, better known as the founder of the Viewers' and Listeners' Association – VALA – which had succeeded her 'Clean Up TV' campaign in November 1965. Her background was what would once have been called 'evangelical' Christianity but which was increasingly known as 'the religious right'. VALA's membership, at some 30,000, was tiny compared with the numbers who viewed or listened; even so, she might fairly claim that support for her general views ran into millions.

Mrs Whitehouse had already detected blasphemy on television. On 17 February 1968, not for the last time, she wrote to the DPP asking him to prosecute the BBC. The culprit was an episode of the situation comedy *Till Death Us Do Part*, broadcast on 16 February. Written by Johnny Speight, it starred Warren Mitchell as the cockney racist and reactionary, Alf Garnett, on this occasion discussing God and evolution. The entire series was something of an embarrassment to the BBC. It had been intended to hold up racism to derision. To the chagrin of the corporation, Garnett with his constant references to coons and darkies became a working-class folk-hero. The programme was discontinued only to be taken up by London Weekend Television.

There was never a chance that the DPP would prosecute the BBC nor that, had he done so, he would have been likely to get a conviction. *Gay News* and 'The Love That Dares Not Speak Its Name' was quite another matter. A large number of Christians would find the poem scurrilous and many non-Christians would have been repelled by the acts and emotions described.

Unlike the Obscene Publications Act 1959, the law of blasphemy made no provision for expert evidence. No witnesses would assure the jury that the Kirkup poem was one all Christians should read. It was left to the jurors to decide whether this was, indeed, a scurrilous and profane effusion or a legitimate poetic fantasy. The prosecution could only suggest that its case was proved immediately to any decent person who read the poem. How could it not be regarded as scurrilous and profane in its treatment of Christian belief? The defence had a far harder task than it appeared to realize when it tried to laugh off the trial as a regression to medieval heresy-hunts.

In the divided society of the 1970s it was perhaps never likely that the jury would return a unanimous verdict. Yet even in the wake of the 'liberated' sixties, and even though homosexual conduct in private had been legalized by the Sexual Offences Act, the practice was still disapproved of by a large majority of people.

It took five hours for the jury to reach a majority verdict, which convicted both Denis Lemon and his newspaper by a majority of 10–2. Judge Alan King-Hall fined Lemon £500 with a suspended prison sentence of nine months. *Gay News* was fined £1,000. Judge King-Hall added, 'This poem is quite appalling and is the most scurrilous profanity.' It showed 'reckless disregard for the feelings of Christians and non-

Christian sympathizers'. Yet the judge was not a backwoodsman of the religious right. This particular defender of Christianity was Jewish.[5]

4

Dramatic though it had been, the *Gay News* trial brought to an end prosecutions for blasphemy as a means of defending the Christian religion or avenging insults against it. Once more, it seemed that the law in a secular society had no business to interfere in such areas of religious dispute.

The shock was all the greater, a decade later, when the world awoke to a future in which a single novel by a British citizen, published by a respected London firm, caused seventeen deaths in communal rioting, the stoning of embassies, the severance of diplomatic relations between Britain and Iran, book-burning and demonstrations in British cities, two firebombs in London, and a bounty of £2,000,000 offered by a foreign state for the murder of a British author, who was probably kept alive by the British authorities for something like the same sum.

That all this might happen as the result of the publication of a novel was far more like a regression to the Middle Ages than the prosecution of Gay *News*. It was more turbulent than regimented book-burning in the Third Reich. In retrospect, it was also to seem like an opening skirmish in a maverick world conflict which took the place of the calculated menace known as the Cold War. The next twenty years would see New York's towers burning, the bombs of democracy falling on Iraq, and London brought to a shocked standstill by suicide bombers who were both Islamic fundamentalists and British citizens.

To a secular society, the first protests over Salman Rushdie's novel *The Satanic Verses* seemed like a fuss about nothing very much. Islam, it appeared, had yet to learn, or to be taught, that religious faith in the Western world enjoyed no automatic deference. Indeed, the First Amendment to the United States Constitution forbad this. The most precious belief was open to insult or injury. The assumption of a democratic society was that if such a belief had anything worthwhile about it, it would emerge strengthened from its ordeal. Even Christianity had won only a majority verdict at the *Gay News* trial. Freedom of expression in the United States had come to the aid of such works of 'art' as Andres Serrano's *Piss Christ*, which was nothing more aspirational than a crucifix photographed in a jar of urine. Compared to that, there was surely not much for Islam to complain of in Salman Rushdie's novel.

The book's author had been born to a Muslim family in Bombay in

1947, which enabled his enemies to add apostasy to his sins. Though his parents later moved to Pakistan, his education was English and patrician, at Rugby School and King's College, Cambridge, where he read history. Until the affair of *The Satanic Verses*, he was best known for his novel *Midnight's Children*, which had won the Booker Prize in 1985.

To the world at large, certainly in the culture of his adoption, *The Satanic Verses* might read rather like an Arabian Nights entertainment which had passed through the gilded thoughts of Ronald Firbank and the dream city of James Joyce. Its opening pages describe two men coming to earth without wings or parachutes from an exploding and hijacked jumbo jet, landing safely as if upon a magic carpet. Gibreel Farishta, part Angel Gabriel and part aspiring Hollywood star, is the focus of the story. His world view embraces figures as diverse as Walter Matthau, Goldie Hawn, Harold Wilson and Ho Chi Minh. In parallel with this modernity, stories of the Prophet Muhammad, told to Gibreel by his mother, are woven into the fabric of the fantasized city of Jahilia, which those who denounced the book identified with Mecca. It was the Jahilia episodes that were to cause most of the trouble.

When the novel was published by Penguin Books, in September 1988, it was well received on both sides of the Atlantic, both in the press and by famous names who endorsed it. Nadine Gordimer thought it 'a staggering achievement, brilliantly enjoyable', while V. S. Pritchett saluted its author as a great novelist. Phrases like 'a masterpiece' or 'a towering work of fiction' detached themselves readily from reviews. There was one such review, by Robert Towers in the *New York Times*, which put Salmon Rushdie into the company of Jonathan Swift as the author of *Gulliver's Travels* and Voltaire as the author of *Candide*. Readers were not reminded that Swift concealed his true identity even from Gulliver's publisher for fear of reprisals, though his publisher was to be indicted a few years later. Voltaire published *Candide* from the safety of Switzerland and it seemed safe to say that his books probably fuelled more bonfires than those of any other author of his day.

At first, trouble came sporadically. *The Satanic Verses* won the Whitbread Award in November. In early October, however, it had been banned by the Indian government of Rajiv Gandhi. Cynics suggested that this was Gandhi's sop to Muslim opinion ahead of a general election. Within weeks, however, the book was being banned across the Muslim world, as well as in countries like South Africa, which found it expedient to balance liberal pretensions against the votes of a significant Muslim minority.

A huge majority of those who protested had not read the book, as its author complained from time to time. It was 547 pages long, divided into nine chapters and most of the outrage had been caused by the contents of Chapter 2, 'Mahound', and Chapter 6, 'Return to Jahilia'. The name 'Mahound' had been used in the Middle Ages and subsequently to denote Muhammad as a false prophet, often in tandem with the villain Termagant. As such it occurs in texts like Edmund Spenser's *The Faerie Queene*, Alexander Pope's *Satires of Dr Donne Versified* and Sir Walter Scott's *The Talisman*. In 1988, however, this name of a 'false prophet of crusading demonology' was used systematically in *The Satanic Verses* to denote Muhammad. The narrator suggests that such insults should be turned into strengths, just as Whig and Tory were political labels derived from mutual name-calling. Unfortunately, it is necessary to the plot that Mahound should also be tricked by the Devil into memorizing and spouting the infamous Satanic Verses, as if Christ had somehow been lured into blasphemy.

Salman Rushdie's portrait of the false prophet Mahound damned the second chapter of the novel in the view of its detractors. The sixth chapter was, if anything, worse. The city of Jahilia now contained a brothel, 'The Curtain', staffed by the nine Mothers of the Believers. Each had assumed the identity of one of Mahound's wives. The youngest, fifteen-year-old Ayesha, 'was the most popular with the paying public, just as her namesake was with Mahound'. In a decade when 'child abuse' hysteria was at its height, Ayesha was also an uncomfortable reminder to the liberal West of a cultural division with the East, millions of whose citizens had by now made their homes in Europe.

By the time the narrative reached 'The Curtain', the question was no longer whether Muslim protests were a fuss about very little but whether freedom of expression meant what it said. On the scale of iniquity, it was not clear that the vices of Jahilia were as revolting as 'The Love That Dares Not Speak Its Name' or indeed the art of *Piss Christ*. Unfortunately it proved impossible, then and subsequently, to weigh such offence to the Muslim world against the right to freedom of expression in the liberal West, including those cities settled by Islam.

By the end of 1988, debate had begun to give way to flame and riot, as the process of law failed. During the autumn, there had been moves by Islamic groups in Britain to get the book banned on the grounds of blasphemy. These began in October with a demand to Penguin Books that all copies of *The Satanic Verses* should be recalled and pulped, while an undertaking was to be given by the firm that Rushdie's novel would not be reprinted in any edition or language for the future. The demand was ignored.

Dr Syed Pasha, secretary of the Union of Muslim Organizations in Britain, then wrote to the Prime Minister, Margaret Thatcher, demanding that the publishers of the book should be prosecuted. The Prime Minister replied that there were no grounds on which the government would consider banning the book. It was perfectly true that as the law stood it made no direct provision for such protection of any religion other than Christianity and that, as a matter of history, there had been no reason why it should. The Public Order Act 1986 extended some protection to all religions but its provisions could scarcely apply to the publication of a novel. The Prime Minister reminded Dr Pasha that 'It is an essential part of our democratic system that people who act within the law should be able to express their opinions freely.' Both the Attorney-General, Sir Patrick Mayhew, and the Lord Chancellor, Lord Mackay, confirmed this view. Solicitors who were consulted by the Muslim Council also advised that neither the Race Relations Act nor the Public Order Act offered them any remedy. On 1 February 1989 Douglas Hurd, as Home Secretary, confirmed that the government did not intend to alter the law of blasphemy. For half a century a growing body of opinion had favoured the abolition of such laws, not their increase.

There was an escalation of the protests at the beginning of December 1988 with a march of 7,000 members of the Asian community through Bolton. It ended with a public bonfire of copies of the novel but passed off without further incident. In the New Year, demonstrations began in Yorkshire among the 60,000 Muslims of Bradford. Another march on 14 January ended with the burning of *The Satanic Verses* outside police headquarters. As *The Times* was to reveal, the Crown Prosecution Service and its director declined to intervene against this disorder on the grounds of 'lack of evidence'.

The general tenor of the British press and public opinion was firmly on the side of the author and his publishers, as if to inform Muslims that they had chosen to come and live in a liberal democracy which valued freedom above all things and which regarded freedom of expression as the non-negotiable frontier of liberty. If they could not accept that, perhaps they were living in the wrong place. Had the matter been put to the test, such a response would probably have received overwhelming national support. On 22 January, in the *Observer*, Salman Rushdie himself hit back at the clerics who had taken over Islam as 'the contemporary Thought Police'.

Five days later there was a protest rally in Hyde Park, drawing Muslims from all over Britain. The numbers were put at 8,000, far less than had been expected. Not for the first time, this raised the question of how representative of the Muslim community the book-burners were. A further attempt at a private prosecution for blasphemy was promised by the Islamic Defence Council and another demand was made to Penguin Books for the suppression of the novel. This time, the specific objections listed were to the naming of the Prophet Abraham or Ibrahim as a bastard and of Muhammad as Mahound; the description of the Prophet as having no scruples, being no angel and his companions being described as 'scum' and 'bum' (*sic*). Finally there were the namesakes of his wives staffing a brothel in Jahilia, itself a satire on Mecca.

Parliamentary support for Salman Rushdie's antagonists was hard to find. The law appeared to be in his favour, the demonstrations had let off a good deal of steam, and there seemed a good chance that the row which had simmered for three months might now die down of its own accord.

In the space of a week the scene was altered beyond recognition as the faithful in Muslim countries rallied against a writer they now regarded as an apostate. On 12 February a crowd of 2,000 tried to storm the US Information Center in Islamabad. The flag was torn down and burnt, along with effigies of Rushdie and Uncle Sam. Police fired on the crowd and six demonstrators were killed. There was another death on 13 February during a similar riot in Kashmir. A further ten people were to be killed in Bombay on 24 February during rioting between Muslims and Hindus. The first reaction of those who looked on was incredulity that a novel by a British author published in London could have caused such events across the world.

Two days after the Islamabad riot, Tehran Radio broadcast an announcement on behalf of the country's fifty million Shia Muslims. To those who heard it in the West, it was sinister and bizarre, reminiscent of 'Lord Haw-Haw' in Berlin almost half a century earlier. The Ayatollah Khomeini, de facto ruler of his country since the overthrow of the Shah, had issued a *fatwa*. For most people, a new word had entered the English language. Those who wondered what it meant were soon enlightened. 'The author of the book entitled *The Satanic Verses* . . . as well as those publishers who were aware of its contents, have been sentenced to death.' All loyal Muslims were urged 'to execute them quickly'. If there were those who had access to Salman Rushdie but were not in a position to 'execute' him, they were to 'refer' him to the people so that he might be punished for his actions. As a final persuasion, an initial bounty of £1,500,000 was offered for the author's death.

A world which congratulated itself on the fall of the Berlin Wall and the end of the Soviet threat soon found that a new and nightmarish page of history had been turned. Up to now, the Khomeini regime had exercised its murderous talents publicly in or near its own territories. Now it claimed the right to pick foreign nationals anywhere from the streets of their cities and put them to death. How many of those hundreds of thousands of immigrants in the West would be among the 'zealous Muslims' to whom the message was addressed?

It seemed as if the savagery of dogma which liberal democracy associated in its own history with the bonfires and racks of the Reformation or Counter-Reformation or the massacres of the Thirty Years War, three or four centuries earlier, was armed with all the technology and trickery of the modern age. President Rafsanjani, titular leader of Iran, suggested on 17 February that the dispute might be settled if Salman Rushdie were to apologize. He apologized next day and was told the day afterwards that his death sentence had been confirmed. He vanished under police protection. 'If I were in Pakistan now I'd be dead,' he told the *Sunday Times* on 19 February 1989. The press dealt robustly with Khomeini, the man who had sidled into power by promising democracy to replace the autocracy of the Shah but had brought a benighted tyranny instead.

Penguin Books were also under armed guard. All known copies of the novel were withdrawn, though W. H. Smith had given up selling it some months earlier and most other booksellers had followed suit. In April two London bookshops, Collets and Dillons, were fire-bombed. In May, a young Moroccan blew himself up in his room at the Beverley House Hotel, Paddington. The Organization of the Mujahedin in Beirut claimed him as the first martyr in attempting to assassinate Salman Rushdie.

In the face of what seemed the ultimate form of censorship, writers and writers' organizations rallied to the cause of free speech. Two members of the Swedish Academy, judges of the Nobel prizes, resigned when the organization refused to condemn the death sentence as what Anthony Burgess called a declaration of war on citizens of a free country.

Resistance to the threats from Iran was robust in the United States, laced with a dash of contempt for Khomeini and his kind. Embarrassingly for Britain, the land of the First Amendment seemed rather more forthright in defending Salman Rushdie than some of his own country's leaders. *The Satanic Verses* was published as intended in New York, those booksellers who declined to stock it being reminded by Norman Mailer that 'serious literature, in a world of dwindling certainties, is the absolute we must defend.'[6]

The United States Congress took the beleaguered author of *The Satanic*

Verses under its wing. On 27 February, while repudiating religious intolerance, the Senate declared that it would 'protect the right of any person to
write, publish, sell, buy and read books without fear of intimidation or
violence'. Senator Daniel Moynihan denounced Khomeini's 'intellectual
terrorism'. Even so, the enemy seemed already within the gates. During
the previous week the *Riverdale Press* had come to the support of Rushdie.
The offices of the paper were promptly fire-bombed.

With every act of violence, Khomeini lost ground in the eyes of the
world. Yet his corrosive bigotry in respect of Rushdie's novel had the
power to destabilize the communities of the West. The carefully woven
policy of 'multiculturalism', which had always been a fragile artefact, began
to unravel. The great majority of Muslims in the West had cause to loathe
the Khomeini regime as much as anyone. Quite a number were refugees
from it. Most were not Khomeini's supporters any more than most
Germans had been members of the Nazi party or most citizens of the
Soviet Union had been members of the Communist party. Indeed, by no
means all the hostility directed towards Salman Rushdie came from Islam.
Roald Dahl, for example, denounced the novel and called its author 'a dangerous opportunist', which was still some way short of demanding his
execution.[7]

Unfortunately it was the loudest and probably least representative voices
which carried furthest. There were demands from Muslim fundamentalists
in Britain for the execution order to be carried out, including the vote of
more than 600 delegates at Walthamstow on 15 December 1989. Though
such incitement to murder was criminal under Section 4 of the Offences
Against the Person Act 1861 and Section 5 of the Criminal Law Act 1977,
the Crown Prosecution Service decided that it would not be in 'the public
interest' to bring proceedings against the inciters.

Had there been a prize for audacity it must have gone finally to Salman
Rushdie rather than to his enemies. In 1990 a Palestinian film, *International
Guerillas*, depicted Mr Rushdie being struck down by a thunderbolt, presumably despatched by Allah, as a punishment for having tortured and
killed Muslims. In July, the British Board of Film Classification refused the
film a certificate on legal advice that it might be a criminal libel, to which
the board would be party if it sanctioned its exhibition. Protests against the
ban were predictably led by Dr Syed Pasha. One of those who supported
the protest was, less predictably, Salman Rushdie himself, on the grounds
that any such ban violated the freedom of expression for which he and his
supporters were fighting.

Khomeini's command was never carried out but, from time to time, there were reminders that the sentence was still in place. In March 1989, the spiritual leader of Belgium's Muslims and his aide were shot dead after the imam had made an apparently conciliatory statement about the Rushdie case on television. In February 1993, President Rafsanjani emphasized to Western reporters that the death sentence 'would never in any circumstances be revoked'. The head of the Iranian judiciary promised in April 1996 that the threat would be carried out 'sooner or later'. Indeed, the bounty payable to an assassin was now raised to £2,000,000. MI5 concluded that no agreement with Iran could be depended upon and that the author must always be at risk from a covert and deranged fanatic.

5

After the terrorist bombings of 2001 in New York and London in 2005, the British government sought to define and control extremist propaganda. At the same time the Crown Prosecution Service was attacked in the press for apparently favouring Islamic fundamentalism and failing to act against it. The assumption was that the service lived in fear of being branded 'racist' if it prosecuted Muslims. In 2005–6, however, two cases helped to define the limits of tolerance.

In August 2005 it was decided not to prosecute Abdul Muhid for inciting racial hatred, after complaints of his open-air preaching in Walthamstow High Street. His remarks included, 'Now is the time for jihad. Now is the time for all British servicemen to be slaughtered', and 'All homosexuals should be thrown off a cliff . . . All homosexuals should be thrown off a tower.' The remarks about homosexuals came in reply to a man who argued with him on the topic.

If freedom of speech included the freedom to be offensive, provocative, insulting and to tell people all those things which they did not wish to hear, that freedom belonged to Abdul Muhid as much as to anyone else. If freedom of speech gave only the latitude apparently permitted by the legislation of the new millennium, he was almost certain to have been convicted. The question was whether his words were an expression of opinion, as in the First World War slogan, 'The only good German is a dead German', or an incitement to his audience to go and kill British servicemen or throw homosexuals from cliffs and towers.

As the great American scholar of constitutional law, Zachariah Chaffee, described it, for incitement to be punishable it must come 'dangerously near success'; it must offer what Justice Oliver Wendell Holmes called 'a clear and present danger'. In Victorian England, as Sir James Fitzjames

Stephen wrote, incitement was only criminal if it produced 'an immediate tendency' to action. Hence John Stuart Mill's distinction between the legality of arguing in the press that corn merchants are the starvers of the poor, and the illegality of the leader of an angry mob exhorting his followers to the same effect outside the house of a corn merchant.

In these terms, there was no chance of all British servicemen being slaughtered as a result of Abdul Muhid's words, nor of all homosexuals being thrown off a cliff or a tower. His words expressed opinion as much as incitement. As Mill's lone voice against mankind, his liberty would entitle him to speak as he did. Equally, those who stood by might engage him in argument, heckle him, or demonstrate that he was talking pernicious and offensive rubbish. Traditionally, the law would only take him by the collar if he provoked violence.

Among Muslims, Muhid's views were shared by very few. They also ran counter to the views of the great majority in a time of emotional national crisis. They resembled opinions which Mr Justice Stable in the far more immediate crisis of May 1940 believed 'the Court should be particularly jealous to protect'. In 1940, the views on trial were those of the *Daily Worker*, a defender of the Soviet Union which was still Hitler's supporter against the West. As for the difference between an opinion and an incitement, Justice Holmes had put his finger upon it precisely: 'Every idea is an incitement . . . The only difference between an expression of an opinion and an incitement in the narrower sense is the speaker's enthusiasm for the result.'[8]

Issues of law gave way to semantics and to speculation. For example, in 2006 a jury found that it was not racial incitement for Mark Collett of the BNP to say, 'Let's show these ethnics the door in 2004.' It was presumably accepted that he did not advocate coercion. Would Abdul Muhid have been considered for prosecution if he was saying figuratively that he hoped Britain would lose the wars in Afghanistan and Iraq or that the Sexual Offences Act 1967, legalizing homosexual conduct, should be repealed?

The CPS had twice declined to prosecute a far more important Islamic subversive, Abu Hamza. He was tried eventually in January and February 2006. This former imam of the Finsbury Park mosque was charged on a total of fifteen counts, nine of them of soliciting to murder. The other six related to his opinions as incitement. Four of these were incitements to racial hatred, one of possessing offensive recordings and one of possessing a 'terrorist manual', *Encyclopaedia of the Afghani Jihad*, an account of the Afghan resistance to the Red Army. None of these charges required the new legislation restricting freedom of speech, which the government had thought indispensable.

The prosecution alleged solicitations to murder at one extreme; at the other were assertions that living in the Britain of Cool Britannia was like living in a toilet. Not only would most people allow Abu Hamza to say the latter, a good many might agree with him. Unfortunately for him, the arsenal found at the mosque gave his comments a far more sinister context. The weapons included three blank-firing pistols, which could have been converted to fire live rounds but had not been, a stun gun, knives, masks, military suits and radios. Whether these were of great practical use or merely the theatrical props of a pantomime ogre was not an issue. It was the incitement of his sermons and speeches which determined the character of the collection.

The first stage of jihad, Abu Hamza had told his followers, is 'Shawkat al-Nekaya . . . the needle of bleeding the enemy'. They were to imagine the enemy as a large animal standing in front of them. 'You have to stab him here and there until he bleeds to death . . . We ask Muslims to bleed the enemies of Allah anywhere by any means. You can't do it by nuclear weapons, by kitchen knife . . . You can't do it by chemical weapons, you have to do it by mice poison.'

Not only had the CPS refused to prosecute him; when Abu Hamza had approached the Metropolitan Police about these recruiting sermons, he had been told, 'You have freedom of speech. You don't have anything to worry about so long as we don't see blood on the streets.' In the event he had quite a lot to worry about, even without blood on the streets. The material in his possession brought him convictions on three counts of inciting racial hatred and six counts of soliciting to murder, and seven years in prison.[9]

The trial of Abu Hamza decided very little about freedom of speech but even before it was over, the world was reminded of what Salman Rushdie and his publishers had discovered. Censorship of the written word or picture was now global and its most effective weapon was terror.

In August 2005 a book described by its author as written 'to promote understanding between cultures' was published in Copenhagen. *The Koran and the Life of the Prophet Mohammed* by Kare Bluitgen was a children's book. It contained twelve drawings of the Prophet. None of these would have seemed disrespectful in Western eyes, especially since the Koran did not forbid depictions of Muhammad and there were a good many in the art of Turkey and Iran. However, the illustrators of the book were uneasy and were only prepared to work anonymously. Long before the book appeared, news of the illustrators' caution reached a Danish paper, *Jyllands-Posten*.

In September 2005, the newspaper reacted to this self-censorship by publishing twelve cartoons commissioned from Danish artists. One of these showed Muhammad on a cloud with Buddhist, Jewish and Christian deities, the last of them saying, 'Don't worry, Muhammad, we all get caricatured up here.' Another showed Muhammad with a bomb and a lighted fuse for a turban. So far as there could be a comparison, the cartoons seemed less offensive than the *Freethinker*'s 'Comic Bible Sketches', in respect of which it had proved difficult to get a conviction at the Central Criminal Court in 1882. The new cartoons appeared in the Danish paper on 30 September.

There was little response to their publication until they were denounced in Saudi Arabia by an Islamic cleric at the end of January 2006. Within days, Danish embassies were burning across the Muslim world and crowds were rioting in major cities. In London, outside the Regent's Park mosque on 4 February, protesters carried banners, some denouncing liberal values, 'Free Speech Go To Hell', while others, if they deserved to be taken seriously, were an incitement to murder, 'Behead Those Who Insult Islam'. The police made little effort to intervene and, indeed, a motorist who slowed down to protest to a police officer at the threats was warned that he would be arrested unless he kept moving.

Newspapers across Europe reprinted the cartoons in solidarity with their Danish colleagues and in defence of freedom against what was denounced as Islamic bigotry. If the façade of multiculturalism seemed to fragment over the next few months, these were its first significant fissures. Despite the five million Muslims in France, *France Soir* was one of the first major European papers to reprint the cartoons, one of them on its front page, on the grounds that no 'religious dogma' should be allowed to impose itself on a democratic and secular society. It was accompanied by *Die Welt* and *Berliner Zeitung* in Germany, *La Stampa* and *Corriere della Sera* in Italy, *ABC* and *El Periodico* in Spain, and *De Volkskrant* in the Netherlands. In Britain, the cartoons appeared on television in Channel 4 News and in Cardiff in the student newspaper *Gair Rhydd*, which despite its name, 'Free Speech', hastily recalled 9,800 of the 10,000 copies.

Some newspapers talked of 'a clash of civilizations' or cultures. Some, including the *Daily Telegraph*, suggested that if Muslims or others found that the standards of freedom in a liberal democracy were unacceptable to them, they might be living in the wrong country. Others, like the *Independent*, urged the need for respect. The government acknowledged freedom of speech but warned nervously against causing offence. Freedom to offend had traditionally been upheld in almost every judicial ruling. Since it would otherwise hand the powers of censorship to anyone claiming to be offended, it could hardly be otherwise.

In response to these demands for respect, the Israeli media inquired why those who now made them remained silent when the Arab press carried cartoons of hook-nosed Jews, their leader drinking the blood of Palestinian children, and anti-Semitic caricatures which *Haaretz* on 6 February compared to those featured in Julius Streicher's notorious Nazi newspaper *Der Sturmer*.

Even before the mutual antagonism had died down, the long history of hostility between Muslim East and Christian or secular West was revived when Pope Benedict XVI delivered a lecture at Regensburg University on 12 September 2006. Benedict had a particular claim to Islamic scholarship, though his subject on this occasion was the reconciliation of reason and divine revelation. In the course of his lecture he quoted what he called a 'somewhat brusque' repudiation by the Byzantine emperor Michael Paleologos II who had ruled in Constantinople from 1391 to 1425.

In the course of a dialogue with a Persian opponent, Paleologos is recorded as saying: 'Show me just what Muhammad brought that was new and there you will find things only evil and inhuman, such as his command to spread by the sword the faith he preached.' Benedict agreed with Paleologos only as far as to add that 'Violence is incompatible with the nature of God and with the nature of the soul.' Once again there was uproar, some of it allegedly government sponsored, across the Islamic world.

There was no denying that the Koran recommended violence or that the quotation was accurate. The protests were at the Pope's 'offence' by which he set out to 'attack the glory of Islam' or to 'hurt the sentiments of Muslims' or to cause 'a lot of dismay and hurt'. In London, the offended picketed Westminster Cathedral with placards reading 'Jesus is the Slave of Allah' and 'Islam Will Conquer Rome'. The protest was permitted by the police, unlike the exhortation of John Banda who had been stopped at London Bridge in December 2005 for carrying an offensive placard – 'Jesus is Lord'.

A significant legacy of this quarrel was a brief lesson in history from the popular press. In identifying Paleologos II, the newspapers explained to their readers that Islam had expanded at sword-point. The Crusades were launched in response to this. By 732 the first invasion of the West had brought the Moorish armies from Gibraltar to Poitiers, hardly two hundred miles from the English Channel. Here the common enemy of Europe was routed at last by Charles Martel, 'The Hammer'. Greece and the Balkans had not been liberated from a despotic and decadent Turkish rule until the nineteenth century. It was naive to expect that thirteen centuries of mutual hostility between East and West should be expunged by a few pious declarations of respect and laws against causing offence.

Relations were not helped in such situations by demands for apologies over misconduct in previous centuries. In 2000 Pope John Paul II had apologized for the Crusades, among other 'errors' of the Church. At the same time, British politicians were being urged to apologize for the Atlantic slave trade of the seventeenth to the nineteenth centuries. It was suggested that the topic should be taught as a compulsory subject to children. It had always been taught when history was a systematized mainstream subject. Taught once more in its context as part of the British historical development, it might have done a great deal of good. Taught as a single compulsory subject, showing how badly the British or the Europeans had behaved, it carried considerable risks.

It was not clear whether the topic would be carefully balanced. Children who were invited to feel ashamed of their past might feel considerable resentment if they were allowed to discover that slavery of a brutal kind had not only been endemic among Africans and Asians but that it still existed. It might not do for them to discover, while being urged to deplore their own past, that for example in the new millennium girls who were little more than children were still being sold for £5 each at the Marché des Jeunes Filles in the capital of the Ivory Coast. Worse still, the command to feel remorse for something beyond their own responsibility or their ability to alter, also invited the fulfilment of a warning by Tacitus, 'It is human nature to hate those whom you have wronged.'[10]

6

The case of *The Satanic Verses* and those controversies which followed it did more than internationalize censorship. As surely as a legal judgment they shifted the ground of debate from the historic rights of speech and expression to the right not to be offended. Semantically, it was the difference between 'freedom to' and 'freedom from'. This had long since enabled Communism, for example, to claim a moral superiority for its collective freedom from hunger or from fear, as opposed to the self-indulgent individualism of freedom to liberty of expression. During the Cultural Revolution of the late 1960s inquiries after the health of free speech in

China were greeted with an assurance that of course there was free speech – so long as it did not cause offence to others. No dictator need worry over 'inoffensive' freedoms.

In the case of *The Satanic Verses*, religious fanaticism had more bluntly asserted the rights of believers not to be offended, whatever the cost to freedom of expression. By the end of the Victorian period, it seemed that liberal democracy had outgrown this view during two centuries of ideological argument. In that respect, some forms of fundamental Islam in the twentieth century seemed to stand where some forms of Christianity had stood in the sixteenth or seventeenth. Was Mill's argument now to be upended, so that if all mankind minus one were not offended and only one person took offence, mankind would be no more justified in allowing that one person to be offended than he, if he had the power, would be justified in offending the whole of mankind? If not, whose offence would take priority in a conflict of religious or cultural beliefs?

In the wake of *The Satanic Verses*, human rights in the West moved closer to the hostile view taken of Salman Rushdie's fiction. In 1994, for example, a film was made, *Liebeskonzil* or *Council in Heaven*, based on Oscar Panizza's play over which Geoffrey Russell and Lady Birdwood had unsuccessfully tried to bring a prosecution for blasphemy in 1970. The new film was to have been shown in Austria, at the Otto Preminger Institute. When it was seized by the Austrian authorities, the institute appealed to the European Commission. The Commission upheld the institute's complaint that the prohibition on the film infringed the right to free speech under Article 10 of the European Convention on Human Rights. The Austrian authorities thereupon appealed to the European Court of Human Rights. They argued that interference with free speech is necessary to protect the vulnerable from gratuitous insults to their feelings, in this case to their religious beliefs. The court upheld the appeal and confirmed the ban on the film.[11]

The importance of avoiding offence was reinforced in December 1996, in the case of Nigel Wingrove's eighteen-minute film *Visions of Ecstasy*. This had been refused a certificate in 1988 by the British Board of Film Classification, on the grounds that its portrayal of St Teresa of Avila's alleged erotic obsessions would 'outrage the feelings of Christians'. The European Court of Human Rights considered that the English law was devised to protect Christians from offence and that the English censors had been best placed to make the decision. The ban on the film was also confirmed.[12]

Such rulings in favour of avoiding offence seemed a symptom of what was increasingly denounced as a form of censorship by 'political correctness'. As the culture of one millennium shaded into the next, this correctness and its powers of control became the focus of debate and hostility. The phenomenon had seemed something of a novelty in the 1980s and 1990s. Yet, as with so many apparent novelties, it had always been there for those who cared to look. Sometimes it had been described as courtesy and sometimes as humbug, according to preference.

Its present ingredients were not new, for example in their euphemistic terms for race or sex or physical disability. The overworked word of censure, 'inappropriate', seemed to veil every unspeakable act from the trivial to the life-threatening. A defendant was charged with having touched a complainant's bottom 'inappropriately'. In a more sinister context, parents were to lose their children to the social services because they behaved 'inappropriately' in front of them. The cliché struggled to spread moral neutrality evenly across the downright criminal and the merely impolite.

Political correctness as the language of euphemism was Anglo-American and drew most recently upon the American tradition of courtesy. American servicemen in Britain during the Second World War, for example, set a standard that compared favourably with their British comrades-in-arms. Children who grew up in Britain prior to the 1960s and who knew America only through the cinema were apt to believe that Americans never swore. More generally, Americans spoke politely of a 'bathroom' rather than a 'lavatory' or a 'toilet', let alone a 'privy'. They said 'rock' rather than 'stone' because 'stone' had been seventeenth-century English – and American – for 'testicle'. This meaning became obsolete in the Old World but survived in the New. For a more obvious reason, the New World said 'rooster' rather than 'cock'.[13]

A second ingredient lay in the English evangelicalism of the early nineteenth century and, to some extent, in those Societies for the Reformation of Manners which had begun in 1692. Like its late twentieth-century successor, this philosophy encouraged a vocabulary of moral reform and its influence was seldom far below the surface of English public life. 'At this moment cant and puritanism are in the ascendant,' noted Charles Greville gloomily in February 1856, from the vantage point of his Clerkship to the Privy Council.

From the first, its opponents suspected the movement would distort language to moral or political ends. In 1839, Lord Brougham recalled the distaste of Sir Philip Francis, the viper-tongued 'Junius' of political journalism, for the new politeness or correctness. Sir Philip, for example, defended the 'good manly words of assent and denial, the *yes* and *no* of our ancestors'. He loathed the way in which mealy-mouthed and sanctimonious claptrap undermined the vigour and accuracy of English words or phrases. The earnest young, anxious to be as non-judgmental as possible, preferred, 'I rather think' or 'I rather think not', often adding, 'to a degree'. 'Gracious God!' cried the old man at one of them, 'does he mean *yes*? Then why not say so at once like a man?' From such conversational aberrations, Dickens drew inspiration for Chadband or Podsnap, while Samuel Butler created Theobald Pontifex in *The Way of All Flesh*. In the hands of the National Vigilance Association, the same moral predispositions sent the publisher of Zola and Maupassant to prison.[14]

Evangelicals and the politically correct of a later century might have seen eye to eye over issues of language. Those who roused the anger of Sir Philip Francis would most surely have rallied to the 1997 campaign to make Merriam-Webster's *Collegiate Dictionary* remove the word 'nigger' from its pages. The definition was 'a black person – usually taken to be offensive'. The publishers stood their ground, acknowledging that the word was a slur but reminding the petitioners that 'it is none the less part of the language, and it is our duty as dictionary makers to report on it.' Two years later, American Indians joined the campaign, demanding the removal of 'squaw' not only from dictionaries but from names of geographical features, on the grounds that its hitherto unsuspected meaning was 'whore'.

Once a word had escaped from the specimen jar of the dictionary and was running free through the pages of fiction, standards of censorship grew stricter. In 1993, five American states instructed libraries to remove all copies of Mark Twain's *Huckleberry Finn* from their shelves because the novel contains the word 'nigger'. *Huckleberry Finn* had been banned from public libraries in Massachusetts as early as 1885, under pressure from the notorious book-burner Anthony Comstock, as 'trash suitable only for the slums'. In 1930 copies had been confiscated in Stalinist Russia. The state censors who targeted Mark Twain in 1993 were in good company.[15]

In Britain that year a PEN survey found that publishers were encouraging the removal of the pig from children's books for fear of angering the Muslim community. As for authors of the past, the best method of dealing with them was laid down by the Dorset Social Services guidelines for literature: 'Any old-fashioned books should be destroyed, i.e., any showing the female as the weaker sex, male as stronger.'[16]

The opponents of such diktats seldom wished offence to those who were alleged to be susceptible to it. If they wished to offend anyone, it was probably an elite who appeared set upon achieving a 'hegemony' for a new vocabulary and its literature in the media, schools, universities, and various arms of government. Like Orwell, the disaffected feared this linguistic purge as 'the party's' first tool of censorship.

For the dissidents, as for Victorian rebels like George Moore and George Gissing, a movement for greater courtesy and humanity took on a stifling and sinister self-righteousness. The voices which denounced Mark Twain or 'old-fashioned books' echoed those who had denounced Vizetelly, Zola and 'classics'. The photographer Helmut Newton in 1995 watched political correctness develop in this respect and thought of his youth in Nazi Germany. On 21 March 2001 the Common Serjeant of the City of London, Judge Neil Dennison, described a threat to the independence of the judiciary.

> Over all this hangs the cloud of political correctness. In some of its more lunatic aspects, political correctness is merely ridiculous. But in the thinking behind it, there is something more sinister which is shown by the fact that already there are certain areas and topics where freedom of speech, in the sense of the right to free and open discussion, is being gradually but significantly eroded.[17]

Often the effect of the new philosophy was simultaneously menacing and farcical. In October 1999, for example, it was reported that Professor Jared Sakren had been dismissed from the Theater Department of Arizona State University. The current form of correctness was a general denunciation of any literature produced by a 'dead white European male' and an eager reception for almost anything produced by the contrary. It was this which had goaded Saul Bellow. 'Who is the Proust of the Papuans and the Tolstoy of the Zulus?' Jared Sakren's offence was in making use of works for his students 'from a sexist European canon that is approached traditionally'. More specifically, he had taught at Yale and the Juilliard School in New York, and had a distinguished record as producer of Shakespeare and Greek tragedy.[18]

He was uneasy at the response of his students to the *Medea* of Euripides, which they had adapted as *The Medea Experience* to minimize the presence of its dead white European male dramatist. The first part of Euripides' play was approved, showing the callous and unfaithful husband Jason, with the text adapted to include Medea as a variety of abused wives, albeit a woman wise in herbs and benevolent magic, as well as part of an ethnic minority in Corinth. It was not acceptable to them to include the second part of the play in which Medea murders her own children, poisons the King of Corinth and his daughter, and departs for Athens to live under the protection of King Aegeus. The students considered that this portrayed a 'negative' image of womanhood.

The joke, if it was one, was on the students, who were 2,500 years late in denouncing Euripides' image of women. In 410 BC Aristophanes had exploited such criticism in his knockabout comedy *Thesmophoriazusae* ('The Women Celebrating the Thesmophoria'). Euripides fears being condemned to death by an Athenian festival of women whose rites are forbidden to men, also on pain of death. His elderly male relative, who would be no great loss, is dressed up as a pantomime dame and attends the Thesmophoria to explain, among other things, the far worse vices of womankind which Euripides might have portrayed had he chosen to.

Back in Arizona, Professor Sakren was warned again that 'the feminists are offended by the selection of works from a sexist canon.' The students demanded instead a production of what sounded like a knockabout farce of their own but was an intensely serious and earnest piece, *Betty the Yeti: An Eco-Fable*. This depicted a wise woman of the forest living an ecologically sustainable life in proximity to a redneck lumberjack, winning him over by her wholesome wiles and converting him into an eco-warrior. When Professor Sakren insisted on preferring Shakespeare over what he called 'this ridiculous play', he was 'let go'.

Censorship on behalf of moral or cultural relativism was also by no means new. Since the 1960s its voices had asserted the impossibility of proving that the Beatles were not, in their way, as great as Bach or Mozart or, in this case, presumably that Shakespeare and Euripides were superior to *Betty the Yeti*. Some non-judgmental rules went back further. When Hitler's Germany had already seized the Rhineland, Austria, and occupied the remainder of Czechoslovakia whose independence had been guaranteed at Munich the year before, it remained an offence to mock this illustrious head of state on the British stage. As late as March 1939, the Lord Chamberlain took direct action to prevent it. If all mankind had the right not to be offended, presumably one of them must be Adolf Hitler.

It was at this level of moral relativism that the values of the politically correct or the non-judgmental floundered. Whether or not it caused offence to say so, there was an undeniable difference in values between punishing a woman for adultery by burying her to the neck in sand, prior to stoning her to death, and the withering injunction to such a woman's accusers, 'He that is without sin among you, let him first cast a stone at her.'

Political correctness seemed formed to be plagued by irony, if only because it disregarded those who preferred to answer back for themselves. Very often such people found it morally repellent to see themselves as 'victims' protected by an array of government regulations and statutory bodies. Those bodies were naturally vigilant for situations in which offence might occur, as when fringe political parties were invited to address senior pupils at Dulwich College in March 1998. This was done, as the Master of Dulwich later said, 'in the context of a series of meetings exploring the extremes of British politics'. The Socialist Workers' Party was a guest on one occasion, the Anti-Nazi League on another. They faced questioning and argument from two hundred senior boys.

As representative of the far right, the British National Party had also been invited. The chairman of the Commission for Racial Equality publicly criticized the school for giving the BNP credibility it did not deserve. It was also a matter for concern that Dulwich College contained a fair number of Asian pupils, surely vulnerable to offence. Embarrassingly for the commission, it was 'sixth formers of Asian background' who had issued the invitation because they wanted to hear and confront their antagonists. Having heard them they courteously but vigorously attacked the policies and the explanations of a discomfited BNP representative.

During September 1997, a *Sunday Times* journalist was threatened with prosecution by the same commission for describing North Wales as 'hellish', its inhabitants as 'ugly, pugnacious little trolls' and the resort of Rhyl as a place 'only a man driving a crane with a demolition ball would visit with a smile'. The CRE Commissioner for Wales saw nothing funny in this and promised to assemble a file for the commission's litigation department. The culprit replied that he could not be 'less bothered', that he believed in freedom of speech and was not to be intimidated. It also seemed offensively patronizing that CRE officialdom, who might not be Welsh anyway, judged the land of Lloyd George incapable of answering back – or were unaware that it was possible to be Welsh and find the comments funny, or true, or both.

7

'Of course there is freedom of speech but there is no obligation to be gratuitously offensive.' The words of the British Foreign Secretary at the time of the Danish cartoons furore might have suggested that freedom was now running second in the race. By contrast, a man who knew better than most writers or politicians what it was to be censored had no qualms in the matter. With a *fatwa* still threatening Salman Rushdie, a playwright who was now President Vaclav Havel of Czechoslovakia addressed the 61st Congress of International PEN in Prague on 6 November 1994. He had been banned, and indeed imprisoned, under the puppet Communist regime which followed the Soviet invasion of 1968. He had a far better right to respect than the supporters of Betty the Yeti or even a Foreign Secretary.

President Havel did not hedge over offence or provocation in this case. He called on all participants at the congress to fight repression and particularly to raise their 'joint voice' in support of 'our colleague and friend Salman Rushdie' at whom the 'lethal arrow' of Khomeini's fanaticism was aimed. With the Iranian *fatwa*, he bracketed the tyranny of the Nigerian government and its treatment of the Nobel Prize winner, Wole Soyinka, as well as 'the criminal fanaticism of ethnic cleansers' in Bosnia, against which the country's writers were fighting. In dealing with such abuses of liberty, Vaclav Havel showed the cavilling over 'offence' or 'provocation' or a 'sexist canon' for what it was.

If there was one overriding misgiving at the beginning of the new millennium it was not that freedom of expression would be abolished at a stroke but that it might be gradually diminished by a throttling network of government restrictions. An unpleasant little word entered the vocabulary of politicians when cases involving freedom of expression went against them. In the case of the prosecution of the British National Party, for example, the first acquittals in February 2006 caused a government MP to suggest that since the verdict was unwelcome, the law was one which his government would have to 'revisit' in order to get the required result in future. The truth was that his government was seen as having bungled the case and, indeed, had now engineered a situation in which one in five people polled by Democratic Audit two months later said that they would 'consider' voting for the BNP in the forthcoming local elections. Before the trial publicity this would have been unbelievable.

At the further acquittals in October the prospective prime minister of 2007, Gordon Brown, despite the mass of recent legislation affecting freedom of speech, also promised to re-examine the law in order to silence the views of such defendants. It was not necessary to have the least sympathy with the BNP in order to wonder who else was intended to be silenced or intimidated, as a result of repeated 'revisiting'. If the sceptics were right, this had less to do with national security or community relations than with making the nation do as it was told, by repeated changes in the law.

Most censorship, in the end, had traditionally required the verdict of a jury. That had been and remained the guarantee of democratic freedoms. However unwelcome to a government a verdict might be, there was considerable danger in that government telling jurors to go away and think again by tinkering with the law. It was always open to jurors to return a perverse verdict, acquitting a defendant who had broken the law but with whose views they sympathized. Something of the sort seemed certain to have happened in the *Belgrano* trial of Clive Ponting in 1985.

Such responses were certainly not unprecedented. The press in the eighteenth century enjoyed greater political freedom because sympathetic juries, backed by advocates like Thomas Erskine, returned bloody-minded verdicts of 'not guilty' in the face of the evidence when defendants were prosecuted for their political views. At that time, the only question a jury was supposed to answer in cases of seditious libel was whether the defendant had published the words complained of, which was seldom in doubt. Whether or not they were criminal was a matter for the judge alone to decide, at a time when the judiciary had been brought effectively to the government's heel.

Questioned and browbeaten from the bench, jury foremen declined to budge, merely repeating the same verdict of acquittal to every question. A campaign began in the country under the banner 'The Liberty of the Press and the Rights of Jurymen are the Bulwark of the English Constitution'. It was a lesson that governments were obliged to learn until the law was changed in favour of press freedom in 1792. Until then the advocates of that freedom had anticipated the answer suggested in the twentieth century by the Spanish poet Juan Ramón Jiminez as the only response to censorship and autocracy: 'If they give you ruled paper, write the other way.'[19]

Jiminez wrote of pens and paper, innocent of the world-wide web or the Internet. At first it had seemed that this new technology opened the doors of freedom and wisdom, beyond the power of national governments to control. Yet freedom was not always accompanied by wisdom. By the 1990s a counter-technology was needed to police obscenity of the most repellent kind. Once in place, that technology became the master rather than the servant of the new science.

The danger of believing governments who impose censorship, promising that it is to be a temporary measure, is exceeded only by accepting their assurance that censorship will apply solely to material which all right-minded people must abhor. By 2007, it was political censorship rather than liberty which had become active in cyberspace. The OpenNet, comprising Harvard Law School, plus the universities of Oxford, Cambridge and Toronto, found an increasing number of countries who monitored those citizens using websites to spread political disaffection. As a result, for example, a Turkish court had ordered the blocking of YouTube to prevent its people reading unwelcome comments about the creator of modern Turkey, Mustafa Kemal Ataturk. Censorship in China was far more comprehensive. The technology of curbing obscenity was also to be the means everywhere of tracing political dissent by 'keyword filtering', which simply tracked down individuals using 'sensitive' words.[20]

The bright promise of artificial intelligence had not, after all, delivered liberty to its consumers. Both Aldous Huxley in *Brave New World* and Ray Bradbury in *Farenheit 451* had described fugitives and dissenters who escaped the oppression of uniformity by a more remote and primitive life. Like Jiminez, they ignored the ruled paper and wrote the other way. The poet's metaphor rang true. Perhaps, through one of the ironies of censorship, it would only be the private world of the pen rather than the shared universe of the keyboard which would in the end prove mightier than the sword.

Notes

Chapter 1. Watch Your Lip: The New Millennium

1. George Orwell, *Nineteen Eighty-four*, Part I, Chapter 2.
2. High Court, 5 October 2006.
3. John Stuart Mill, *On Liberty*, London: Watts & Co., 1929, pp. 12–13.
4. Ibid., p. 64; cf. Peter Quennell, *Four Portraits: Studies of the Eighteenth Century*, London: Collins, 1945, p. 209n.
5. *Daily Telegraph*, 5 February 1999.
6. *Evening Standard*, 19 October 1951.
7. Norman St John Stevas, *Obscenity and the Law*, London: Secker & Warburg, 1956, p. 189n.; T. H. White, *The Age of Scandal*, Harmondsworth: Penguin Books, 1962, p. 229.
8. Raymond Durgnat, 'Horror, Violence, Catharsis: Jolly Monsters', *Censorship*, No. 2, 1965, p. 54; J. P. Mayer, *British Cinemas and their Audiences*, London: Dennis Dobson, 1948, p. 89.
9. Adelaide Police Court, 5 September 1944; Michael Heyward, *The Ern Malley Affair*, London: Faber & Faber, 1993, pp. 189, 191.
10. *Gitlow v. New York* (1925); Zachariah Chaffee Jr, *Free Speech in the United States*, 2nd edn, 1942, rep. New York: Atheneum, 1969, pp. 318–25.
11. Ray Bradbury, *Fahrenheit 451*, London: Corgi Books, 1957, Part I, pp. 61, 62.
12. *Daily Telegraph*, 31 January 2006.
13. *Metro*, 11 December 2005.
14. *The Chronicle*, 26 April 1816; *Blackwood's Magazine*, December 1879, p. 175; *Daily Telegraph*, 10 February 1996.
15. House of Lords, 25 June 1857; *The Times*, 22 June 1877.
16. *Daily Mail*, 22 April 2006.
17. *Independent on Sunday*, 16 October 2005; *My Secret Life*, Vols. 1–4, London: Arrow Books, 1994, p. 396.
18. *Daily Express*, 1 November 2006.
19. PRO KB 28/363/1.
20. *Irving v. Penguin Books & Deborah Lipstadt* (2000), High Court Queen's Bench Division, 11 January–11 April 2000.

21. *Sunday Telegraph*, 4 April 2004; *Independent*, 19 January 2001.
22. *Sunday Telegraph*, 26 June 2005.

Chapter 2. In Retrospect: 'The Perfect Day'

1. William Stubbs, *Letters of William Stubbs, Bishop of Oxford, 1825–1901*, ed. William Holden Hutton, London: Archibald Constable, 1904, pp. 137–8, 145, 165, 178.
2. William Stubbs, *The Constitutional History of England in its Origin and Development*, Oxford: The Clarendon Press, 1878, IV, 615–16.
3. T. B. Macaulay, *History of England*, London, 1849–61, IV, 540; H. T. Buckle, *History of Civilization in England*, London, 1857-61, I, 353.
4. Donald Thomas, 'Press Prosecutions of the Eighteenth and Nineteenth Centuries: The Evidence of King's Bench Indictments', *The Library*, Fifth Series, XXXII, 315-32.
5. *State Trials: Treason and Libel*, ed. Donald Thomas, London: Routledge & Kegan Paul, 1972, pp. 99–124.
6. John, Baron Campbell, *Lives of the Lord Chancellors*, 4th edn, London, 1857, VII, 273n.; H. T. Buckle, *History of Civilization in England*, I, 457; Elizabeth Gaskell, *The Life of Charlotte Brontë*, London, 1857, I, 114.
7. Leigh Hunt, *Autobiography*, London, 1850, II, 78.
8. Benjamin Disraeli, *Coningsby: or, The New Generation*, London, 1844, I, 154.
9. James Fitzjames Stephen, *History of the English Criminal Law*, London: Macmillan, 1883, II, 300; Zachariah Chaffee Jr, *Free Speech in the United States*, pp. 46–7.
10. Benjamin Franklin, 'An Apology for Printers', *Pennsylvania Gazette*, 10 June 1731.
11. Sir James Fitzjames Stephen, *A Digest of the Criminal Law*, London, 1877, p. 189; Lord Burnham, *Peterborough Court*, London, 1955, pp. 14–15.
12. Cecil Woodham-Smith, *Queen Victoria: Her Life and Times; 1819–61*, London: Hamish Hamilton, 1972, p. 124.
13. PRO KB 28/565/16.
14. PRO KB 28/547/1.
15. PRO KB 28/596/4.
16. PRO KB 28/527/25.
17. PRO KB 28/551/9.
18. *Law Reports* (1881) 7 QB 244–59; PRO DPP 4/14; Donald Thomas, *A Long Time Burning: The History of Literary Censorship in England*, London: Routledge & Kegan Paul; New York, Praeger & Co., 1969, pp. 226–7.
19. PRO KB 28/555/9–10, 12–13; William C. Townsend, *Modern State Trials*, London: Longman, 1850, II, 356–91.

20. *The Trial of Charles Southwell for Blasphemy*, London, 1842, p. 4.

21. Mansion House Court, 21 July 1882; Central Criminal Court, 27 February 1883; Donald Thomas, *A Long Time Burning*, pp. 233–4.

22. *Law Reports* (1867–8) 3 QB 360.

23. Central Criminal Court, 19–21 June 1877; E. W. Cox, *Reports of Magistrates Cases*, London, 1882, III, 221.

24. H. H. Asquith, *Memories and Reflections 1852–1927*, London: Cassell, 1928, I, 89.

25. Middlesex Sessions, 16 February 1870.

26. Central Criminal Court, 31 October 1888, 30 May 1889; Henry Vizetelly, *Glances Back Through Seventy Years*, London: Kegan Paul, 1893, II, 432.

Chapter 3. Testing the Limits

1. Central Criminal Court, 10 September 1909; 'Indian Martyrdom in England', *Indian Sociologist*, 1909; Guy Aldred, 'Guy Aldred's Trial for Sedition', in *Representation and the State*, London: The Herald of Revolt, n.d.

2. PRO KB 28/704/1; Central Criminal Court, 1 February 1911.

3. Leeds Assizes, 5 December 1911, 11 January 1912; West Ham Police Court, 21 November 1921; Central Criminal Court, 7 December 1921, 9 December 1921; Court of Criminal Appeal, 16 January 1922; Ernest Pack, *The Trial and Imprisonment of J. W. Gott for Blasphemy*, Bradford: The Freethought Socialist League [1912], pp. 24–74. In December 1911 Gott was tried with Thomas William Stewart, President of the Freethought Socialist League, who was sent to prison for three months. In December 1921, a first jury failed to agree; a second jury convicted Gott but recommended 'clemency'.

4. Evidence of Robert Standish Siever in Report from the Joint Select Committee on Lotteries and Indecent Advertisements, 1908, paragraphs 1113–29.

5. Ibid., Evidence of Chief Inspector Edward Drew, paragraphs 421–70.

6. Central Criminal Court, 1 June 1919.

7. *Studies in the Psychology of Sex: Sexual Inversion*, Philadelphia: F. A. Davis, 1917, Preface to the First Edition.

8. John Sweeney, *At Scotland Yard*, London: Grant Richards, 1904, pp. 179–80.

9. Ibid., pp. 191–7.

10. Report from the Joint Select Committee on Lotteries and Indecent Advertisements, paragraphs 539–46; *Glyn v. Western Feature Film Company Ltd* (1915).

11. Robert Montgomery, *Poetical Works*, London, 1836, p. 276; E. H. Ruddock, *The Lady's Manual of Homoeopathic Treatment*, 6th edn, London, 1876, p. 25; John Thompson, *Man and his Sexual Relations*, Scarborough, n.d., pp. 159–60; Sylvanus Stall, *What A Young Boy Ought to Know*, Philadelphia, 1909, p. 152.

Stall also advises: 'Never read, handle, or listen to the reading of a book or paper which you might not ask your Mamma or Papa to read aloud to you' (p. 130).

12. *R v. Thompson* (1900) 64 JP 465.

13. Henry Vizetelly, *Extracts Principally from English Classics*, London: Vizetelly & Co., 1888, p. 2.

14. The Reports are reprinted in Donald Thomas, *A Long Time Burning*, pp. 481–4.

15. George Moore, *Literature at Nurse: or, Circulating Morals*, London: Vizetelly, 1885, pp. 3–4, 18.

16. *Spectator*, 19 October 1907.

17. *Spectator*, 20 November 1909.

18. '*Salome* at Covent Garden', *Harper's Magazine*, Vol. 186 (1943), pp. 464–72.

19. Report from the Joint Select Committee on Lotteries and Indecent Advertisements, paragraph 472.

20. *Star*, 3 July 1936; Charles Davy, *Footnotes to the Film*, London: Lovat Dickson, 1938, pp. 268–70.

Chapter 4. The Defence of the Realm

1. E. T. Cook, *The Press in Wartime*, London: Macmillan, 1920, p. 17; Christopher Hibbert, *The Destruction of Lord Raglan*, Baltimore: Penguin Books, 1963, pp. 192–3.

2. Winchester Assizes, 14 November 1910.

3. Admiral of the Fleet, Lord Fisher, *Memories*, London: Hodder & Stoughton, 1919, pp. 4–5.

4. Exeter Assizes, 3 November 1911.

5. Winchester Assizes, 9 February 1912.

6. Central Criminal Court, 17 January 1913.

7. Cook, *The Press in Wartime*, p. 177; Frederick, Second Earl of Birkenhead, *F. E. Smith First Earl of Birkenhead*, London: Eyre & Spottiswoode, 1959, p. 265.

8. Cook, *The Press in Wartime*, p. 162.

9. Lord Fisher, *Memories*, p. 45.

10. Peter Fryer, *Private Case – Public Scandal*, London: Secker & Warburg, 1966, pp. 139–40, 154–5.

11. Tom Clarke, *My Northcliffe Diary*, London: Victor Gollancz, 1931, pp. 75–9; Trevor Royle, *The Kitchener Enigma*, London: Michael Joseph, 1985, p. 294.

12. *Spectator*, 15 December 1917, 29 December 1917, 'Mr Lloyd George and his Stewardship'; David Lloyd George, *War Memoirs of David Lloyd George*, London: Ivor Nicholson & Watson, 1936, V, 2797–8.

13. Ibid., V, 2802; Lt-Col. C. à Court Repington, *The First World War 1914–1918*, London: Constable, 1920, III, 229.

14. Ibid., III, 231, 234.

15. Lloyd George, *War Memoirs*, V, 2804; Frank Owen, *Tempestuous Journey: Lloyd George His Life and Times*, London: Hutchinson, 1954, p. 451.

16. H. Montgomery Hyde, *Famous Trials Ninth Series: Roger Casement*, Harmondsworth: Penguin Books, 1964, pp. 72–3, 158; *The Trial of Sir Roger Casement* [Notable British Trials], ed. H. Montgomery Hyde, London: William Hodge, 1960, p. 3.

17. Sir Basil Thomson, *The Scene Changes*, London: Collins, 1939, p. 305.

18. *The Black Diaries of Sir Roger Casement*, ed. Peter Singleton-Gates, London: Sidgwick & Jackson, 1959, pp. 10–13.

19. E. D. Morel, *The Secret History of a Great Betrayal*, London: [Caledonian Press] n.d., p. 27; Elizabeth Longford, *A Pilgrimage of Passion: The Life of Wilfrid Scawen Blunt*, New York: Alfred A. Knopf, 1980, p. 400.

20. Arthur Ponsonby, *Falsehood in Wartime*, London: George Allen & Unwin, 1928, p. 11.

21. Ibid., pp. 126–7; London Gazette Supplement, 12 August 1918.

22. *The Autobiography of Bertrand Russell 1914–1944* (Volume II), London: George Allen & Unwin, 1968, pp. 31–2.

23. *The Persecution of E. D. Morel: The Story of his Trial and Imprisonment*, Glasgow: Reformers' Bookstall, n.d., p. 9.

24. *A Misrepresentation Exposed*, compiled by Arthur Ponsonby and E. D. Morel, London: The Union of Democratic Control, 1918, p. 7.

25. E. D. Morel, *The Horror on the Rhine*, London: The Union of Democratic Control, 1920, pp. 11–16, 20.

26. Central Criminal Court, 29 May 1918.

27. Central Criminal Court, 30–31 May 1918.

28. Central Criminal Court, 31 May 1918.

29. Central Criminal Court, 1 June 1918.

30. Cook, *The Press in Wartime*, p. 148.

31. Central Criminal Court, 15 November–15 December 1926.

32. *The Times*, 1 November 1940.

33. Austen Morgan, *J. Ramsay MacDonald*, Manchester: Manchester University Press, 1987, p. 116.

Chapter 5. Between Two Wars

1. C. M. Bowra, *Memories 1898–1939*, London: Weidenfeld & Nicolson, 1967, p. 87.

2. Evelyn Waugh, *Vile Bodies*, London: Chapman & Hall, 1930, Chapter 2.

3. *United States v. One Book Called Ulysses*, District Court, New York, 1933; Morris L. Ernst, *The Best is Yet*, West Drayton: Penguin Books, 1947, pp. 110–16.

4. PRO Mepol 3/390.
5. Radclyffe Hall, *The Well of Loneliness*, Paris: Pegasus Press, 1928, Chapter XIII.
6. Ibid., Chapter XIX.
7. Ibid., Chapters XXXVIII, LVI.
8. Bow Street Magistrates Court, 9 November 1928.
9. West Riding Assizes, 3 December 1934.
10. Central Criminal Court, 8 February 1932.
11. Montague Summers, *The Gallanty Show*, London: Cecil Woolf, 1980, pp. 182–5.
12. Jack Kahane, *Memoirs of a Booklegger*, London: Michael Joseph, 1939, p. 212.
13. *Paddington News*, 5 February 1938.
14. West Ham Magistrates Court, 24 March 1938.
15. *Daily Sketch*, 30 September 1936.
16. Ibid., 25 May 1936, 31 July 1936.
17. Ibid., 2 April 1936, 27 November 1936.
18. Aldershot Magistrates Court, 13 June 1940.
19. *Daily Sketch*, 24 April 1936.
20. High Court King's Bench Division, 7 June 1937.
21. High Court King's Bench Division, 26 April 1937; Curzon Papers, Charles Eliot to Curzon, India House Library, 1 May 1922, 23 May 1922.

Chapter 6. Total War: The Home Front

1. Rear-Admiral George P. Thomson, *Blue Pencil Admiral*, London: Samson Low, Marston, 1947, p. 3.
2. Ibid., pp. 60, 67.
3. Ibid., p. 127.
4. The Earl Jowitt, *Some Were Spies*, London: Hodder & Stoughton, 1954, pp. 46–7, 77, 70–73.
5. Ealing Magistrates Court, 27 May 1940.
6. *Manchester Guardian*, 24 March 1942.
7. Hugh Cudlipp, *Publish and be Damned: The Astonishing Story of the Daily Mirror*, London: Andrew Dakers, 1953, p. 180.
8. High Court King's Bench Division, 13 June 1941.
9. High Court King's Bench Division, 18–31 July 1941.
10. Thames Magistrates Court, 6 November 1939.
11. Old Street Magistrates Court, 5 January 1940.
12. Central Criminal Court, 6–7 April 1943.
13. Liverpool Magistrates Court, 20 May 1943.
14. Wood Green Magistrates Court, 18 April 1941, 25 April 1941.
15. Clerkenwell Magistrates Court, 16 April 1941.
16. Croydon Magistrates Court, 25 June 1943.

Chapter 7. Total War: A Sort of Traitors

1. William L. Shirer, *The Collapse of the Third Republic*, London: Pan Books, 1970, p. 977n.
2. *Le Monde*, 20 January 1945.
3. *Le Monde*, 7 February 1945.
4. Malcolm Muggeridge, *The Infernal Grove* [Chronicles of Wasted Time, Vol. 2] London: Fontana Books, 1975, p. 253.
5. P. G. Wodehouse, *Performing Flea: a Self-Portrait in Letters*, Harmondsworth: Penguin Books, 1961, p. 126.
6. Iain Sproat, *Wodehouse at War*, London: Milner & Co., 1981, pp. 147–67.
7. William Joyce, *Twilight over England*, The Hague: Oceanus, 1942, pp. 46, 171.
8. Ibid., pp. 25, 46, 52–3, 56, 170.
9. William L. Shirer, *Berlin Diary: The Journal of a Foreign Correspondent 1934–1941*, Boston: Little, Brown, 1941, p. 529.
10. Robert Skidelsky, *Oswald Mosley*, London: Macmillan, 1981, pp. 401–2.
11. Cecil Roberts, *And So To America*, London: Hodder & Stoughton, 1946, pp. 22–3.
12. The descriptions occur in a neo-Augustan satire, 'Verses to an Impolite Reformer', in the Birkbeck College Magazine, *The Lodestone*, Spring 1927.
13. Joyce, *Twilight over England*, pp. 20, 68.
14. Ibid., pp. 51, 57, 162.
15. Ibid., pp. 63, 66, 166, 171.
16. Ibid., pp. 110–11, 182.
17. Ibid., p. 7.
18. *Trial of William Joyce* [Notable British Trials], ed. J. W. Hall, London: William Hodge, 1946, p. 36.
19. F. R. Leavis, *New Bearings in English Poetry*, London: Chatto & Windus, 1950, p. 149.
20. *The Cantos of Ezra Pound*, London: Faber & Faber, 1964, p. 10; Leavis, *New Bearings in English Poetry*, p. 236.
21. Ibid., p. 236.

Chapter 8. Tales of Mean Streets

1. Minutes of Evidence Taken Before the Select Committee on the Obscene Publications Bill and Appendices in Session 1956–7, paragraph 101.
2. *Classical Association News*, No. 24, July 2001, p. 8.
3. Minutes of Evidence, paragraphs 17–19.
4. Bow Street Magistrates Court, 22 April 1942; Central Criminal Court, 18–19 May 1942.

5. *People of State of New York v. Viking Press Inc.* (1933) 147 Misc N.Y. 813, 264 Supp. (534).
6. Fredric Wertham, *The Seduction of the Innocent*, London: Museum Press, 1955, p. 176.
7. *Winters v. New York* (1948).
8. Wertham, *The Seduction of the Innocent*, p. 264; Mickey Spillane, *One Lonely Night*, London: Transworld Publishers, 1960, p. 84.
9. Wertham, *The Seduction of the Innocent*, pp. 168–9.
10. Ibid., pp. 343–50.
11. Tottenham Magistrates Court, 25 March 1941.
12. Tottenham Magistrates Court, 21 January 1949.
13. Uxbridge Juvenile Court, 9 October 1953; Southampton Juvenile Court, 28 March 1960; Plymouth Magistrates Court, 6 August 1960.
14. Central Criminal Court, 10 December 1952.
15. Central Criminal Court, 11 December 1952.
16. Sir Harold Scott, *Scotland Yard*, Harmondsworth: Penguin Books, 1957, p. 74.
17. Central Criminal Court, 4 November 1953.
18. Brighton Magistrates Court, 6 May 1954.
19. *Evening Standard*, 12 November 1954.

Chapter 9. New Laws for Old

1. *Cw. v. Forever Amber* (1947) 32 Mass. LQ, No. 2, 79 (Massachusetts Superior Court).
2. Minutes of Evidence Taken Before the Select Committee on the Obscene Publications Bill, paragraphs 317–21.
3. Ibid., paragraph 623.
4. Sheffield Magistrates Court, 28 February 1950.
5. Swindon Magistrates Court, 29 July 1954.
6. Wiltshire Quarter Sessions Appeal Court, 15 September 1954.
7. Clerkenwell Magistrates Court, 20 May 1954.
8. Central Criminal Court, 29 June–2 July 1954.
9. Central Criminal Court, 24 September 1954.
10. Central Criminal Court, 2 December 1954.
11. Central Criminal Court, 29–30 November 1954.
12. Minutes of Evidence Taken Before the Select Committee on the Obscene Publications Bill: Home Office Memorandum, paragraphs 19–21.
13. PRO KB 28/3705; Central Criminal Court, 12–21 September 1960.
14. *Shaw v. DPP* (1962).
15. *Knuller v. DPP* (1973).

Chapter 10. The Policing of Literature

1. H. D. F. Kitto, *The Greeks*, Harmondsworth: Penguin Books, 1951, p. 124.
2. Aristophanes, *Lysistrata, An English Version by Dudley Fitts*, London: Faber & Faber, 1955, pp. xi, 14, τὸ τοῦ φερεκράτος κύνα δέρειν δεδαρμένην. The joke of Pherekrates referred to the uses of a dog-skin penis. Hence Brunk's commentary in the eighteenth century, 'penem coriaceum intelligit.'
3. Central Criminal Court, 20 October 1960.
4. Central Criminal Court, 20 October 1960.
5. Central Criminal Court, 27 October 1960.
6. Central Criminal Court, 27 October 1960.
7. Central Criminal Court, 28 October 1960.
8. Central Criminal Court, 28 October 1960.
9. Central Criminal Court, 1 November 1960.
10. Central Criminal Court, 1 November 1960.
11. Central Criminal Court, 2 November 1960.
12. PRO SP 36/111/157, 158.
13. Bow Street Magistrates Court, 20 January–9 February 1964.
14. Hubert Selby Jr, *Last Exit to Brooklyn*, London: Calder & Boyars/Corgi Books, 1970, p. 9.
15. House of Commons, 2 March 1966.
16. *Regina v. Hicklin* (1868) LR 3 QB 360; *Obscene Publications: Being a series of articles reprinted from the Justice of the Peace and Local Government Review*, Chichester: Justice of the Peace Ltd, 1955, p. 3.
17. Central Criminal Court, 13–24 November 1967; Court of Appeal, 31 July 1968.
18. *My Secret Life*, Vols. 1–4, pp. ix–x.
19. Leeds Magistrates Court, 21 April 1968; Leeds Assizes, 14 January–3 February 1969; Court of Criminal Appeal, 28 November 1969.
20. Chester Assizes, 21 April 1966.
21. Central Criminal Court, 28 January 1976.
22. Central Criminal Court, 21 January 1976, 28 January 1976.
23. *Pornography: The Longford Report*, London: Coronet Books, 1972, pp. 417–18.
24. Ibid., p. 48.
25. Minutes of Evidence Taken Before the Select Committee on the Obscene Publications Bill: Memorandum Submitted by the Commissioner of Police of the Metropolis, Section 2 paragraph 8.
26. Ibid., Section 2 paragraphs 8–10.
27. *Cox's Criminal Law Cases*, London, 1846, I, 229.
28. Sir Robert Mark, *In the Office of Constable: An Autobiography*, London: Collins, 1978, p. 155.

Chapter 11. Beyond the Pale

1. Vladimir Nabokov, *Lolita*, London: Transworld Publishers, 1961, p. 32.
2. Minutes of Evidence Taken Before the Select Committee on the Obscene Publications Bill, paragraphs 71–3.
3. Nigel Nicolson, *Long Life*, London: Weidenfeld & Nicolson, 1997, pp. 198–9.
4. *The Times*, 2 August 1968; *Daily Telegraph*, 13 February 1970; *Evening Standard*, 5 April 1963.
5. Minutes of Evidence Taken Before the Select Committee on the Obscene Publications Bill: Memorandum Submitted by the Commissioner of Police of the Metropolis, Section 2 paragraph 8.
6. Stuart Bell MP, *When Salem Came to the Borough: The True Story of the Cleveland Child Abuse Crisis,* London: Pan Books, 1988, p. 51.
7. *On Liberty*, p. 68.
8. Bristol Crown Court, 19 November 1999.
9. Arno Schonberger and Haldor Soehner, *The Age of Rococo*, London: Thames & Hudson, p. 381.
10. House of Commons, 14 March 1988.
11. *The Times*, 12 February 1987.
12. *Financial Times*, 24 September 1994.
13. *The Times*, 13 March 1990; *Independent*, 17 March 1990.
14. *The Times*, 8 August 1990.
15. *The Times*, 8 May 1993; *Western Mail*, 8 May 1992; Newport Magistrates Court, 1 February 1993; *South Wales Echo*, 23 February 1993; *South Wales Argus*, 9 November 1993; Swansea Crown Court, 12 January–12 June 1994; Byron Rogers, 'The Child Snatchers', *Sunday Telegraph*, 10 January 1999.

Chapter 12. The Enemy Within

1. Douglas Hyde, *I Believed*, London: Pan Books, 1953, p. 190.
2. Constantine Fitzgibbon, *Secret Intelligence in the Twentieth Century*, London: Granada Publishing, 1978, p. 320.
3. Central Criminal Court, 16–18 July 1958.
4. Central Criminal Court, 12–20 February 1962.
5. *Attorney-General v. Jonathan Cape Ltd* (1976) QB 752 (High Court).
6. *The Times*, 16 February 1968.
7. Jonathan Aitken, *Officially Secret*, London: Weidenfeld & Nicolson, 1971, p. 148.
8. Central Criminal Court, 12 January–3 February 1971.
9. Clive Ponting, *The Right to Know: The Inside Story of the Belgrano Affair*, London and Sydney: Sphere Books Ltd, 1985, p. 138.
10. Central Criminal Court, 6 February 1985.

11. Central Criminal Court, 6 February 1985.
12. Peter Wright with Paul Greengrass, *Spycatcher*, Richmond, Victoria: William Heinemann Australia, 1987, p. 56.
13. House of Lords, 13 August 1987.
14. *R v. Secretary of State for the Home Department, ex parte Briand and others* (1991) 2 WLR 588 (House of Lords).
15. H. L. Mencken, *A Carnival of Buncombe*, ed. Malcolm Moos, Baltimore: Johns Hopkins Press, 1956, p. 74.
16. *New Statesman*, 28 January 1928.
17. High Court King's Bench Division, 25 March 1949.
18. High Court Queen's Bench Division, 12 April 1957, 3 May 1957.
19. Woolwich Crown Court, 21 January 1997.
20. High Court, 8 August 1992.
21. *The Times*, 19 January 1993, 4 November 1997.

Chapter 13. 'Enoch Says What Everyone Thinks'

1. Rt Hon. C. R. Attlee, *As It Happened*, London: Heinemann, 1954, pp. 174–5.
2. Leonard Burt, *Commander Burt of Scotland Yard*, London: Heinemann, 1959, pp. 126–9.
3. Liverpool Assizes, 17 November 1947.
4. Boston Herald, 13 January 1920; Anne Sharpley, 'The Little Hand-Kisser', *Evening Standard*, 1 August 1962.
5. House of Commons, 22 December 1969.
6. Reading Quarter Sessions, 17–18 October, 9 November 1967; Marlborough Street Magistrates Court, 25 September 1967, 19 October 1967; Donald Thomas, *Dead Giveaway*, London: Michael O'Mara Books, 1993, p. 172.
7. Oxford Crown Court, 30 January 1979.
8. Exeter Magistrates Court, 25 October 2002.
9. Central Criminal Court, 12 March 1997.
10. Southwark Crown Court, 11 September 1997.
11. *Western Daily Press*, 13 December 2005.
12. Swindon Crown Court, 5 January 2006, 27 January 2006.
13. Leeds Crown Court, 17 January–2 February 2006, 10 November 2006.

Chapter 14. God Is Not Mocked

1. Dorothy L. Sayers, *The Man Born to be King*, London: Victor Gollancz, 1943, p. 224.
2. Bernard Levin, *The Pendulum Years*, London: Pan Books, 1972, p. 103.
3. Ibid., p. 103.

4. John Robinson, *Honest to God*, London: SCM Press, 1963.

5. Central Criminal Court, 4–12 July 1977.

6. *Independent*, 23 February 1989.

7. *The Times*, 28 February 1989.

8. *Gitlow v. New York* (1925); Zachariah Chaffee Jr, *Free Speech in the United States*, pp. 318–25.

9. Central Criminal Court, 11 January–7 February 2006.

10. *Sunday Telegraph*, 9 September 2001; Tacitus, *Agricola*, 42, 'Propium humani ingenii est odisse laeseris.'

11. European Court of Human Rights, *Otto Preminger Institut v. Austria* (1994).

12. European Court of Human Rights, *Wingrove v. UK* (Case 19/1995).

13. 'Stone' is used in this sense throughout such seventeenth- and eighteenth-century texts as *The School of Venus: or, the Ladies Delight reduced into rules of practice* – a translation of Michel Millot and Jean L'Ange, *L'Ecole des Filles* (1655). The English version, which Samuel Pepys bought from his bookseller on 8 February 1668, was lost after the prosecutions of 1745–6. However, long passages of it survive in the manuscripts of King's Bench, notably the indictment of John Stevens who published it in 1744. Pepys added that he read his copy once, 'a lewd book but what do no wrong once to read for information sake', and then he burnt it, 'that it might not be among my books to my shame'. Cf. PRO KB 28/176/20.

14. Henry, Lord Brougham FRS, *Historical Sketches of Statesmen Who Flourished in the Time of George III*, Second Series, London: Charles Knight & Co., 1839, pp. 91–2; Charles Cavendish Fulke Greville, *The Greville Memoirs*, ed. Lytton Strachey and Roger Fulford, London: Macmillan, 1938, VII, 203. Greville attributes this cant to 'the Evangelical and Sabbatarian interest'.

15. Anne Lyon Haight, *Banned Books*, London: George Allen & Unwin, 1955, pp. 66–7.

16. *The Author*, Vol. CIV, No. 1, Spring 1993.

17. *Daily Telegraph*, 21 November 1995; Central Criminal Court, 21 March 2001.

18. *Guardian*, 16 November 2006.

19. 'Press Freedom and the Rights of Juries' in Donald Thomas, *A Long Time Burning*, pp. 107–12.

20. *Financial Times*, 15 March 2007.

Index

Banda, John, 11, 12
Bankhead, Tallulah, 215
Barber, Anthony, 240–1
Bardot, Brigitte, 271
Barnekow, Major von, 159
Barnes, Dr Ernest William, Bishop of
Birmingham, *The Rise of Christianity*,
342
Barrie, Angela, 122
Barry, Dr William, 64–5
Bartholomew, Harry, 141
Barzun, Jacques, 244
Bastian, John, 219
Bastwick, John, 28
Baudelaire, Charles, *Les Fleurs du mal*, 54
Baxter, Walter, 235; *The Image and the
Search*, 222–3, 227–9, 235; *Look Down
in Mercy*, 227
Beach, Sylvia, 103
Bean, John, 322, 333
Beatles, the, 364
Beatty, Dr Richard, 151
Beaumont, Francis, *The Maid's Tragedy*, 62
Beckett, John, 128
Beckett, Samuel, *Watt*, 231, 232
Beckford, Jasmine, 276
Bedborough, George, 58–60
Beecham, Sir Thomas, 66–7
Begin, Menachem, 318
Belfast, HMS, 133–4
The Bell Curve see Hernstein, Richard J.
Bellenger, Fred, 142
Bellow, Saul, 363
Benedict XVI, Pope, 358
Benn, Tony, 327
Bennett, Arnold, 104, 112
Bennett, Joan, 245
Benson, Gale, 326
Bentley, Derek, 200–1, 203
Bentley, E. C., 162–3
Bentley, Richard, 26
Béraud, Henri, 156; *Gringoire*, 156
Berlin, Sir Isaiah, 270
Bertony, Charles, 281
Besant, Annie, 43–6, 57, 60
Bethmann Hollweg, Theobald von, 77
Betjeman, John, 122
Bevan, Aneurin, 143, 289

Bevin, Ernest, 139, 289
Bhatti, Gurpreet Kaur, *Behzti*, 15
Birdwood, Lady, 345, 360
Birkett, William Norman, 1st Baron
Birkett, 112–13, 236, 320
Biron, Sir Chartres, 112–13
Bismarck, Otto von, Duke of Lauenberg,
26
Black, Sir Cyril, 252–4
Blackburn, Raymond, 263
Blackwell, Sir Basil, 252–3
Blackwell, B. H., 232–3
Blackwell, Sir Ernley, 89
Blair, Tony, 15, 20, 23, 336
Blake, Major F. W., 98
Blake, George, 293, 296
Bland, Margot, *Julia*, 222–3, 224, 229
Bluitgen, Kare, *The Koran and the Life of
the Prophet Mohammed*, 356–7
Blundell, Sir Robert, 249
Blunt, Anthony, 292
Blunt, Wilfrid Scawen, 90
Blyton, Enid, 274
Boccaccio, Giovanni, *Decameron*, 62, 69,
217, 220–1
Bodkin, Sir Archibald, 112
Bolam, Sylvester, 311
Bonham-Carter, Mark, 234
Bottomley, Horatio, 315
Bourgeois, Christian, 231
Bourget, Paul, 44
Bowen, Elizabeth, 122
Bowra, Sir Maurice, 101, 270
Boyd, Air Vice-Marshal Owen Tudor, 160
Bracken, Brendan, 144–5
Bradbury, Ray, *Fahrenheit 451*, 10, 15, 368
Braddock, Bessie, 309–10
Bradlaugh, Charles, 43–6, 57, 60
Brady, Ian, 259–60
Brailsford, H. N., 90
Bramley, Ted, 148
Bramston, James, *The Man of Taste*, 254
Brandon, Lieutenant Vivian, 75
Brantôme, Pierre de Bourdeilles, Abbé,
Lives of Fair and Gallant Ladies (*Vie des
dames gallantes*), 117
Brasillach, Robert, 156; *Je suis partout*, 156
Bremner, Moyra, 260–1

Cockburn, Sir Alexander James Edmund, 42–3
Cockburn, Claud, 139
Coleridge, Bernard John, Baron, 47
Collett, Mark, 335, 336, 338, 355
Collins, Sir Andrew David, Hon. Mr Justice, 4
Commission for Racial Equality, 10, 365
Comstock, Anthony, 362
Comyn, James, 300–1
Conan Doyle, Sir Arthur, 87–8; 'The Naval Treaty', 72; 'The Bruce-Partington Plans', 72; *The Adventures of Sherlock Holmes*, 194
Congreve, William, 27, 65
Connell, Vivian, *September in Quinze*, 222, 225–6
Connelly, Marc, *Green Pastures*, 121–2, 342
Connolly, Cyril, 122
Conqueror, HMS, 302
Cook, Sir Edward, 79, 80, 85–6
Cooper, Alfred Duff, 1st Viscount Norwich, 161–2, 164, 170
Corelli, Marie, 94
Correggio, Antonio Allegri da, *Jupiter and Antiope*, 41
Cousins, Sheila, *To Beg I Am Ashamed*, 118
Coward, Noël, 169
Craig, Christopher, 200–1, 203
Crewe, Robert Offley Ashburton, 1st Marquess of, 89
Crippen, Hawley Harvey, 52, 57, 86
Croce, Benedetto, 104
Cromer, Evelyn Baring, 1st Earl of, 47
Crompton, Richmal, *Just William*, 274
Cromwell, Oliver, 22
Crossman, Richard, 297, 309
Culme-Seymour, Laura Grace, 49–50
Culme-Seymour, Mary, 49–50
Culme-Seymour, Sir Michael, 48–50
Curll, Edmund, *Venus in the Cloister: or, The Nun in her Smock*, 39
Curzon, George Nathaniel, 1st Marquis of Kedleston, 47, 61, 82–3, 126
Cussen, E. J. P., 164–5

Dalyell, Tam, 302–3
Darling, Charles John, 1st Baron, Mr

Justice, 95–7
Daudet, Alphonse, 44, 45
Davis, Sammy, 325
Dawes, C. R., 254
Day-Lewis, Cecil, 117
Deeley, Peter, *Beyond Breaking Point*, 292
Defoe, Daniel, 61; *Moll Flanders*, 213, 248
De Freitas, Michael, 325–6; 'Michael X', 325–6; Michael Abdul Malik, 326
De Gaulle, Charles, 156, 270
Deighton, Len, 304
Delbrück, Professor, 85
De Mille, Cecil B., *King of Kings*, 342
Demosthenes, 181
Denning, Rt Hon. Alfred Thompson, Lord Justice, 16, 263
Denning, Sir Norman, 300
Dennis, Geoffrey, *Coronation Commentary*, 125–6
Dennison, Judge Neil, 363
Derby, Edward Henry Smith Stanley, 17th Earl of, 86
Devlin, Rt Hon. Patrick Arthur, Lord Justice, 202, 228
Dew, Chief Inspector Walter, 57
Dewey, Governor Thomas Edward, 197
Dhingra, Madan Lal, 47
Diana, Princess of Wales, 313
Dickens, Charles, 251–2, 257, 262, 362
Dietrich, Marlene, 123
Disraeli, Benjamin, 1st Earl of Beaconsfield, 29, 32–3, 73
Dobson, Arthur, 255–6, 258
Dodson, Sir Gerald, Judge, 206, 222, 224, 226, 234, 238
Donahue, Judge Frank J., 214
Donleavy, J. P., *The Ginger Man*, 234
Dopagne, Jacques, 231
Dors, Diana, 192, 219
Dostoevsky, Fyodor, 44, 45
Douglas, Lord Alfred, 57, 96, 315; 'All's Well With England', 97
Douglas, James, 102, 103–4, 111–12
Downes, J., *Roscius Anglicanus*, 117
Downey, Lesley Ann, 259
Drakard, John, *Stamford News*, 31
Drew, Chief Inspector Edward, 53–7, 68
Dreyfus, Colonel Alfred, 45

Ker, John, 39
Kermode, Frank, 252
Keyes, Admiral Sir Roger, 145–6
Khomeini, Ayatollah, 351, 352, 353
Khrushchev, Nikita, 6, 143
King, Cecil, 140
King-Hall, Judge Alan, 346–7
Kingsley, Charles, *The Water Babies*, 274
Kipling, Rudyard, 80, 274
Kirby, Mr Justice Michael, 305
Kirkup, James, 'The Love That Dares Not
   Speak Its Name', 345–7
Kirman, George, 52
Kitchener, Field Marshal Herbert
   Horatio, 1st Earl Kitchener of
   Khartoum, 81–4
Kitto, H. D. F., *The Greeks*, 240
Knowlton, Charles, *The Fruits of
   Philosophy*, 43–4, 60
Krafft-Ebing, Richard von, *Psychopathia
   Sexualis*, 46, 57–8, 94, 96
Kroger, Helen, 292–3
Kroger, Peter, 292–3

Laden, Osama bin, 331
Lalcaca, Dr Cowas, 47
Lamb, Charles, 36
La Mettrie, Julien Ofray de, *L'Homme
   machine*, 259
Lane, Sir Allen, 239, 242–3, 245
Lane, John, 107
Lang, Andrew, 62; *Brown Fairy Book*,
   274
Lansdowne, Henry Charles Keith Petty
   Fitzmaurice, 5th Marquis of, 92
Larkin, Philip, 117
Laski, Harold, 315
Laski, Marghanita, 222, 249
Laurel, Stanley, 7
Laval, Pierre, 156, 181, 182
Lawrence, D. H., 63, 101, 104, 191; *The
   Rainbow*, 65, 102, 111; *Lady Chatterley's
   Lover*, 108–9, 113, 186, 213, 233,
   239–50, 267, 271; *Pansies*, 109
Lawrence, Geoffrey, 311
Lawrence, Stephen, 10, 337
Lawton, Rt Hon. Sir Frederick Horace,
   Lord Justice, 223, 224

Leavis, F. R., 247; *New Bearings in English
   Poetry*, 177, 178, 182
Le Carré, John, 304
Lee, Gypsy Rose, *The G-String Murders*,
   193
Leese, Arnold, 127–8, 318; *The Fascist*,
   127–8
legislation: Bill of Rights (1689), 309;
   Blasphemy Act (1698), 36–7, 341;
   Blasphemy Laws (Amendment) Bill
   (1930), 341; British Nationality and
   Status of Aliens Act (1914), 174;
   Broadcasting Act (1981), 308–9;
   Censorship of Plays (Repeal) Bill
   (1949), 217; Children and Young
   Persons (Harmful Publications) Act
   (1955), 209–11, 285; Cinematograph
   Act (1909), 68; Civil Partnership Act
   (2004), 11; Contempt of Court Act
   (1981), 314; Criminal Law Act (1977),
   353; Criminal Law Amendment Act
   (1885), 111; Customs Consolidation
   Act (1876), 112, 234; Defence of the
   Realm Act (1914), 77–8, 80, 82, 86,
   91–2, 99; Defence General Regulations
   (1939), 138, 144, 151, 157, 164;
   Emergency Powers (Defence) Act
   (1939), 132, 150; Larceny Act (1861),
   72–3; Libel Act (1843), 32; Licensing
   Act (1737), 65; Local Government
   Miscellaneous Provisions Act (1982),
   266–7; Matrimonial Causes Act (1938),
   210; Naturalization Act (1870), 174;
   Newspaper Libel Act (1888), 31;
   Obscene Publications Acts (1857)
   (1959) (1964), 39–45, 88, 111–12, 186,
   197, 221, 234, 236, 237, 250, 252, 255,
   264, 271, 277, 282–3, 346; Offences
   Against the Person Act (1861), 35, 317,
   326, 331, 353; Official Secrets Acts
   (1889) (1911) (1920) (1939) (1989),
   70–4, 97–8, 129, 130, 289, 292, 294–5,
   296, 301, 303, 304–7, 308; Paper Order
   (1942), 184; Parliamentary Papers Act
   (1840), 31; Prevention of Terrorism
   Act (2005), 2, 9; Protection of
   Children Act (1978), 275, 277, 279,
   280; Public Order Act (1936), 321–2;